SOCIOLOGY
A Way of Seeing

SOCIOLOGY
A Way of Seeing

Richard L. Benkin
Illinois Department of Mental Health
and Developmental Disabilities
and
De Paul University

Wadsworth Publishing Company
Belmont, California
A Division of Wadsworth, Inc.

Sociology Editor: Curt Peoples
Editorial/Production Services: Phoenix Publishing Services, San Francisco
Designer: Brenn Lea Pearson

Cover art: Ron Davis "Cube and Four Panels,"
1975, acrylic on canvas, 110½ x 130¾".
Albright-Knox Art Gallery, Buffalo, New York.
By exchange, National Endowment for the Arts
Purchase Grant and Matching Funds, 1976

2 3 4 5 6 7 8 9 10   85 84 83 82 81

Library of Congress Cataloging in Publication Data

Benkin, Richard L
Sociology, a way of seeing.

Bibliography: p.
Includes index.
1. Sociology. 2. Social psychology. I. Title.
HM251.B4524   301   80-24480
ISBN 0-534-00929-8

Photo Credits

To Toby Zallman Benkin,
who taught me about growth.

Contents in Brief

Contents

Preface

The late C. Wright Mills wrote about the *sociological imagination* as a quality of mind that takes us beyond the confines of our personal problems to a broader view of the social world around us. I always felt that Mills captured the essence of sociology in this view of it as a way of seeing. For although all of us participate in social life, few people can objectively analyze whatever social issue they happen to be looking at—be it reinstating capital punishment, making abortions safe and available, busing schoolchildren to achieve racial integration, or cutting social programs to balance the federal budget. Sociology provides that objective ability. And that is what this book is about.

All of us are subject to some very powerful forces. I am often amazed by, sometimes frightened by, and usually concerned about their impact on our lives and destiny. Some of these forces, such as government, are apparent. But what particularly interests and troubles me are the powerful unseen forces that allow us, in Erich Fromm's words, to obey without being commanded and to want to do what we have to do. Such forces might manifest themselves in the form of people (parents, media stars), processes (job hunting, education), or ideas (loyalty, views of women and men). Whatever their form, they are reflections of social structures and structural controls that few people are aware of and that sociology can make apparent to us. At the same time, sociology teaches us how necessary some controls are for our ability to communicate and live with one another. In short, we can appreciate the need for some controls while questioning the particular forms they take and those who control them.

In using this book, you should master the tools that you will need to pierce the curtain that surrounds these forces and come to see what others miss. You will become familiar with sociology's basic vocabulary, which is essential for putting this "way of seeing" to work for you. Beyond that, I hope that you will also begin thinking of things in a new way so that you will question those powerful social forces rather than passively accept them. As you do this, you will find that sociology can be a valuable tool for the rest of your life.

The Tone

In 1980 the World Future Society predicted that, if current behavior patterns persist, the earth in the year 2000 will be a particularly unhappy place for all of us, with widespread poverty and starvation, far less farmland to produce the food we will need; tremendous overcrowding; poisoned air and water; an even greater risk of war; fewer animal species; and all manner of increased social ills. These predictions need not come to pass (and I'm optimistic enough to believe that they will not—at least not in their entirety). Technology will not avert them; neither will military action nor repressive government. That clear vision of social relationships that sociology offers is our best shot. This means that a sociological perspective will become vital for our long-term survival as we approach the close of this century. And we will never make it unless others in addition to professional sociologists have grasped this way of seeing.

The Book's Special Features

Each chapter in this book builds upon the one preceding it, while drawing out the implications of its topic for our view of various social issues. The first chapters concern our individual development into social beings; the next ones are about social organization and inequality; and in the concluding chapters we will look at the broader processes of social change and persistence. To help us along I have incorporated certain features into the text.

THE SOCIAL CONTROL THEME For me nothing so thoroughly captures what I have been talking about as does the concept of social control. That concept is the underlying thread of this book—the recognition of unequal social power that is wielded through basic social structures. Whether social control is a force for good or for ill—and it can be both—it is important that we acknowledge the presence of existing inequalities before accepting or rejecting them. Thus, the book has an active, critical tone: regularities in our behavior cannot be coincidental, and I find not knowing the source of these regularities uncomfortable.

BOXED EXCERPTS   Each chapter contains at least two boxes of material set apart from the rest of the text, which apply the social control theme to specific social phenomena (welfare, juvenile arrests, childrearing styles, sex roles, and so on). Whether they are based on formal research or journalistic observations, the boxes give an added reality to my contention of social control's pervasiveness.

CHAPTER BACK MATTER   Because I believe that the sociological vocabulary is so important, each chapter lists the key terms introduced in it. Following the key terms, each chapter has several questions that I've included for review and discussion. And for any student who wishes to explore a particular topic further I have included lists of pertinent readings at the close of each chapter.

SOURCES   When I was in graduate school, one of my professors once said that any discipline that looks for information only in its own products is doomed to perpetual narrowness, if not stagnation. He was right, and I have drawn my data from a number of sources in addition to sociological books and articles. I have used a range of books (fiction and nonfiction), the foreign presses, and a great deal of government data to bring the material alive.

When I first moved to Chicago, I spent a lot of time driving around most of the city's neighborhoods, riding the various subways and elevated routes, and generally exploring the place. Some of my friends did not quite understand my fascination with what many saw to be "dangerous" or "run-down" areas. But others—most of them sociologists—knew immediately what drew me all over the city: my sociological way of seeing the world. I'm not trying to say that any "right-minded" sociologist would have done the same. The point is that I—and my sociologist friends—saw an urban wonderland that others missed. We saw conflicting interests, changes and resistance to change, social history, and much more. I sincerely hope to communicate to you my fascination with the world that a sociological perspective brings.

Acknowledgements

I had not realized what a collective effort was involved in writing a textbook before now and can hardly claim complete responsibility for this one. Several colleagues helped make it possible with their insights, comments, and anecdotes at various points in the book's birthing. My thanks go to E. Digby Baltzell, Grace DeSantis, Neal Gross, Lester Kurtz, and Charles Suchar. I would also like to thank the reviewers, whose analysis and commentary played a major role in producing the final product: Kathryn Barchas, Skyline College; B. A. Bolanos, College of the Desert; David Dobos, Santa Ana College; John W. Foley, Sangamon State University; Paul Johnson, Bethel College; Doug Klegon; Reece McGee, Purdue University; William Mayrl, University of Wisconsin at Milwaukee; Russ Purdy, Corpus Christi State University; Martin Scheffer, Boise State University; Stephen Winn, Marshall University. Special thanks to Toby Zallman Benkin for her analysis of the female sex role, nurturance, and powerlessness. And thanks to De Paul University's Sociology Department, which provided essential secretarial services.

Neither could my vision of a book have become a reality without the combined talents and hard work of a number of people at Wadsworth Publishing Company. I could not have been luckier than I was in having Steve Rutter and Curt Peoples as my two successive editors. I value my relationship with them as much as I do their skills. Thanks to their assistants, Barbara Cuttle and Judith McKibben, for their help, too. Sheryl Fullerton and Jonathan Cobb gave invaluable help in writing, rewriting, and editing the book. And John Enright, of Phoenix Publishing Services, carried the book—and me— through the final, all-important production stage.

Finally, our endeavors would be tremendously more difficult—if not impossible—without the support and encouragement of friends. For me, Toby Zallman Benkin stands far above the crowd. She has always pushed for excellence—in her work and in mine—and helped me focus on the truly valuable aspects of writing and scholarship. Steve Dubin and Les Kurtz have been unique as friends and colleagues; and Marilyn Morris has given me her support and insights into myself that I would otherwise have missed. A special thanks to them.

Richard Benkin
Chicago
1980

PROLOGUE
Why Sociology?

Many times, as a student, I swore that if I ever wrote a textbook, it would not have an introduction. Later, as a sociology instructor, I read countless introductions to countless texts and reaffirmed this conviction, and I would tell my students to go straight to the first chapter. It was always evident that, despite the author's good intentions, introductions often burdened students with unnecessary material—unnecessary because it did not aid them in their study of sociology. When my "moment of truth" arrived, however, rather than carry out my intention, I decided to write an introduction that would be worth reading—worthy of both students' and instructors' time and effort.

This prologue presents important components of the *sociological method*—how we will practice sociology—and it provides a rationale to unite the many different topics in this book. It also sets an important tone for the book by focusing on how we can use sociology in our own lives.

WHAT IS SOCIOLOGY?

Since the dawn of human history, at least, men and women have wondered about and tried to make sense of their relationships with each other. Why are some groups of people treated better than others? What holds a community together? What causes it to break apart? How do people learn to accept the manners and morals of their society? Why don't people who are oppressed revolt more often? What causes populations to rise and fall, wars to break out, and crime rates to vary?

Attempts to answer questions such as these in a coherent way had, until comparatively recently, been the concern of social and religious philosophers. Since the late nineteenth century, however, workers in the field of sociology have provided some answers. Simply put, **sociology** is the scientific study of the social relationships among human beings. It begins with the recognition that human life is social life (see Chapter 1)—sociologists study just about every aspect of human activity. Take a look, for instance, at the titles of sociology courses: the family, the industrial city, race relations, and criminology, to name a few. A single issue of the *American Journal of Sociology* (November 1977) contained articles on the relationship between different careers, the job market, and personal advancement; elites in a community; prestige among peasants; religious conversion; arrest probabilities for marijuana users; and drugs that alleviate stress. Not only are these topics fascinating but they concern issues we encounter personally or through

1

the mass media. Sociology is flexible enough to take in just about anything that is important, troubling, or interesting in our lives, and in the life of our society.

Sociology and Social Sciences

Sociology, of course, is not the only discipline to concern itself with the relationships of humans with each other. All the social sciences—economics, political science, psychology, and anthropology, as well as sociology—have this as their subject. What, then, differentiates sociology from these other disciplines? Sociology can be distinguished from economics and political science by the broadness of its scope: sociology encompasses humans as political and economic animals, but as much more besides.

We can broadly characterize the difference between psychology and sociology as a difference in focus: psychologists tend to concentrate more on the individual, sociologists on the group. In general, sociologists are concerned only with those aspects of behavior that are affected by the existence of others and that are likely to change when relationships with those others change. For instance, sociologists will study why people have children, but not the process of childbirth itself; they will want to know why city life produces anxiety in many people, but they will not look at the process of anxiety itself. Sociologists are not concerned with the biological or psychological aspects of human behavior, per se. These aspects refer to our internal goings-on that operate with or without the presence of others. (Our heart continues to pump blood; it doesn't matter whether we are in the company of our parents, a group of steelworkers, a priest, or a tribe of New Guineans.) Sociologists, on the other hand, are very interested in **social structures**—the customary patterns of interaction evident in institutions, groups, occupations, and the like—that significantly influence behavior. Understanding these structures is central to sociology but only peripheral to psychology.

Of all the major disciplines, sociology has most in common with anthropology, and the concerns of workers in these two fields often overlap. Historically, anthropologists have tended to concentrate more on primitive civilizations and on culture, while sociologists have tended to focus more on industrialized societies and on social structure. Nevertheless, in principle the domain of anthropology is as broad as that of sociology—nothing less than the nature of human social relationships.

The Usefulness of Sociology

The subject of sociology is so broad that some people charge the discipline with having little practical use for students—unless they want to become professional sociologists. This accusation reflects a common misconception about what can be gained from studying sociology.

Students usually enroll in an introductory sociology course because it is required, it is supposed to be less difficult than physical science and commerce courses, its subject matter vaguely interests them, or because it involves working with people. Unlike accounting or calculus, sociology does not generally draw students who expect to learn a "skill" that they can use after school. Yet, in fact, you can learn many useful skills from your study of sociology.

Sociologists are concerned with real people and problems. Here are some questions sociologists ask: Does capital punishment deter homicide (Reckless 1969)? What effects will urban renewal have on the people of a particular community (Jacobs 1969)? Has civil rights legislation helped equalize the relationship between blacks and whites (Featherman and Hauser 1976)? How do male executives adapt themselves to having female colleagues (Kanter 1977)? What are the effects on worker productivity of employee relationships (Blau 1963)? The sociological method, used to find answers to these questions, is a composite of many useful skills. By learning these skills we gain the potential to understand the bases of buying behavior, voting patterns, family conflicts—in fact, of any human behavior.

Learning sociology skills is useful in another sense as well. By exploring some of the conclusions sociologists have come to about the nature of society and how we as individuals fit into it, we can learn something about our own lives. By learning sociological concepts and methods, we can provide ourselves with the necessary tools to make our own judgments about society, our place in it, and what reforms may improve it.

Finally, sociology's practical value has become increasingly evident in the employment opportunities outside of the university (see Figure P.1). Government agencies have hired sociologists to do research on various aspects of crime. Sociologists have also served on special commissions such as the President's Commission on Obscenity and Pornography and the President's Commission on Law Enforcement and the Administration of Justice. Other agencies, such as the National Institute of Health and the Department of Health and Human Services (formerly Health, Education, and Welfare), have sponsored sociological research, and a number of sociologists have helped design the government's social welfare programs (see Horowitz and Katz 1975).

Many other sociologists are employed full or part time by "big business." Some examine the relationship between worker output and the work setting, while others study labor unions, problems associated with certain types of office organization, and interaction among executives. Sociologists also examine family relations, urban problems, and minority relations.

Sociology, then, is a recognized skill; the tools are in this book. And as with hammers and saws you do not have to be a "professional" to find them useful.

SOCIOLOGY AS A SCIENCE

Sociology is a form of scientific analysis. The statement "In Soviet Georgia, many people live past the age of 100" describes a state of affairs in that part of the USSR; it tells us *what* exists there. But the statement "In Soviet Georgia, many people live past the age of 100, *because they eat yogurt*" attempts to state *why*—to analyze why—so many Georgians live so long. The first statement is an example of description; the second is the product of analysis. Through analysis, we attempt to give meaning to raw facts.

We use the process of analysis to find answers to questions, but we do so only part of the time. Most of us tend to be am-

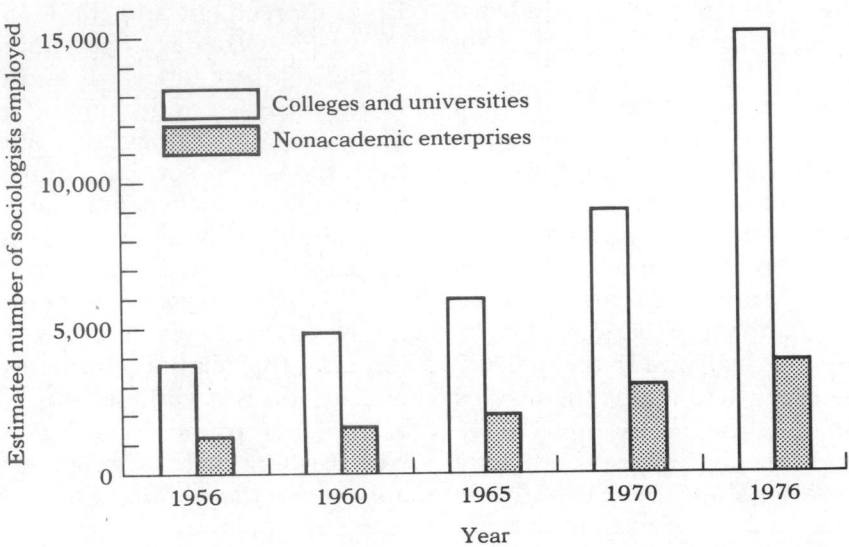

Figure P.1 Sociologists In and Out of the University

SOURCE: *U.S. Department of Labor, Bureau of Labor Statistics,* Occupational Outlook
Handbook *(Washington, D.C.: Government Printing Office, 1957, 1961, 1966–1967,
1970–1971, 1972–1973, 1978–1979*

ateur sociologists and psychologists and continually make up "explanations" as to why an individual acted in a certain way or, with less surety, why a particular person was elected president, why the media pay so much attention to the crime rate, or why everybody leaves the classroom ten minutes early. Many of our "explanations," however, aren't based on an analysis of the facts but on our opinions and beliefs.

There are real difficulties with basing explanations on our opinions and beliefs. First, these explanations might seem to be based simply on common sense but actually are often riddled with unprovable assumptions (e.g., people all have their own, unique ideas), myths (e.g., harsh punishment is what we need to stop crime), and prejudices (e.g., when blacks move

into a white neighborhood, it has to degenerate). Second, there is no way to decide which explanation is the most reasonable. My opinion is simply that, *my* opinion. In a democracy, we might agree, each person has an equal right to his or her explanation, but that won't help us to determine whose explanation is closest to the facts of the case.

What differentiates sociological analysis from our own musings and opinions about society is that sociologists, at least in principle, do not rely on common-sense explanations of social phenomena or on their own opinions and beliefs. Instead, they try, through systematic observation of the world, to build their explanations from facts, and they use a method that tests these explanations and allows others to evaluate them. It is the use of this process of establishing facts and testing explanations that allows sociologists to claim the status of a science for their discipline.

The Scientific Method

By calling their discipline a science, sociologists do not mean that they work only in laboratories or only with numbers. The idea of a science means, above all, adherence to the **scientific method,** that is, to forms of inquiry and rules of evidence that are designed to minimize the investigator's subjective influence as much as possible. Three basic principles underlie this method: (1) the research must follow the dictates of logical reasoning; (2) the research must be based on facts rather than opinions; and (3) the procedure of investigation must be fully stated and publicly accessible so that others can test the proposition themselves. As Kenneth R. Hoover has observed:

Ultimately, good science provides its own check on the influence of values in inquiry. If the method by which the study has been done and the evidence for conclusions are clearly and fully stated, the study can be examined for the fit of conclusions to evidence. If there is doubt about the validity of what has been done, the study itself can be double-checked, or "replicated," to use the technical term. This feature distinguishes science from personal judgment. (1976, p. 10)

Sociologists, like other scientists, are not slow to criticize one another when they

disagree, and that's important for improving the quality of sociological explanation. There are many examples of these disagreements in the major sociological journals. The two most prestigious publications, the *American Journal of Sociology* and the *American Sociological Review,* devote sizable portions of each issue to criticism of specific articles that have appeared in the journals, plus the original authors' responses to their critics.

This kind of public debate is important for another reason. Because sociologists are human beings, they are influenced by their past histories, their present ambitions, their culture, and their society. It is therefore impossible for them to completely exclude personal biases and beliefs from their analyses—that is, it is impossible for them to be completely *objective.* Although the way in which sociologists work tends to minimize these distortions, some always remain. In carrying out sociological analysis, we all need to become as aware as possible of our biases in order to ensure that they do not cloud our perception. Public debate helps us develop this awareness.

The importance of separating our opinions from our evidence in science doesn't mean that sociologists must ignore everything of personal significance to them. Valuable sociological insights have come from the work of sociologists who have studied groups or conditions that were of great concern to them. For instance, E. Digby Baltzell, who coined the expression WASP (White Anglo-Saxon Protestant), made a superb study of the upper-class Protestant establishment in America, of which he is a member; Jessie Bernard, Ann Oakley, and other feminist sociologists have made important contributions to our understanding of sexism; and many sociologists have made incisive studies of their own ethnic groups—for instance, Marshall Sklare (Jewish), Michael Novak (white ethnic Slav), and Andrew Greeley (Irish Catholic). What the rules of scientific inquiry do require is that we make clear where the evidence ends and our opinions begin. There is nothing wrong with stating our values or our personal opinions in sociology—so long as we state that they are *personal* and not *scientific* judgments. Because no matter how hard we try to avoid it, some of our value judgments will creep into our analysis, some sociologists argue that we have a responsibility to inform our readers (or students) of those values so that they will be aware of them when reading the work.

Conclusions in the Social Sciences

What has been said so far applies not just to sociology or just to the social sciences but to the natural sciences as well. Sociology and the other social sciences differ from the natural sciences such as chemistry and physics in an important aspect, however. The object of analysis in the social sciences is *human* behavior. This has two important implications for considering sociology as a science. First, human properties and behavior cannot be manipulated, dissected, and subjected to laboratory tests the way a rock or plant or rat can. (Revolutions obviously don't happen in the controlled conditions of the laboratory.) This absence of scientific control means that conclusions in the social sciences are usually not considered as well established as many conclusions are in the natural sciences.

Second, because there is so much variation in the human species, conclusions about human behavior in general are not as easy to arrive at as are conclusions in the natural sciences. A chemist announcing that a molecule of water is composed of one oxygen and two hydrogen atoms is not likely to hear: "Wait a minute! You found that in one molecule of water, but that says nothing about other molecules of water." But a sociologist making a comparable statement about human behavior would immediately be presented with counter cases. Because of this variability of human behavior, the generalizations of sociology are usually more contested than the findings of the natural sciences. But that variability—the richness of human behavior—is what makes sociological analysis so fascinating and challenging.

Having seen something of the subject of sociology and the general method of social scientific inquiry, let's turn now to a more specific consideration of how sociologists view society and the methods by which they investigate social phenomena.

PERSPECTIVES ON SOCIETY

The aim of scientific endeavor, whether in physics or sociology, is, as we've seen, the explanation of facts in a manner that helps us understand our world. In making these explanations, sociologists, like other scientists, use *concepts* and *theories.*

Concepts

The concepts sociologists use, along with their methods of gathering data and their general perspectives, help distinguish sociology from other disciplines. Some of these concepts appear in the chapter titles: social control, socialization, value, norm, role, performance, deviance, conformity, social organization, social institution, social stratification, collective behavior, social change, social disorganization—and, of course, society. Concepts are simple names for complex items and ideas. For example, the single word *socialization* sums up the multitude of ways in which an individual learns how to accept society's rules as her or his own; and the concept of *norms* includes all of the many rules of right and wrong behavior—from formal laws to informal customs. Concepts help us organize our perceptions. They help us to see the links between what at first appear to be quite unlike phenomena. For example, the concept of socialization draws our attention to the similarity between television commercials and the dictates of parents: both act as messages that teach children how to behave in society. Our concepts, however, can also prevent us from noticing some phenomena—because of the concepts we hold, we tend to attend to some things and not to others.

Our daily conversations are filled with concepts. "Job market," for example, is a concept that we use to organize perceptions about changes in the economic state of the nation, the supply and demand of labor, and who gets a job and who doesn't. "Political machine" is another concept, this one organizing certain perceptions about the concentration of power in a city, acts of corruption, payoffs, and so forth. You will, I expect, find the concepts in this book useful as you develop your own understanding of human behavior.

Concepts by themselves don't explain anything. Theories do. A **theory** is an explanation: it is a proposition that organizes and emphasizes certain concepts, showing the relationships among them. At their broadest, theories provide us with general frameworks we can use to make sense of reality and to generate our sociological concepts. Scientists have always looked at the objects they study in light of particular theoretical perspectives. Some perspectives were accepted as "truth" for a time but were later discredited, giving way to more plausible ones. For example, until around 1543, European astronomers used a theory that placed the earth at the center of the universe, with the sun revolving around it; and until well into the last century, most biologists and anthropologists used a perspective that did not include evolution.

Most sociologists rely on one of three major theoretical perspectives for analyzing social life and events: **functionalism,** which focuses on the interrelationship of social structures and groups; **conflict theory,** which sees groups competing for values and resources; and **symbolic interactionism,** which concentrates on interacting individuals.

The Functionalist View

The functionalist perspective in sociology has its intellectual roots in the work of one of the founders of modern sociology, the nineteenth century French theorist Emile Durkheim (1858–1917). To adequately explain a social phenomenon, Durkheim wrote in *The Rules of Sociological Method* (1964a [1895], p. 95), we must know not just its cause but the part it plays in social life as well. He argued that if we want to understand human social behavior, we must be able to detach the behavior we observe from those we see doing it and look for the **social facts** underlying the behavior. He defined a social fact as "every way of acting which is general throughout a given society, while at the same time existing in its own right independent of its individual manifestations" (1964a [1895], p. 13). For example, a sociologist might explain table manners in terms of the social fact of inherited custom. That is, the custom of putting your napkin in your lap when sitting down to dinner has a reality independent of any particular person who performs the ritual. And the constraint we feel to follow that custom is not derived from any single person; instead, we feel compelled by "society." In Durkheim's view, society has a reality all its own, apart from the individuals in it.

Not all functionalists would concur with Durkheim's definition of a social fact, but they would likely agree that to understand a social phenomenon we must understand its use, and that society is more than the sum of the individuals who compose it. In the view of Durkheim and most of today's functionalists, society is made possible by collectively shared ideas and values, and the individual is, in many respects, the plaything of these larger social forces. As Durkheim put it in his classic study of suicide, "The individual is dominated by a moral reality greater than himself: namely, collective reality" (1951 [1897], p. 38).

To functionalists, the most important thing to know about a social phenomenon—whether it be the family, the prison system, or table manners—is the function it serves in society. The function of the police in society, for instance, is to maintain order, that of the schools to transmit knowledge and train the next generation. If a sociologist were looking at table man-

ners from this point of view, for example, he or she would be interested in showing how these rituals bind people together.

From the functionalist point of view, society is a *system of interrelated structures* (such as the university, the government, the public schools, the economic system, and the religious institutions) which operate together to preserve order and stability. Early sociologists illustrated this concept by comparing the elements of society to the systems of a living organism. Just as the heart, respiratory, and circulatory systems have to work together for the organism to live, so must the elements of society work together for it to survive.

Although the organic metaphor is not ordinarily invoked by functionalists today, they, too, perceive that society is made possible by a rather delicate balance among its component parts. The parts of society, like the organs of an animal, are all interrelated. A change in one part of the organism/society touches off disturbances in other parts, and this continues until a new balance, or equilibrium, is established. For instance, an increase in abandoned children is likely to spur an increase in adoption services, plus increased agitation for the passage of laws designed to prevent such abandonment and to take care of those already left homeless.

The functionalist perspective has been the dominant one in American sociology, although in recent decades it has undergone considerable attack. Critics point out that functionalists, by emphasizing the need for order and integration, often tend to support the status quo; that theirs isn't a particularly useful perspective from which to understand social change; and that, by simply describing some social process or action as "functional" for society, adher-

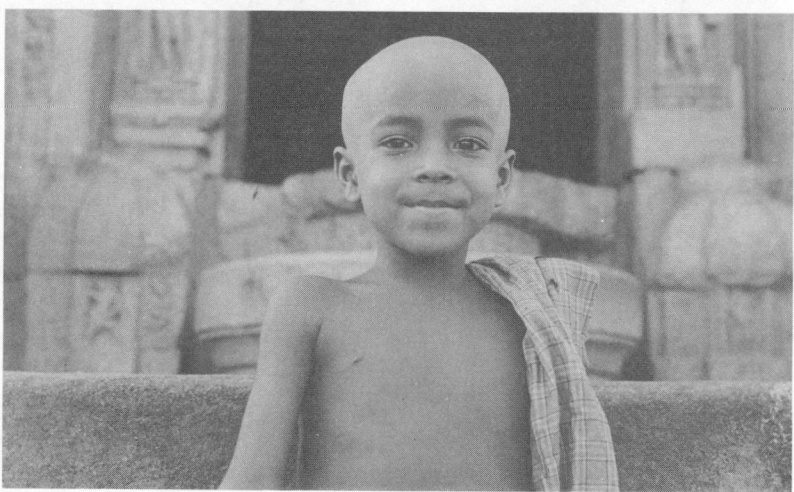

ents of this perspective blur exactly who in society benefits from that process or action.

The Conflict View

The intellectual roots of the conflict perspective lie in the writings of the German social philosopher and communist Karl Marx (1818–1883), who viewed the struggle between economic classes (peasant vs. lord, worker vs. owner) as the major determinant of history and the shape of society. Many of those who analyze society from the conflict perspective today, however, are not Marxists.

Conflict theorists see society as the outcome of conflict among groups competing for values and resources (money, land, education, and so forth). Because most resources and values are *scarce* (that is, limited in supply), conflict theorists understand society not as shared values (functionalism), nor as shared meanings (symbolic interactionism), but as a contest of groups for power and control. Conflict arises because those groups and individuals who are dominant at any one time try to hold onto their power and the resources they control, while those who have less try to gain more power in order to gain more resources.

At first glance, conflict might seem to be only destructive of social order. But some contemporary sociologists working within the conflict perspective, for example, Lewis Coser (1956) and Ralf Dahrendorf (1959), have shown that conflicts not only can tear society apart but can help hold it together as well. For instance, conflicts often tend to draw members within each of the contending parties closer together.

Conflicts also may spur attempts to solve the underlying problems that have given rise to the conflict, which may ultimately increase order and stability.

In contrast to the functionalists, who emphasize the broader values and beliefs that people of a society share, conflict theorists stress what divides different groups. The appearance that everyone shares the same values, they argue, is often an illusion; behind the facade lies the ability of one segment of society to impose its beliefs on the rest through control of institutions such as the mass media, the criminal justice system, and the major corporations. As you might imagine, functionalists often accuse conflict theorists of finding conflict where there is none and thereby missing the larger tacit agreements that people do share, while conflict theorists accuse functionalists of ignoring the reality and consequences of domination by one group of another.

The Symbolic-Interactionist View

Unlike functionalists, who focus on the grand institutions of society, such as education, the state, and religion, symbolic interactionists tend to focus on individuals and how they interpret the world and communicate with each other. According to symbolic interactionists, social life is made possible by the exchange of symbols among individuals. A **symbol** is simply something that stands for something else. Language and gestures are the most obvious forms of symbols. Thus, while the functionalist would ask what the consequences of an action are for the group or for society, the symbolic interactionist would ask how participants in the action interpret it and how

Table P.1 Three Views of Society

	Functionalism	Conflict Theory	Symbolic Interactionism
Basic question to understand a social phenomenon is	What is its function for society?	What are the group interests involved?	What is its meaning for the interacting individuals?
Society is	Interrelated structures	Competing interests or groups	Interacting individuals and symbols
Social interaction is possible on the basis of	Shared values	Group interests and power	Shared meanings of symbols
Essence of society is	Order; equilibrium	Conflict	Dynamism; constant redefinition in interaction

these interpretations influence their social relationships.

The interactionist perspective owes much to the work of the German sociologist Max Weber (1864–1920). While Weber didn't view society exclusively from any one of the major modern perspectives, his emphasis on the subjective aspects of social life, on the importance of understanding how people interpret their own lives in order to properly understand their actions, provides the foundation on which contemporary symbolic interactionism is built.

Symbolic interactionists emphasize that communication is possible only to the extent that participants agree on the meaning of the symbols used, and that these agreements are subject to continual reinterpretation and change. While we are the source of these agreements and can and do change them, symbolic interactionists point out that we are as much formed by the meanings we come to share with others as these meanings are formed by us.

The special domain of symbolic inter-actionism is *socialization*—how we learn the cultural meanings of our society and come to adopt them as our own. These meanings include our expectations about how others should act and what these acts signify. In the view of George Herbert Mead (1863–1931) and Charles Horton Cooley (1864–1929), two sociologists who are generally considered the earliest major exponents of this theoretical perspective, socialization occurs through our interactions with others, as does the development of our minds and our sense of self. (For a summary of these three views of society, see Table P.1.)

Implications of the Three Views of Society

Functionalism, conflict theory, and symbolic interactionism each emphasize different aspects of social life. Depending on the perspective you use in approaching some social event or problem, you are likely to notice some elements but not others, and you may come to quite different conclusions. Throughout this book, we'll see many instances of these different points of view. By way of summarizing the different perspectives, let's see how a functionalist, a conflict theorist, and a symbolic interactionist might analyze the following situation: Recently, a state university located in a major city requested that it be allowed to tighten its standards for admitting students. It claimed that under its current policy, a significant number of admitted students read and write at the eighth-grade level. This makes their education difficult, slows the pace of learning for everybody, and results in students being graduated with deficient verbal skills. For the most part, the students referred to come from low-income, black families, and a local civil rights leader has charged that much of the blame belongs to the city's public schools for not providing the students with a sufficient education.

A sociologist working within the functionalist perspective might argue that the university exercises an important "doorkeeping" function for our society. It helps assure that only those with certain qualifications occupy the most highly skilled positions in our country. Proficiency with verbal skills (reading, writing, speaking ability) is needed for: keeping up with the large amount of new information constantly coming out in all fields; communicating with co-workers; making an impression as a competently educated individual; and handling complicated ideas. If students are allowed to graduate without these skills, the doorkeeping function will be impeded. The capacity of graduates to perform in the skilled positions society needs will decline,

and society as a whole will suffer. Therefore, this sociologist might conclude, the university is merely requesting that it be allowed to do its job.

A conflict theorist, by contrast, might focus on the different interests of the participants involved, perhaps seeing the issue as part of a larger conflict between blacks and whites over equality. She or he might analyze the interests of the university administrators in restoring proper "standards"—upholding the prestige of the university, for instance—and emphasize the degree of power and control the university administrators hold over who does and does not get into school. The university, by restoring certain standards regardless of the backgrounds of the students applying for school, will, in effect, bar poor black students from getting the education necessary to gain more powerful and better-paying positions in society—positions that would help ensure that their children would receive quality education from the start. This sociologist might therefore conclude that, in order to meet the needs of poor blacks, the university should not be allowed to raise its entrance standards but instead should develop special remedial programs to help those whose preuniversity schooling was below standard.

A sociologist working within the symbolic-interactionist tradition might concentrate on quite a different set of elements in the same situation, perhaps by investigating how the university administrators, students, parents, and civil rights leaders interpret the situation and the motives of each of the other groups involved. The investigator might then go one step further and try to relate these interpretations with the nature of the groups' interactions. Or the symbolic interactionist might investigate the meaning of the bachelor's degree to the various parties involved and to other interested parties. Prospective employers, for instance, would likely expect individuals with a bachelor's degree to have demonstrated competence at a range of skills, but the present policy allows students to graduate without having achieved this competence. Thus, the degree's meaning is unclear. Such confusion about the significance of a degree could undermine the meaning of the educational process, this sociologist might conclude, and, as a personal suggestion, add that the parties involved might get together and try to develop a consensus on the degree's meaning.

It should now be clear that the particular viewpoint we adopt influences what we see and our final analysis. Depending on the perspective we choose, we are likely to define the same situation quite differently, although not necessarily contradictorily.

In our hypothetical example, we suggested some policy positions that each sociologist might advance. Of course, much social science research is not done with policy in mind; still, when it is, are the positions taken similar to the ones we've suggested—conservative for the functionalist, more liberal for the conflict theorist, and relatively neutral for the symbolic interactionist? Yes and no. We might draw an analogy with the Democratic and Republican parties. While a rule of thumb is that the Democrats tend to be the more liberal party and the party of labor while the Republicans tend to be more conservative and the party of big business, there are many exceptions, such as the Southern Democrats, for example. Similarly, the functionalist approach, with its emphasis on order and stability, tends to be conservative, but

there are radical functionalists, and there are conservative conflict theorists. For example, a conflict theorist might argue that it is legitimate for the university to change its rules. Another sociologist might look at the university from a functionalist point of view but criticize the institution for not living up to its function with regard to children from poor black families. For an example of a study in which the authors took a functionalist perspective but came to some radical conclusions, see The Functioning of Welfare.

Having sketched the three major points of view with which sociologists look at society, let's now examine the methods sociologists use to test the more specific theories they develop from these perspectives.

METHOD OF SOCIOLOGICAL INVESTIGATION

In undertaking a sociological investigation, sociologists, like all scientists, use a three-step process:

Step 1: Carefully define the question or problem to be investigated in a way that is testable.
Step 2: Gather the relevant data.
Step 3: Analyze the data and compare the results with the proposition (or "hypothesis") with which you started.

In this section, we'll look at the logic that lies behind how sociologists define the question they want to investigate and how they analyze the results. Then we'll look at the methods they use to gather the evidence.

THE FUNCTIONING OF WELFARE

In their book *Regulating the Poor: The Functions of Public Welfare*, Frances Fox Piven and Richard A. Cloward illustrate the insights that can be gained through use of the sociological method, and they demonstrate that functionalist analysis doesn't necessarily lead to conservative conclusions.

Why do governments set up welfare programs? Many people think such programs are established primarily for charitable and humanitarian reasons, that they amount essentially to massive giveaway programs. A study of the role of welfare in Europe and the United States, however, convinced Piven and Cloward that the primary aim of welfare has always been to regulate labor and, in doing so, to minimize public unrest. They reached that conclusion after an extensive study of government reports, histories, and other written material pertaining to welfare policy in the United States in the twentieth century. In trying to explain changes in welfare policy, they considered such sociological variables as political stability and unrest, economic conditions, unemployment, protest organizations and action (from committees to public demonstrations), and the like.

Piven and Cloward concentrated on relief practices during three periods: the Great Depression, 1929–1939; World War II and the Cold War years, 1940–1960; and 1960–1970. While the nature of their material did not lend itself to quantitative analysis, the two researchers were still able to uncover some broad patterns in public welfare policy. They found that as social unrest or the threat of it increased (as during the Great Depression and the 1960s), government welfare expanded. When general stability and prosperity returned (the Cold War years), the welfare rolls were reduced by imposing more

The Logic of Sociological Investigation

Sociologists, like other scientists, work by *abstracting* certain elements from the situations they observe and then investigating the role these elements play in the situations. **Abstraction** is the process of identifying the element(s) common to several situations. To get a feel for this process, consider the following.

Imagine that one night, after dining in an Italian restaurant, you become ill. Your first reaction might be: "I'm never going to

stringent eligibility requirements. During these latter periods, moreover, the welfare system helped to keep wages low. It did this by drastically limiting the amount of relief money available to recipients and by stigmatizing the recipient as a "valueless person"—a drain on society. Individuals were motivated to accept low wages because the alternative of going on welfare was too shameful to consider. The point here, Piven and Cloward suggest, wasn't that people shouldn't work, but that they get adequately paid for doing so.

> Our argument, however, is not against work. We take it for granted that all societies require productive contributions from most of their members, and that all societies develop mechanisms to ensure that those contributions will be made. . . . And so the issue is not the relative merit of work itself; it is rather how some men are made to do the harshest work for the least reward. (1971, p. *xvii*)

In general, Piven and Cloward conclude, relief systems function to bring social and political stability when expanded and motivate people to work for low wages when contracted. But in performing this functional analysis, the authors went one step farther: they showed how the welfare system tends to benefit the interests of business owners. Piven and Cloward's analysis thus allows us to say to the antiwelfare partisan who perceives welfare as a social waste: See, society is getting something in return. And of prowelfare partisans we can ask: Are you sure that the present system of welfare adequately looks after *your* interests?

---

that ptomaine village again!" Perhaps you try another Italian restaurant, but you again become sick. You then vow never to eat Italian food again! What you have done is abstract one of the many elements common to the two situations—the element of cuisine—and decide that that is the cause of your upset. No doubt, you are quite confident about your theory as you put relish and ketchup on your "good old American" hamburger the next day. But when your stomach rebels later that evening, you're confused. You had abstracted the most obvious element; if that isn't the cause, what is? The next day, the only thing you can bring yourself to eat is a small salad—and when that makes you sick, you decide on a new strategy: What, you ask, did I eat at every one of these meals? You remember that there was tomato sauce on the Italian food, tomato ketchup on the hamburger, and tomatoes in the salad—one element common to every situation. Your analysis—tomatoes make you sick! You'd probably quit right there, but if you were a proper scientist (and didn't mind getting sick again), you would see how your stomach would respond to the restaurants' foods without tomatoes and with some more tomatoes before drawing a conclusion.

Although abstraction in science is not usually that simple, the example demonstrates two common aspects of the process: (1) we make abstractions all the time; and (2) in seeking an answer we begin by examining only the most obvious elements common to the situations. Similarly, the way we define and study any social problem is not going to include every element involved—that would be impossible. (Try and imagine *everything* involved in the commission of a crime or in a riot!) The elements we choose are called **variables** (any characteristic that can change and be measured) because we study them by observing how they change, or *vary* (see Table P.2).

In science, or even in finding the source of our stomachaches, we test whether or not, when one element varies, another one would also. For instance, when we vary our diet in a certain way, does our feeling of good health decline? In other words, is there a match (or *correlation*) between the change in one variable and that of another? For example, Piven and Cloward (1971) discovered that as the variables of social disorder (strikes, riots, protest rallies, and such) increase, so does the amount of wel-

Table P.2 What Is a Variable?

Variables	What Could Be Studied
Age	The proportion of youth, middle-aged adults, and elderly in the labor force
Educational background	The average number of years of schooling for people at different income levels
Ethnicity	Educational achievement of Jewish, Irish, and Italian Americans
Marital status	The number of married, divorced, or never-married individuals in a given area
Race	White and nonwhite income
Sex	The number of women vs. the number of men as corporate executives
Social class	The number of blue-collar and white-collar workers voting Democratic in an election

fare payments, another variable (see pages 14 to 15).

In the same way, Charles Y. Glock and Rodney Stark (1965) were able to expand our understanding of religious behavior by asking over 3,000 northern Californians such questions as: Do you believe in God? How often do you attend church? Can you list the Ten Commandments? Have you been "reborn"? Taken together, religious behavior is a complicated social phenomenon, but the sociologists' questions identified and abstracted four general categories linking them all. The four categories, or *dimensions*, of religiosity—belief, ritual, knowledge, and experience—are components that affect how "religiously" we be-

Individual qualities can go forever unnoticed without the "right" combination of sociological variables. What variables have affected this man's chances for success in life?

and then examining data on Western European suicide rates during the nineteenth century. What could explain the changes in suicide rates that he discovered? Through a process of selecting one variable after another (climate, nationality, religion, level of education, and so forth) and matching variations in these characteristics with variations in the suicide rates, Durkheim was able to show that persons who committed suicide tended to share certain social characteristics. For example, suicide was more common among Protestants than Catholics or Jews, among the upper rather than lower classes, and among widowed rather than married persons.

Having made this initial analysis, Durkheim went on to investigate what similarities existed among these characteristics. He suggested that many of the variations in suicide rates could be explained by characteristics that reflected looser social bonds among suicides than among nonsuicides. (For example, Protestantism stresses individualism more than Catholicism does, while widows are suddenly left alone.) The real cause of many suicides, Durkheim suggested, was social; it lay in relatively weak relationships of individuals to society.

Durkheim didn't "prove" that loose social bonds were the major cause of suicide. What he did do was show that there was a correlation between certain social characteristics of the victims and the incidence of suicide, and he provided a theory to account for this correlation. Other researchers could then test Durkheim's theory in various other situations to see if it held up as an explanation of the facts.

Durkheim's investigation represents a model of the interplay between theory and research in sociology: Understandings gained through research of particular be-

have. These findings enabled the researchers to explain the social facts of religious behavior. (For the study's results, see Chapter 6.)

The process of abstraction, then, helps us to find the social facts behind behavior. The classic demonstration of this type of analysis is Emile Durkheim's study of suicide (1951 [1897]). Durkheim began his study by defining what he meant by suicide

Table P.3 Major Research Methods

Method	Use
Survey research 　Face-to-face interviews 　Questionnaire surveys	To describe a population with regard to some variable, in order to explain the connections among variables.
Observation 　Participant observation	To understand behavior or social processes that can't be obtained simply by asking the participants in a survey.
Experimentation 　Laboratory experiments 　Field experiments	To analyze behavior that does not normally occur in any regular, observable way.
Content analysis	To analyze material in documents, books, official reports, tape recordings, and so on.
Historical research	To uncover social processes and social facts from the past.

haviors are used to form general principles of social action that are woven together to build theories that explain similar behaviors. These theories are then tested through further research, which lends support to them, causes their refinement, or leads to the introduction of new theories.

Research Methods

Thus far we have been talking about the logic of scientific research, but there are also specific methods sociologists use when gathering data. Here we'll look at the five major methods: survey research, observation, experimentation, content analysis, and historical analysis (see Table P.3).

SURVEY RESEARCH Perhaps the most popular method of research among sociologists today is that of *survey research.* In this method, the researcher asks members of a given population a set of questions about their attitudes, beliefs, or habits. The questions may be asked in face-to-face interviews, over the phone, or through the use of mailed questionnaires. Opinion polls, market research, the United States census, and television ratings are all examples of this method. These researches are conducted in order to *describe* a population with regard to some variable. For instance, a population might be described by political party affiliation (the number of Democrats, Republicans, and independents), by the proportion of virgins and nonvirgins in a population of singles, or by attitudes toward feminism. Most survey research in sociology, however, is carried out in order to help *explain* the connections among variables. For example, the researchers might subdivide the population asked about feminism according to the sex, age, income, and occupation of the respondents. They would then try to explain why the results varied (if they did) from one group to another.

Except in instances where the responses of only a small number of persons are of interest to the researcher (for instance, how members of a local boy scout troop feel about their organization), sociologists must rely on the answers of a *representative sample* of the larger population they wish to study. For instance, when George Gallup or Louis Harris conducts one of their nationwide polls, they usually question only a few thousand people, yet they are often able to make quite accurate predictions (about, for example, a presidential election) because they carefully choose what types of people to contact. They select people from different areas of the country, occupational categories, income groups, educational levels, and so forth in proportion to their numbers in the larger population.

Especially in large-scale surveys, there is a limit to the flexibility of answers that survey researchers can conveniently utilize if they want to be able to compare the responses of different people. For this reason, survey questionnaires tend to be highly structured. For example, public opinion pollsters would not ask people: What do you think of the president's economic policy? Instead, they might ask: With regard to the president's economic policy, do you (1) Approve; (2) Disapprove; (3) Feel neutral? Survey research can be useful for revealing general patterns of attitudes and conscious behavior, but asking questions in this way obviously doesn't allow the researcher to capture the subtlety and intensity of people's attitudes.

Survey research is also not of much help in understanding behavior that the respondents take for granted or don't understand themselves. Much of our behavior is habitual to the point where it is almost unnoticed—for instance, wearing clothes in public; the special ways we react to people of different races, ages, or sex; the bases on which we form close attachments with others; and so on. Our answers would be based on habit and therefore fail to reflect the range and intensity of our stance on the issue or the motives behind it. For these kinds of behaviors, other research methods must be used.

OBSERVATION When investigators are interested in understanding complex behavior or social processes, which can't be obtained by simply asking the participants in a survey, they frequently use the method of direct *observation*—that is, they go out and carefully and systematically observe the group or interaction or social process themselves. For instance, sociologists Donald Black and Albert J. Reiss, Jr. used this method to help them explain why, among those detained for questioning, black youths are more likely to be arrested than whites (see Picking Up Delinquents).

One variant of the observation method is the *participant-observation* method, so named because the researcher actually participates in the social behavior under study. This method is particularly useful when the researcher wants to get a fresh look at some aspect of social life and understand the feelings of those involved.

Consider, for instance, the complex relationships in the streetcorner life of black men studied by Elliot Liebow (1967) in *Tally's Corner*. If Liebow had pursued his subject by surveying such things as unemployment rates; the amount of time spent at the corner hangout; and marriage, divorce, and desertion rates, he would have missed the richness of the streetcorner relationships. To get at these patterns of social behavior and explain why people engaged in them, Liebow spent eighteen months on the streetcorner, becoming part

PICKING UP DELINQUENTS: AN OBSERVATION STUDY

Why are black youths more likely to be arrested for minor crimes (nonfelonies) than their white counterparts? To explore this question, two researchers, Donald Black and Albert J. Reiss, Jr. (1970), engaged thirty-six observers to ride in police cars and carefully note police encounters with white and black juveniles in three cities: Boston, Chicago, and Washington, D.C. Without such direct observations, we might speculate that the different arrest rate could be explained by the racial prejudices of the police or because blacks commit more serious misdemeanors than whites. Through their systematic observations, however, the investigators discovered that neither of these suppositions explained the pattern of arrests.

In cataloging reports of the nearly 6,000 incidents observed, Black and Reiss found that the disparities between the arrest patterns varied with whether or not the victim-complainant was present at the encounter between police and the juvenile. In situations where the complainant was absent, researchers found that, of the youths detained for questioning, blacks were arrested a higher percentage of the time, but the discrepancy wasn't great (14 percent for blacks, 10 percent for whites). However, when the complainant was present, blacks were arrested almost three times as frequently as whites (21

---

of its life. His aim, he said, was not to test a particular hypothesis but to gain a first-hand picture of lower-class black men. By using the participant-observer method, Liebow was able to gain some new insights into the culture of the ghetto. We'll look at some of his findings in Chapter 2.

EXPERIMENTATION In the *experiment*, a sociologist manipulates variables in a controlled environment and observes the reactions of the subjects. Experimentation

is particularly useful when the behavior does not normally occur in any regular, observable way. For instance, a now famous experiment we will discuss in detail in Chapter 4 was set up to test how willing people are to harm others on command—behavior we cannot easily observe systematically outside the laboratory. The experiment was constructed so its subjects believed they were giving electric shocks to other individuals as part of a "learning exercise" (Milgram 1963). The major drawback of the laboratory experiment is that we can never be certain that be-

percent vs. 8 percent). Why did this happen? Black and Reiss note that the police are generally responsive to the demands of victim-complainants for arrests. No youths were arrested for minor offenses if the victim was present at the police-juvenile encounter, unless the victim demanded the arrest. The researchers found that the crucial factor in explaining the different rates of arrests in situations where the complainant was present was that black complainants (usually living in black, high crime areas) were more likely to demand the suspect's arrest than whites were. Since suspect and victim are usually of the same race, this meant that a higher percentage of blacks would be arrested.

Alan Orenstein and William R. F. Phillips (1978, pp. 199–200) have noted that one reason the Black and Reiss study is important is that it takes the encounter as its basic unit of analysis. The study demonstrates that the outcome of a police-suspect interaction can depend on the situation itself rather than on any personal characteristic of the individuals in the encounter. Prejudice may play a role in these encounters, but the study suggests that, overall, it is not the crucial variable. Only by systematic observation were researchers able to uncover the significant data that led them to this conclusion.

havioral patterns observed in the laboratory are the same as those found in the "real" world.

Experiments can also be performed "in the field," that is, outside the laboratory. In *field experiments*, we introduce a variable into a real situation and watch people's reactions to it. For instance, in one study an accomplice crossed the street against a traffic light while others observed how many people followed (Lefkowitz et al. 1955). Experimenters have also had accomplices act as if they were badly hurt in order to find out what factors encourage or inhibit people from aiding others in need (Latane and Rodin 1969).

CONTENT ANALYSIS *Content analysis* is another important method of investigation. It is particularly useful when researching material in documents, books, official reports, tape recordings, and so on. The researcher has a particular social or cultural principle in mind and looks for relevant data in the materials. If, for example, the researcher were interested in how females are viewed in America, he or she might review newspapers, magazines, books, and other written documents for statements that reflect what woman's role was and is and how people have viewed it over time; or the researcher might watch television for several months and count the number and kinds of roles in which women appear.

HISTORICAL ANALYSIS In historical analysis, as you have probably gathered, researchers attempt to uncover social processes and social facts from the past. Obviously, researchers cannot directly observe them, and so rely on such sources as archival materials, old letters, census reports, or on the recollections of participants in, for example, a strike of a previous era. Emile Durkheim's *Suicide*, which we have cited so often in this chapter, is also a classic instance of historical analysis in sociology.

THE PROMISE OF SOCIOLOGY

Sociology as an academic discipline began to take shape in the middle of the last century as a response to the revolutionary social changes wrought by the democratic and industrial revolutions spreading across Europe and the United States. Peasants, farmers, and artisans were transformed into factory "hands," and captains of industry and commerce arose to share power with the great European landowners. Challenges to autocratic rule and to the spread of the factory system erupted in the European revolts of 1830 and 1848. The population of cities both in Europe and the United States mushroomed; the pace of technological change accelerated; religion

and traditional values were frequently attacked; new social problems arose and many old ones increased in complexity.

In these circumstances, many individuals voiced the feeling that they were being buffeted about by forces that they could neither control nor explain, nor sometimes even name. The promise of sociology, as expressed by early workers in the field, was to make sense of these forces and, by so doing, to make possible their more rational control. A central theme of the early sociologists was the influence of social forces on the individual. We already noted Durkheim's statement that the individual is dominated by a collective reality. Weber showed how the ideas people generate to give meaning to their world subsequently impose order on their actions and ways of thinking as individuals, and Marx showed how individual lives are dominated by conflicts between economic classes. Today's major perspectives in sociology—functionalism, conflict theory, symbolic interactionism—also share the view that powerful social forces dominate the lives of individuals, often without their knowledge.

Order and Society

Long before anyone had ever heard of sociology, an English philosopher named Thomas Hobbes (1588–1679) proposed a theory to account for the dominance of society over the individual. Hobbes believed that people have always been engaged in a perpetual struggle for power over others—"a restlesse desire of Power after power, that ceaseth onely in Death" (1968 [1651], p. 161). He recognized that there is generally a smaller number of any given item than what people want—this is the concept of *scarcity*—and our inclination has always been to compete for the goods we want.

In his book *Leviathan*, Hobbes asks us to imagine a time when no type of government or laws existed to restrain our behavior in any way. In such a condition, there would be no boundaries on how we might attempt to get what we want. There would be, Hobbes wrote:

> no place for Industry; because the fruit thereof is uncertain: and consequently no Culture of the Earth; no Navigation, nor use of the commodities that may be imported by Sea; no commodious Building; no Instruments of moving, and removing such things as require much force; no Knowledge of the face of the Earth; no account of Time; no Arts; no Letters; no Society; and which is worst of all, continuall feare, and danger of violent death; And the life of man, solitary, poore, nasty, brutish, and short. (1968 [1651], p. 186)

We could never feel safe in that condition because we would lack all protection from the hostile acts of others pursuing their interests. There would be, in Hobbes's famous phrase, a war of all against all. Hobbes assumed that most people would desperately want to get out of this condition, and he hypothesized how: namely, by allowing a third party (government) to lay down the rules that tell us what we can and cannot do. It is essential that we be powerless against this party, so we cannot change the rules just because they do not suit us. (That would mean that anyone could change the rules and we would be back where we started.) We would each give up our total freedom to do anything that

personal passions lead us to do, and we would relinquish any power that the government demands of us (for instance, government has a monopoly on the legitimate use of violence). And we would feel that the exchange of some freedom for security is worth it.

Although Hobbes was certain that the world was much better with governments than without them, he did not believe that this purged society of all conflict. The crucial difference he saw was that in the original state of affairs we fought unprotected, as individuals; now we fought in groups that protected "the Industry of their Subjects; [and] there does not follow from it, that misery" that accompanies the war of all against all (1968 [1651], p. 188). In short: now the conflict is organized.

Hobbes's imaginary world—filled with individuals but no society—could never have existed because without society, as we'll see in subsequent chapters, there can be no individuals. But his vision provides us with two important insights. First, he shows us that social life is organized life. Without some semblance of organization, regularity, and cooperation, society would not be possible. Second, Hobbes alerts us to the role of the state and other institutions of society in controlling and regulating our behavior. These institutions are equipped with a number of very powerful means for accomplishing this task. These means include the police, the prison system, and the system of laws. They include the power of parents to command obedience of us, the power of teachers to pass or fail us, and the power of corporate managers to hire and fire us.

It is important to realize, however, that the organized behavior that flows from the state and the laws of a society represents only one aspect of social order and regu-

Order is important for society to work. But it doesn't just happen, and we give up a lot of individual freedom in exchange for it.

lation and only one aspect of the influence of society over the individual. Regulation of behavior involves more than simply someone telling us what to do. We make agreements with each other, implicitly or explicitly, to regulate our own behavior. For instance, we move out of the way of each other when approaching on a busy sidewalk, and we try to follow regular patterns in conversation so that others can understand us. We act in ordered ways also out of custom or to gain approval. We seldom experience these forms of cooperation as constraints on our personal interests and actions. They are of a different order than someone standing over us with a billy club,

and we may be only dimly aware of the social forces that induce them.

If we must accept the necessity of order and regulation, we do not necessarily need to accept the particular forms this order takes. Although we will be emphasizing powerful social mechanisms that guide our behavior, that does not mean that the particular state of affairs they protect (e.g., a particular distribution of wealth, specific behaviors encouraged or prohibited, or individual leaders) is inevitable or necessarily the best one. It can be changed; however, we need first to understand what social forces impinge on our lives. Sociology can help us gain that understanding.

The Sociological Imagination

Sociology is—as much as it is anything else we have mentioned in this chapter—a state of mind and a way of thinking. C. Wright Mills (1959) called it the *sociological imagination* and described it as a quality of mind that helps us achieve a clear understanding of what is going on in the world *and* what may be happening within ourselves. Nowadays, he said, people "often feel that their private lives are a series of traps. They sense that within their everyday worlds, they cannot overcome their troubles, and in this feeling, they are often quite correct" (1959, p. 3). This sense of being trapped comes because the changes we observe in our society and across the world seem to occur with no reference to what we want out of life; and so we concentrate on our personal loss. The major advantage that sociology and the sociological imagination offer is that they can take us beyond our particular concerns by pointing to the structural—or social—origins of our problems (Mills 1959, pp. 2–11).

All of us participate in social life, but not very many of us can adequately explain it. Mills addressed this in *The Sociological Imagination* when he noted that any participation proceeds within our own "private orbits," that is, within the many defined sectors of life—family, school, job, and so on—that direct our behavior and imagination to narrow ends. In other words, unless we make a special effort, our powers of explanation and understanding will be severely limited in scope. Ralf Dahrendorf has summed up well the nature of this effort. It requires that we develop the capacity to look on our own lives and the society around us as a stranger might. As he says: "Whoever attempts a fundamental and comprehensive interpretation of his own society must be capable of some detachment from the world of his daily life. . . . Detachment from the familiar and habitual, the stranger's view, is not always easy to bear. It is never comfortable, but I have always felt it to be a pure gain" (Dahrendorf 1967, p. *x*).

As social actors, we are constantly involved in problem solving: how to secure a job, how to successfully negotiate the perils of an expressway at rush hour, how to have a quiet dinner time, how to ensure an active "social life," how to find salvation, even how to get out of bed in the morning. As a result, we generally fail to distinguish our own personal troubles from the problems of society. The major feature of personal troubles is that they occur within individuals (*I* was robbed) or within their immediate vicinity (which includes their immediate relationships with others). Mills's description of social problems stands out in contrast. Social problems, he says, "have to do with matters that transcend these local environments of the individual and the range of his inner life. They have to do with the organization of many such [environments] into the institutions of an historical society, as a whole, with the ways in which various [environments] overlap and interpenetrate to form the larger structure of social and historical life" (1959, p. 8). Making this distinction is the necessary first step to a successful understanding and analysis of the conditions that gave rise to individual and social problems. (Recall our discussion of objectivity.) If my concern is how much money *I* can afford to spend on food, can I expect to find an answer to the underlying economic problem of inflation? Does the social problem of unemployment cease to exist when *I* have a job? Is there no need for abortions if *I* don't have to carry and bear the child?

Is there no crime problem if there is hardly any crime in *my* town or suburb? Is busing a good thing as long as *my* children can attend their neighborhood school? If a group of people lose some or all of their civil rights is it a problem if *I* have my rights? There are an infinite number of examples, but the idea should be clear—we are often too involved with overcoming the countless barriers we encounter in daily life for an objective understanding and analysis of society. The irony is that only through such an objective understanding will we be likely to successfully cope with our personal problems.

The importance of understanding society, finally, lies in the fact that social forces are not just outside of us, but in us. Georg Simmel (1858–1918)—like Marx, Weber, and Durkheim, an important early sociologist—observed that we are the sites of an inner conflict between two different sets of demands. One set concerns our personal lives—eat, sleep, go out tonight, spend lots of money; and the other concerns us as members of a particular society, following a set of specific rules—stay up and study, stay home with your family, go to church, make lots of money, and don't kill that person no matter how angry you are (Simmel 1950). As you can see, the two sets are often in conflict (sleep vs. stay up and study). Individuals are always confronting this conflict: how about those Monday mornings when you are exhausted but have an early class—do you gratify your desire to sleep, or go to class; or how about those beautiful spring afternoons when everybody is outside and you have a class or have to go to work.

In sum, sociology gives us the ability to explain the relationship between the individual and society—often through analyses of important social issues. Our concern is thus shifted from personal troubles to the social issues that ultimately underlie them. For example, consider abortion—whether or not an individual can obtain a legal abortion ultimately rests on the resolution of conflicting values and interests of different social groups.

Our perspective requires that we question what others find obvious; for instance, why a university has particular admissions standards. And we not only ask, we attempt an objective analysis to find an answer. The sociological imagination is critical, not in a judgmental sense of determining good and bad, but as an ability that can uncover hidden patterns and intelligently challenge the stock answers we are given by parents, teachers, clergy, bosses, political leaders, influential business leaders, oil company executives, and the like. Instead, we seek our own.

The Plan of This Book

The organization of this book is designed to help you develop a sociological imagination about our own society. Part One deals with how the individual is related to society, starting in Chapter 1 with socialization—the process by which we become functioning members of society. Chapters 2 through 4 continue to show the extent of society within the individual and discuss the elements of social structure that define right and wrong and "proper" behavior. Chapter 2 examines their cultural context; Chapter 3 looks at the consequences of these structures in social action; and Chapter 4, on conformity and deviance, talks about our reactions to this behavior and their impact.

Chapters 5 through 8 examine the

structure of society. Chapter 5 looks at the power organization brings and at its coercive nature on the individual. Chapter 6 examines some powerful social institutions and some challenges being launched against them. This critical examination of society is continued in Chapters 7 and 8, on inequality. Chapter 7 explores the social bases of inequality, and Chapter 8 is concerned with injustices perpetrated against specific groups (blacks and other ethnics, women, youth, and the aged).

Chapters 9 through 13 are about societal and group change. Chapter 9 contrasts the processes that pull societies apart (social disorganization) with those holding them together (social solidarity). Chapter 10 discusses collective behavior (crowd behavior) and social movements. Chapter 11 looks at social change in general; it focuses on theories of social change and some of the major sources of change (population growth, urbanization, and technology).

Throughout this prologue, we have indicated the usefulness sociology has for understanding important social issues (e.g., abortion, affirmative action). As you go through this book, test the value of each idea and concept as it is covered, by asking exactly how well it works for *you*, to what extent it increases your understanding of the public controversies you confront, and by how much it increases your knowledge and understanding of the human world around you.

Key Terms

sociology (p. 1)
social structure (p. 2)
scientific method (p. 5)
concepts (p. 7)
theory (p. 7)
functionalism (p. 7)
conflict theory (p. 7)
symbolic interactionism (p. 7)
social fact (p. 8)
symbol (p. 10)
abstraction (p. 14)
variable (16)

Review and Discussion Questions

1. What skills do you hope to get out of your sociology course? How do you expect to use them later in life?
2. Are the stands you take on public issues based more on analysis or on your personal opinions? How do personal opinions prevent the analysis of certain public controversies (the gay rights debate, for instance) on the basis of objective facts?
3. What are some of the important concepts in your daily routine? How do you use them? What do they describe?
4. Grading seems to be an essential part of our educational system, although many people have questioned its utility over the years. How would you analyze the grading system in school from each of the three major perspectives on society?
5. How can a sociological imagination help you see your personal problems in a social context? Give an example or two.

For Further Study

SOCIOLOGY IN SOCIETY One of the major points this prologue has tried to make is that sociology is not only a scientific study of society but also an active part of social life. A comprehensive review of the impact of sociology on various areas of public life can be found in Paul F. Lazarsfeld, William H. Seward, and Harold L. Wilensky, eds., *The Uses of Sociology* (New York: Basic Books, 1967). Sociological findings have had a particularly strong impact on the design of government social services; for that aspect of sociology in society, see Irving L. Horowitz and James E. Katz, *Social Science and Public Policy* (New York: Praeger, 1975).

THREE VIEWS OF SOCIETY For a more comprehensive look at each of the three perspectives on society you might consult the following. For functionalism, there is Robert K. Merton, *Social Theory and Social Structure* (New York: Free Press, 1968). For conflict theory, see Ralf Dahrendorf, *Class and Class Conflict in Industrial Society* (Stanford, CA: Stanford University Press, 1959). For symbolic interactionism, see Herbert Blumer, *Symbolic Interactionism: Perspective and Method* (Englewood Cliffs, NJ: Prentice-Hall, 1969). For an important critique of functionalism's conservative bias, see Alvin W. Gouldner, *The Coming Crisis of Western Sociology* (New York: Avon, 1970).

GENERAL A publication that is of great aid in the pursuit of sociology is Pauline Bart and Linda Frankel's, *The Student Sociologist's Handbook* (Morristown, NJ: General Learning Press, 1976). It offers practical advice on such things as writing sociology papers, doing library research, and using periodic literature and data sources. Another useful book is Kenneth R. Hoover's *The Elements of Social Scientific Thinking* (New York: St. Martin's, 1976). This is a comprehensive review of basic social scientific terms and concepts (e.g., concept, variable, and theory). On methodology, see Alan Orenstein and William R. F. Phillips, *Understanding Social Research: An Introduction* (Boston: Allyn and Bacon, 1978). Finally, C. Wright Mill's *The Sociological Imagination* (New York: Oxford University Press, 1959) is well worth reading for a good orientation to the study of society.

PART ONE

Each part of this book has a
specific aim. The major goal of the prologue was to provide
some idea of what society and its study (namely, sociology) are
about. Hopefully, it also started us thinking about our use of
abstractions in our lives—the things we cannot grab hold of
but that are powerful nonetheless. With this general
understanding, we are ready to tackle the substance of
sociology—its special vocabulary, its insights and theories, and
some of its studies. Part I has as its aim, appropriately enough,
the specification of what makes each individual a social being—
that is, how we each fit into society and how society exists
within us. This is the link between the concrete individual and
the abstraction, society. That might sound a bit vague, but it
should become clear as we look at the topics explored in Part I.

Each chapter in Part I offers a basic insight into the social
nature of the world around us. Each pinpoints a way that most
people view important aspects of human behavior (such as
individuality, right and wrong, creativity and individual
freedom, and responsibility) and offers instead a sociological
viewpoint that considers some powerful forces that people
frequently ignore. (You probably got some idea of these forces
in the prologue.) Chapter 1 takes issue with the way many
people understand their own nature and where it originates.
Without denying the unique component in each of us, the
chapter shows that the self does not come into the world full-
blown but rather is essentially a social product. Each of us

The Individual
and Society

develops our sense of self through society in a process known as socialization. Everything that we subsequently do is in relation to other people, if not to society in general. In short, although people tend to emphasize individual differences, we should also be aware of the similarities in the way we think and behave. We want to understand the basis and implication of these similarities.

In Chapter 2, we will explore the subtleties of right and wrong and learn that they are social determinations rather than eternal standards, as they are frequently treated. We will also look at the rules of behavior we follow (both consciously and unconsciously) to discover where they come from, how we internalize them, and what happens if we try to violate them. Chapter 3 examines the way these rules are often organized in the form of roles, or parts, we play. We tend to see only the people playing these parts and to forget that the range of behaviors they are allowed is severely limited by social rules, with the result that we often overestimate the extent of our freedom in these roles. Sociology gives us the tools to more realistically assess our position. Finally, in Chapter 4, we will use these insights to explain why people generally obey the rules and to see what happens when they do not. We will find that the way in which society reacts to a disobedient act may be as important as the action itself. Chapter 4 also emphasizes the social forces that enforce obedience. Our obedience is not necessarily a result of the rules being right. ▦

CHAPTER ONE
Socialization and the Nature of Social Control

I usually give a class in which the students are asked to select a single social problem and research it *as a group.* They are told ahead of time that they will have to do this without the instructor's help. The students can study whatever topic they agree on—but they have to agree on it by themselves. That's not so easy; and without fail, students voice their apprehensions that without the teacher's direction, they will have to contend with seventy different suggestions from the seventy different individuals in the class. After all, they claim, all of us have our own ideas. Fairly soon, however, it is apparent that we do not. There are nowhere near seventy different topics; there may only be a dozen; and soon thereafter, only a few, and in a short time, the single topic is agreed on. What do you think accounts for this amazing lack of difficulty?

The answer to that question is entwined with the answer to another, more general one that we'll be exploring in this chapter: Why is there so much order and predictability in social life?

SOCIAL ORDER AND SOCIAL CONTROL

As we noted in the prologue, through the process of abstraction sociologists look for regularities—common behaviors—among individuals. If we take each individual in isolation, as a person, we might emphasize the unique qualities that have led to her or his present behavior. But when we consider society as a whole, we get quite a different picture. We are likely to see that, in general, people behave quite like one another: most "individuals" do not commit murder or theft, and they agree that it is "wrong" to do so; most "individuals" work at jobs; almost everybody eventually gets married; just about everyone, at least in the United States, watches television (and generally a great deal of it).

These similarities in human social behavior are so numerous and so predictable that we have all come to depend on them. Each of us has some notion of how another person will react to our actions, and we act on the basis of these notions constantly. When we are with others, we know that their responses will almost certainly be restricted to a limited number of alternatives: we know that they are likely to be impressed by wealth, certain professions, and higher education, even if the only thing we know about them is their membership in our society. We know that "street" language will not go over very well in class, church, or at family dinners; but we also know that our friends will not be at ease with us if we use only very refined speech with them. And you use this same knowledge any time you "dress up" for a job interview, expecting to make a good impression. Of course, our expectations about behavior aren't always borne out. When, for example, I sold women's shoes, the store manager told the salespeople to make sure we complimented the customers on how good the shoes looked on them. In general, it worked; people enjoyed the compliments. Sometimes, however, I might say something like, "That really gives your foot a nice look," and the customer would tell me to cut out the sales talk, she would make up her own mind. Even so, our predictions are usually accurate.

You can no doubt think of many other examples of more or less predictable behavior. If the multitude of individuals in our society (including you and me) behave in a similar way, there is a reason *why* they do. It cannot be a coincidence.

Social Control

In the sociological view, the similarities in behavior that we have been discussing are primarily the product of **social control**—the containment of our behaviors within socially approved of boundaries. If you are like most people, you probably associate the term *social control* with such things as prisons and the police. Yet, with a little math, you could determine that the ratio of police officers to members of society is so small that they could not possibly regulate all behavior. Of course, you might then argue that the physical presence of these law enforcers is not necessary. Their mere existence poses an ever-present threat of detection and its unpleasant consequences.

Formal social control mechanisms, such as the police, often are effective. Threatening students with an F, for instance, usually gets them to do the assigned work. And such formal control mechanisms as the blacklist, which employers used against union organizers and which the old House Committee on Un-American Activities used against supposed Communists and Communist sympathizers in the early 1950s, also forced people to stop what they were doing or to avoid certain kinds of activities. Formal mechanisms enforce social order, but even as threats they are not enough in themselves—you cannot go around threatening *everybody* with blacklisting, an F, or jail *all the time.* Yet, all around us, daily social life—the world of business, education, and recreation—proceeds in a very ordered fashion. The highly publicized violations of the social order represent only a small percentage of the innumerable individual actions in our social world. Thus any attempt to locate the source of society's orderliness must see *self-enforcement* of society's rules as crucial. That is, even though hostility builds up in everyone over time—each day, for example, we fight traffic or for a seat on the bus; argue with a friend or fellow student or fellow worker; or compete with someone for a grade, job, or sale—we control ourselves and find acceptable ways to release this hostility (see Table 1.1). But why do we? Why is it that social enforcement and self-enforcement often come to the same end? To answer this question, sociologists suggest that we examine not just the overt methods of social control but also the process of *socialization*—the process whereby we internalize the informal methods of social control we encounter as we grow up and interact with other people.

Table 1.1 Expression of "Legitimate" Hostility

Activities	Ways Hostility Is Released
Business	Conflict can be escalated at will (e.g., price changes, "cutthroat competition")
Dress	Loud and/or noticeable clothes are aggressive. Parental wishes can be disobeyed
Media	Identification with stars' aggressiveness
Music	Loudness of rock music is aggressive. Musicians also speak of "attacking" their instruments
Politics	Obviously competitive
Sex	Some aspects of the behavior are aggressive. Parental wishes can be disobeyed. Some see it as a form of competition and try to be "best" or "most active"
Sports	Obviously competitive, also involves physical contact. Provides an overt enemy and defined goals (winning)

Socialization and Social Control

One objection you might make to what has been said so far is that a concept like social control isn't needed to explain the similarities in our behavior because we are similar by nature. You might argue that our ability to live with others—that is, to speak, eat with utensils, sit in a room with another person, walk upright, and even use a toilet—emerges "naturally," as part of our physical development; that all of these skills are basic to us as human beings. Yet, as the occasional discovery of a child who

has been living isolated from others demonstrates, little is "natural" about our behavior. One such case is that of a six-year-old illegitimate girl named Anna. Her family wanted to hide their "shame," so they confined Anna to a small room, with almost no human contact. Kingsley Davis, who studied her case, writes:

> Anna was left almost without attention. Ordinarily, it seems, Anna received only enough care to keep her barely alive. She appears to have been seldom moved from one position to another. Her clothing and bedding were filthy. She apparently had no instruction, no friendly attention. . . . It seems little wonder that, when finally found and removed from the room in her grandfather's house . . . the child could not talk, walk, or do anything that showed intelligence. (1947, p. 433)

Only nine months after Anna was discovered, authorities found another six-year-old girl, Isabelle, in a similar condition. Anna was indifferent to other humans, whereas Isabelle was extremely fearful of them. The absence of social interaction had not stopped the biological growth of these girls, but it had made their social development impossible. Neither of them was feeble-minded (although Anna's confinement had caused some retardation), and both of them made progress with training.

What these unfortunate individuals had missed was **socialization**, which we can formally define as the social process through which we gain our sense of self and learn the values of our society. Socialization usually implies that we don't simply

When people misbehave, formal control mechanisms react, as are these umpires in ejecting this quarrelsome Yankee manager. But the umpires' power is not what keeps the other players in line. What does?

memorize our society's values, or even just accept the necessity of following their dictates; instead it means that we take them on as our own.

Socialization has two sides. On the one hand, it enables individuals to live in society—that is, it makes social life possible. Without socialization, we would be unable to communicate with others, unable to work or play with them. But socialization also limits individuals. It is a much more important component of social control than laws and their enforcement. Through socialization, we learn society's standards for deciding among possible behaviors (for example, throwing out a piece of food that falls on the floor, rather than eating it; wearing "good" or formal clothes to an office job, rather than wearing old or very casual clothes; speaking English, rather than Serbo-Croatian; becoming a Democrat, Republican, or independent, rather than a socialist; having only one spouse and sex partner, rather than many; preferring work to welfare, and so forth. Socialization explains my students' experience with choosing a problem topic. They are as individual as anyone else, but because they are members of the same society, their ideas tend to fall within the same social limits.

Socialization not only sets limits on our behavior but also shapes our motivations for action. Whether we seek fame, money, sexual favors, power, or salvation, each is a socially defined goal. We have to *learn* to value (or want) them. Do you think we could automatically appreciate the beauty of a Beethoven symphony or a Rembrandt painting, or prefer to live in one suburb or neighborhood rather than another? These motivations depend on social definitions and, ultimately, on how we view ourselves—selves which, as we'll see, develop through socialization.

Variations in Socialization

The critical part played by socialization in what we do and think doesn't mean that everyone turns out the same. You know that isn't so from your own experience. There are several reasons why they don't.

One reason why people don't all think alike is that whereas socialization takes place in *all* societies, its precise content differs from one society to another. In a peasant society, for example, individuals are taught to fit into the system of agricultural labor and suppress their individual desires. In our society, by contrast, according to Erich Fromm, we are trained to fill the needs of industrial capitalism:

> Modern capitalism needs men who cooperate smoothly and in large numbers; who want to consume more; and whose tastes are standardized and can be easily influenced and anticipated. It needs men who feel free and independent, not subject to any authority or principle or conscience—yet willing to be commanded, to do what is expected of them, to fit into the social machine without friction; who can be guided without force, led without leaders, prompted without aim—except the one to make good, to be on the move, to function, to go ahead. (1956, p. 72)

Socialization can also vary widely within a given society, and recent research has revealed some of the differences between the socialization of black and white children in the United States. The researchers have stressed that there is a unique Afro-American component to black life, which black children must learn during this early process (Lewis 1978). Traditionally, black children have learned to develop and present a dual personality—one for the white world, one for the black. They learn to offer a facade of conformity to those white teachers, caseworkers, employers, and police they encounter, while emphasizing their sense of self as unique personalities to other blacks (Lewis 1978, pp. 222–23). The second aspect of that dual personality is encouraged from infancy.

According to anthropologist Virginia Heyer Young (1970), black parents, unlike whites, tend to interpret the behavior of

PERMISSIVE VS. AUTHORITARIAN SOCIALIZATION

You have probably heard proponents of permissive and authoritarian socialization debate over how we should raise our children, with the latter emphasizing parental supervision and control of children's activities. In particular, proponents of authoritarianism blame many social ills on "permissive parents." It seems that the loudest rhetoric comes from such politically conservative groups as religious fundamentalists, antifeminists, and conservative politicians. For the most part, these groups favor tighter controls on adult behavior as well. But if there is a link between support for these positions and authoritarian parenting, what is it? And how can we demonstrate it? We cannot do it with just personal feelings or scattered observations. Fortunately, however, a team of sociologists has done so with research and analysis (see Ellis, Lee, and Petersen 1978).

Considerable research has indicated that people of lower socioeconomic classes tend to value conformity more than self-reliance in their children, and authoritarian over permissive socialization. This has been explained by the conditions of their work, in which they are closely supervised and must follow established procedure. In short, satisfactory performance is strongly related to accepting the direction of some authority, rather than independent decisions. Ellis and his associates went beyond the single variable of socioeconomic status to look at the extent that people are closely supervised in other areas of their lives. For instance, the sociologists found that under autocratic political structures (which closely monitor people's lives) there is a strong emphasis on strict socialization. Ellis and his colleagues concluded that parents will tend to value

even young infants as having some specific motive behind it. So they view infant exploration with hands and mouth as hitting or biting and see the child as "mad" or "mean." Whites, says Young, are more likely to see such actions as instinctive. Young claims that black parents thus cultivate strong-willed children. In addition, other children in the house are socialized to view babies in this way, thereby supporting the image and continuing it into the next generation.

Researchers have continually found that American parents treat girls as though

conformity in their children and be authoritarian to the extent that they themselves are supervised by others.

From this conclusion, they generated hypotheses and tested them with data on 122 nonindustrial societies, contained in the Human Relations Area File (HRAF). (The HRAF is a compendium of data on cultures throughout the world and is available to all scholars.) After coding the data, the researchers found that the value parents place on their children's conformity varied according to the complexity of economic and political systems, religious beliefs and practices, and control over mate selection (that is, when parents control their children's choice of a mate, they will likely be authoritarian). In the case of each hypothesis, the researchers found that as supervision over the parent increased, so did her or his value on conformity in children.

The point of the study for us is twofold. First, we find that socialization values, which are often presented to us as if they were matters of right and wrong, are held by people on the basis of various sociological factors. (Note, though, that socialization is never the same throughout a society and that the researchers are reporting *tendencies*.) This is a very important insight to carry throughout our study of society. Moreover, we can see the part that authoritarian socialization plays in social control. For Ellis, Lee, and Petersen demonstrate that authoritarian socialization is more likely to produce individuals who are generally willing to accept supervision in their lives and direction from an authority.

Ask yourself if you will react any differently now, when you encounter an argument over which mode of childrearing is "best" for your society.

---

they were much more fragile than boys (see, for example, Maccoby and Jacklin 1974). For instance, Alice Lake (1975), in reviewing the research, found that mothers used adjectives like tiny, soft, and delicate to describe their newborn girls, and strong, alert, and well coordinated to describe their infant sons. The result is a society in which women and men themselves believe that women are fragile, and in which a woman who appears otherwise (for instance, by being assertive) is not considered "feminine."

And even within broad social cate-

"What are you really teaching me?"
Socialization is loaded with messages about
"proper" sex-related behavior. Girls learn
passivity, while boys play actively and learn
to work in groups.

Democrat. Socialization, furthermore, is never completely successful. There is always a difference between what people are taught and what they end up actually believing or accepting.

Socialization, then, while a basic element of social control, does not turn people into carbon copies of one another, nor does it eliminate social conflicts. Individual variations still occur, but ordinarily within socially defined limits.

SOCIALIZATION AND THE DEVELOPMENT OF THE SELF

Socialization entails the learning of society's values and symbols. It enables us to participate in society, while at the same time limiting our behavior and values and structuring our wants. Sociologists also generally agree that early socialization is inseparable from the development of the self. The concept of **self** is open to many different interpretations, but we shall define it as the conscious sense of who we are, including our perception of how others see us. For example: I am rich, intelligent, attractive, and have a great social life; I'm ugly, and nobody cares what happens to me; I go to college, have a good job, am insecure, and just like my mother.

In the beginning, we have no sense of self separate from the world around us. Without distinguishing between our own beings and the world, we have no sense of other selves either. Theorists disagree on how we eventually become integrated into society and develop a perception of individuation, although there is a consensus that it occurs through our interactions with others. We will look at the psychoanalytic explanation of Sigmund Freud and

gories such as those of race and sex, socialization can vary considerably. Not all females or all males, all blacks or all whites are brought up the same way, for example. And even when individuals are brought up to share a certain value, they often interpret this value quite differently. Look, for instance, at how many ways there are of being a Democrat. You can be a liberal Democrat, a moderate Democrat, a conservative Democrat, a city machine Democrat, a New Deal Democrat, or a socialist

Table 1.2 The Id, Ego, and Superego

	Id	*Ego*	*Superego*
Considers	What gives pleasure	What works	What is right
Will satisfy	Biological needs	Id and superego	Society
Operates on basis of	The pleasure principle	The reality principle	Internalized social control

then turn to the view of the early American symbolic interactionists Charles Horton Cooley and George Herbert Mead.

Freud's Theory of Personality

Sigmund Freud (1856–1939) was a Viennese physician and the founder of psychoanalysis. In his view, the self develops through conflict between the instinctual drives of the individual to satisfy basic needs and society's inability to directly gratify those needs.

Freud divided the personality (the self + behavior + unconscious thoughts and feelings) into three major parts—the *id, ego,* and *superego*—that he believed constantly competed with one another for control of the individual's actions (see Table 1.2). The id is our basic, unconscious urge for satisfaction which lies behind all our attempts to obtain gratification of any sort. It operates on the *pleasure principle,* constantly demanding of us that we satisfy its wants for food, drink, sex, sleep, and so on. You know that's not always possible. So to gratify the id safely, that part of the personality Freud calls the ego develops. The ego is partially conscious—it includes our sense of self. It attempts to satisfy the demands of the id by directing these urges into so-

cially acceptable channels, for example, hit a tennis ball instead of another person; buy the used Chevy you can afford instead of the Porsche; pay for your food instead of stealing it. In other words, the ego mediates between the id's irrational demands and the constraints imposed by the real world; it operates according to the *reality principle.*

Actually, the ego must seek to satisfy not only the needs of the id but the demands of the superego as well. The superego is, most simply put, the conscience; it is society's representative in the individual. According to Freud, our actions result from the conflict between the urges of the id, society's constraints as represented by the superego, and the efforts of the ego to mediate between them. Socialization consists of the superego's development and the improved ability of the ego to satisfy these often contradictory demands (Freud 1953 [1916]).

Freud's views on personality formation have had a powerful effect on subsequent thinkers. But in trying to make sense of the socialization process, sociologists are more apt to turn to the writings of Cooley and Mead, who place more emphasis on the importance of society in the development of the self than Freud does. Like Freud, Cooley and Mead see personality as a complex unity. But whereas Freud emphasizes conflict between the drives of the id and the requirements of society (as represented by the superego), Cooley and Mead view the self as made up of two complementary components, identified by Mead as the "I," or the individual and innovative aspect of the self, and the "me," or the social aspect of the self. Let's look at this more sociological view.

The Interactionist Perspective

From the interactionist perspective, as one might suppose, the self develops through symbolic interaction. Social interaction involves communicating shared symbols, the most common of which are those of language. Language makes possible, as sociologists Robert A. Nisbet and Robert G. Perrin have written, the development of the human mind and the sense of self, culture, "and that very fundamental capacity . . . of being able to adopt one or more of the social roles that confront each newborn infant in human society" (1977, p. 48).

Language makes it possible for us to share knowledge that is not part of our immediate experience—through books, for example—and to understand the reactions of others and give our own responses.

We can best examine the theory of socialization developed by Mead and Cooley from the symbolic interactionist perspective by analyzing it in four steps: obtaining a self-image through society, learning from our significant others, internalizing the lessons we have learned, and taking the role of the generalized other.

OBTAINING A SELF-IMAGE THROUGH SOCIETY Cooley's (1924) basic contribution to our understanding of the socialization process is to point out that we never really see ourselves directly, but only as reflected in the responses of others to us. To capture this insight Cooley coined the term *looking-glass self.*

Cooley conceptualized the looking-glass self as being composed of three parts: (1) our belief about how we appear to others, (2) our understanding of the way in which others evaluate that appearance, and (3) our own feeling about that evaluation (shame or pride, for instance). Of course, we can be mistaken about either of the first two parts of this process. We may incorrectly interpret how others see us or how they evaluate what they see. Furthermore, our self-concept will not be simply a reflection of what others think of us because obviously not everyone views us in the same way—although their interpretations are likely to fall within a relatively narrow range of disagreement because they were probably brought up in the same society and subjected to the same set of values. Despite this latitude for interpretation, however, it is clear from Cooley's description that what we come to think of as our individuality is to a large degree a social product. Although children sometimes disagree with the judgments others make of them or misinterpret those judgments, for the most part they come to accept those social definitions as the definition of who they are.

LEARNING FROM OUR SIGNIFICANT OTHERS Children learn about society in the same way they learn about themselves—through the actions of others, especially "significant others." **Significant others** are those individuals who, because of our emotional attachment to them or their control over resources we need, exercise the greatest influence on our self-concept. Parents, older brothers and sisters, and teachers are the most likely candidates to fill these positions in our lives.

We learn from others in three ways. The first is through *passive observation*, which begins to occur even before children can speak or comprehend most of what they hear. All around them, children find evidence of behavior patterns (or regularities): in mealtimes, bedtimes, bathing and dressing rituals, celebrations (birthdays, anniversaries, holidays); and in personality traits like politeness, sympathy for the sick, and respect for authority (see Elkin 1960, p. 26). So, even while children are still sitting on the sidelines of social life, they begin to learn what will constitute their daily routines.

Children also learn about behavior from the *reactions of others* (especially, significant others) to specific actions, in the form of rewards and punishments. If the baby does not want any more food and turns its head, the mother stops feeding. If, instead, the baby throws the food on the floor, the mother might respond with a slap on the wrist, and the baby will learn a lesson. Rewards and punishments need not be physical; for instance, the mother's approval of the child's action constitutes a reward in itself.

Finally, the child learns by *direct admonition.* "We don't take without asking." "We say 'thank you' when someone gives us a present." In this way, we also learn about various types of people: "big boys don't cry"; good Americans put out a flag on July 4th; teachers are supposed to know everything. Such lessons are likely to have both immediate and long-range effects on the way we view ourselves in the many parts we play in society: male, female, stu-dent, Jew, Christian, Muslim, doctor, professional athlete, president, or any other you can think of. Major notions about right and wrong are also communicated through direct admonition.

INTERNALIZING THE LESSONS WE LEARN During our socialization, we grow to accept many elements of "proper" behavior—behavior our parents tell us is correct. Whether it is how to dress ourselves, how to chew with our mouths closed, or how to get along with other children, at some point we tend to **internalize** this learned behavior—that is, we take it on as our own. So, instead of a child not stealing from the cookie jar *only when her or his mother is looking* (and taking the cookies when the coast is clear), she or he comes to believe that it is wrong to take the cookies in any case.

Internalization takes place because of the highly emotional attachments we have with significant others, such as our parents. As children, we *identify* with them—that is, we imitate the things they do and say—hoping to be just like them. Later in life, too, internalizing values and behaviors tends to be our strongest and most permanent response to important authorities.

The importance of this internalization process for social control should be clear: it removes the need for external controls (e.g., watchful parents) and substitutes our own self-controls. Through internalization we learn to want to do what we have to do.

TAKING THE ROLE OF THE GENERALIZED OTHER Socialization is a process of generalizing from specific situations; from "I hit my brother and mommy yelled" to "Mom always gets angry when I hit my brother." The crucial development in socialization comes when we can interpret our behavior in light of not just our significant others but society as a whole: "nonviolence is preferable to violence"—or "*everybody* gets angry when I hit another person." Mead (1934) called this development the ability to internalize the demands of the **generalized other:** our impression of society as a whole, on which we base our expectations of individual behavior.

When we gain that ability to conceptualize the generalized other, we are no longer dependent on individual others for our identity—we can see ourselves in relation to our society in general. For Mead, this implied that we can also understand many different points of view—to understand why people are angry, why they vote Republican, or whatever. Moreover, we can even *take the role of others*—imagine ourselves in someone else's shoes—an ability, according to Mead, which more than anything else distinguishes human beings from other animals. We can also understand how we fit into an organized whole, consisting of many different individuals playing different roles.

AGENCIES OF SOCIALIZATION

The process of socialization and development of the self that we have been discussing occurs throughout society, but some individuals and institutions play more important roles than others. In our society, the major **agencies of socialization** (groups and institutions that carry out socialization) are the family, the school, the peer group, and the media. (There are others,

such as the church and the community, but we will cover only the four major ones.)

The Family

The principal agency of socialization in most societies is (and has been) the family. It is in the family that most of us must learn the basic lessons of physical life: how to eat, dress ourselves, walk, talk, use a toilet, and so on. To the extent that these lessons entail obligations to others (don't wake up crying at 3 A.M., and don't eat the cat's food, to name two), they are also our initial lessons in social behavior. The family is a minisociety in which children have their first contacts with others. Here also, we encounter the first (and most enduring) notions of right and wrong. Furthermore, the family provides children with their initial social identity: we first identify ourselves—and are similarly identified by others—as members of our particular families. And through the family, we get our ethnic status and initial class and social standing. The family is also our introduction to conflict, as individuals and in groups: parents vs. children; parent with custody of child vs. parent without custody; men vs. women. In industrial societies, that area of socializing children which is exclusively the family's has been steadily shrinking. The school has not only taken over the functions of basic education and job training to meet industrial society's demands for skilled laborers, but it now teaches sex education and other moral lessons, as well.

Though its sphere of influence has been decreasing, the family still remains the most powerful socializing force in society. Parents provide the context for and help interpret the child's early encounters with the world, which are the most formative of personality, and they exercise nearly complete control of the child's immediate environment. Parents have economic, emotional, and physical power over their children. Through the use of rewards and punishments, the granting and withholding of approval, parents exercise a crucial influence over their children's development and conception of themselves. Consider, for example, how important parental love is for a child—what it means to receive it and have it withheld. Joseph Pleck (1976) has described the agony he went through after a miserable showing at a father-and-son softball game:

> I was the only person on both teams, the fathers and the sons, not to get a hit; I struck out every time. I don't think I have ever felt so ashamed of myself as I felt then, or felt that anyone was so ashamed of me as my father was then. In the picnic which followed, my father and I avoided each other completely. Driving home with him was excruciating. (1976, p. 256)

The family's basic force, then, remains intact. Some modern critics, while admitting that the family's extensive part in socializing the young has been restricted, even argue that the modern family provides a more intensive socialization than in the past because children tend to remain at home longer and because the nuclear family (father, mother, child(ren)) provides the child with fewer people to be dependent on and a narrower range of experience than provided by the extended family (nuclear family plus other relatives) which was more

prevalent in past centuries. We'll examine the family in greater detail in Chapter 6.

The School

The school socializes in two ways: overtly, by teaching specific skills; covertly, by teaching social values and accustoming students to fitting into a social hierarchy. The school also serves as an arena for interaction among youngsters. Although it is not part of the child's life until about the age of five or six, the school generally presents adult models of behavior which are the first alternatives to those encountered in the family. Generally, the school is supportive of the family's behavior patterns, but it teaches children to orient their behavior toward a wider society, beyond the narrow confines of family. The teacher, as the primary socializing agent, is an adult authority like the parent (my first-grade teacher continually told us to regard her as our "classroom mother"), who ordinarily demands respect, order, and discipline. By their own actions, teachers demonstrate the culturally preferred forms of behavior. They impress students with the personality traits that are admired in our society— traits like honesty, correct speech, hard work, politeness, respect for property and authority, and neatness.

Like the family, the school wields enormous power as a socializing force. Its "blessing" is now necessary for access to almost all but the least rewarding occupations. By granting or withholding approval for our educational accomplishments, as well as overt encouragement, the agents of schooling play an important part in directing us to different occupational

Schools not only provide specific information but also transmit cultural traditions and values.

areas. (Stop a moment to contemplate the role of your educational institutions in determining the choice of *your* own goals.) The constant ranking and comparisons with companions through grades and "tracking" and the public blame and praise that goes on in schools usually has a strong impact on our individual feelings of self-worth—be they positive or negative, as we'll see in Chapter 6.

The Peer Group

A **peer group** is three or more people of about the same age and social rank who associate with one another. A group of friends is an example. As a socializing force, the peer group differs greatly from the family and the school. It is centered on immediate concerns—there is no "later" for which the group is explicitly preparing the

child. There is no officially recognized hierarchy, membership in the group is voluntary, and all members have approximately equal roles in socializing each other.
Peer group interaction includes the be-
stowal of rewards (attention, approval,
leadership) and punishments (contempt,
ostracism, disapproval), but contrary to the
other agencies mentioned, in a peer group
all participants have comparatively equal
control of the distribution of rewards and
punishments. Although it doesn't have the
formal power of the family or school, the
peer group does exert strong pressure on
the individual to conform to its ways, as we'll
see later in this chapter and in Chapter 4.

The peer group is the child's first experience with social relationships not controlled by adults. Leaders are chosen from
among approximate equals; they do not
present themselves to be accepted without
choice (as parents and teachers do). It is
here "on the street" that we usually learn
about taboo subjects like sex and techniques for avoiding the demands of adult
authorities. Peer groups inform the child
of alternatives in society about which parents may not wish to teach, and they offer
behavior models who are not solidly en-
trenched in the adult power structure.
More than anything else, however, the peer
group teaches us to respect the wishes of
our equals and how to get along with others
in a group. We also learn what is fashionable for people like ourselves to wear, say,
and do.

The separate research of two sociologists, David Riesman (1950) and James
Coleman (1961), indicates that you do not
have to belong to a specific peer group in
order to be socialized to accept peer values.
Riesman and Coleman both found that
people in general turn to their peers for
direction.

In his book *The Lonely Crowd,* David
Riesman argues that peer group approval
and pressure are the most powerful deter-
minants of behavior in our modern society
for children and adults alike. Riesman
maintains that societies tend to produce
one of three different personality types.
Traditional societies produce *tradition-
directed* individuals, who look to the past
for guidance; societies undergoing rapid
change (such as the United States around
1900) produce *inner-directed* people, who
look within themselves for guidance; modern Americans, on the other hand, are *oth-
er-directed,* and we look to our peers. In a
society like ours, traditional authorities do
not carry the weight that immediate approval from our social equals does (Riesman 1950). So we are more likely, for example, to choose an occupation that will
bring us our peers' admiration than follow
a parent's footsteps or take a job simply
because we like it.

James Coleman's (1961) study of 7,-
500 Midwestern high school students in
the early 1960s adds support to Riesman's
contention about the importance of youth
peer groups in modern society. Coleman
found that despite the *official* ideology and
values of the school and the community,
students had developed a set of values, customs, and beliefs of their own. He conducted his study in the varying atmo-
spheres of a small town, a working-class
suburb, and a wealthy suburb. Students'
attitudes toward education and toward
what other students expected of them remained constant across all communities—
and were always in opposition to the values
of the school, which did vary according to
the particular community (Coleman 1961).
For example, when boys were asked to
choose among becoming a jet pilot, a na-
tionally famous athlete, a missionary, and

an atomic scientist, they overwhelmingly picked athlete (the pilot was a close second); when girls were asked to choose among the careers of actress, artist, nurse, model, and schoolteacher, they chose model. Furthermore, less than 25 percent of the small-town boys questioned, and less than 10 percent of the city and suburban boys, wanted to go into their father's occupation. From these and other surveys, Coleman concluded that high school students tend to value glamour and athletic ability, although parents and teachers encourage them to prefer studiousness (Coleman 1961).* In other words, youth are socialized to the values of their peers—into his or her generation (see Table 1.3).

You can also see the power of the youth peer group as a socializing force in the development in recent decades of a youth "counterculture" that mandates its own standards of morality (most notably with reference to dress, sexual activity, and the use of drugs or liquor). Its influence is unbounded by social position or geographical region. It has also been instrumental in changing fashion, as well as in influencing opinions about the Indo-Chinese war.

The Mass Media

The *mass media* are forms of impersonal communication aimed at large, or mass, audiences. Radio, television, movies, and newspapers are major examples. The mass media provide an important supplement to

---

Table 1.3   Determining Popularity: Peer Group vs. School and Family*

Attribute	Average Rank
Being an athletic star	2.2
Being in the leading crowd	2.6
Being a leader in activities	2.9
Having high grades, being on honor roll	3.5
Having a nice car	3.9
Coming from the right family	4.5

*Coleman (1961a) asked the boys at nine public high schools to rank from 1 to 6 (1 being the best rank) those attributes that go into making a boy popular. Their answers clearly indicate that peer group values (e.g., athletic prowess) have a far greater influence on popularity than either school or family values (e.g., high grades) do. They were given six traits to rank.

SOURCE: James S. Coleman, "Athletics in High School," The Annals of the American Academy of Political and Social Science 338 (Nov. 1961): 33–43. Reprinted by permission.

---

the traditional agencies of socialization. Through the mass media, we learn about a vast number of additional role models, situations, and, ultimately, experiences outside of our personal experience. Television in particular has become an integral component of daily life, for both children and adults (see Figure 1.1). As the authors of *A Populist Manifesto* put it: "If it is possible to pick out a single act, other than eating or sleeping, that most Americans do more often than any other, it is watching television" (Newfield and Greenfield 1972, p. 126).

Television socialization (along with other forms of mass media socialization) differs from that carried out by the other agencies we discussed in two important ways. First, it is *impersonal* communica-

---

*At the time of writing this book, a more extensive followup by Coleman and others was in the early stages of preparation.

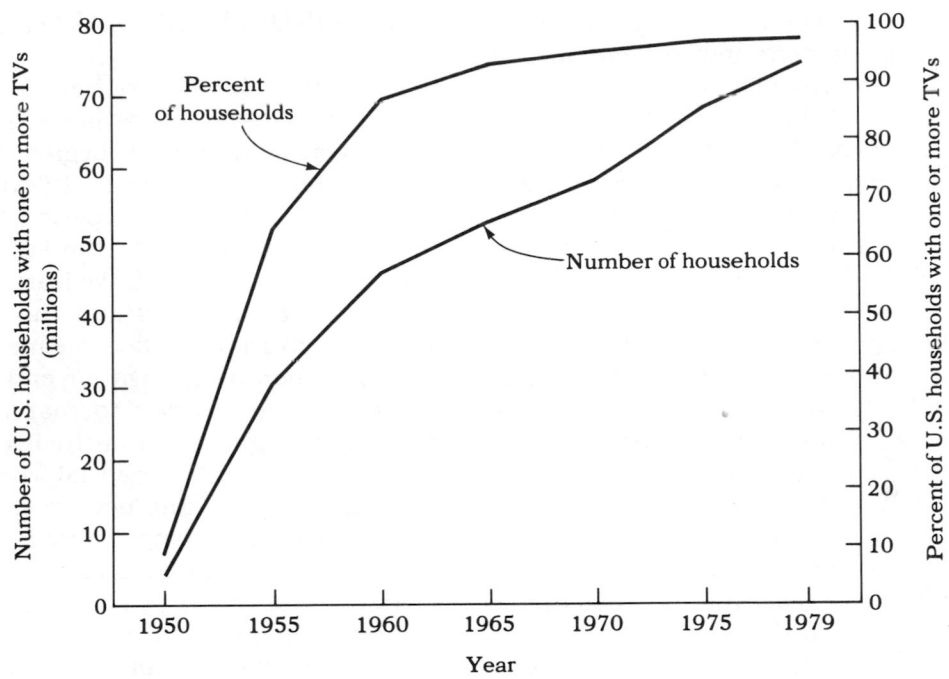

Figure 1.1. The Growing Presence of Television in the U.S. Household.

SOURCE: U.S. Department of Commerce, Consumer Population Survey: Consumer Income, Series
P-60, Number 118 (Washington, D.C.: Government Printing Office 1979, p. 587).

tion, addressed not to us per se, but to a mass audience, without regard to any individual factors. Second, the communication is almost entirely one way. We viewers are subject to the information provided, yet, except for an occasional token editorial response, we do not have the opportunity to talk back to it. This is particularly true on commercial networks—there is no "channel" for questioning or challenging the portrayal of reality we are given. Yet, the portrait we are shown is frequently not realistic. Think about the "good marriages" and "happy homes" of the situation comedies, the superhuman dedication of certain professionals and public officials, and the results of "scientific studies" on aspirin and bran presented by sponsors.

The power of the mass media—again, particularly television—to influence children's views of reality and their behavior has led to a number of criticisms of media content. The rise of the feminist movement has brought with it an examination of how television teaches children sex roles. (They found, to cite just two examples, Harriet Nelson of the 1950s "Ozzie and Harriet Show" and "Maude" in the 1970s typically portrayed women in subservient positions. And, for all Archie Bunker's flaws, he was king in his household.) Other groups have pressured the federal government to ban advertisements (usually for sweets) aimed specifically at children. Also, many Americans have become concerned about the effects of media violence on children (adults, too)—a concern that included a national campaign by the PTA and an actual reduction in the level of television violence. However, the current evidence concerning a direct link between violence observed in the media and actual violent acts has not been definitely established, although there has been some scientific evidence suggesting that tie (see Eysenck and Nias 1978; Surgeon General 1972).

On the more positive side, public television in recent years has begun to be used as a direct teaching tool. Children's shows like "Sesame Street," "The Electric Company," and "Zoom" reach millions of children regularly. Researchers have found that children, particularly those from poor, nonwhite, and Spanish-speaking families, who watch these programs improve their basic skills significantly (e.g., recognizing numbers and letters and putting items into categories—elementary analysis) (Ball and Bogatz 1970).

When a group of junior high school students were polled in 1975, the majority said that television was the major influence in their lives. Two years later, the Encyclopædia Britannica Educational Corporation asked 2,000 high school students the same question. This time, 55 percent named someone in their family (most often the father). Whether this means that the family is regaining influence lost to the television is unclear (this is certainly *not* proof of such a trend). In any case, the pollsters did not dispute the fact that television, movies, and the other mass media have a tremendous impact on our lives.

SECONDARY SOCIALIZATION

So far in this chapter, we have focused on what sociologists call **primary socialization**—socialization that begins at birth and continues throughout childhood and adolescence. During this period, we gain our first introduction to the social order and its rules of conduct. We learn to walk, talk, respect authority, and through primary socialization, we become members of society. But does socialization end with adolescence? The answer to that is no—it goes on throughout our entire lives, as we mature and expand our social world by attending college, taking new jobs, meeting new people, marrying, voting, viewing "adult" entertainment, and solving problems. (As a student, you are being socialized right now, for your future place in the economic world.) Sociologists call the socialization that occurs beyond adolescence **secondary socialization.** Secondary socialization is necessary whenever we take a new job, move our homes, or meet a new group of people. Each of those situations requires that we learn new skills, new formal rules, new "unwritten laws."

Secondary socialization is also necessary for us to accommodate technological advances. Changes in mass transportation and communication (air travel, long-distance telephone service, highway and expressway systems), for example, have made it possible for family members to remain in contact while living hundreds of miles away from one another and have made possible new life-styles. (If you have ever gotten frustrated at an elderly person's refusal to accept your modern life-style, you know first hand that social changes do indeed require some getting used to or socialization.)

In recent years, American adults have

Total institutions resocialize by destroying the individual self so far as that is possible. Even without the use of "brutal guards" these monks have probably internalized most of the institution's basic values about life.

gone through some socialization in response to the two great human rights movements of this period: the civil rights movement and the women's movement. We have come to know that those who were "Colored" and then "Negro" are now "black"; and we have learned that adult females are "women," not "girls." These changed labels reflect new social relationships. Each time we take on a new sphere of activity, or whenever changes in society alter familiar ones, socialization continues.

The socialization of adults ordinarily proceeds gradually—and largely unnoticed. Some people, however, experience a rapid "resocialization" as well.

Resocialization

In the film *A Clockwork Orange*, the main character is a violent youth whose life consists of terrorizing and victimizing others. While in prison, he is forced through a treatment program that produces incapacitating nausea when he even thinks of violence. As a result, he becomes the defenseless victim of those he once brutalized. In sociological terminology, he was "resocialized." **Resocialization** is a frequently rapid and intense process, requiring a radical change in behavior and attitudes, often making the "new" self incompatible with the former one.

People enter into some forms of resocialization voluntarily. Examples include signing up for the U.S. Marines, entering a monastery, undergoing psychoanalysis, or having a religious or political conversion. Other forms of resocialization are quite involuntary. Attempts to rehabilitate criminals and, under some circumstances, mentally disturbed persons; to degrade and destroy the sense of self among concentration camp inmates; or to convert political prisoners through brainwashing are examples here. In these latter instances, individuals are incarcerated for violating the standards of the given society in some way (robbing, acting irrationally, being a Jew, trying to undermine the current political system).

Resocialization often occurs in what the sociologist Erving Goffman (1961) has called **total institutions**—places where individuals are cut off from the rest of society and put under constant supervision. Mental hospitals (see Figure 1.2), prisons, and boot camps are all total institutions. While the details vary from one type of total institution to the next, the essential process of trying to remold the self is the same. To begin with, total institutions refuse to recognize individual identities: inmates wear the same clothing and eat the same food at the same time; their occupational and social standing on the outside go largely unrecognized; and they are cut off from all familiar, individual activity by which they formerly recognized "their" own day. A break with the past occurs, and in the place of their former social world, inmates substitute their common "society," with a belief system that denigrates the old self in comparison to outsiders or to the yet-to-be-created new self. The total institution also sets up a barrier with the outside world whose influences might reinforce the old

self. If the institution is a rehabilitative one, the custodians try to motivate inmates to internalize a new set of values and thereupon build a new sense of self. (For a description of an experiment in resocialization, see Abuse and Resocialization in a Total Institution.) Of course, these attempts at resocialization, like attempts at other forms of socialization, do not always accomplish what they were designed to. There is, for instance, a growing recognition of the mental hospital's failure to resocialize its patients for life in society. Newer treatment methods and ideologies emphasize the need for patients to maintain ties with the community. In addition, the total institution is impractical for accommodating the larger number of people seeking help in recent years. Thus, the proportion of total institutions for treating the mentally ill has declined sharply. The Italian parliament has even abolished mental hospitals in its country (de Zulueta 1980).

IMPLICATIONS AND DISCUSSION: THE INDIVIDUAL AND SOCIETY

In our discussion in this chapter, we have seen how much of society there is in the individual and how this can account in large part for the usual orderliness of social life. Most individuals, because of their socialization, do not need obvious, external control to get them to act according to society's values. They have internalized those values and consequently regulate their own behavior. We have also seen that socialization structures our personal desires and strivings. Erich Fromm captured the essence of socialization when he wrote that society shapes our reality so "people *want*

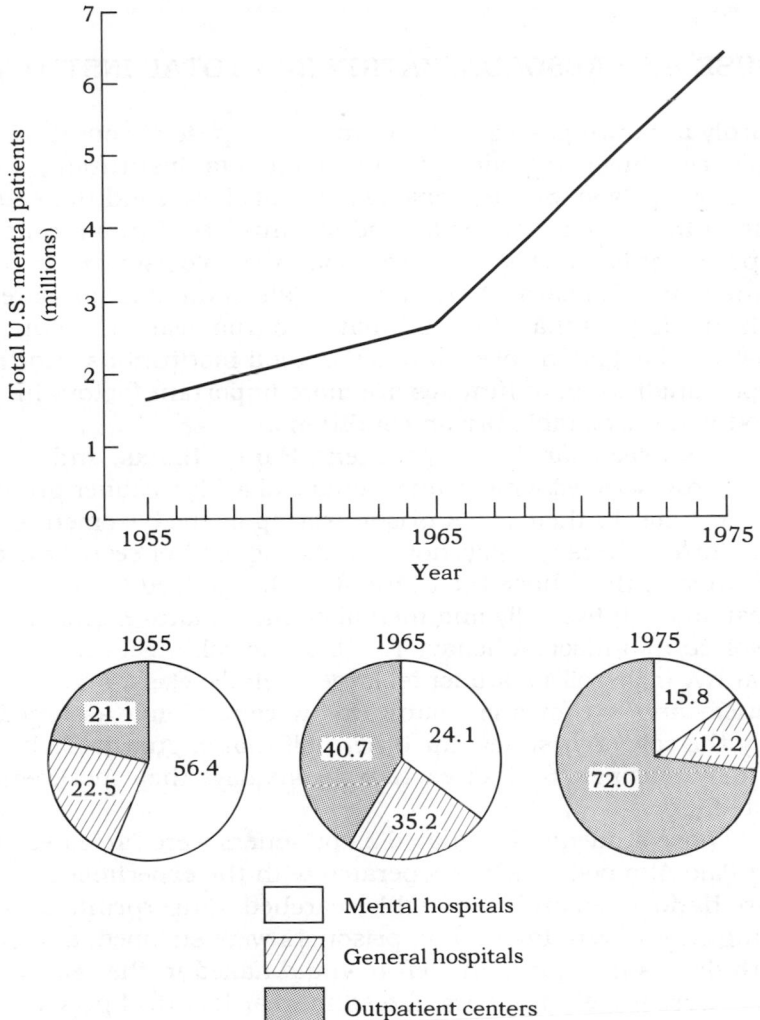

Figure 1.2 Mental Care and Total Institutions
in the United States, 1955–1975

SOURCE: *U.S. Department of Commerce*, Statistical Abstract of the
United States, 1979 *(Washington, DC: Government Printing Office,
1979 p. 117).*

to act as *they have to act* and find gratification in acting according to the requirements of culture" (1949, p. 5). The end
product is a "self-controlled" individual,
which enables society to continue without
spending its resources in watching its
members. Ironically, these internal controls, while ever present, operate without
our knowledge of their existence.

The term *individual* is constantly used

ABUSE AND RESOCIALIZATION IN A TOTAL INSTITUTION

Hardly a month passes without another exposé of conditions of violence, abuse, and corruption in some total institution, usually a prison. Some people argue that these conditions are due to the "caliber" of the individuals involved. But a recent experiment conducted by three social psychologists (Haney, Banks, and Zimbardo 1973) on resocialization in a simulated prison suggests that the combination of the nearly absolute power of custodians over inmates in total institutions and the depersonalization of inmates are more important factors in producing deplorable prison conditions.

As subjects for their experiment, Haney, Banks, and Zimbardo selected what many would call a *high*-caliber group to "do time" in their mock prison, set up in the basement of Stanford University's psychology building. Out of seventy-five volunteers, they chose the twenty-two they judged to be "the most stable (physically and mentally), most mature, and least involved in antisocial behavior." All of the volunteers were healthy, male college students, largely middle class, and Caucasian (save for one Asian). Half were randomly assigned to play the role of prisoner, the other half that of guard. Each student was paid $15 for each of the six days the experiment lasted.

Those students designated as prisoners were "arrested" by the Palo Alto police, who cooperated with the experiment, and were handcuffed and thoroughly searched. Fingerprints and "mug shots" were taken; and prisoners were stripped, sprayed with delousing liquid, and left to stand naked in the cell yard. They were issued numbers, forced to wear identical prison

in casual conversation, but our discussion has cast doubt on what exactly "individuality" is. We might have vague notions that there is a "self" that develops along with the socialized being, that there must be some substance to socialize and control. Yet, our understanding that our very self-definition is a social product now makes that substance difficult to specify. Where does society leave off and the individual begin?

The temptation after reading this chapter might be to assume that society is everything and the individual nothing, that we are completely socialized, "self-controlled" creatures. But to give way to this

uniforms, and then confined to the "prison" twenty-four hours a day during the experiment (guards worked on three-man, eight-hour shifts).

Except for the absence of activities expressly prohibited by the experimenters—physical violence, rape, drug use, and the like—the behavior of the student subjects began to approximate that of "real" prisoners and guards. Prisoners became passive and guards hostile. Exchanges between guards and prisoners were impersonal, with few references to individual identity. When guards spoke to prisoners, it was usually to give a command, and verbal assaults were frequent. Some of the guards acted quite brutally, and some even conspired to keep a prisoner in "solitary" for the night without telling the experimenters—who the guards thought were "soft" on the prisoners. The guards appeared to be completely caught up in the world of the experiment. In private conversations, they would discuss "problem prisoners" or other prison information, or they would not talk at all.

Prisoners reacted to their situation with crying, rage, acute anxiety, emotional depression, and even rashes. Recorded conversations among the prisoners revealed that they also were not merely "playing a part" for the experimenters. Even in private, they rarely talked about life outside the prison, which reinforced the sense of oppressiveness of their situation rather than providing a means for relief. In their conversations, they tended to deprecate both their own selves and their fellow prisoners. The experimenters concluded that the subjects had responded way out of proportion to the "minimal" nature of their imprisonment, demonstrating pathologies similar to those found in actual prisons.

temptation would be to miss all the resistance to socialization that occurs and the potential for at least a partial breakdown of internalized controls. Think, for instance, of the attempts to socialize us by placing limits on our behavior when growing up. Very often, we were faced with demands that seemed unreasonable to us at the time. "Go to bed (early)"; "Eat your greens"; "Do your homework"; "Don't fight!" We didn't always give in; we sometimes resisted, even if only verbally. We would, for instance, appeal to social custom ("Everyone else is allowed"), equality ("If you can smoke, why can't I?"), self-preservation ("He hit me first"), or personal tastes ("I don't like sitting in church every week").

Resistance to socialization is also evident in Freud's theories; he frequently found conflict between individual desires (id) and social constraints (imposed by the superego), which he believed to be at the root of neuroses (Freud 1953 [1916], pp. 358–59). Georg Simmel (1950) has told us that an individual's "purely personal qualities—strength, beauty, depth of thought, greatness of conviction, kindness, nobility of character, courage, purity of heart— have their autonomous significance . . . entirely independent of their social entanglements" (p. 62). And Mead, remember, left room in his theory for an unsocialized I along with a socialized me, to account for the sources of conflict between the individual and society.

We have emphasized how dependent the individual is on society. Any reevaluation of individuality, however, must also consider society's dependence on the person. It is obvious that individual survival requires us to play by our society's rules; but it also should be recognized that if individuals refuse to do so, our society's means of perpetuating itself is dealt a severe blow. The social order would become dependent on the limited resources of overt controls, which are usually quite repressive—intended, as they are, to fill such a large and critical gap.

You have probably observed how repression often accompanies modern revolutions. Revolutions require a refusal of a large proportion of the populace to obey some basic social rules: to remain within the law, to listen to "legitimate" leaders, and to support the country (by supporting the government). If the revolution is successful, the problem for incoming leaders is clear. They must attempt to enforce their leadership with overt controls and try to develop a new set of internalized controls through resocialization. The institution of "reeducation" camps by Vietnam's Communist government for former South Vietnamese officials is one example of this kind of effort.

The relation between individual and society is, then, not simple. But through sociology, you can begin to understand that relation and the ways in which society affects you.

SUMMARY

In this chapter, we've looked at why, in the face of individual differences, there is so much order and regularity in society. The containment of behavior within the limits set by a society could never be accomplished through the relatively small number of law enforcers, who do not have the resources for it. The social process that assures that most people will control themselves instead—and that enables them to live in society at all—is called *socialization*. Although our primary socialization in childhood is most important, socialization continues throughout our lives (secondary socialization).

The process of socialization has been conceptualized in different ways. Sigmund Freud began by dividing the personality into three parts: the id, ego, and superego. Representing our animal urges, the id makes demands on us that are controlled by the ego to accommodate reality and the superego (or conscience); socialization occurs through the development of the superego. Most sociologists follow Charles Horton Cooley and George Herbert Mead and see socialization more in terms of cooperation between a social and a personal self. In this view, the socialization process has four steps:

1. Obtain a self-concept from society (*looking-glass self*).
2. Learn basic social lessons from our *significant others*.
3. *Internalize* these lessons as our own.
4. Take the role of *generalized others*.

In any case, socialization is carried out by special agencies, which wield an enormous amount of power over the individual to be socialized. The major agencies in our society are: the family, the school, the peer group, and the mass media. The last differs from the others in two key ways: communication is impersonal (not directed at an individual) and it is one-way (there is no opportunity for questioning its contents). Also, the other agencies—and especially the family—utilize significant others. Their relationship with the child is based on emotional bonds and the latter's total dependence on them for the necessities of life. The child learns through passive observation of their behaviors, their reactions to his or her behavior, and their direct admonitions.

Sometimes individuals who have already received their primary socialization are required to undergo resocialization. This can be distinguished from secondary socialization by its rapid and drastic nature, and by its attempt at a replacement of the "self," not an addition to it. Resocialization often takes place in total institutions (such as prisons), which have complete control over the individual. If resocialization is successful, the old self is destroyed and a new one is created through isolation from all outside sources of information, denial of familiar sources of personal identity, and intense peer group pressure.

Key Terms

social control (p. 34)
socialization (p. 35)
self (p. 40)
significant others (p. 42)
internalize (p. 43)
generalized other (p. 44)
agencies of socialization (p. 44)
peer group (p. 46)
primary socialization (p. 50)
secondary socialization (p. 50)
resocialization (p. 51)
total institutions (p. 52)

Review and Discussion Questions

1. In what ways has social control begun to break down in the United States? What are the more basic ways, however, in which social control is at least as powerful as ever?
2. There are some differences between women and men that cannot be traced to socialization, although many can. How many of the differences between American women and men can you identify as socialized—that is, learned—differences?
3. We most often speak of parents socializing their children. However, their children often socialize them, too. What are some of the ways that children socialize their parents? How have you socialized your parents? If you are a parent, how have your children socialized you?
4. If you were a subject prisoner or guard in Haney, Banks, and Zimbardo's experiment, how might you have behaved differently from the actual subjects? How do you account for the behavior they chose to engage in?
5. How do television commercials socialize us? What are some of the messages we receive from them—about women, men, the energy crisis, beauty, and the like?

For Further Study

SOCIALIZED SEX DIFFERENCES Sociologists have found that we cannot trace many of the differences between people to heredity, that these differences come quite specifically from socialization. Extensive studies of socialized sex differences have been carried out in recent years, and you can find summaries of their findings in most new books on sex roles. Particularly recommended are: Eleanor Maccoby and Carol Nagy Jacklin, *The Psychology of Sex Differences* (Stanford, CA: Stanford University Press, 1974); and Laurel Richardson Walum, *The Dynamics of Sex and Gender: A Sociological Perspective* (Chicago: Rand McNally, 1977).

SOCIALIZATION AGENCIES For the sociological view of the family, two good readers are: Jacqueline P. Wiseman, ed., *People as Partners* (San Francisco: Canfield, 1979); and Roger Libby and Robert N. Whitehurst, eds., *Marriage and Alternatives: Exploring Intimate Relationships* (Glenview, IL: Scott, Foresman, 1977). Also see E. E. LeMasters, *Parents in Modern America* (Homewood, IL: Dorsey, 1977). Two of the finest works on the influence of peer groups on adults remain David Riesman's *The Lonely Crowd* (New Haven, CT: Yale University Press, 1950) and William H. Whyte, Jr., *The Organization Man* (New York: Simon & Schuster, 1956). Two good summaries of research on the mass media's impact on socialization are: G. Comstock et al., *Television and Human Be-* *havior* (New York: Columbia University Press, 1978); and the Surgeon General's Scientific Advisory Committee on Television and Social Behavior, *Television and Growing Up: The Impact of Televised Violence* (Washington, DC: Government Printing Office, 1972).

ADULT SOCIALIZATION Psychologist Erik Erikson laid the foundation for conceptualizing the stages of adult socialization in *Childhood and Society* (New York: Norton, 1963). A popular and illuminating treatment of these stages is Gail Sheehy, *Passages: Predictable Crises of Adult Life* (New York: Dutton, 1974). Finally, Irving Rosow has written a book about the socialization process that occurs as we reach old age: *Socialization to Old Age* (Berkeley: University of California Press, 1978).

RESOCIALIZATION The seminal work on resocialization within total institutions is Erving Goffman, *Asylums: Essays on the Social Situation of Mental Patients and Other Inmates* (Garden City, NY: Doubleday, 1961). Jan Morris's *Conundrum* (New York: Harcourt Brace Jovanovich, 1974) is an interesting account of one person's attempt to radically change his/her sexual identity. Finally, see Samuel Chaukin, *The Mind Stealers: Psychosurgery and Mind Control* (Boston: Houghton Mifflin, 1978).

CHAPTER TWO
Culture: Content for Social Control

Socialization is effective in producing individuals who behave in a way that most others define as correct. By "correct," though, we really mean in conformance with the many rules of right and wrong that govern all social behavior—including our own. Some of these rules are very formal and specific (e.g., written laws) but others are informal and vague (e.g., how you are supposed to act at various times during the evening when on a date).

For the most part, we grow accustomed to these rules and can hardly imagine living in accordance with any other standards. But acceptance does not always happen. In fact, much social progress would never have occurred if individuals hadn't broken rules. One of these important violations occurred on the evening of December 1, 1955, when a black woman in Montgomery, Alabama, refused to give her bus seat to the white man who demanded it. In doing this, the woman defied one of the many rules that had kept southern blacks second-class citizens for decades (in this case, the rule that blacks must comply with any white person's demand to give up their bus seats). With this "illegal" act, a civil rights movement was born in the United States that saw many other blacks—and whites—deliberately violate numerous laws that they considered unjust and discriminatory. But other Americans were outraged by these "illegal" activities, and some (including the FBI) considered them acts of treason against the United States. Not many years later another large group of people, Vietnam War protestors, deficd laws they considered unjust. They burned their draft cards, refused to pay taxes, and demonstrated in defiance of court orders and local ordinances. They, too, were called traitors by their opponents, many of whom claimed to be bothered more by the illegal tactics of the protestors than by their opposition to the war. In other words, the protestors violated the accepted rules for conduct, specifically, those governing the proper forms of dissent.

Since that time, however, there have been some important shifts in the behavior of many Americans. Many people who were outraged by the law-breaking activities of civil rights activists and antiwar protestors have probably since disobeyed the law themselves. For instance, public employees (such as police and firefighters) have gone out on strike in cities where it is illegal for them to do so. They claim that the rules are stacked against them—without the right to strike, they lack the one weapon that can bring them success. Other union workers have repeatedly defied court orders (injunctions) to return to their jobs. They feel that such orders favor management in their disputes, and these otherwise law-abiding citizens believe that such inequality gives them the right to break the law.

It is significant that civil rights workers, antiwar protestors, and union members committed their crimes openly. By doing so, they were saying that their actions were justified. Like them, most of us also try to justify our own actions when they run counter to society's rules, even if only by using the excuse of many income tax cheaters that "everyone does it."

Parents, bosses, teachers, clergy, government officials, and others are always ready to explain to us, and to protestors, why we should obey the rules of our society. Some people tell us to obey all laws simply because they are laws, some invoke God or "God's will" in the matter, while others refer to the power of those who enforce the law and to the consequences of violation. Still others explain to us that we should obey the laws because if a law continues to exist, it must have some value for society.

People on both sides of the issue of obedience to the rules of society judge actions by certain standards of what they consider right and wrong. In this chapter, we are going to look beyond the issue of whether any action conforms to this or that standard of right or wrong to explore the social origins of the standards themselves. Where do our standards of right and wrong come from? To answer this question, sociologists say, we need to investigate the nature of *culture*—that more general array of human products of which our standards for correct conduct are but one part.

WHAT IS CULTURE?

All of our notions of right and wrong come out of a particular context—and that context is culture. As with many other concepts you will encounter in this book, the way a sociologist or other social scientist uses this term differs from the way we or-

dinarily use it. Generally, most people use the term *culture* to mean the finer things in life—classical music and literature, art, refined speech, perhaps a knowledge of fine wines, and so on. We even say that people who use and appreciate these things are "cultured."

When sociologists use the term *culture,* however, they mean by it something broader. To them, culture is not something possessed by an elite alone; it is shared by all members of the species. Culture includes music, but the Rolling Stones as well as Beethoven; it also includes art, theater, and literature of *all* types. In fact, **culture** includes all human products and activities that are not strictly biological in origin (knowledge, belief, art, morals, law, and custom)—all the nobler sentiments *and* the mundane ways of behaving.

Culture and Society

The term *culture* is often used interchangeably with *society* in everyday speech, and sometimes by sociologists, too. However, there is a difference in the meaning of the two words. Whereas *society* generally refers to people and the organized relationship they share with each other, *culture* refers to human creations (including the way in which humans organize themselves). In each instance, the terms can be used as broad concepts to describe human life in general or to describe specific constellations of human products—"a culture"—or a specific people who share a common set of relationships and pattern of social organization—"a society." Just as we refer to "French society" and "Indonesian society," so we can discuss "French culture" and "Indonesian culture." Each culture has its

The people at this Harlem park dedication are gathering to reaffirm their cultural bonds, rooted in the social categories of neighborhood and race.

own values, beliefs, and customs, which sometimes differ dramatically from those of another culture. In the study discussed in the box, Mark Zborowski (1953) found that the differences between cultures even extend to how we react to pain (that is, whether we yell out or pretend that nothing is happening to us).

Culture and Social Control

Culture makes human society possible. Because men and women can transmit knowledge and other products of their ef-forts to their children, each generation does not have to start from scratch in learning to survive. Instead, it can build on the accomplishments and experiences of those who came before. But if culture allows us to live and to thrive in society, it also limits us. To a large extent, the particular culture in which we grow up determines, often without our knowledge, our way of life and also the way we evaluate that life. In this respect, culture provides the content for social control.

Culture gives us those standards for appropriate behavior we are likely to hold: the do's and don't's, the rights and wrongs, the goods and bads, the betters and

CULTURE AND THE WAY WE FEEL PAIN

A primary aim of this book (and sociology itself) is to point out the many *social* elements in our "individual" selves and actions. Mark Zborowski's (1953) study, "Cultural Components in Responses to Pain," provides some impressive evidence to further that aim. It demonstrates that our culture even directs such "biological" responses as our reactions to pain, with values, norms, and sanctions.

Human societies give most biological processes some cultural meaning—hence the child's intensive toilet training and the extensive norms about sex, to cite two examples. Likewise, culture conditions the way we react to pain.

To uncover culture's role in these reactions, Zborowski conducted a study where people regularly experienced pain (a hospital) and where there would be patients with different cultural backgrounds (New York City). He selected a veterans hospital because it offered a range of adult age groups as well. This selection also meant that there were no female patients.

Zborowski compared the reactions of Jewish, Italian, Irish, and "Old American" (WASP) patients. He chose the first three groups because of their reactions to pain, as described by medical personnel in prestudy interviews. Italians and Jews were said to "exaggerate" their pain, while Irish patients were said to be able to take a great deal of pain. The WASPs were chosen because their values dominate the country and the medical profession.

The primary methods employed in the study were interviews with patients from the four groups; observation of their actual reactions to pain; and discussion of individual cases with "doctors, nurses and other people directly or indirectly involved in the pain experience of the individual." Each interview lasted about two hours, and its questions were *open ended*—that is, asking for a general description, rather than specific, limited responses (e.g., agree or disagree). Open-ended questions are often less precise and more difficult to translate into numbers, but they offer more information.

Zborowski also interviewed nonpatients from the four cultural groups.

Information obtained in the prestudy interviews was confirmed. Complaining, crying out when in pain, and so on were proscribed by both Irish and WASP norms and cultural values. When faced with unbearable pain, the WASPs reacted in private—that is, by withdrawing from society. American males, especially, should be familiar with some of the sanctions for breaking these norms—they might be called a "cry baby," their masculinity might be questioned, and so on. On the other hand, Jewish and Italian cultures encourage emotional responses. Jews and Italians both "feel free to talk about their pain, complain about it and manifest their sufferings by groaning, moaning, crying, etc. They are not ashamed of this expression" (Zborowski 1953).

But Zborowski showed that the common emotional reaction of Jewish and Italian patients did not stem from the same cultural attitudes. For example, Italian patients were concerned with the immediate sensation of pain and discomfort; Jewish patients saw pain as symptomatic of future disaster, and worried about its threat to their health and welfare. So, Italians more readily accepted pain-relieving drugs, which did not relieve the Jews' anxieties; physicians gained their Italian patients' confidence when they relieved pain, while Jewish patients did not see pain relief as evidence that the doctor was able to take care of their illness. Jewish and Italian responses appeared similar, but stemmed from different cultural attitudes.

Because both the Italian and Jewish cultures encourage free expression of feelings through words, sounds, and gestures, their members also feel free to express feelings of pain. In short, emotional expression is a prescribed norm for them and not for the Irish or WASPs, which accounts for the differences in behavior. Zborowski is not saying that reactions to pain are entirely social, but he has demonstrated that society and culture have a significant role in these seemingly biological reactions.

worses—all have their source in culture. When somebody greets us with "How are you," we know not to respond with a catalog of aches and pains, even if we feel terrible. When dressing to go outside, we know which parts of the body must be covered just as an Arab woman knows she must veil her face as well as cover her body, and a Japanese woman knows not to expose the back of her neck.

Culture also determines the way we carry out our daily activities. Take eating, for instance. We eat different kinds of meals at specified times of the day: breakfast in the morning, lunch at midday, dinner in the evening. Many southern Europeans, by contrast, eat their heaviest meal in the middle of the day and follow it with a few hours of rest, and the people of certain tribes have no regular mealtimes at all but eat whenever they happen to be hungry. We also find only some foods appetizing. For example, most Americans would have a tough time eating dog, which was a favored food of many American Indians. We eat off of plates and use metal utensils; yet in medieval Europe, areas scooped out of the table surface were used instead of plates, and forks did not become common in Europe until the early eighteenth century. Now that we have a general understanding of culture, let's look at the particular elements of culture.

THE ELEMENTS OF CULTURE

For purposes of analysis, sociologists often divide culture into two levels, material and nonmaterial. **Material culture** is made up of the physical objects that members of a human society make use of, from knickknacks to nuclear reactors. Without the *things* of a culture—the implements for growing food, the materials for housing, and so forth—human society could not survive.

Nonmaterial culture is composed of intangibles—beliefs, values, rules of behavior (or norms)—that shape our understanding of the world around us and of ourselves. These ideas are tremendously powerful—probably much more so than you would think at first glance. They provide us with a way of interpreting the events we witness, and the way of interpreting any single event can differ radically from one culture to the next. For instance, the culture of late medieval France defined Joan of Arc's "voices" as a direct communication from God and considered her a saint. But how would you, living in the United States today, define a person who claimed to hear voices telling her or him how to save the world? On the basis of your culture, you'd certainly not consider that person a saint.

International conflicts, and the difficulty of their resolution, attest to the force of nonmaterial culture. In the Middle East, for instance, Israelis see their nation as the realization of a two-thousand-year-old dream and as a return to their homeland; while Palestinian Arabs see an invasion of their native land. Irish Catholics feel that all of Ireland is the land of a single people, and its division is unjust; whereas Irish Protestants and the British in Northern Ireland support that division and believe that their actions protect the rights of a religious minority. Those who hold these contrasting views do so on the basis of their own culture's concepts. In each case: *one* situation, *two* interpretations.

In this section, we'll look first at material culture and then at the components of nonmaterial culture.

Material Culture

Material culture refers not only to the physical objects that members of human society produce but to all the physical objects they use, whether they made them or not. Many of the objects in this last category are natural ones that are given a special meaning by their use. For example, in prehistoric times someone might take a stone from a stream and display it as an art object, giving it a cultural meaning (Janson 1970). In a more dramatic example, we incorporated the giant Colorado River—a natural object—into our material culture. Since the building of the Hoover Dam, the river has produced enormous quantities of the hydroelectrical power our society needs.

These illustrations suggest that the objects of our material culture aren't just a collection of things but are also reflections of nonmaterial culture. They are part of our culture because we have invested them with meaning. We can see this intertwining of material and nonmaterial culture perhaps most clearly in the role of technology in culture.

TECHNOLOGY AND MATERIAL CULTURE Animals—human and nonhuman—and plants live in a "natural" environment of temperature, altitude, precipitation, atmosphere, soil, water, light, darkness, and, of course, other plants and animals. Technology consists of the many ways in which people adjust to this environment. In a society, **technology** is the sum total of all the methods that its members use to accomplish their tasks. Machines and computers are the most obvious part of our technology, but the term refers to much more. It includes, for instance, the way that manufacturers organ-ize laborers on an assembly line, the needles that tailors use to sew our clothes, the typewriter I used to write the manuscript for this book, the simple and complicated tools farmers use, and every type of housing you can think of (from caves to tepees and grass huts to project high rises). Not all of technology, in other words, is part of our *material* culture; technology includes nonmaterial elements as well. Capitalism, bureaucratic organization, and division of labor, for example, are essential components of Western technology. They are ideas, or principles, used to organize work.

As you might expect, a society's technology can tell us a great deal about what that society is like. Anthropologists for this reason understand and classify prehistoric societies by the tools that their people used. We, too, understand societies in this way when we refer to "the Stone Age" or "the Iron Age."

Technology, for instance, can tell us about the likely extent of inequality in a society, at least according to the studies of sociologist Gerhard Lenski (1966). In his analysis of inequality in different societies, Lenski concluded that technology was the single most important factor in determining the amount of social inequality, more important than either the role of the military or the amount of a government's constitutionalism (or rule by law, instead of by unrestrained individuals). In general, because societies with more primitive technology produced very little, they had to distribute their goods on the basis of need in order to keep their members alive, and thus were relatively egalitarian economically. Modern technology, on the other hand, makes possible the production of a large surplus of goods over and above what is needed for subsistence. The generation of this surplus has led to great inequalities

The individual often seems lost amidst the giants of modern technology. But hand tools, buildings, theories, even capitalism are also part of American technology.

Of course, you would not want to explain *all* social processes and events in terms of technology. Yet its importance should not be overlooked. For example, consider the tremendous influence that the development of new products through technology can have on our lives. The development of "the pill," for instance, improved our methods of family planning and enabled many women to join the labor force for long periods of time. Evidence also suggests that it has increased the rates of marital sex. One sociologist states: "Effective contraception which is sexually unobtrusive provides both sexual and economic autonomy, effects that were not part of the original idea" (Gagnon 1977, pp. 407–8). Think of the social forces reflected in this piece of technology!

Now let's turn to the components of nonmaterial culture—beliefs, values, and norms.

Beliefs

Beliefs are the ideas people hold about what the world is like. For instance, some common beliefs of our culture are that the earth is round, that disease spreads through germs, and that if you leave a pot of water boiling on the stove, it will eventually boil dry. Cultures different from our own hold many different beliefs about the world. For instance, people of some tribes believe that their crops will be more likely to thrive if they perform religious rituals while we are more likely to put our energy into spreading fertilizer.

Beliefs include not just what we think is true of the present but also what we think will happen in the future or when conditions change. For instance, many

because those who control it are not willing to share it equally (Lenski 1966, pp. 46–50, 434–46). By looking at who has access to a society's technology, we can also learn something about who is most likely to exercise control within it. For example, in the United States, the wealthier political candidates can afford to buy television time, and can thus reach millions of potential voters. And you can imagine the advantage this gives such candidates.

Americans believe that it is necessary for their nation to maintain a strong military force to prevent the Soviet Union from attacking noncommunist states. A good many Soviets similarly believe that a strong military is their country's only hedge against its being invaded (as in the past) or having its vital interests threatened.

Values

The parties in the Middle Eastern and other conflicts each have a personal stake—or vested interest—in the outcome. In the Israeli-Arab dispute, for example, Jews and Palestinian Arabs continue to kill one another over the issue of who will occupy and control a particular and very tiny piece of land. Outsiders, like ourselves, might consider this an awful waste of lives. Isn't there enough room in the Middle East for everybody? Well, there is, in the sense that the land area would support both Arabs and Jews. But by looking at the conflict in this mechanical way, we miss the crucial role that *values* play in culture.

The culture of each group provides it with a set of **values**: broad social definitions of what is good, right, or preferred. People would not voluntarily obey rules of conduct (remember, self-enforcement) if the rules didn't rest on a recognizable set of principles—that is, if it didn't make sense to do so. In his historic speech to Israel's parliament on November 21, 1977, Egyptian President Sadat called all "Arab land" (including that occupied by Israel since 1967) sacred—not one inch is negotiable, he said. At the same time, Israeli Prime Minister Begin has time and again proclaimed his nation's "biblical right" to the occupied territory. In other words,

every party to the conflict believes in the *rightness* of their claims and believes in it so strongly that they are willing to die for their beliefs.

AMERICAN VALUES   American society has its values, too. Many of them tend to fall into identifiable clusters:

- capitalism — free enterprise — hard work—self-help (not taking charity)—social Darwinism (those in power are biologically superior to those ruled; the poor and powerless are biologically inferior)
- action (time is money)—antiintellectualism—practical skills (superior to theoretical knowledge)—rationality
- congregationalism (local autonomy, states' rights)—political democracy—voluntarism (being free to choose from among many alternatives)

Others are in conflict:

- individual achievement (achieved inequality) vs. equality for all Americans
- individual freedom vs. puritan morality
- individualism (enlightened self-interest) vs. sovereignty of popular opinion
- optimism (e.g., science will solve all problems) vs. realism
- "pioneer" spirit (progress, more means better, what's new is best, future-orientation, youthfulness) vs. traditionalism (conservatism, nostalgia, Americana, "old fashioned" virtues, Judeo-Christian values)

A word of caution is necessary at this point. By labeling these values "American," we do not assume that their acceptance is automatic. Also, it is incorrect to think that everyone shares the same values, as we'll see shortly. Even those who do share the same values often have differing interpretations of what they mean, for in choosing values, people respond in light of their own personal circumstances (e.g., being a corporate president or being on welfare), which are likely to differ from one individual to the next. Social conflicts over civil rights and sexual freedom in our society, for example, reflect basic disagreements about how to interpret such major values as equality and morality. But, despite these variations in values, every society's social structure—the interrelationships of the family, the state, the church, the economy, the mass media, and so forth—must, in order for the society to survive, rest on a relatively coherent and consistent set of values and their rationalizations, that is, on an *ideology.*

IDEOLOGY   Max Weber termed the values and rationalizations that support social structure *legitimations* because they "legitimize" (for us) our obedience to others. We feel morally bound to act in conformance with these values (Weber 1946, pp. 78–79). The system of legitimations that characterize a particular society is called its *ideology.* The concept of ideology is crucial to our study of society, so we should be sure of its meaning.

What does it mean when you say "That's just communist ideology" or "That's capitalist ideology"? For one thing, it probably suggests that you do not think the statement is very objective. You are saying that the speaker's statement is influenced by some set of values, and you may therefore doubt the statement's validity. That is only

one aspect of what I mean by ideology, however. In this book **ideology** will refer to a comprehensive view of the world justified by an appeal to basic social values. Karl Mannheim, who helped to develop this concept, noted that even when there is a strong conflict within a society, the parties involved frequently agree on the same set of basic values. They usually disagree on specific points and try to destroy the specific arguments of their opponent. But they almost never attack the foundations on which their opponent's argument is based (Mannheim 1936, pp. 64–65). For instance, although participants in the American civil rights movement demanded many important social changes, few challenged the basic values of American society; instead they were more likely to complain that those values weren't being lived up to. As another illustration, consider how likely you are to read an editorial that favors child abuse, idol worshipping, cannibalism, or returning Texas to Mexico.

Almost all our discussions occur within the context of our own ideology. People appeal to these values constantly in order to get others to act the way they want them to. Appeals to values, for instance, lie behind the power of the advertising industry. We can understand business competition as a conflict among manufacturers for a scarce resource—your purchase. To obtain that, the competing parties use their knowledge of American values to make their products more attractive to consumers. For example, when an East Coast fast-food chain added fried chicken to its hamburger menu, its advertisements read: "Gino's gives you freedom of choice." Of course, not all of these campaigns succeed, but the fact that many do emphasizes something we discussed earlier: understanding the ideology of any society is the first step in understanding the way its members behave.

In using the concept of ideology, we should keep the following points in mind:

1. The ideology of a group or society indicates its priorities.
2. Ideology is part of the social system, not the device of temporary leaders.
3. Ideology supports social control, so that, for example, people in a society accept that some members will dominate others.
4. Ideology is the justification of the socialization system and its confirmation by social interaction.
5. Ideology (because it is composed of ideas) is difficult to identify; the demands of life in society keep people focused on actual behaviors.
6. Thus a critical, questioning stance is necessary to gain an objective understanding of ideology.

Norms

As important as shared values are, without some way of translating them into what people should and should not do—into behavior—society would collapse. **Norms** are shared standards of behavior rooted in values and enforceable. They are elements of the social structure, and have the following characteristics: they define specific behaviors—not general values; they define how people should behave, even if that is not the way everybody actually acts; they are shared by a substantial portion of society's members; and they can be enforced.

Norm Characteristics

NORMS DEFINE SPECIFIC BEHAVIOR During the process of socialization, we adopt the major ideas and values that characterize our culture. Yet, that acceptance would have little significance if it were not reflected in our behavior. Society's values alone do not ensure proper conduct because they are too general. Norms, however, give us a social definition for specific behaviors. For example, we might believe in nonviolence as a general value, but norms against murdering translate it into definite do's and don't's of individual behavior.

Because most people generally obey social norms, in our continued interaction with others we come to *expect* certain specific behaviors from them. For example, if in class you voice your disagreement with the instructor, you expect some sort of civil response, such as a rational argument or explanation. You do not expect the instructor to take out a gun and shoot you. Even if her or his feelings tended in that direction, such behavior would (almost) never occur.

NORMS TELL US WHAT "SHOULD BE" Norms define proper and improper behavior for a group or an entire society. As such, they can tell us what the ideals of the group or the society are. For instance, in 1954, the U.S. Supreme Court ruled that racially segregated schools were unconstitutional because they violated the principles of fairness and equality upon which the nation was founded.

The ideal behavior specified in norms,

however, is frequently not the same as the behavior that actually takes place. In 1954, racial segregation was a common practice, and it was supported by many local laws, particularly in the South. But, since the Supreme Court ruling, while segregation has not been completely wiped out, it is now considered wrong by most people. There are established penalties, and violators are recognized as lawbreakers.

To take another example, the norms that appear in the Constitution of the Soviet Union, specifying the rights of Soviet citizens to due process and equal access to public office and public services, regardless of past activities, race, nationality, or religion, are often violated in practice. *Normative* behavior, or the actual behavior corresponding to the norms of a society, in other words, isn't necessarily *normal* behavior, or behavior that is typical or common. For example, if *most* arguments were settled with one party killing the other, it would be *normal* behavior. However, that wouldn't make it *right* by the standards of the society in question. The catch—and the reason why the terminology may be confusing—is that, in many instances, people associate what occurs most frequently with what is right.

NORMS ARE SHARED AND ENFORCEABLE Norms are rooted in the social structure. My *personal* feelings about right and wrong are not norms because there is no commonly accepted way of enforcing them. Norms must be enforceable, through either formal or informal means. For example, the Watergate criminals made the mistake of acting on their beliefs; they justified their crimes by saying they felt their actions were in the "national interest." Former White House Chief of Staff H. R. Haldeman clarified this position when, after his conviction, he stated that only he could possibly determine his guilt or innocence. But society saw otherwise (that social norms had been violated) and punished him.

Most of a society's members share major norms that refer to national loyalty, marriage, murder, and work, as well as many more norms that regulate our daily routine. Other norms, however, apply only to members of particular groups: only Catholics have the norm of ritually confessing their sins to priests; members of national "right-to-life" groups generally obey norms to vote against candidates who support abortion on demand; and union members usually observe the norm of not crossing a picket line. All norms, though, can be enforced, either through informal pressure of the group or through formal means such as expulsion from the organization or imprisonment. And that quality—not the number of people who agree with a particular belief—makes a norm.

Norms are enforceable because they involve sanctions. A **sanction** is that part of a norm—stated or not, specific or general—that indicates a proper reaction to either the violation of or adherence to the norm.

Sanctions for the same behavior can vary greatly from one culture to another. For instance, in the United States, business executives are rewarded for shrewd financial speculation (buying a product for the sole purpose of selling it again at a higher price—with no intention of putting it to use). In the USSR, by contrast, the very same action is a crime because it costs the members of society money and does not give them anything in return.

Most people feel strongly about certain objects because they represent the norms they hold dear—whether the items are a Mercedes and a conservative suit . . .

. . . or Big Mike's tatoos, motorcycle posters, and bare midriff.

Sanctions do not necessarily involve penalties, nor are they always applied. All urban subway and elevated trains, for example, have laws—with specific sanctions—prohibiting smoking in the cars. The norm is almost never enforced, however, and anybody who rides these trains regularly will tell you that smoking is not all that uncommon. So, annoyed passengers are often unsure how to react. Some people will ask the offender to stop, others will simply show their displeasure, but most will remain silent.

Norm Types

How strongly we feel when a norm is violated gives us a good idea of its importance in our society; and sanctions generally indicate how strongly we feel about the norm violations. Norms can be classified by whether they tell us what to do or what *not* to do, and they can be further divided by whether they entail mild or severe sanctions.

Norms that tell us what to do are called *prescriptive norms.* Some prescriptive norms are taken very seriously; they are "musts." For example, we must serve in the military if drafted. Violations of prescriptive norms like this one generally bring harsh sanctions—for instance, heavy fines, jail terms, or beatings. But what about norms such as those that instruct us to thank someone who gives us a gift? We do not "have to" follow this rule, though we should. The sanction for not obeying is not likely to be severe (a dirty or hurt look, perhaps).

Norms that specify what *not* to do are called *proscriptive norms.* As with the prescriptive norms, the penalties for violating some of these norms are high. The classic proscriptive norms carrying severe sanctions appear in the Ten Commandments: Thou *shall not* murder, steal, commit adultery, or bear false witness. Finally, there are behaviors that we shouldn't do but that usually carry only mild sanctions: combing our hair at the dinner table, scratching certain parts of our body in public, talking extremely loudly, and so on. Violating these norms does not result in severe penalties, though it does upset the flow of casual social interaction and thus the smooth working of society. On the other hand, adhering to these "good manners" implies that others should do the same—and they usually do.

The American sociologist William Graham Sumner (1840–1910) has provided us with a classification of norms according to their function in society (1906). He grouped norms according to four types: folkways, laws, mores, and taboos (see Figure 2.1).

FOLKWAYS In their films, the Marx Brothers violate many rules with their odd styles of speech and dress, their sarcasm, and their refusal to take life seriously, but people only find them "crazy" not "bad." They break **folkways**—the customary ways of doing things—but they're obviously not menaces to society. Recently, I asked students how they thought people would react to someone who came to a dinner party wearing faded jeans and a T-shirt. The most common response was: "People would look at him funny." That's all. The violation was not seen to be serious. As Sumner notes, the content of a particular folkway

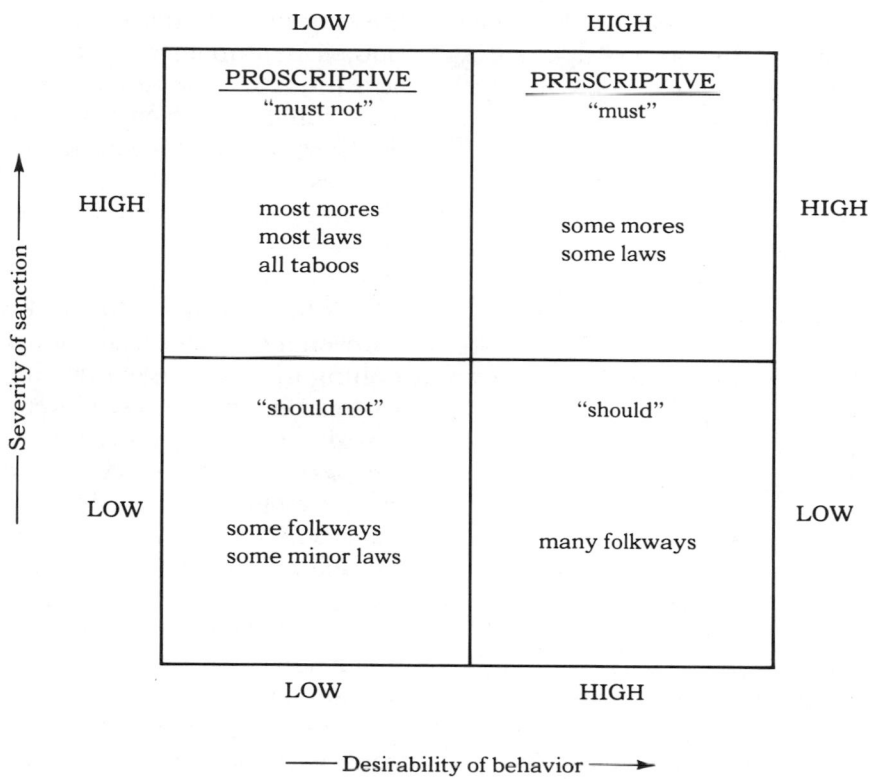

Figure 2.1 Types of Norms

is never important; it is only convenient that we have some rule (Sumner 1906, p. 64). Compared with other types of norms, sanctions for folkways are fairly mild.

LAWS Laws are also norms. They regulate behaviors that are felt to be necessary for the smooth running of society. We can distinguish laws from other norms because laws define both the behavior involved and the sanction for its violation with some precision. Even when judges in the United States are given discretion in deciding what sentences should be im-

posed, for instance, they must remain within specifically defined boundaries. Laws also differ from other types of norms in that they specify *who* can punish transgressors and what the process is for determining guilt or innocence. For this reason, vigilantes (groups of citizens who take the law into their own hands) can never be upholding *any* law. Vigilantes have been guilty of countless injustices, but even if they act against real murderers, rapists, and thieves, in doing so they are violating an integral part of the norm—its specified sanction. Thus their "war on crime" is criminal to the core.

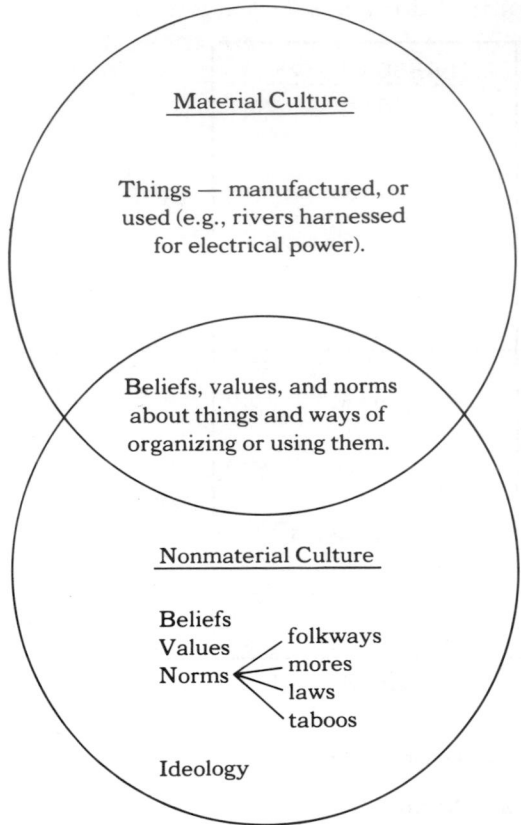

Material Culture

Things — manufactured, or used (e.g., rivers harnessed for electrical power).

Beliefs, values, and norms about things and ways of organizing or using them.

Nonmaterial Culture

Beliefs
Values
Norms → folkways
mores
laws
taboos

Ideology

Figure 2.2 Components of Culture

the *mos* (the singular of mores) of wearing clothes in public, become established as law, but most go unrecorded. Thus it is often difficult to recognize many of them. Yet they are there, as we learn anytime we witness their violation or anytime we encounter a society with different mores.

TABOOS Taboos, a fourth kind of norm, are even more basic than mores to the functioning of society. We find their violations so terrible that we see them as serious threats to society's moral foundation. Moreover, taboo violations arouse very strong feelings in us. Take a moment to imagine the violation of any specific taboo. Think, for instance, about how you would handle a violation of the now near-universal cannibalism taboo. Could you maintain a normal social relationship with anybody who did such a thing? In fact, the customary fate of apprehended taboo violators has been exclusion from normal social interaction! To violate a taboo is so contrary to our notions of "normal" and "human" that we redefine any person who does so as very different from us.

MORES Mores regulate moral behavior, and their sanctions are usually relatively severe. Mores can be either prescriptive or proscriptive. Consider, for example, what would happen if somebody came into class next time with nothing on. No doubt, the reaction would be stronger than raised eyebrows, and it is certainly unlikely that the offender would be allowed to remain in class. What about a male lawyer who appeared in court wearing a dress? That behavior might very well be defined as conduct unbefitting a professional and result in his disbarment. Some mores, such as

VARIATIONS IN CULTURE

The actual content of the elements of culture we have been examining varies enormously from one society to another. Some peoples still use Stone Age tools while others use computers; some practice periodic cannibalism, others vegetarianism; some practice the Islamic religion, others Christianity, Buddhism, or one of hundreds of folk religions. Many of the beliefs and practices of peoples around the world may seem quite irrational or immoral to us, even silly (if not unappetizing). But if we look more closely, we can detect that these foreign ways often do make sense, at least within the terms of their own culture. In this section, we'll look at the "sense" behind cultural differences, then at the attitudes people have toward these differences, and, finally, we'll look at cultural variations within a single society and how we can make sense of them.

Practical Origins of Cultural Differences

Many of the customs and beliefs that most of us see only as "bizarre" have very practical origins, as the anthropologist Marvin Harris (1974) has pointed out. Consider, for instance, the spectacle of "sacred" cattle roaming free among a starving Indian population and the prohibition against eating pig meat among both Jews and Moslems.

Those "useless" cows are actually vital to the Indian economy. They are the main source of draught animals, which are in short supply in India. Their manure is one of the most versatile commodities you can think of: it is an excellent fertilizer; a source of cooking and heating fuel; and mixed with water, it can be used as a flooring material. More importantly perhaps, unlike Western society, India has almost no chemical fertilizers or fossil fuels. And even if the society could convert to the kind of intensive machine agriculture we have in the United States, 250 million small farmers would be forced off the land into the already overcrowded cities, which cannot support their current populations. But if those cows stay sacred, most Indians will be less tempted to gain a few meals by killing them, thus averting long-range agri-

cultural and urban catastrophe (Harris 1974, pp. 11–32). Now do those stray cows seem useless?

To understand the prohibition on pork, Harris suggests we look at the role of climate in the Middle East where both the Moslem and Jewish religions originated. For people living in desert conditions, pigs have few uses. Unlike goats, sheep, and cows, they do not provide milk, which is a major commodity for the area's inhabitants. Besides that, people in this region generally lived nomadically, wandering over great distances, and pigs are extremely difficult to herd for long distances. Finally, there is almost no forestland in the Middle East, meaning that pigs compete with humans for scarce food resources. A pig, then, would be a dangerous (as well as costly) item to support. Because some people are invariably drawn to such "forbidden foods," only the word of God or Allah could keep them away (Harris 1974, pp. 35–46).

Perhaps even more fascinating is the fact that many Jews and Moslems who do not live in the Middle East continue to obey the ban. Even though the original practical reasons no longer apply, a "good Jew" or a "good Moslem" abstains from eating pork. As an element of Jewish and Moslem culture, the rule does not have to be a "good idea." Obeying it becomes simply a matter of right and wrong.*

While explaining such practices in light of culture, we must keep in mind that cultures do not develop on a strictly rational basis—no person or group "thinks" out the most logical or logically beneficial

---

*Most Jews you know probably do not follow this rule of diet; it has lost much of its importance for Jews in the United States. The more religious Jews, however, do uphold it as essential to Jewish living, and the prohibition remains part of Jewish culture to varying degrees.

Why is this man so calm? Although cows play a vital role in India's economy, it is their cultural meaning that keeps them sacred when their economic benefits are not apparent.

practices to follow. Customs and beliefs are the products not only of human reason but of feelings, nonrational attachments, and unrelated conflicts. And, as we have seen, they can persist long after their original rationales have disappeared.

Now turn the analysis on yourself—what "bizarre" practices do you engage in regularly? How could you justify them to someone with no knowledge of American culture? Could you explain why the moment before putting food in your mouth, you switch your fork from your left to right hand—unlike most Europeans who omit this seemingly useless step? Can you explain why it is very important that men do not wear skirts, when the Scotsman feels fine in his kilt, and the ancient Greeks and Romans were never uncomfortable in their tunics? And whether or not you can explain why these rules persist today, you will probably say that, reason or not, the rules must be followed.

Cultural Attitudes

The reason we see cultural practices of other societies as incomprehensible—or merely as "strange" or "primitive"—anthropologists and sociologists say, is related to our attitude toward our own culture and its values. For instance, what is your reaction to Horace Miner's description of the Nacirema's mouth rituals?

> The Nacirema have an almost pathological horror of and fascination with the mouth, the condition of which is supposed to have a supernatural influence on all social relationships. Were it not for the rituals of the mouth, they believe that their teeth would fall out, their gums bleed, their jaws shrink, their friends desert them, and their lovers reject them. (Miner 1956, p. 504)

So, according to Miner, they perform a mouth rite daily: "inserting a small bundle of hog hairs into the mouth, along with certain magical powders, and then moving the bundle in a highly formalized series of gestures." Once or twice a year, they also seek out the "holy-mouth-man" whose "exorcism of the evils of the mouth involves almost unbelievable ritual torture of the client."

If these rituals sound either exotic or irrational, you should worry, because Miner is describing American culture. (*Nacirema* is *American* in reverse.) Your reaction at this point might be somewhat skeptical: what a foolish description of some very "rational" practices! In fact, Miner wants us to see just how strange *any* culture can appear.

People generally view other cultures with one of two attitudes: ethnocentrism or cultural relativistism. **Ethnocentrism** is the tendency for people to see their own culture as superior to others; **cultural relativism** is the belief that we can understand the customs, beliefs, and values of other cul-

tures only on the basis of the culture's own standards and not our own. We saw an example of cultural relativism in Harris' analysis of the sacred cows of India and the Jewish and Moslem ban on eating pig. Harris shows that those practices we might consider nonsensical can be traced to causes we can easily understand and often agree with.

Watching for ethnocentrism in ourselves is crucial if we're going to understand cultural practices other than our own. Observers are bound by the ideology of their particular culture, and that ideology probably will not be shared in full by the culture being observed. Examples of ethnocentrism are everywhere. Across the United States, for example, ethnocentrism exists between Southerners and Northerners, Easterners and Midwesterners, urbanites and rural dwellers, blue collar workers and executives, and many others. Its most glaring manifestations, however, occur between nation and nation. People of many third world nations seem to look down on Americans as degenerate and completely obsessed by material things, and willing to exploit other countries to obtain them. By the same token, Americans (and other Westerners) have tended to see the civilizations of developing countries as inferior to their own because these nations have not achieved the technological progress attained in the West. For years, Westerners have exploited their resources with little restraint in the belief that these countries would be incapable of using them anyway. Although ethnocentrism is worldwide, the spread of nuclear weapons and the interdependence of nations on limited food and energy supplies would seem to require that an ethnocentrist view of the world in simplistic dualities of good vs. bad, communist vs. capitalist, East vs. West, white vs.

ETHNOCENTRISM ON TALLY'S CORNER

In *Tally's Corner* (1967), a participant-observation study, Elliot Liebow gives us a unique picture of black streetcorner men in Washington, D.C, from "the inside out." He challenges the assumptions outsiders make about these men; for example, those made by a hypothetical pickup-truck driver, cruising the ghetto in search of day laborers:

> The truck stops as it comes abreast of a man sitting on a cast-iron porch and the white driver calls out, asking if the man wants a day's work. The man shakes his head and the truck moves on up the block, stopping again whenever idle men come within calling distance of the driver. At the Carry-out corner [the hangout, which is the site of most of Liebow's research], five men debate the question briefly and shake their heads no to the truck. The truck turns the corner and repeats the same performance up the next street. In the distance, one can see one man, then another, climb into the back of the truck and sit down. In starts and stops, the truck finally disappears. (Liebow, 1967, p. 29)

Liebow asks us to think about what we just witnessed; namely, out of somewhere between twenty to fifty contacts, the driver finds only two or three willing to work for him. What *he* saw was clear: able-bodied men unwilling to do a day's work. This may be true for some of the men, but the point is that the experience confirms the driver's *ethnocentrist* stereotypes about *all* black men. He entered the ghetto that morning already believing—from things he had heard and read—that black men simply do not want to work. In reality, the men were reacting to a complex of economics, social values, and personalities.

The only way to understand what happened is for us to examine how and under what conditions the men responded to these forces. To the pickup driver, all men on the street during "working hours" were unoccupied. In fact, this was not so; many of the men did have jobs: one belonged to a suburban trash collection crew and was off that day; another worked nights cleaning office buildings, restaurants, and other public places; some worked in retail stores (e.g., liquor stores) that opened later in the day; and so on. Other employed men were off the job for personal reasons—to attend a funeral or answer a subpoena. Some of the men were not able-bodied, but the driver did not know that. Still other men were recently jobless and collecting unemployment insurance that paid more than the driver would have. When you add in the numbers runners, pimps, fences, and such, only a small number of men were still unaccounted for.

Some do fit the driver's stereotype. Yet, although a small minority, the don't-work-and-don't-want-tos are particularly visible to outsiders. First of all, they represent the clearest expression of the different social values found in degrees throughout the ghetto—and the subject of work is central in American society. Moreover, this group is made visible by people who exploit their existence for their antiwelfare and/or anti-civil rights ends. Although it is ethnocentrist to evaluate the actions of streetcorner men by these notions, that is just what many other people do.

By taking a culturally relativistic approach and not viewing these actions simply in terms of white middle-class values, we can see that streetcorner men evaluate their jobs the same way that others do—judging their social worth by the amount of money they command (Liebow 1967, p. 57). So they—and the pickup driver—would agree that the job offered was not worth doing. In cases like that, employees show their contempt by not keeping such jobs, and employers show theirs by paying workers too little to support a family. And they all agree that these jobs offer no prestige, respect, interest, or opportunities for advancement.

As you would expect, this takes its toll in self-esteem (Liebow 1967, pp. 61–62). There is almost no talk on Tally's corner about jobs, because jobs fail these men where they succeed for middle-class persons—in gaining for them a positive evaluation by society. So, for a number of reasons—both objective (low pay, physical strain of some jobs, seasonal nature) and subjective (dirty work, low self-esteem, no future advancement)—jobs are often subordinated to nonjob considerations in the individual's life. But, because of his ethnocentrist bias, the driver of the pickup truck failed to see these more complex dynamics. Our culturally relativistic look, however, enables us to identify the social factors at the root of this social problem.

black, and Judeo-Christian vs. Moslem diminish if we are to survive.

Subcultures

So far we have treated the culture of a society more or less as a single entity. But looking at a society's culture in this way can obscure important variations within it. To discuss those variations within a more general, or dominant, culture, sociologists use the term *subculture*. A **subculture** is a distinct way of life practiced by a group living within a larger society. In general, members of a subculture will live in accordance with many of the norms and values characteristic of the society as a whole, but in some respects, their lives will be distinguished by a number of distinct behaviors and norms. Among the different types of subcultures are criminal subcultures, ethnic subcultures, and countercultures. Each subculture presents an alternative set of norms and values to the rest of society.

CRIMINAL SUBCULTURES In the 1931 film *M*, Peter Lorre portrays a child murderer whose crimes terrorize an entire German city. The police are unable to find the murderer, but their efforts disrupt the "business" of the city's other criminals. In defense of their common interest (their illegal livelihood) and out of their beliefs that this criminal's actions are evil, the city's pickpockets, safe-crackers, burglars, con-artists, beggars, and prostitutes decide to capture the child murderer themselves. Each "trade group" selects a representative to a central committee, which then decides how to best mobilize their collective resources. Eventually, as you might expect,

the criminals capture the murderer and try him themselves.

The criminals in *M* represent a well-developed *criminal subculture.* Members belong to cultural organizations (based on trade), they participate together in leisure activities, and the subculture's members share a very definite idea of right and wrong. "Honest crime" is all right; killing a defenseless child is detestable.

Whenever we talk about "the underworld," we are referring to a subculture. American criminals, for instance, obviously reject some of their society's values, such as those emphasizing fair dealings with others and obedience to the rules. Their rejection of these values helps support a distinctive way of life, which offers criminals an ideology that justifies their behavior to themselves—something that would be almost impossible for a lone individual to sustain over time (Becker 1963, p. 38; Sykes and Matza 1957).

At the same time, criminals are actually quite supportive of many generally held values, such as those emphasizing individual achievement, experimentation, ingenuity, and the learning of practical skills. According to some sociologists, many criminals are individuals who believe in basic American goals but don't have legitimate means to reach them. For instance, in his study of delinquent boys, Albert Cohen (1955) concluded that gang activity among working-class youth was a result of the inadequate preparation they received to compete with middle-class youths at "legitimate" enterprises. He interpreted gang behavior as an alternative route to socially accepted rewards, like wealth.

ETHNIC SUBCULTURES One of the most important forms of subculture is that of ethnic groups. **Ethnic groups** are groups whose members are held together by race (e.g., blacks), religion (e.g., Mormons), national origin (e.g., Germans), or some combination of these (Gordon 1964, pp. 27–28). Black Muslims combine race and religion in their identity; Korean Americans combine national origin and race; American Jews combine religion and national origin, as do Polish, Irish, and Italian Catholics; while Chicanos (Mexican-Americans) form their subculture on all three dimensions. You may also have noticed that most nations have a dominant ethnic culture, as well as many subcultures. In the United States, the dominant ethnic culture is that of the WASP—or White Anglo-Saxon Protestant.

Americans are generally proud of the fact that their country is made up of many different ethnic units (see Table 2.1). But we should remember that many other countries contain diverse groups as well. For instance, in the Soviet Union only about half the population is Russian. Chester L. Hunt and Lewis Walker (1974, p. 57) estimate that there are people of over seventy-five different non-Russian nationalities living within the Soviet Union. There are Ukrainians, Uzbeks, Tartars, Lithuanians, Jews, Armenians, Georgians, Germans, Kirgiz, Moldavians, Estonians—and that's not even all the *major* ones (see Table 2.2). Belgium, a nation that cannot maintain a single official language, was formed by a Dutch group (Flemish) joining with a French group (Walloon). And most African nations are populated by tremendously diverse tribes, who speak different languages, worship different gods, and had little to do with one another until they were thrown together by a colonial power.

Ethnic groups vary in how distinctive their way of life is. In the United States, for instance, most people of German ancestry

Table 2.1 Selected Major Ethnic Groups in the U.S., 1973

Ethnic Group	Population (in thousands)
English	25,993
German	20,517
Irish	12,240
Italian	7,101
Mexican	6,293
French	3,939
Polish	3,686
Russian	1,747
Puerto Rican	1,548
Other*	100,329
Not reported	22,902
TOTAL U.S. POPULATION	206,295

*Includes groups from eastern Europe (Greek, Rumanian, Lithuanian, and others); western Europe (Dutch, Portuguese, and so on); Latin America (Cuban, South American); and Asia (Chinese, Japanese, Korean, Iranian, Arab, and more). Also includes blacks and native Americans.

SOURCE: U.S. Department of Commerce, Statistical Abstract of the United States, 1979 (Washington, DC: Government Printing Office, 1979, p. 33).

have, for the most part, so blended into the dominant culture as to become virtually indistinguishable from it. They share the same language as the bulk of the population, they intermarry with them, and they can be found at every level of income and occupation. Chicanos, on the other hand, retain values, language, and a way of life that set them apart from the predominant culture.

Some ethnic subcultures are formed and maintained because the members of the group want to remain distinct from the larger culture of which they are a part. The Amish are a good example. Other groups

Table 2.2 Major Ethnic Groups in the U.S.S.R., 1970

Ethnic Group*	Population (in thousands)
Russian	129,015
Ukrainian	40,753
Uzbek	9,195
Belorussian	9,052
Tartar	5,931
Kazakh	5,299
Azerbaijani	4,380
Armenian	3,559
Georgian	3,245
Moldavian	2,698
Lithuanian	2,665
Jewish	2,151
Tajik	2,136
German	1,846
Chuvash	1,694
Turkmen	1,525
Kirgiz	1,452
Latvian	1,430
Dagestan	1,365
Mordvin	1,263
Bashkir	1,240
Polish	1,167
Estonian	1,007

*There are forty-one additional ethnic groups with populations greater than 10,000, including: Chechens and Ossetics; Bulgarians, Greeks, and Turks; Gypsies and Hungarians; Iranians, Assyrians, and Kurds; Kalmyks and Yakuts.

SOURCE: Edward Allworth, ed., Soviet Nationality Problems (New York: Columbia University Press, 1971, pp. 282–83).

develop and maintain distinctive traditions and values because they are denied full access to the larger culture. American history is filled with examples of prejudice and discrimination against various ethnic groups who have arrived on our shores from Africa to Puerto Rico, from Italy to Iran. And even some members of white ethnic groups complain that they are treated unfairly and looked down upon because their ideology emphasizes values such as preserving the community, rather than the "American" value of individual achievement (see Novak 1971).

The distinctive ethnic group ideologies set their members apart from the rest of the society and provide support for their unique subcultural way of life. The existence of these competing subcultural belief systems within a society can be the source of much conflict. On the national scale, for instance, groups can attempt to break away from the larger culture that they feel incompatible with. This is what caused a brutal civil war in Nigeria when the Ibos attempted to form their own nation, Biafra. And this has happened in Ethiopia, where both the Eritreans in the north and the West Somalis in the south have battled for their own independent nations. On the individual level, conflict can occur when the same individual is expected to satisfy both the norm of one subculture and the different norm of another (often the dominant culture). Many young Americans experienced this conflict in the 1960s (and early 1970s) when the youth subculture asserted its norms about sex, drugs, our hectic lives, and the Vietnam War, among others, which differed radically from the traditional norms of adult American society.

Countercultures

The youth subculture of the 1960s and early 1970s is referred to as a *counterculture.*

As the label implies, the norms and values of a counterculture are substantially opposed to those of the dominant culture, although many overlaps still exist.

The members of the sixties' counterculture seemed to oppose everything that America stood for. They ignored traditional folkways by dressing in blue jeans and other clothes that "respectable" Americans would not wear. The women did not wear makeup, and they were not obsessed with bathing often. All protested Americans' concern with appearance.

Counterculture members also violated many mores of conventional society. Their use of language was not bound by conventional taboos, which they claimed stifled expression. They said that Americans were sexually repressed, and they preached "free love" and openness toward sex.

Some segments within the counterculture rejected some fundamental values of American culture:

- They rejected capitalism and the material goods that it brought. They chose to live without possessions.
- They rejected hard work. They chose leisure and idleness rather than constant activity.
- They rejected the glorification of achievement. They chose to concentrate on personal happiness and interpersonal relationships rather than take jobs.
- They rejected faith in rationality, science, and technology. They chose to place their trust in direct experience.
- They rejected progress. They chose a nontechnological, less-complicated style of life, often in a rural setting.

Despite their apparent complete rejection of American society, members of the counterculture retained many traditional values. Fred Davis (1967), for instance, who wrote about the American counterculture in its heyday, did not find its members totally opposed to their original culture: "The hippies, in their collective, yet radical, break with the constraints of our present society, are—whether they know it or not—already rehearsing *in vivo* a number of possible cultural solutions to the central life problems posed by the emerging society of the future" (Davis 1967, p. 12). In other words, they offered middle-class Americans an alternative way of living. Dean MacCannell (1976, p. 100), in his book about modernity, also sees the counterculture as a stage in our society's evolution—rather than as a complete break with the dominant culture.

These assessments of the American counterculture help make sense of its demise. The counterculture of the sixties and seventies is no more. Its members grew older, social mores changed, the war ended, and the movement ran out of steam. In the end, many counterculturalists embraced the dominant culture. But despite its disappearance, the counterculture did have an enduring influence on American society. For instance, through its mobilization of youth, voting and drinking ages were lowered, younger political candidates were elected, and norms concerning sexual behavior and drug use were revised.

CULTURAL CHANGE

The absorption of countercultural elements into the central stream of American culture, and the subtle changes that resulted, points to one of the major processes by which cultural change occurs. Without such changes, cultures would ill prepare their members to cope with new conditions.

Cultural Diffusion and Innovation

When one culture acquires elements of another, we call the process **cultural diffusion.** Ralph Linton (1936) notes its importance:

> If every human group had been left to climb upward by its own unaided efforts, progress would have been so slow that it is doubtful whether any society by now would have advanced beyond the level of the Old Stone Age. The comparatively rapid growth of human culture as a whole has been due to the ability of all societies to borrow elements from other cultures and to incorporate them in their own. (p. 324)

Linton found that just about all the elements in an American's daily routine originated elsewhere: pajamas are from India; neckties from seventeenth century Croatia; umbrellas from Southeast Asia; waffles from Scandinavia; smoking from American Indians (pipes from Virginian Indians, cigarettes from Mexico, cigars from the Antilles) (Linton 1936, pp. 326–27). Capitalism, socialism, Judaism, Christianity, classical music, sociology, the English language, democracy, tennis, and many *people* who call themselves Americans—all are imports from abroad.

Diffusion also occurs within a society. Much of this cultural diffusion takes place downward, from the upper classes to the middle classes to the lower classes. But

Nutritionally speaking, the diffusion of fast foods might not be a boon to the Japanese; but it has given them a method for preparing and marketing food that fits the modern, industrial lifestyle they have developed.

some elements diffuse upward. In the 1960s, for example, rock music, associated with American youth, and having roots in the jazz and blues music of black Americans, became a strong influence on white adult popular music. Marijuana use spread from Chicano farmworkers and urban ghettos to middle-class suburbs. Whites adopted styles of speech, dance, and dress from blacks. Finally, a look at the popular media will show us many elements taken directly from Jewish, Italian, and other subgroups (e.g., foods and expressions) and adopted by the larger culture.

Of course, cultures also produce things of their own, a process called **innovation.** In the United States, this has brought us jazz, the assembly line, and cocktails, among other things. But diffusion is a more important source of culture than innovation.

Even baseball, although developed in New York, derives from the English games of cricket and rounders.

Innovation is hindered because all inventors operate within the restrictions of their culture. And each culture provides its members with a limited number of ways of looking at the world. In 1932, for example, Americans found that they were incapable of solving their economic difficulties, given their understanding of economic processes. That understanding stressed individual initiative, for example, and did not include government intervention in the economy. The Great Depression, however, created a condition where private initiative did not work. To meet the crisis, the Roosevelt administration turned for inspiration to the new ideas of a British economist, John Maynard Keynes. More recently, we have found that the American ideology—with its emphasis on bigness and expressions of individual taste—did not provide a favorable climate for the development of a small car. Gasoline shortages, on the other hand, made such cars desirable. We needed a *foreign* perspective, which the Germans and Japanese provided.

No society is self-sufficient, and a society without diffusion would stagnate. After they settled in the western hemisphere, the American Indians lost contact with the rest of the world, and most tribes' technology remained in the Stone Age until Europeans arrived on the American continents. (The Maya and Incas built their brilliant civilizations without the wheel.) Complex, modern cultures are unlikely to become stagnant, however, since advanced methods of transportation and communication bring their members into contact with peoples from every part of the globe. This interaction infuses each culture with ever new elements and alternatives for daily contact. When gasoline prices skyrocketed, American auto manufacturers were forced to build more small, nonluxury cars in order to meet the competition from Europe and Japan. And an American idea, fast food, is spreading throughout Europe; in fact, a new McDonald's has become the most popular eating spot on Paris's famous Champs Elysées!

Cultural Lag

One final point about cultural change. A change in one sector of a culture does not necessarily stimulate an immediate change in all the other sectors that may be affected. Our technology, for example, has been evolving at an astonishing rate; often more rapidly than our ability to react to the social changes it brings in its wake. As a result, our values often refer to conditions that no longer exist. This is an instance of **cultural lag.** It takes place when one part of a culture—usually the material—changes more rapidly than another—usually the ideological. The lag often causes a period of maladjustment (see Ogburn 1964). For example, medical technology can now keep a human being technically alive beyond the point when the diseased or injured patient has any possibility of ever regaining consciousness. In an internationally followed court case, the parents of a young New Jersey woman, Karen Ann Quinlan, who was in that condition, asked to have their daughter's life-sustaining machines turned off so she could "die in dignity." The problem arose because our culture's definition of death (and of life) still focuses on the heartbeat—which can now be prolonged almost indefinitely.

Technological changes are not always for the better: cultural lag may be a factor in industry's pollution of air and water. With this and other social problems, our values and norms have not kept up with the physical changes that our technology brings.

SUMMARY

Culture—material and nonmaterial—provides a society with the values, beliefs, knowledge, and customs that legitimize the enforcement of its standards. Culture consists of all human creations. Its main elements are material things, beliefs, values, and norms.

Beliefs are ideas people hold about what the world is like. Values are general assumptions about what is right and wrong, good and bad, better and worse. Norms translate values into relatively concrete rules. They are shared standards of behavior that contain sanctions—definitions for the proper response to their violation. By looking at a society's sanctions, and at how well they are enforced, we can learn much about what is important to that society. Of the major types of norms the content of taboos and laws are the most important, folkways (or customs) the least, and mores (from morality) in between.

Norms and values are sometimes called legitimations because they legitimize our obedience to others. Together, the legitimations that characterize each society or group make up its ideology. Ideology is a comprehensive view of the world. It plays an important part in social control because it provides a justification for that group's or society's rules.

We can look at other cultures with two different attitudes. We can adopt the viewpoint of cultural relativism and judge other cultures on the basis of their own conditions of existence. Or we can find certain practices silly or barbaric, judging them according to the life we know, from the perspective of ethnocentrism. As the term *ethnocentrism* is generally used, it refers to our interactions with exotic and foreign cultures. However, we can be ethnocentric about the many different subcultures within our midst as well. These subcultures include criminal subcultures, ethnic subcultures (which are built on ties of common race, religion, national origin, or a combination of these factors), and countercultures, among others. In every society, there is a dominant culture, whose values and norms may conflict with those of a subculture.

There are two main processes of cultural change—diffusion and innovation. Diffusion is the spread of material things, ideas, or practices from one culture to another, and innovation is a culture's own creation of cultural elements. All parts of a culture seldom change at once. The period between the time that one part of a culture changes and the adjustment to that change by the rest of the parts, is called cultural lag.

Key Terms

culture (p. 62)
material culture (p. 66)
nonmaterial culture (p. 66)
technology (p. 67)
values (p. 69)
ideology (p. 70)
norms (p. 71)
sanction (p. 72)
folkways (p. 74)
mores (p. 76)
taboos (p. 76)

ethnocentrism (p. 79)
cultural relativism (p. 79)
subculture (p. 82)
ethnic groups (p. 82)
cultural diffusion (p. 86)
innovation (p. 86)
cultural lag (p. 87)

Review and Discussion Questions

1. How do executives of competing businesses (and ad agencies) use their knowledge of American values to make their products more attractive to consumers?
2. Make a list of all the norms you have violated in the past five years. What kind of norms were they? How serious were they? Did other people know about the violations? How were you sanctioned—or why weren't you?
3. Describe some well-known activity in which you engage regularly à la Miner's description of Nacirema mouth rituals. Does it seem odd? How would you explain its utility?
4. Which of your favorite everyday items would be missing from your life were it not for cultural diffusion? What are some American cultural elements that have entered the lives of other people around the world?
5. What gave rise to the youth counterculture of the 1960s? What lasting impact has it had on society (and on your life)? Do you expect to see the rise of another? Why or why not?

For Further Study

CULTURAL NORMS IN OUR LIVES We often miss the importance of cultural norms in our lives because we tend to obey their dictates without thinking about them. Some sociologists and anthropologists have, however, been able to clearly show us their significance. One of the best books on this topic—and also one of sociology's basic works—is Emile Durkheim's *The Division of Labor in Society* (New York: Free Press, 1933). Durkheim's basic thesis is that we can understand how societies stay together by looking at the nature of their laws. Another important book is Herbert Gans, *Popular Culture and High Culture* (New York: Basic Books, 1974), which relates our conceptions of good taste and notions of what culture is to a host of social indicators. Finally, see the collection by Milton Rokeach, ed., *Understanding Human Values* (New York: Free Press, 1979).

CULTURE AND SEX ROLES How we behave as either male or female is also something we rarely question. Of course, norms are changing in this area, and the social and cultural basis of this behavior is increasingly being studied. Although first published in 1935, Margaret Mead's *Sex and Temperament in Three Primitive Societies* (New York: Dell, 1968) remains among the best comparative studies. Another interesting study is *Women of the Forest*, by Robert F. and Yolanda Murphy (New York: Columbia University Press, 1974), about sex roles in an isolated Brazilian tribe. *La Chicana* (Chicago: University of Chicago Press, 1979), by Alfredo Mirande and Evangelina Enriquez, focuses on Mexican-American women. Finally, Sarah B. Pomeroy's *Goddesses, Whores, Wives, and Slaves: Women in Classical Antiquity* (New York: Schocken, 1975) reviews the way women behaved in ancient Greece and Rome and traces our own images of women to ancient literature and mythology.

LOOKING AT OTHER CULTURES The Case Studies in Cultural Anthropology series published by Holt, Rinehart and Winston consists of brief monographs on such cultures as: the Cheyenne, Mexican-American, rural Irish, Yoruba of Nigeria, and New Guinea tribal. Ruth Benedict's *Patterns of Culture* (Baltimore: Penguin, 1946) compares three primitive societies (Pueblo Indians, Indians of northwest America, and a tribe of New Guineans) and provides many insights on the nature of all cultures. Also see Ashley Montagu, ed., *Learning Non-Aggression: The Experience of Non-Literate Societies* (New York: Oxford University Press, 1978). Finally, we have Marcel Mauss's classic 1925 study of Indian tribes of northwest America, *The Gift* (New York: Norton, 1967). Mauss explores the "odd" economy of the Indians' culture, in which the destruction of property was valued rather than its accumulation.

CHAPTER THREE

Roles, Performances, and Sociability: Types of Social Behavior

I f everyone simply acted according to cultural norms, we would all behave the same. This would not only make social life extraordinarily dull but also render it impossible. Without some differentiation in what members of a society do at a given time, society could not exist. For this reason, many cultural norms delineate different parts—or roles—we should play in society. In this chapter, we will look first at the way in which social roles regulate and organize our behavior. Then we will look at two additional dimensions of our behavior: the expressive side of our role behavior; and sociability, our tendency to suppress our individual interests in order to get along with others.

THE NATURE OF SOCIAL ROLES

Most of us understand *social roles* in a general way to mean the "parts" people play in society—like actors' roles in a drama. We learn a number of roles—for instance, those of student, teacher, wife, husband, police officer, comic, plumber, medical technician, lover, town drunk (or skid-row wino, depending on location). That's simple enough, but by leaving it at that, we run the risk of confusing roles with the people who play them. We observed this confusion among Richard Nixon and some of his supporters during the Watergate affair. Presi-

dent Nixon, the individual, was accused of misconduct by substantial segments of the press, the Congress, and the American public. Nixon and his supporters, however, repeatedly protested that those who attacked this particular president were, in fact, attacking *the presidency itself.* In other words: they claimed that the *role*, not the *individual*, was being threatened. His accusers, however, did not attack the presidency of pre-Nixon days, and they left the office unchallenged after his resignation, even though the charges against him proved essentially correct. Nixon the individual resigned that office—he had not performed the role according to its norms. That role is defined in the Constitution, and this, not the actions of a particular individual, is the basis for its existence.

A role cannot rest on the fortunes of a single individual because it is rooted in the social structure. We can easily miss this fact in casual observation because we only see roles in the form of the people playing them. But a **role** is not a person; rather it is a collection of activities regularly performed by the occupant of a specific social position (like that of president).

Role Expectations

The collection of activities that make up a role are governed by norms. The norms that define a role for everyone who might play it, want to play it, or observe it are called **role expectations**. Thus a person playing the role of judge is expected to be knowledgeable about the case being tried, remain attentive and dignified in court, keep order, and listen and rule impartially according to law. Similarly, you expect your instructors to come to class regularly and on time, deliver well-reasoned and informed lectures, assign appropriate readings, maintain order in class, and evaluate your work. You do not expect your instructor to grade you on the basis of how she or he feels about you as a person, which is subjective, but with objective criteria (exam scores, papers, class participation). You also expect these criteria to be applied equally and consistently to everyone in the class. You have had many teachers, and some were no doubt a lot better than others. But you probably expected all of them to obey a particular set of norms. Actions and words, not individuals, make up the position of instructor.

Of course, social life is not simply a matter of everyone uniformly following a set of rules regarding proper roles. For one thing, we don't always enact our roles according to what others expect of us or even according to our own expectations. We saw an example of this in the discussion of Nixon as president. Nevertheless, there is generally some accuracy to our expectations. Otherwise, they would never have occurred in the first place or would give way to different ones.

For another thing, we each interpret the roles we play. Role norms are necessarily vague in order to allow some flexibility in execution and to accommodate different circumstances. We take advantage of this vagueness to put our own stamp on our actions. You may have ob-

served this in police officers. Some seem to take their authority as a justification for being brutish while others play the role in a more restrained way.

Finally, and perhaps most importantly, there is often disagreement over what the proper expectations of a role should be. Many attorneys, for instance, feel that they should be allowed to advertise to attract customers and inform prospective consumers of what they can expect. Other lawyers disagree, believing that it would create an undignified atmosphere in the profession and possibly lead to cutthroat competition and "bargain basement" type selling. Or consider that most Americans feel that the role of spouse demands sexual exclusivity (that you have sex only with your spouse) and that without it, the role cannot have the intimacy required to play it. A minority of couples take the opposite view. They feel that the benefits of a sexually open marriage make for a more intense and loving relationship between spouses (see Clanton and Downing 1975; Libby and Whitehurst 1977).

Roles and Social Structures

Roles cluster to form *social positions,* for example, college instructor. The various role behaviors—lecturer, examiner, and so on—combine together to create the position of "instructor." And roles and positions—unlike people—are units of the social structure. They organize our behavior, they provide categories for understanding it, and they define power relationships between individuals.

Roger Brown, a social psychologist, calls roles the "real social categories" in the United States: "We are conscious of them,

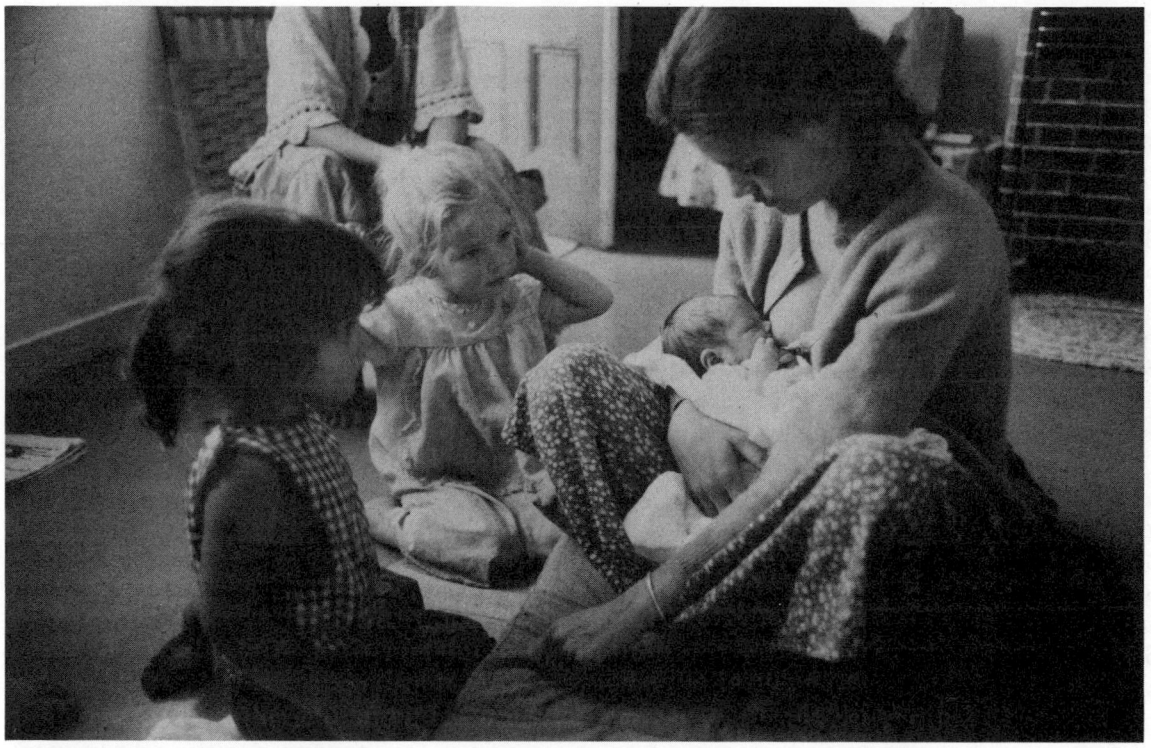

Roles are performed in different ways, and performance is always changing. In 1971 about a fourth of all American mothers breast fed their babies. By 1978 almost half did.

they structure interaction, and they govern style of life" (Brown 1965, p. 134). These same categories allow us to accept all sorts of behavior from some people that we would generally find terrible violations coming from others. Robert A. Nisbet (1977) offers a good illustration:

We take it for granted that the physician, in his role of physician, is entitled to make the most intimate of examinations, to handle our bodies in ways that would be entirely offensive were the same individual dealing with us outside his role of physician. Even in our present, relatively liberated age, nudity . . . our own or another person's—can make us acutely uncomfortable when it is out of role. . . . But nudity in the artist's model, in the stripper and actor on the stage, in the patient undergoing medical examination or being bathed by the nurse in the hospital ward, to use but a few examples, is nudity-in-role and is regarded as legitimate. (p. 141)

But let's not get the wrong impression. People do not all agree on what constitutes legitimate nudity-in-role—or on other role expectations, for that matter. In 1978, for example, a female reporter for *Sports Illustrated* was barred from the New York Giants football team locker room, where she wanted to conduct postgame interviews and where many of the players were undressed. She sued the team, claiming that its action prevented her—solely on the basis of her sex—from performing her role as reporter. Seeing the nude athletes, she contended, was simply part of her role. The Supreme Court agreed, saying that the team's action put her at a "competitive disadvantage with her male colleagues."

Because the norms associated with our roles define what is and what is not legitimate for us to do, they also define the power relationships between people in different social positions. For instance, as long as they play their role properly, the police are allowed to kill other members of our society. Also, think of the power your instructors have: they can demand certain performance from you, correct you when they think you are wrong, and give you grades that significantly affect your future. Finally, in traditional American families, consider the power granted the man who, in his role as husband, is expected to control the family's wealth and make its major decisions, while the wife is expected to serve him (see Walum 1977, pp. 137–218; Mainardi 1970, pp. 265–68; Weitzman 1975; Syfers 1973).

Role Sets

Our roles are not usually played in isolation, but often in groupings called *role sets*. A **role set** is the pair or cluster of roles in which each role takes its meaning from its relationship to the others and cannot

exist without them. We recognize an endless number of role sets in our world: students and instructor; doctor, nurse, and patient; judge, defense attorney, prosecutor, jury, and defendant; union negotiator, business representative, and federal mediator; airplane hijacker, hostages, official negotiator, police officers or soldiers, and spectators.

Role sets entail reciprocal obligations and rights (privileges and rewards). Consider, for instance, the much simplified representation of the role set of a student (Figure 3.1). In general, students have an obligation to pay their tuition to the administration and hand in assignments to the faculty. In return, they receive academic knowledge and consultation from the faculty and an organized structure of classes and requirements from the administration. Notice that, in this instance, the role set of the student overlaps the role sets of the faculty and administration. The role set of the faculty includes the administration and vice versa. The faculty must submit competent reports on student progress to the administration, which must pay the salaries of the faculty. Of course, all of the possible role sets of students don't necessarily overlap with faculty and administrative role sets. For instance, a student role set might include being a member of an off-campus group, but this is not likely to be part of the role set of a faculty member.

Because roles involve an exchange in which we fulfill certain obligations in return for specific privileges or rewards, successful performance of any role requires the participation of the other roles in the set. Imagine, for instance, a teacher without a class, or an actor without an audience. In such cases, trying to play the role would probably be pretty comical. But what about student boycotts to protest an in-

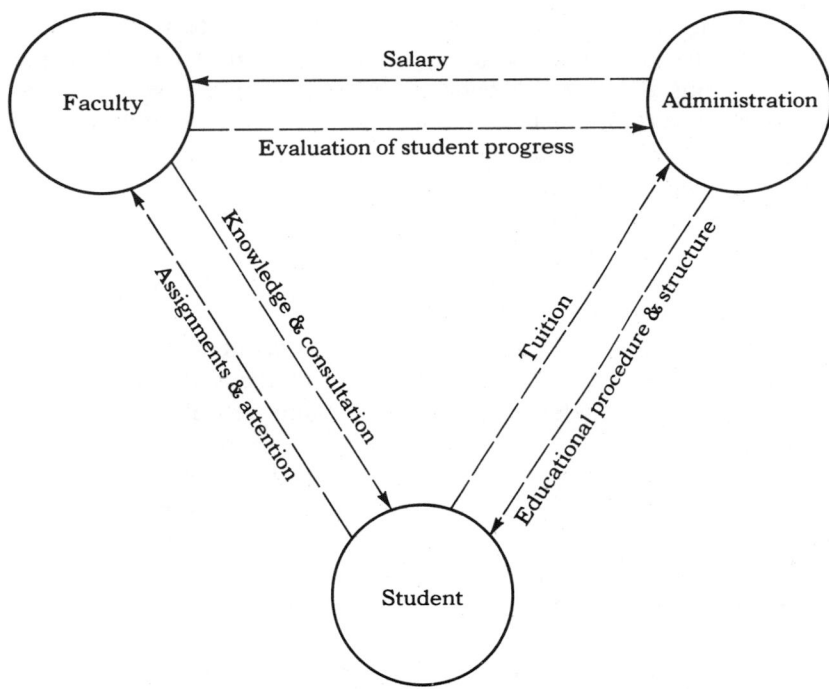

Figure 3.1 Overlapping Roles Sets of Student,
Faculty, Administration

structor's political stance? There, the students use their power to refuse to participate in the role set, and they make the role of instructor impossible.

In sum, generals need soldiers to obey their orders, quarterbacks need receivers to catch their passes, and store cashiers must have customers who are willing to give them money. Most roles are organized and can only be played if the other members of the role set play too.

Roles and the Self

How would you describe yourself to a total stranger? Would you say that you are an intelligent, good-natured individual who enjoys art museums, dislikes seafood, and drives a Porsche? Or would you say that you are a student at X University or a management trainee at Y Company? Chances are, you would choose the latter way, using your social roles. Roles, in fact, are really built into our identity because people react to us on the basis of the social role we appear to be playing. This is how we understand who we are.

The roles that we play, then, have a lot to do with what we think of ourselves. They also affect our behavior, in that we tend to behave in ways that are consistent with this self-perception—much more so than the "individualist" might think. For instance, in the "prison" experiment described in Chapter 1, we saw how ordinary college students, simply because of the roles they were assigned in the experiment, turned into brutal guards and servile prisoners almost indistinguishable from real prison inmates and guards (Haney et al. 1973). With regard to sex roles, sociologists have found that women learn to act less intelligent and competent when interacting with men, and a number of studies show that many women fear that success in a career would make them less feminine (Horner 1972; Weitz 1977, p. 138; Knudson 1974). And you can see on Figure 3.2 how our sex roles generally tend to channel us into certain occupations.

We judge ourselves not only on the basis of what roles we play but also according to *how well* we think we are playing them. If the others in our role set do not think we are playing our role legitimately and properly, says one sociologist, "it usually does not take very long before the self-image collapses" (Berger 1963, p. 100). Teachers know that students who are only criticized for their faults, and never praised for their good points, for instance, develop low self-images and often drop out. Our general interest in performing our roles well is what makes criticism by others often so effective. Many a husband has undermined his wife's attempts to earn money or go to school after a number of years of marriage, for instance, by complaining that she is neglecting her job as mother to their children.

ROLE ACQUISITION

How do we come to play the social roles we do? This question is really two: (1) How do we gain access to roles in our society? (2) How do we learn to play those roles to which we have gained access? Let's explore the answers to these two interrelated questions.

Access to Roles

We play certain roles and not others in society because of the social rankings, or statuses, that we hold. Sociologists commonly divide these rankings into two types, ascribed and achieved, depending on how we acquire them. **Ascribed statuses** are those over which we have no control. They are given to us, generally on the basis of biological characteristics, such as race, sex, and age.

Achieved statuses, on the other hand, must be earned in some way. You aren't born a professor or a police officer, for instance; you must work to gain those statuses, and you have some control over whether or not you retain them. It is often said that achieved statuses are paramount in our society but, as you can see, many positions remain ascribed and people are expected to abide by them. For instance:

- Age roles: child, adolescent, youth, adult, elderly
- Ethnic roles: Irish, Italian, Jew, Latino (Chicano, Cuban, Puerto Rican), Pole, and so on
- Family roles: belonging to a family known as rich (the Kennedys or Rockefellers, for example) or poor or evil becomes an ascribed role
- Racial roles: Asian, black, native American, white
- Sex roles: male (man, boy) and female (woman, girl)

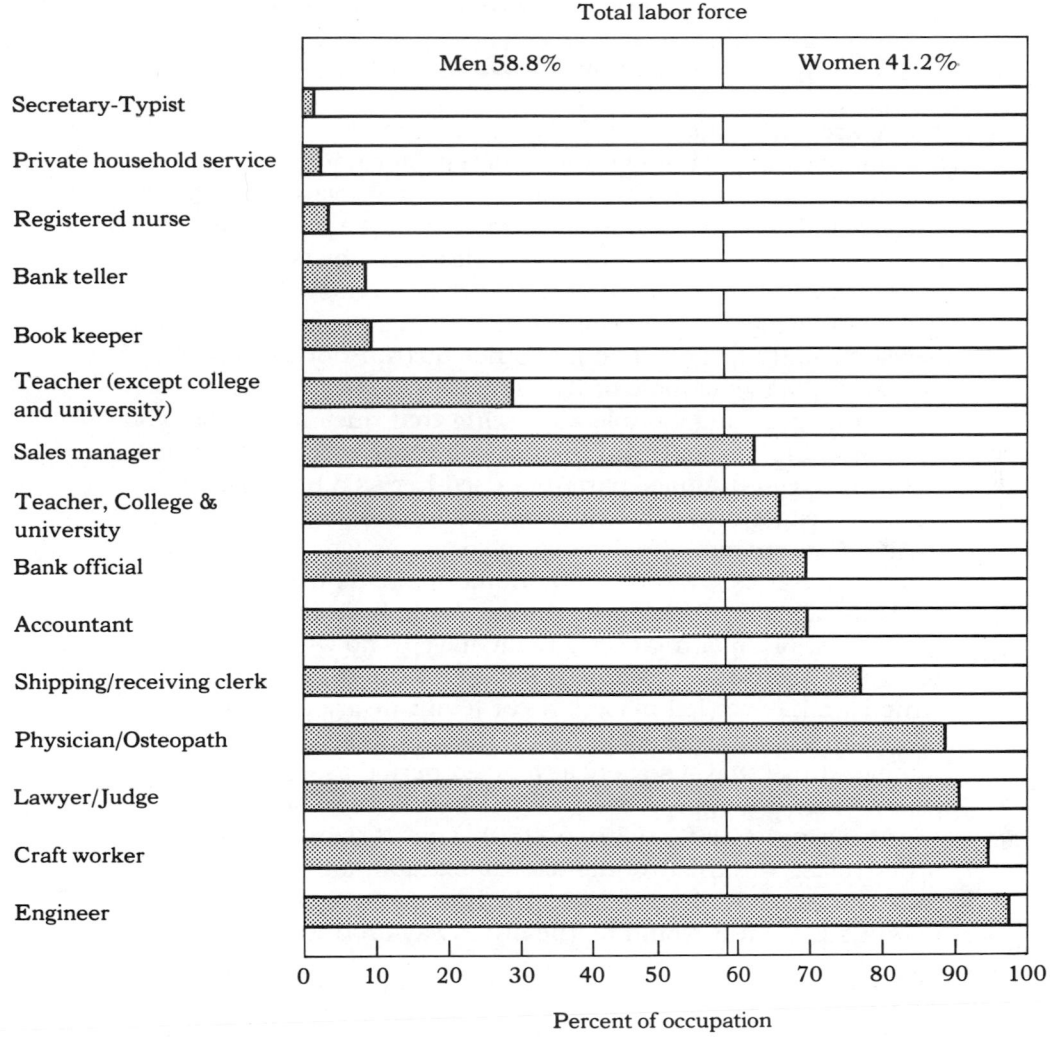

Figure 3.2 "Man's" Work; "Woman's" Work

SOURCE: *U.S. Department of Labor, Bureau of Labor Statistics*, Women in the Labor Force: Some New Data Series *(Report 575, 1979, p. 3).*

Access to most achieved statuses is limited, and, obviously, some statuses are more restricted than others. To become president of the United States, for example, you must first be elected, a process that demands time, effort, desire, recognition, political support from others, and money. These requirements are enough to keep most people out of the competition; for one thing, how many Americans can afford to

SEX ROLES

There are some differences between women and men that are not socialized. Biologically, different hormonal and chromosomal structures—in addition to genitals—distinguish the sexes. But what happens when these differences are not clear? Such was the case of Agnes, described by Harold Garfinkel (1967) as very attractive and well endowed. At age nineteen, surgeons removed the set of male genitalia—by then developed—that Agnes had had since birth. Prior to that operation, was she male or female?

Are you having trouble answering that question? If so, you are not alone: not only did the doctors incorrectly identify her sex at birth, but Agnes' parents raised her as a boy. Agnes herself accepted that identification, adjusting to her situation until, at seventeen, she decided to "pass" as female. Although cases like Agnes are rare, they should make us wonder what such things as running a business, doing housework, wearing cosmetics, or smoking cigars really have to do with our sex. As Margaret Mead says: "Many, if not all, of the personality traits which we have called masculine or feminine are as lightly linked to sex as are the clothing, the manners, and the forms of head-dress that a society at a given period assigns to either sex . . . the evidence is overwhelming in favor of social conditioning" (1968 [1935], p. 260). That is, sex roles—like other roles—are the product of socialization, and it is no more "natural" for a woman to be in the home and a man to be president, than it would be the other way around.

leave their jobs or businesses and devote their full time to running for office?

Access to many important roles in society is restricted by what sociologists call **professionalization**—the process by which the members of a profession or occupation—as a group—acquire the exclusive right to practice a skill (e.g., law, medicine, carpentry) and to train and admit new members. For instance, to become a lawyer, you must graduate from law school and pass a written and oral bar examination—all controlled by lawyers. More than that, the state often enforces this monopoly. For instance, it is illegal to practice medicine without a license, or to represent a client in most courts if you are not a member of the local bar, or to hire nonunion workers for many jobs. This sanction allows the profession to operate by standards it creates, often to protect particular group interests (Collins 1975, pp. 346–49).

Mead based her conclusions on data she collected from extensive field research among primitive societies. Many recent studies also support her contention that society is responsible for many important differences between the sexes. Admittedly, then, our usual way of looking at women and men will not help us understand them. How should we view them?

Even if certain biological differences predispose us to behave in certain ways (and we have no experience of these differences independent of social conditioning), we must add that *all* societies have elaborated a set of roles based on these differences in biology; but in most, if not all, cases, this social component goes far beyond anything built-in. For example, women's fashions—such as spiked heels and tight dresses—have often made it more difficult for women to adequately defend themselves.

We will better understand the nature of men and women if we consider the following change in perspective. Normally, we think about men and women as separate categories—a dichotomy. Instead, we can think of the sexes in terms of a single continuum, with male and female at either end. All of us have some characteristics of the other sex. Most important, a continuum allows movement between the poles; categories do not.

In light of the studies we have cited, and the story of Agnes, do you now conceptualize the sexes as separate categories or points on a single continuum?

We might consider control of access unfair because it's not always foolproof in opening positions to those best qualified to fill them. All of us have at least heard of incompetent doctors and lawyers, for example, despite their official certification. Moreover, we know that a person's ability to take exams does not necessarily make the difference between a good and bad doctor or attorney; yet, that person had better be good at it if she or he wants to get ac-cepted to medical or law school. Finally, we know that many craft unions will use relationship to a union member as the major criterion for deciding on a person's admission. But few of us would feel comfortable with just anybody operating on us or piloting the plane we're flying in. Official certifications of achievement provide some check on competency for us, even though our trust in the process is obviously not always justified.

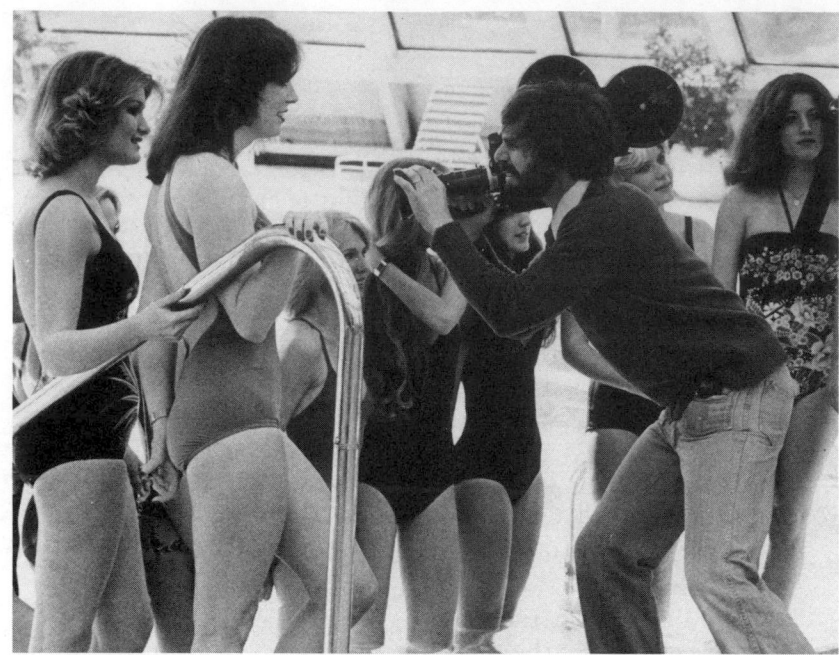

The Miss Virginia Beauty Pageant: Certain activities perpetuate the view of women as sex objects that should be put on display, even though women can be found in most adult roles.

Role Taking

Acquiring any role involves some type of learning. This is true of roles associated with ascribed as well as with achieved success. Take our sex role: sex is a *biological* term, referring to physical characteristics; role is a unit of the social structure. "Sex role" is a *social* definition of part of our biology. And like all social behavior, it is *learned.*

Learning role expectations is a central element in our primary socialization. Role requirements are transmitted to us as children and we internalize (see Chapter 1) these expectations. Of course, everybody does not learn the same roles or the same requirements for them. Our parents (and other agents of socialization) teach us roles

they expect and want us to play. We learn our sex role, our role as daughter or son, our role as an American, perhaps a religious role, and the student role.

As we grow older, our parents might encourage us to take an interest in, for example, medicine by constantly praising the work that doctors do. The mass media may glorify a popular police detective, and with our peers will probably praise sport stars like Muhammed Ali and O. J. Simpson. Later, knowledge of role expectations will allow us to understand the activities that make up certain occupations, so we will have (generally) a more realistic idea of our own ability to perform specific roles.

The specific process by which we internalize role expectations is called **role taking.** It usually involves both some sort of training and some practice at performing the role.

ROLE TRAINING You have probably experienced the training stage during the initial days of a job, when you were assigned only certain chores—probably ones that didn't require much skill. As you learned more about the job and the workplace, you were given more complex tasks.

Sometimes a training period in one specific role prepares people for another. For example, boys are trained to be men, girls to be women, management trainees to be managers, apprentices to be craft workers, interns to be doctors. Learning to play roles involves what role theorists call **anticipatory socialization,** because we anticipate playing our future role and losing the temporary one. You might be experiencing anticipatory socialization right now if you are in school preparing for an occupational role. Neal Gross, one role theorist, has added that the person does not have to go on to an expected role (e.g., law student to lawyer) for anticipatory socialization to take place; it exists whenever a person uses one role to prepare for another (e.g., law student to business executive or politician), whether there is formal training or not.*

ROLE PRACTICE In addition to training, role taking involves practice. The process resembles the one involved in "method acting," which is based on the tenet that for an actor to learn a part, he or she must "live" it. Someone assigned to play Julius Caesar in Shakespeare's play would first learn all there is to know about the character—whom he liked, what his habits

were, whether he was ambitious or greedy, and what life was like in ancient Rome. Then, when the actor stepped on the stage opening night, he would be able to feel as Julius Caesar did, and he would respond to the other performers' words as Julius Caesar. That is, he would not perceive himself as someone *trying to* play a part but would feel he was the character just by being himself.

If you think for a moment about some of the social positions you have recently acquired (obviously, college student, but perhaps also adult, spouse, divorced, or independent person), you probably remember how odd it felt playing the roles associated with them at first. That feeling probably left as people continued to respond to you as a college student, adult, or whatever. I remember my first day as a college instructor. I entered, dressed in a jacket and tie, with my notes all written out, wondering whether I should have the students call me by my first name, and with all sorts of what I believed were provocative comments and learning activities. In other words, it was a conscious effort for me to "be" an instructor. After a number of classes, in which students called me "professor" and reacted to my teaching activities, I learned to act in ways that produced responses in my role set (from students) that confirmed me in my role. I came to see the role as part of my identity—just as they did—and could engage in the behaviors without conscious thought about whether or not I was "really" a college professor.

Role Change

Sometimes we may be required to create totally new roles or to change the norms

---

Personal letter to author, November 8, 1977.

The way we learn our roles varies. We might imitate someone we admire, hoping to live up to social expectations . . .

. . . or learn through a tightly disciplined training program.

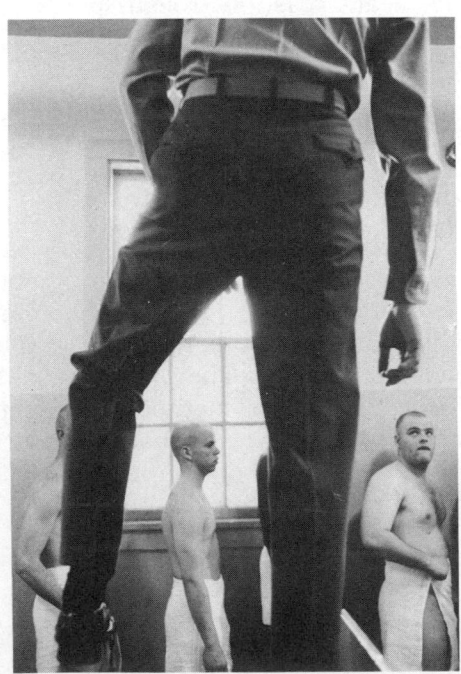

that govern old ones. This is called *role making.* Role making can occur for various reasons. New roles are sometimes created in response to unexpected or emergency situations. For example, increased delinquency in city schools, which was more than teachers could possibly handle, created the need for a new position, that of nonteaching assistant (NTA), whose sole job is discipline. Changes in technology have also spurred the development of new roles (such as computer programmer) and the revision of older ones. Thus when Henry Ford rearranged his Ford plant workers onto an assembly line, where each laborer worked on only part of the product, he not only made automobile production more efficient in his factory, but he revolutionized the role of worker throughout the world economic system.

Like role taking, role making begins in an awkward way, with our being consciously aware of our odd place and of our different ways of acting. Eventually, the new position or new interpretation will probably be recognized and accepted by other members of the role set, and we will become familiar with playing it.

Role making can signify a change for the better, but it can also be a strain because people are expected to abandon or modify roles that may have been central to their self-identity. Modern society, in particular, requires that its members be able to adapt to new roles with some frequency. In recent years, for instance, Americans have had to make substantial changes in the way they play some of their most important roles. The current controversy about sex roles is perhaps the most apparent example, but there have been others. Fathers are told to spend more time with their children, mothers less time than traditionally prescribed, and new guides to

childrearing contradict the Dr. Spock gospel that guided a generation of parents.

The burden of adjusting to potential or actual loss of role has perhaps been most widespread in the economic sphere. In recent years, as many businesses have reorganized, many workers' positions have been eliminated—either through automation or because of "modifications in work methods [which] break down or regroup old craft lines . . . into altered, or even new, occupations" (National Center for Productivity and Quality of Working Life 1977, p. 8). Many labor unions have noticed this trend and have begun demanding provisions in their contracts to guarantee retraining for workers whose jobs are eliminated. Not so long ago, people could reasonably expect to perform the same economic role throughout their lives. Now, flexibility is necessary in case economic roles have to be changed.

If role making often requires adjustments by the persons fulfilling new or changing roles, so does role conflict, the subject of the next section.

ROLE CONFLICT

In an ideal world, perhaps, the various parts we play in society would be coordinated with one another, the norms governing them would be clear, and we would be well adjusted to our roles. But this could only happen if we held just one position with unchanging role requirements, and were completely socialized to fill it. In our own world, however, role coordination is never complete, and when it is not, we are faced with **role conflict**—a situation in which contradictory expectations are made upon us. Sociologist William Goode (1960)

Table 3.1 Types of Role Conflicts

Type of Conflict	Example	Resolution
Interrole: conflicting demands of two or more roles on an individual	A judge who hears a case involving a friend	Separate roles in time and space; change role requirements (role making); choose one over the other, justifying the choice (drop one of the roles)
Intrarole: conflicting expectations over how to fill a single role; conflict between ideal role enactment and role as played	A firefighter who must decide whether to stay on the job or go out on strike with co-workers	Clarify priorities among role requirements; develop more realistic expectations
Self-role: imperfect fit between self and role	A person who is drafted and cannot stand violence	Change self-conception; drop role

has termed the difficulty we feel in trying to reconcile these expectations *role strain.*

You may think that role conflict is something to be avoided because it certainly does cause pain or discomfort. However, role conflicts can provide both individuals and society with a number of benefits because conflicts often stimulate constructive resolution. For individuals, role conflict can clarify alternative priorities (family or career, wealth or happiness, recreation or prestige) so we can make conscious choices. It may also reveal contradictions in the way a person is living, which can take a toll in time and physical and mental health. For society, role conflict can stimulate individuals to reform society in order to reduce the strain. In addition, resolution of conflicts has often meant the creation of new roles, better suited to the conditions of the contemporary society.

As we use the term, there are three types of role conflict: interrole, intrarole, and self-role conflict (see Table 3.1).

Interrole Conflict

Interrole conflict occurs when one of our roles demands certain behaviors that make fulfilling the requirements of another role difficult or impossible. Doctors who play the roles of both physician or healer and entrepreneur at the same time are a good example. We like to think that very few doctors will prescribe surgery *soley* for the money to be made. But when surgery would have only marginal value to the patient, the doctor may feel conflict between her or his roles as healer and moneymaker.

There are three major ways of reducing or resolving interrole conflict. Table 3.1 gives an example of the first type of resolution—*role segregation,* or separation. A judge is expected to hear all cases impartially and to issue decisions based on principles of law and justice. And since friends are expected to help each other when in need, we would expect the friend of someone involved in a lawsuit to hope for his or her victory and help bring that about; friends are not supposed to desert each other in time of need. Thus if a judge is asked to preside over the trial of a friend, a conflict exists because the roles of judge and friend demand contradictory behavior from the same individual. However, there is no contradiction between the requirements of a friend to be helpful and sympathetic and those of a judge to render fair and impartial judgments as long as these roles are separated in time and space. The solution is role segregation—in this case, keeping the judge's friend out of the judge's court. Judges facing this problem disqualify themselves from the case. Note that the solution—judges disqualifying themselves—is one of the norms of this role. Similarly, in order to avoid role conflict, professors are proscribed by the norms of their role from becoming romantically involved with their students.

Role separation cannot always be the answer to interrole conflict. Consider, for instance, the conflict of a woman who is expected to be a substantial contributor to the family's income and a super-mom at the same time. Interrole conflicts like this can be at least partially resolved by altering role norms, or role change, so that the roles can coexist without conflict. For instance, being a good mother can be redefined to not require full-time child care.

Finally, there are instances of interrole conflict that allow neither role making nor rearrangement of roles. These instances are often sparked by changes that throw previously complementary roles into conflict. The resolution may very well have to be a choice between one role or the other. Such a conflict occurred for Spyros Kyprianou, the premier of Cyprus. A group of right-wing terrorists kidnapped the pre-

mier's son, threatening to cut off his head unless a number of rightist prisoners were released. Kyprianou refused, arguing that the life of no single individual, even his son's, could override his duty to protect the nation. Circumstances prevented him from honoring his role obligations both as a father **and** as premier, so he relinquished one of them. (As it happened, his son was eventually released unharmed.)

Intrarole Conflict

Whereas in interrole conflict, an individual is torn between the conflicting demands of two or more roles, in intrarole conflict, the individual feels conflict over how to perform a single role. That is, the individual has incompatible expectations for the same role. Many American parents, for instance, believe that they should teach and discipline their children while also believing that they should be their children's "friends," implying equality in the relationship. Another example is the worker who is torn between getting a job done on time and doing it well. In these instances, the resolution involves clarification of role requirements and the development of more realistic expectations.

Intrarole conflict also arises when a person has internalized competing interpretations of a role promoted by clashing interests in society. For instance, a school superintendent may feel that the role involves doing the best she or he can for teachers and keeping school costs down. In this case, the two positions in the role conflict reflect the opposing economic interests of the different members of the superintendent's role set. The school board expects the superintendent to hold teachers' salaries down, while teachers expect the superintendent to get the greatest increases possible for them (Gross et al. 1957). Here, the superintendent can't so much resolve the conflict as decide how to handle such situations and how to choose priorities.

Not all intrarole conflicts involve varying interpretations of a role, however. There can be a conflict between the ideal way to perform a role and the way we are able to carry it out. For instance, we might agree on the proper way to be a mother but lack a helpful mate or enough money to properly care for our child. In order to resolve this strain, we can either attempt to secure the things we need for proper role enactment or reevaluate the ideal.

Self-Role Conflict

Generally, because of our socialization, our sense of self-identity will be compatible with fulfilling the requirements of many of our roles. However, we may feel strain when the roles we are expected to play do not conform to our sense of self. This type of role conflict frequently arises when a person must change roles or when her or his role is redefined (role making). As we saw in our discussion of role change, the increasing complexity that characterizes modern societies often requires that we switch or alter our major roles (e.g., occupational, domestic, or religious roles), which makes self-role conflict ever more likely.

One way to resolve self-role conflict is obvious: drop the role. Unfortunately, however, that isn't always possible. There is little chance that most disgruntled retirees, for instance, will be able to shed that role and rejoin the labor force. The other

method of reducing this type of role conflict is to alter the self-conception to accommodate the role. To this end, some people have sought help through psychoanalysis or counseling so they can understand the deep feelings that may lie at the root of their adjustment problem.

PERFORMANCES

So far in our discussion of roles we have omitted an important dimension of behavior. Consider the following example. If you were asked to list the activities that teachers should perform during the first days of class, you might reply: checking the roll sheet, clarifying the aims of the class, and introducing the major readings. Yet, at least one teacher sees his role in those first days as: "You can't ever let them [the class] get the upper hand on you or you're through. So I start out tough. The first day I get a new class in, I let them know who's boss . . . You've got to start off tough, then you can ease up as you go along. If you start out easy-going, when you try to get tough, they'll just look at you and laugh" (quoted in Becker 1952, p. 459).

Our study of roles until now has ignored behavior of this type. We looked at behaviors that are obviously intended to accomplish certain tasks—what we call *instrumental behaviors,* because we use them like instruments to get things done. In contrast, the teacher we quoted is concerned with the impression his students will have of him; the behaviors he would list are called *expressive* since they are concerned with *performance.*

Each of us, while interacting with others, might have any number of motives for trying to control their impression of us and our situation: to enforce our power to discipline, to impress a potential source of sexual gratification, to sell some land in Arizona or a used car, or to get people to vote for us. The sociologist Erving Goffman (1959) calls the part of our behavior that is solely intended to make an impression on our audience a **performance**. Performances are "communication oriented," while roles are "task oriented." Both performances and roles are often necessary for success, as with a high school teacher who is expected to both keep order and teach the students something. Performances are also sometimes loaded with instrumental value. Quite often, students will make a point of letting their instructor know just how much they "enjoy" the course. They might simply state it, ask for extra readings, suggest a willingness to take on extra work, or compliment the teacher. Some students are sincere in this, others are not. In either case, however, the action is at least partially intended to give the teacher a favorable impression of the student.

The goal of a performance is to control others' *definition of the situation* by managing the impression they have of it. The means for accomplishing this is a favorable presentation of self, or *front.*

Definition of the Situation

Lev Kuleshov, a founder of the Soviet cinema, once conducted a famous experiment in which he inserted a picture of an actor with an "expressionless face" into a film strip at various points: near the image of a plate of soup, next to that of a child playing with a teddy bear, and before a frame showing an old woman lying dead in her coffin. Arthur Knight (1957) describes the

reaction to it: "Audiences shown the experimental reel praised [the actor's] performance—his look of hunger at the bowl of soup, his delight at seeing the child, his grief over the dead woman" (pp. 72–73). How can we explain the audience's different responses to the same expressionless face?

In offering the concept of definition of the situation, W. I. Thomas (1920) noted that people do not really behave on the basis of external, objective factors (e.g., the "real" shape of the actor's facial muscles), but on their own subjective understanding of them. Consciously or unconsciously, we reach our own conclusions about what each particular situation involves. We define a situation, and how we behave is a product of that definition. Because we experience similar socializations, our definitions are generally quite similar, or at least kept within a range of alternatives.

How we define a situation depends on the cues we pick up from it and on the interpretation our culture places on those cues. Thus audiences interpreted the expressionless face in Kuleshov's experiment in terms of common cultural reactions to the various situations. By manipulating and emphasizing environmental cues, playing on generally accepted societal standards and norms, we can influence how other people perceive the situation. See Studying the Definition of the Situation for further discussion of the sociocultural origin of these definitions.

The Front

Goffman uses the term **front** for the part of our performance that we regularly use to define the situation for those who observe

STUDYING THE DEFINITION OF THE SITUATION

Robert D. Stebbins (1969) observed that we do not select our definition of particular situations entirely on an "individual" basis. He further hypothesized that there are a number of cultural definitions for each situation, and that we choose among them—either entire definitions or parts of them—in the following way:

1. Typically, an individual enters a setting with particular intentions (e.g., entering a classroom with the intention to learn).
2. Certain aspects of the setting will confirm these intentions (e.g., the instructor, chairs arranged to face the instructor and blackboard, and so on).
3. *Taken together, those aspects of the surroundings and the individual's intentions will lead her or him to select a cultural definition of the situation.*
4. This definition will then direct the individual's actions (e.g., to follow norms to listen, be quiet, and so on).

To test his hypothesis, Stebbins conducted the following field experiment.

The experiment was conducted in a college class, introduction to sociology and anthropology, during a series of controversial lectures on evolution—controversial because it was in a "community where religious matters are taken seriously." With the instructor's cooperation, Stebbins had two well-dressed male sociology students, aged twenty-two and thirty-eight, enter the lecture hall just before the class and sit in the front row. As the lecture began, one of them interrupted the instructor and accused him of polluting the students' minds, calling him an outsider, an atheist, and a communist. After a heated five-minute debate, the two were expelled from the classroom and the experimenter entered, disclosing that the argument was staged.

The 120 students then filled out a questionnaire containing a small number of open-ended statements (that is, they could elaborate on their answers rather than restrict themselves to filling in numbered responses) asking them to give their impressions of: the two men's identities; the arguments; the pair's intentions in starting the argument; and their personal feelings about the incident. The men were most frequently identified as "religious figures" (20.8 percent) and "nonstudent intruders" (13.3 percent).

Of those who identified them as religious figures, the greatest number felt the lectures threatened the two men's beliefs (the men's arguments); and a majority believed the two wanted to correct the instructor's views (the men's intentions). Finally, many felt that their actions were highly outrageous (students' personal feelings). Those who identified them as nonstudent intruders agreed that the pair believed the lectures to be a bad influence on the students (the men's arguments) and that they wanted to correct the instructor's view (intentions). Their personal feelings about the men were mild disgust. From these responses, Stebbins came up with two cultural—generally held—definitions of that situation, from which the students' conclusions derived:

1. These two men are religious figures of some sort. Their beliefs are being seriously threatened by the lectures, and as a result they want them either corrected or stopped. Their activities are outrageous and highly resented.
2. These two men are only nonstudent intruders. They somehow feel that the lectures are having a bad influence upon us students, and as a result want them either corrected or stopped. Their activities are mildly disgusting.

It is important to note here that Stebbins could not be entirely certain that these two definitions were thoroughly embedded in the culture of that community; he did not have the research methods for demonstrating that. However, he makes a convincing case for the existence of definitions that are standard among the people of that particular place. Perhaps equally important, Stebbins showed that it is possible to find research strategies for studying subjective phenomena such as this.

us in it. Fronts are "cues for our audience, a warning that a particular role is about to be played. They serve as a shorthand to define the situation for us and alert the members of a role set to the duties they will be expected to fulfill" (Goffman 1959, pp. 22–30). For instance, would you know who your instructor was if, on the first day of class, he or she sat among you and did not do anything that a teacher is supposed to do? You probably would wait for someone to take up the front you associate with the role (move to the front of the room, introduce him or herself as Professor/Dr./Ms./Mr., and start class).

Goffman distinguishes two parts of the front. The collection of physical objects in the front—the *scenery* for the performance—is called the *setting*, and the items we associate with the performer make up the *personal front*.

The setting will often include a particular locale for the performance, such as a motel room, doctor's office, or football field. For instance, the setting usually needed for the performance of teacher includes some type of school. There is more to setting than physical locale, however. Consider the hosts who pour a bottle of inexpensive wine into a fancy decanter before serving it to guests to imply that they are serving a fine wine. Or students who leave a number of books—some in other languages—open on their desks to impress people when they come in. And more than a few executives have been known to carry empty briefcases with them.

The personal front, in contrast, is composed of things that we associate intimately with the particular performer: age, sex, clothing, race, looks, physique, academic degrees, facial expressions, and beliefs. Some of these items are elements of our *manner*—that part of our personal front that alerts others to the role we intend to play in an ensuing interaction. For instance, when you meet a person with an aggressive manner, you get ready for someone who will probably initiate the interaction and try to control such things as the topics of conversation, where you will go, and when you will get together again. By contrast, a person who appears withdrawn probably gives you the feeling that you must make these decisions.

We generally expect some consistency between setting and personal front. Just how much we do is brought home by stories of eccentric millionaires who live in very modest settings, by lawyers whose offices are covered with disorganized piles of old and new papers and dirty coffee cups, by professionals with bad manners and sloppy appearances, and by an Ohio judge who held his court in a tent to protest city policies.

Anyone who puts on a particular front is claiming a right to play the role we associate with it. You cannot don a doctor's uniform (lab coat), set up what looks like a "doctor's office," tell people you can cure their illnesses, charge them lots of money, and then tell the police (as they are taking you to jail), "Well, I never *said* that I was a doctor." Your front said it for you, and we generally assume that the front is an honest one. For the most part, that assumption is realistic, but it allows a phony front to be all that someone needs to play a role illegitimately. Land swindlers have successfully posed as real estate agents, by imitating their manner, advertisements, and glossy brochures. Businesses have been lured into purchasing advertisements in nonexistent publications because someone put on a good front over the phone. And many urban criminals pose as gas meter readers, phone repairers, police,

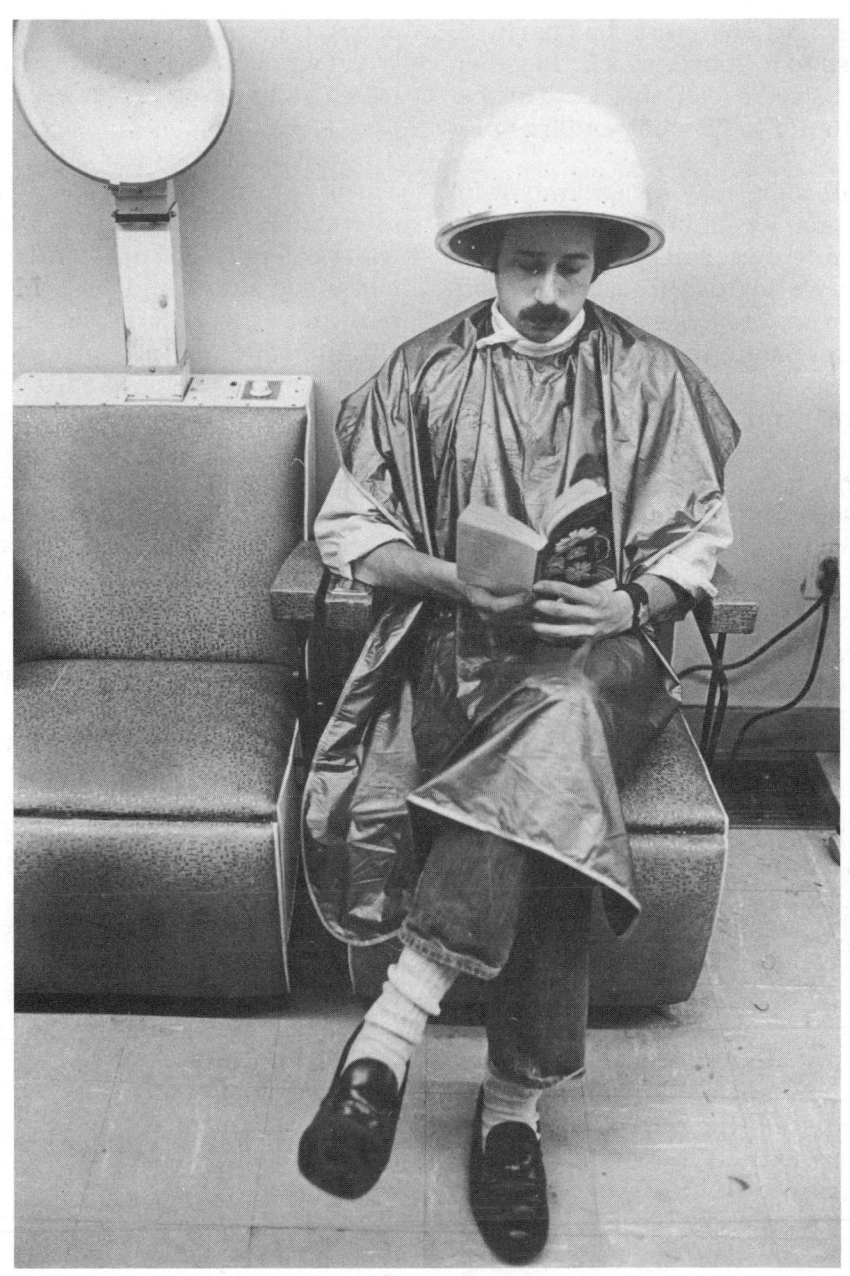

In a changing society traditional pairings of fronts and roles are not always good predictors of behavior.

sales people, and collectors for charity to obtain access to a house, which they then burglarize. Lawyers call this kind of behavior—claiming to be what you are not—fraud.

Although there may be few land swindlers among us, we all find it in our interests to commit minor acts of fraud from time to time. We do this through what Goffman calls *impression management*—manipulating (managing) the impression others have of us. You have engaged in it in a subtle way if you have ever tried to look interested during a tremendously dull lecture. Job applicants are often told to appear aggressive and self-confident for interviews, even if they are actually very nervous, and lovers will sometimes play "easy or hard to get," regardless of their feelings at the moment.

SOCIABILITY

When enacting our roles and managing the impressions others gain of us, we usually try to conform to generally accepted societal norms. Our willingness to perform according to social expectations is part of a general tendency we call *sociability*. You probably associate being sociable with being nice and being around people. As a sociological concept, **sociability** refers to any situation in which the participating individuals suppress their individual interests and concerns in order to assure relatively conflict-free interaction. People are sociable at parties: you go from person to person, making light conversation, preserving a pleasant atmosphere. Chances are that if you hear a remark with which you disagree, you let it pass rather than start an argument. Of course, we seldom agree

about everything with those around us. When we define the situation to involve sociability, however, we at least pretend we do.

Unlike much of our other behavior, we expect to bring nothing away from sociable interaction—our sole aim is just to interact with people. The terms *small talk* and *dinner conversation* indicate sociability; you remember the experience in terms of the situation and not its content. Our sociable performances are marked by a reluctance to include anything about ourselves or to advance any of our interests that could cause disagreement. Georg Simmel (1950, pp. 40–57) further developed the concept of sociability to refer to a state of affairs that is socially ideal in that there should be little or no clash between individual and group goals.

Some situations are entirely sociable; our interaction is only meant to fill time. When waiting for a bus, people will talk about subjects like the weather, how slow the bus is, and the quality of the bus stop bench (if there is one), but they will rarely speak of anything serious. People have similar experiences at funerals, where their very presence tends to be awkward and uncomfortable. As a result, interaction among the mourners becomes an important way of dispelling the gloom of the situation. Of course, the talk will rarely have a great deal of content; its job is simply to fill that time. Also, we constantly engage in nonverbal sociable behavior. For instance, while riding elevators we "know" that people often get uncomfortable if we start talking to them, so we look at the floor numbers in sociable unison with everyone else.

To the extent that we allow the demands of propriety to determine our behavior (over and above the content of our performance and our goals), we are being sociable, and other people will support our sociable behavior. You have probably often been in situations where somebody said or did something that offended you (or that you didn't like or agree with), but instead of expressing your displeasure, you decided not to "make a scene" that would spoil the pleasant atmosphere. People might even compliment your restraint as "tactful." According to Simmel, it is *tact*, and not personal impulses, that regulates our behavior. It tells members of the group just how far they can go in pressing themselves on others before they would be violating their rights (Simmel 1950, pp. 45–46). Thus we would be tactless by bringing up uncomfortable subjects (e.g., death) or by criticizing something that others support.

Sociability shields us from much cruelty as well. Studies of students in encounter groups show that abandoning the sociability we are used to can have devastating effects. Encounter groups actively try to eliminate sociability from interactions, in order to allow the spontaneity that people otherwise suppress. Irvin D. Yalom and Morton A. Lieberman (1971) observed 170 students during 30 hours of group time and found that 16 of them suffered negative and enduring psychological consequences from the group experience.

This does not mean that sociability is always a good thing. Manners and sociability do teach us to suppress behavior that might hinder conflict-free interaction. Thus we get used to *not* challenging actions that we do not like or agree with, instead accepting their presence. Awareness of this social control element in sociability may be a reason why members of several American social movements have intentionally violated rules of tact in their rejection of the middle-class way of life. The bohemians of the 1920s, the beatniks of the 1950s, and the hippies of the 1960s were all recognized by their *antisociable* actions—their manner of dress and speech, their vocal rejection of "the American dream," and their play activities—more so than by their broader goals. In sum, an element of tact appears in most of our performances, making them instruments of social control. But this control does not remove the conflicts themselves, only particular expressions of them, so that they may still surface again.

SUMMARY

Roles are elements of the social structure and are made up of clusters of activities governed by norms—role expectations—that we associate with people in various social positions. Roles organize our behavior and define power relationships of individuals. They are not played in isolation, but must be played in groups called role sets. Successful role enactment requires the participation of the other members of the role set (the students have to come to class for the teacher to teach). We incorporate our various roles into our identity, and any self-evaluations we make depend considerably on how well we perform in our roles.

Learning role behavior begins during socialization, but the specific process by which we internalize role expectations is called role taking. Sometimes, role taking involves a role that prepares you for some future role (e.g., student, child); this is called anticipatory socialization. The norms that make up each role are necessarily vague, and some circumstances require that we take advantage of unclear behaviors to change role requirements—or even create new roles. That process is called role making.

There are also three types of role conflict: interrole, which occurs when two or more roles make conflicting demands on the same individual; intrarole, which results from conflicting expectations about how to play a single role, or a conflict between an ideal of role enactment and how it is actually played; and self-role conflict caused by a poor fit between our self-conception and a role we take.

Also related to role behavior is the concept of performance—behavior that is intended to influence any of the people with whom we are interacting. Whereas roles are task oriented, or instrumental, performances are communication oriented, or expressive. According to Erving Goffman, successful performers will succeed in imposing their definition of the situation on everyone else. The front serves to define the situation for those who are observing the performance. Its two components are a physical setting and a personal front. Finally, there is one dimension of our interactions with others—sociability—in which performances are given for no external purpose. In order to be sociable, we agree to suppress our individual interests and concerns to ensure a conflict-free situation.

Key Terms

role (p. 91)
role expectations (p. 92)
role set (p. 94)
ascribed statuses (p. 96)
achieved statuses (p. 96)
professionalization (p. 98)
role taking (p. 100)
anticipatory socialization (p. 101)
role conflict (p. 103)
performance (p. 107)
front (p.107)
sociability (p. 112)

Review and Discussion Questions

1. What possible role has professionalization of the medical profession played in the soaring costs of health care? How has professionalization of certain trades (through unionization) driven up the cost of their work? Has either process brought any positive results?

2. Which people are most likely to grow up to become president of the United States? Who is least likely to occupy that role? How can you account for this?

3. How many new roles have been created in the past few years? In which roles have you witnessed dramatic change? What are some possible new roles for the future?

4. Because we tend to associate our self-image with the roles we play, the loss of a major role (e.g., becoming unemployed, getting divorced) can have a profound impact on us. What major roles are the elderly forced to give up? How have they adjusted to the loss?

5. If you were on trial, which of the following attorneys would you prefer: one with an excellent knowledge of the law and a rather dull performance or one with only a fair knowledge of the law and a very good performance? How would you explain your answer in terms of the judge's and jury's motives?

For Further Study

THE MALE SEX ROLE By far the lion's share of attention to sex roles has focused on the woman's sex role. But recently, the man's role—its problems for both men and women—has also been analyzed. Deborah S. David and Robert Brannon, eds., *The Forty-Nine Percent Majority* (Reading, MA: Addison-Wesley, 1976) is a fine collection of readings on the role. Mirra Komarovsky, who studied the female role, has analyzed the male role in *Dilemmas of Masculinity* (New York: Norton, 1976). She surveys the sex lives of college males, their images of male and female, social relations, and so on. Herb Goldberg, in *The Hazards of Being Male* (New York:

Signet, 1976), discusses the male role from a therapist's viewpoint. In 1978, the *Journal of Social Issues* (34:1) devoted an entire issue to the male sex role. Its twelve articles analyzed a range of issues: physical health, attitudes about men, friendship between men, and reactions to atypical male behavior. Finally, anyone interested in exploring the role extensively should see K. Grady, R. Brannon, and J. Pleck, eds., *The Male Sex Role: A Selected and Annotated Bibliography* (Washington, DC: Government Printing Office, 1979).

PERFORMANCES AND SOCIABILITY The best introduction to performances and the numerous motivations behind our behaviors is Erving Goffman's *The Presentation of Self in Every-day Life* (Garden City, NY: Doubleday, 1959). A very solid presentation of sociability is in the work where it was first enunciated: Georg Simmel, *The Sociology of Georg Simmel* (New York: Free Press, 1950), chap. 3. There is also a very good study of both performances and sociability in Joan P. Emerson's "Negotiating the Serious Import of Humor," *Sociometry* 32:2 (1969): 169–81. Emerson shows how we use humor to introduce hidden messages and potentially controversial topics into conversations and how others respond. Finally, a novel that aptly illustrates the uses of impression management is Thomas Mann's *Confessions of Felix Krull, Confidence Man* (New York: Vintage, 1969), the story of a man whose entire existence is built on deception.

CHAPTER FOUR

Deviance and Conformity

We began Part One by talking about socialization and then discussed cultural norms, values, and roles. Throughout this discussion, we have examined the basic mechanisms of our social control—socialization, the formal controls of prisons and the police, and the informal ones of learning to behave in a way that will please our significant others and be acceptable to the other members of our role set. In this chapter, the final one in this section on the individual society, we will consider how social organization and control result in our general conformity, but also how they may, paradoxically, cause our deviance.

DEVIANCE AND CONFORMITY: AN OVERVIEW

At the simplest level, to conform means to obey society's rules, and to deviate means to break some of them. In general, **devi-ance** is the failure to live up to socially held expectations. Crimes are only the most obvious violations. Others are more subtle. I used to know someone who put french fries and ketchup in milkshakes; believe me, my associates and I considered that practice deviant. My friend violated a well-established eating norm for our group. Most Americans consider homosexuals, crimi-

nals, eccentrics, communists, Jesus Freaks, panhandlers, and tramps, among others, deviant because their behavior violates one or more important social norms.

Social conformity and deviance, however, are considerably more complex than they appear in the simple definitions just given. The first complication is that conformity and deviance are culturally relative. An act that is consistent with society's norms in one culture may be deviant in another. In Iran recently, a European man was arrested and fined $400 for kissing his Iranian female companion in public (Padgaonkar 1978). Although he clearly violated the nation's law, by the standards of his own culture, his actions would hardly be considered deviant. People sometimes assume that all deviant behavior is inherently "bad." Deviance, however, does not involve objective and eternal standards of good and evil but violations of defined norms of particular social groups at particular times.

A second difficulty arises from the fact that there is often no sharp dividing line between deviance and conformity. As we saw in the last chapter, role norms are necessarily vague in order to allow for some leeway in playing any role. Consider, for example, two women who disagree about how to play their sex roles: one has a husband and family, has no thought of personal advancement outside the home, and thinks that feminists are subversives; the other is a successful politician, plans not to have children because they will interfere with her career, and believes that the traditional role is repressive. Which one is the deviant, which the conformist?

A third complication is that even within a society the same action won't always be considered either deviant or conforming. If you walked into an American Legion meeting and tried passing a marijuana joint around, you would expect the Legionnaires to consider you a deviant. At the same time, in many college dorms, the one or two students who refuse to smoke pot are seen as the deviants. Similarly, while killing is considered a deviant act, a combat soldier's refusal to kill is not only deviant, but we treat it as a major crime. Finally, many people see handicapped persons as deviant because their behavior often violates social norms (e.g., they may take up too much room on a sidewalk or a bus; deaf people wave their hands to communicate, and so on). In other words, deviance and conformity depend on the social context.

Labeling and Deviance

As you can see, defining conformity and deviance in a way that helps us understand them is not so simple. In general, however, most of us define a deviant as someone whom others call a deviant. And a conformist is someone they—and we—call a conformist. This might indicate that exactly what people consider deviance and conformity is intimately tied up with what they understand as normal. Normality, you might remember, refers to frequency: in general, something is normal if it occurs

more times than not. Specifically, what we see most of the time in our social and cultural environment is normal to us.

But many rare behaviors are nevertheless not labeled deviant. No one labels the astronauts deviants for having landed on the moon, for instance. Similarly, criminals are considered no less deviant when the crime rate goes up. Instead, we tend to reserve the label deviant for behavior we consider significant and disgraceful in some way. It is these more significant norm violations that set the individuals so labeled off from the rest of us, and it is these violations that are the main interest of sociologists.

Use of the labels deviant and conformist threatens to mislead us, however, because no one is simply "normal" or "conforming" or "deviant." In the first place, all of us are deviant in some ways, although our deviance may go unrecognized by others or be ignored by them. We may engage in pot smoking, tax fraud or evasion, illicit sex (generally, any sex between a man and a woman not married to each other), shoplifting, illegal gambling, or any one of a number of other norm-violating acts. In the second place, as we saw in the last chapter, even the most hardened criminal is a conformist in many respects. We apply the labels only when we take notice of a certain aspect of someone's behavior that has violated a significant cultural norm.

To sum up: no action is inherently deviant or conformist. For an action to be deviant, it must violate social norms, we must respond to it in a negative fashion, and it must be labeled as deviant by the society. As Howard Becker (1963) has pointed out, this means that deviance is truly a creation of society. Only social groups, Becker tells us, create the rules whose violation we call deviant. Social

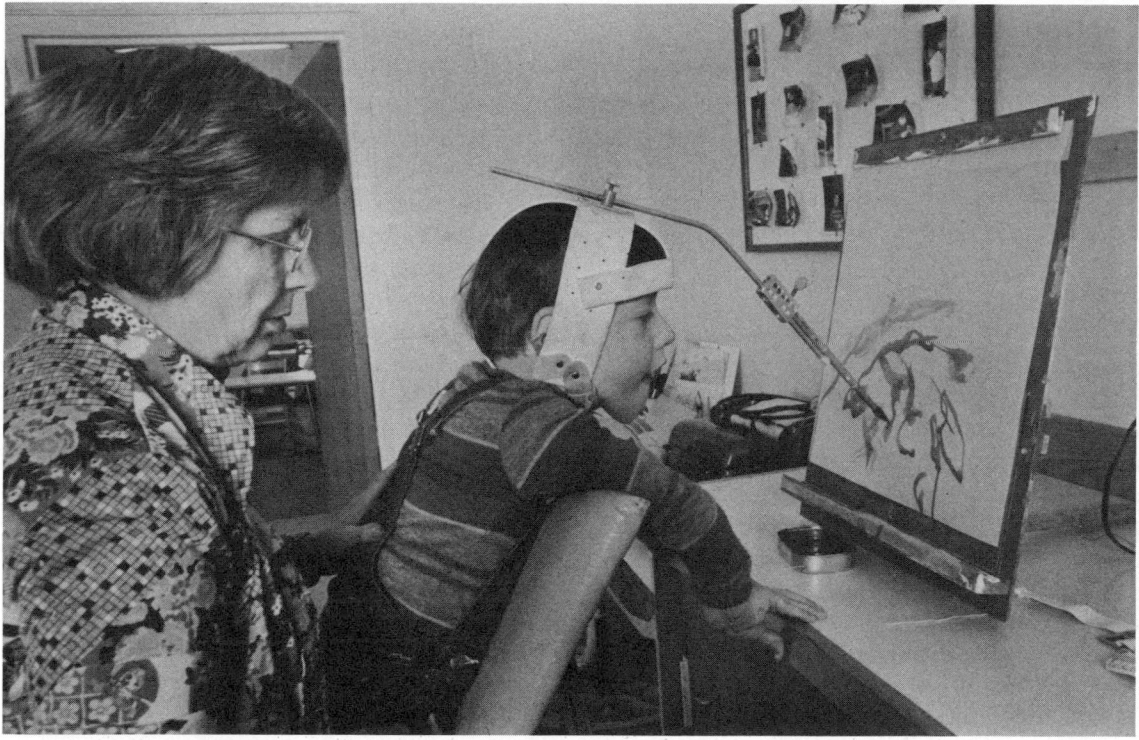

Almost everyone agrees that handicapped children like this one are deviant in their way of doing things. Where we differ is in our reactions to that deviance.

groups apply these rules to particular people, then label them; in that sense, society creates deviance (Becker 1963, pp. 8–9). It creates deviance as the definition of a situation. Take the Saudi Arabian woman who walks around without a veil over her face; she is a deviant in her country because others define her as one. But *we* do not apply that definition to American women who do the same thing.

With this overview of conformity and deviance in mind, let's look more closely at the nature of conformity. Then we'll explore various explanations of why people depart from the ranks of the conforming, and fi-

nally, we'll look at the consequences of deviance for society and social control.

CONFORMITY

The most interesting point to notice about conformity is that it is so seldom discussed. It is not uncommon for us to ask about law-breaking, even though that is only a tiny percentage of anybody's actions. We conform in most of the things we do—even criminals conform most of the time—but few people seem to wonder why. One possible reason for this lack of interest is that conformity appears dull compared to crime and other forms of deviance. A related reason is that conforming behavior is so common that we almost never notice it. This is what three social psychologists (Lefkowitz, Blake, and Mouton 1955) discovered when they tested the reactions of pedestrians waiting at a "Walk/Don't Walk" traffic signal. They ran their test under three conditions: under one, they had an experimenter violate the signal; under another, they had the experimenter obey it; and under the third, they ran tests with no experimenter at all (control group). Many subjects followed the experimenter in his violation in the first set of trials. However, there was no difference in the number of subjects who obeyed the rules in the tests with a conforming experimenter and those without. It seems that no one actually *saw* the experimenter conforming; his behavior was simply what they were accustomed to.

Deviant behavior grabs our attention; conformity, on the other hand, seems to "just happen." Some people even say that it is "natural" to conform. However, what we have seen so far in this book is that conformity does not "just happen." We have become aware of the tremendous efforts of society to ensure our relative conformity—in our socialization, by the use of sanctions, by the expectations of others.

To be sure, we know that there are some good reasons to conform. If we did not conform, any kind of extensive interaction would be impossible—considerable conformity is necessary for social life. At the simplest level, it helps if we speak the same language to each other. There was an "international incident" at Warsaw's airport in 1977, when President Jimmy Carter told the Polish crowd—in English—that he desired warm relations between Poland

and the United States. Unfortunately, the translator told the crowd—in Polish—that Carter "lusted after the Poles." Without conforming to that society's use of language, Carter could not communicate his point.

We conform to countless social norms from the moment we get out of bed in the morning to the moment we get back in at night. But you might feel: "What does all that matter? It generally makes sense to behave like that anyway." That is a legitimate challenge, but we learn to conform to social norms regardless of what their content is. This point has been brought out by two important social psychological experiments, one showing the influence of group pressure on our conformity and the other, the influence of authority.

Conformity and Group Pressure

Suppose you are sitting with a group of friends after all of you have seen the same movie. Although you liked it, everybody else thinks it was terrible. In a situation like that, wouldn't you change your opinion, at least outwardly, and go along with the majority? If you ever have, then you understand some of the power of group pressure to conform. In a set of famous experiments, the social psychologist Solomon Asch (1955) was able to demonstrate under controlled conditions that individuals in a group will often abandon even their obviously correct judgments if everyone else in the group takes another position.

For his experiment, Asch assembled seven to nine male college students. Actually, only one of these was a true subject; everybody else was working for the experimenter. The students were shown several

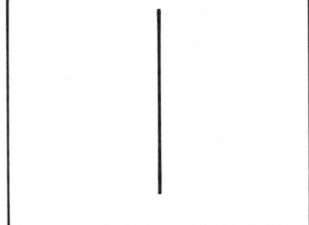 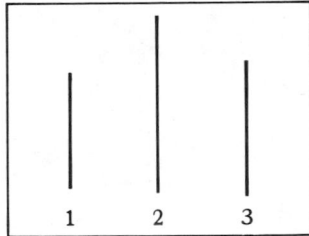

Figure 4.1 Test Cards in Asch's Experiment

pairs of cards like those in Figure 4.1 and asked to state which of the three lines on the right-hand card was equal in length to the one on the left. Asch drew the lines so that the answers were quite obvious; however, after the first few pairs, everybody but the subject purposely gave the same incorrect answer. How do you think you would react, if you were the subject? The 123 subjects tested gave the incorrect answer 36.8 percent of the time. Considering that individuals left by themselves will normally be wrong less than 1 percent of the time on the same test, almost all of the wrong answers in the experiment can be attributed to the effects of group pressure. Of course, not everyone succumbed to the majority's perception. About 25 percent of the subjects did not accept the majority opinion and consistently answered correctly. However, the experiment does show that when we are faced with group pressure to act in a particular way, we often conform, even against our better judgment.

Conformity and Obedience to Authority

Consider the case of Adolf Eichmann, the SS officer responsible for administering

the murder of millions of Jews. At his trial in 1961, Eichmann pleaded "not guilty" and asserted over and over that he harbored no personal malice toward the Jews, that he had only followed orders. After observing the court trial, Hannah Arendt said that Eichmann "left no doubt that he would have killed his own father if he had received an order to that effect" (Arendt 1963, p. 22). Eichmann was conforming to the laws of his own state and the norms of his role set.

Social psychologist Stanley Milgram (1963) has given us some insight into our readiness to conform to norms in situations somewhat similar to Eichmann's. In his "Behavioral Study of Obedience," forty males between the ages of twenty and fifty agreed to participate in an experiment in which they were to administer electric shocks, of varying intensity, to another individual ("learner"). Shocks were to be given for incorrect responses in a word-pairing exercise, and each wrong answer was to be followed by a more powerful shock. Subjects were told that "although the shocks can be extremely painful, they cause no permanent tissue damage." Milgram found that no one refused to administer the shock, and every subject continued administering the shocks to at least 300 volts. At that level, "the learner pounds on the wall

Conformity is so pervasive that we almost never notice it. Few people can resist group pressure to conform, regardless of the specific behavior in question.

ministering real shocks. Yet, they obeyed the experimenter anyway—at least to a point (Table 4.1)—assuming the role they were expected to without question. Milgram comments:

> Subjects have learned from childhood that it is a fundamental breach of moral conduct to hurt another person against his will. Yet, 26 subjects abandon this tenet in following the instructions of an authority who has no special powers to enforce his commands. To disobey would bring no material loss to the subject; no punishment would ensue. (1963, p. 376)

How can we account for the subjects' behavior? Milgram believes that certain features of his performance in the experiment help explain the high amount of obedience he observed. The first was the setting—a laboratory at Yale University. We are likely to assume that scientists working in such places have a high degree of integrity. (This explanation was supported by later experiments, which repeated the procedure in other settings.) Another feature was the subjects' implicit belief that their actions could be rationalized because they presumably contributed to some worthy purpose—in particular, the advancement of knowledge.

Milgram also noted some other factors that influenced his subjects. Neither the victims nor the subjects appeared to be forced into their roles; the subjects were paid in advance to participate; they believed they had an equal chance of being the victim (they drew rigged lots); and the experimenter claimed that, although painful, the shocks would not cause permanent damage to the victim. Milgram also

of the room in which he is bound" and sometimes screams, too. The learner ceased making any response after the 315-volt shock, but still, 26 of the 40 subjects continued to administer shocks until the maximum of 450 volts was reached (see Table 4.1).

In reality, the "learner" received no electric shocks. He was a confederate of Milgram's, and the electrical shock device was not connected to a power source. However, the subjects believed they were ad-

Table 4.1 Milgram's Obedience Experiment*

Voltage Description	Voltage Indication	No. of Subjects for Whom This Was Maximum Shock
Intense shock	300	5
Extreme shock	315	4
	330	2
	345	1
	360	1
Danger: severe shock	375	1
	390	0
	405	0
XXX	420	0
	435	0
	450	26

*Milgram described the experiment to Yale seniors and faculty before actually conducting it, and asked for their predictions of the subject's behavior—when they would refuse to continue to administer shocks. There was a high level of agreement among the people he questioned: they generally felt that few if any of the subjects would go beyond the Very Strong Shock (240 volts). Actually, none of the subjects stopped before the Intense Shock (300 volts).

SOURCE: Stanley Milgram, "Behavioral Study of Obedience," Journal of Abnormal and Social Psychology **67** (1963): 371–78.

mentioned that subjects were given no time to reflect on their decision to administer the shocks. Asch's subjects likewise had to make snap decisions. Although many suspected that "the majority were 'sheep' following the first responder, or that the majority were victims of an optical illusion; nevertheless, these suspicions failed to free them at the moment of decision" (Asch 1955, p. 33). That is, they were influenced by group pressure anyway. Group pressure to conform need not be direct and coercive. We are likely to feel very uncomfortable being the "odd man out" in a group, and we are therefore unlikely to contradict its unanimous decision. Some of Asch's subjects, for example, interpreted their "deviance" as an indication of some personal deficiency in themselves. As a result, they tried desperately to merge with the majority.

Americans' valuation of public opinion, and of majority rule, certainly reinforces such attitudes. By conforming, we respond to internalized norms and attachments developed during socialization; that is, we respond to social control. There are even cultural sources of our degree of conformity; for instance, Milgram (1961) found that Norwegians are more likely to conform than are people from other countries. Unless we are presented with a great deal of evidence not to, these studies suggest, we will go with the majority. Conformity is so second nature to us that none of the subjects in Asch's experiment realized how often they yielded to the majority.

Obedience is rarely free of inner conflict, however, and many of Milgram's subjects showed signs of the conflict they were experiencing. One subject was so upset over causing pain to the "victim" that he was "reduced to a twitching, stuttering wreck who was rapidly approaching the point of nervous collapse . . . And yet he . . . obeyed to the very end" (Milgram 1963, p. 377). Thus, although the Milgram and Asch experiments both provide us with some powerful insights into our readiness to conform, they do not suggest that we are simply robots, always prepared to obey any

DON'T GET INVOLVED!

Our tendency to conform sometimes manifests itself in rather disturbing ways, such as the reaction of thirty-eight people to the murder of a New York City woman. All were neighbors of the victim, Kitty Genovese, and while they rushed to their windows upon hearing her screams, they just watched the attack for the full thirty minutes it lasted. No one so much as called the police. Why didn't they help? Were they too foggy-headed at 3 A.M., when the incident occurred? Did they fear the attacker would turn on them if they tried to help? Were they stunned— or hardened by the glut of urban crime? Still, none of these answers explain Eleanor Bradley's predicament. She fell down on Manhattan's Fifth Avenue, in broad daylight, and broke her leg. Yet, for forty minutes, she lay on the sidewalk while hundreds of people walked by.

To find out why people don't intervene in situations like these, Bibb Latane and Judith Rodin (1969) created similar circumstances in an experiment. They had subjects wait either alone or in pairs to participate in what they were told would be a market research study. While waiting, they heard someone fall and cry out (actually, they heard a tape recording). Did they help the "victim"? That depended: 70 percent of the subjects waiting alone did intervene, but only 20 percent of those waiting in pairs did.

Bystanders to an emergency must first define the situation as one requiring their help before they will offer it. Those subjects who did nothing said later that the situation did not seem serious to them—a conclusion they formed partly on the basis of their partner's inactivity. Put otherwise: Not getting involved is an act of conformity. We're supposed to be "cool" in public and not display undue emotion or concern. This means that taking action can be costly in terms of self-image. What if

command or accede to group pressure. Those American males had to overcome their own better judgment in order to give those electric shocks and to switch to obviously incorrect answers. Besides, social psychologists have found a number of factors that reduce the impact of group pressure. For example, if a group's position is not unanimous, we are less likely to go along with the majority (Moscovici, Lage, and Naffrechoux 1969). The impact of group pressure also varies with how cer-

you got excited and there really was nothing wrong? Both individuals in the pairs looked for some cue from the other end and were misled by what they took as unconcern. Moreover, they both accepted the other's apparent definition of the situation.

Although necessary for any kind of social life, conformity can be overdone. Authority figures have defined situations that their followers accepted with severe consequences. Many Germans now regret their fervent and massive support for Adolf Hitler. More recently, hundreds of people committed mass suicide in Guyana at the behest of their religious leader, Jim Jones. There are many other examples. As Asch concludes:

> Life in society requires consensus as an indispensible condition. But consensus, to be productive, requires that each individual contribute independently out of his experience and insight. When consensus comes under the dominance of conformity, the social process is polluted. . . . That we have found the tendency to conformity in our society so strong that reasonably intelligent people are willing to call white black is a matter of concern. It raises questions about our ways of education and about the values that guide our conduct (1955, p. 34).

In other words, the ideology and social institutions that shape our individual selves can sometimes go overboard in their efforts at social control. Our best check against extreme conformist tendencies is support—and maybe even encouragement—for deviant behaviors.

tain we are of our deviant answer. This certainty is determined by our self-esteem and sense of personal independence, our ability at the task at hand, and our feelings of power and status with reference to others in the group.

You can see, then, that conformity does not necessarily signify agreement. It can be an attempt to obtain rewards (e.g., a raise or approval) or avoid punishments (e.g., negative labels), but it says nothing about our belief in the demand's validity.

If you see me "give" my money to someone who has a gun at my head, you're not likely to say, "That person obviously favors a redistribution of wealth in society." I would give up that money no matter how strongly I believed I deserved it or that it should go in the bank. I was only giving in to a stronger power.

Even though we may only go along with the group or obey authorities because we find it in our self-interest to do so, the pressures on us to conform to society's rules would seem so strong that it is remarkable that deviance occurs at all or occurs with as much frequency as it does. (You can see some implications of this in Don't Get Involved!, above.) How can we account for this deviance in the midst of so many pressures for conformity?

EXPLANATIONS OF DEVIANCE

From the beginnings of recorded time, humans have attempted to explain why some individuals violate significant social norms. In this section, we'll look at the major theories of deviance, starting with some prescientific, biological, and psychological explanations, and then examine the major sociological theories. Our discussion will focus more on specifically criminal forms of deviance than on noncriminal forms, because crime is the explicit subject of many of the theories.

Nonsociological Explanations

EARLY PERSPECTIVES The earliest schools of thought, the *demonological* and the *classical*, were developed indepen-

dently of the scientific method; the first was based on a religious view, the second on a philosophy. The demonological school's basic proposition was that the devil (or demons) commit all crime, by taking over a human body and using it. This idea has a long history, and there have been many variations on the theme. Preliterate tribes believe that evil spirits often have human accomplices in the form of tribal sorcerers who practice "black magic." For the ancients, the possessed body did not have to be a human's but could be another animal's or even an insect's. Thus we read in the Old Testament (the basis of the ancient Hebrews' legal code): "And if an ox gore a man or a woman, that they die, the ox shall be surely stoned, and its flesh shall not be eaten" (Exodus 21:28). This view was still prevalent in the Middle Ages. In Victor Hugo's novel about that period, *The Hunchback of Notre Dame,* a goat is tried and convicted of murder. And in trials that actually took place, insects were convicted of carrying the plague. According to the criminology of that period, the devil could take possession of a person's body only if there were already something morally wrong with him or her. This placed the blame for the deviant's actions squarely on the individual, not the devil. As you can imagine, such reasoning sanctioned all sorts of irregular trials, such as "trial by ordeal," in which God was thought to save the innocent among the accused, who were subjected to a life-threatening ordeal. Unfortunately, the demonological principle did not fade with the Middle Ages. Defendants at the Salem witch trials and the Spanish Inquisition were also judged according to this theory, and we recognize it still in the millions who flocked to see *The Exorcist,* a film about a young girl possessed by the devil.

Early theorists believed that individuals were entirely responsible for any crime they might commit and could never be rehabilitated; sociologists today think that society plays an important role in crime.

The *classical* school was informed by the principles of utilitarianism. Adherents of this philosophical view believe that human beings are rational, have free will to choose between alternative behaviors (in this case, right and wrong), and are responsible for their actions. In addition, they hold that we are all self-seeking and choose our actions according to how much pleasure we expect these actions to give us, compared to the pain involved. Thus we might refrain from eating a favorite food, if we found the extra pounds it brought just too "painful." These tenets were applied to the study of crime by Cesare Bec-

caria (1738–1794) and the English philosopher Jeremy Bentham (1745–1832). They reasoned that if we make the pain of punishment exceed the pleasure of a crime, any rational person will refrain from breaking the law. In this, they differed from the demonologists because their reasoning led them to see the problem of crime primarily as a matter of criminal law. True, they said, some individuals happen to be weak willed, but because people are rational, the incidence of crime could be controlled by manipulating the law. Thus Bentham (1948 [1776]) wrote that it was the task of criminal law to make clear that "mischievousness" (deviance) was the direct opposite of "happiness."

BIOLOGICAL EXPLANATIONS The value of these two early perspectives for understanding crime and other forms of deviance is limited, given their nonscientific basis. Many people trace the beginning of the modern, organized study of crime to the Italian *biological* school, under the leadership of the physician Cesare Lombroso (1836–1909). This group of criminologists is also known as the *positivist* school because Lombroso and his colleagues used the methods of science and not the speculative approach of the earlier criminologists. Members of the positivist school rejected the classical school's notion of free will. Since biological factors, they said, determine whether we are criminals, there is nothing we can do about it. Ironically, this placed responsibility for deviant acts back on the individual's shoulders, where the demonologists had located it.

Members of the biological school also took issue with the classical school's calls for prison and legal reform. Rather, Lombroso held that criminals were born—not made—that they were throwbacks to earlier evolutionary forms. With primitive bodies and minds, criminals acted like people of the remote past; unfortunately, their behavior violated modern norms. For example, primitives might kill when threatened or take anything that they want. This behavior might make sense in a dangerous jungle, but it was criminal in modern society.

Lombroso based his beliefs on years of research in the prisons and asylums of Pavia, Italy. He examined both the living and the dead and claimed, in 1876, when he published his findings, to find "atavistic anomalies"—biological characteristics like those found in lower animals—in many of them. Because there is thus no way we can change the criminal's "defective" biology, criminal justice lies in determining who committed the offense and making sure that he or she is unable to do it again.

Many of Lombroso's contemporaries attacked his theory and attempts at proving it failed. Lombroso himself repudiated his theory of the born criminal in a later book. Still, in *The Jukes* (1877) Richard Dugdale, an inspector for the New York Prison Association, analyzed a family (the Jukes) with a history of many criminals and concluded that the tendency to criminality (or degeneracy) was genetically inherited. However, he went on to explain this transmission of criminality not in genetic terms but in terms of the child's environment, where the "parent makes an example which greatly aids in fixing habits of debauchery on the child" (quoted in Quinney 1970, p. 66). Other studies have tried to link crime and biology by comparing identical twins, by looking at different body types (Sheldon 1949; Glueck and Glueck 1956), and, more recently, by correlating criminal behavior with certain chromosome structures (Amir and Berman 1970). None of these studies, however, provides a convincing case for the primacy of the biological factor in causing crime.

Psychological Approaches

Partisans of the psychological approach to deviance seek the cause of crime in the offender's personality. In the nineteenth century, theories of "mental degeneracy" and the speculations of physician Benjamin Rush (a signer of the Declaration of Independence) dominated the psychological explanation. Rush believed criminal behavior resulted from an injured "moral faculty," a disease he called *anomia.* It was Charles Goring's (1913) statistical tests of Lombroso's theory, however, that signaled the shift to a more strictly psychological explanation of crime. In his survey of 3,000 English male convicts, Goring claimed to find: "that, on the average, the criminal of English prisons is markedly differentiated by defective physique—as measured by stature and body weight; by defective mental capacity—as measured by general intelligence" (p. 370).

However, while not totally disagreeing with Lombroso, Goring concluded from his test that the "born criminal" did not exist, as Lombroso assumed: "This anthropological monster has no existence in fact" (Goring 1913, p. 370). In doing so, he focused attention on the criminal's alleged defective intelligence, which inspired Henry Goddard's studies of feeblemindedness (1914). Goddard felt that criminality itself was not inherited, but that the low intelligence which caused it was. He estimated that over 50 percent of all criminals were feebleminded and that the greatest single cause of delinquency and crime was low-grade mentality. These views suggest that criminals are mentally inferior to the rest of us and imply that the criminal can never be reformed. Subsequent research, however, has mostly discredited the belief that low intelligence leads to crime.

Modern psychological theorists of deviance begin with the proposition that criminals are part of the general, normal population. Among these theorists, psychoanalytic psychiatrists in particular have developed elaborate explanations of crime as "substitute" behavior. For example, a rapist might be motivated by the desire to hurt his domineering mother. Following the work of Sigmund Freud, these criminologists often see crime in terms of "repression." Repression, according to psychologists, is a psychological defense mechanism to block painful and embarrassing experiences from memory. It helps the person cope with anxiety, but the memories remain at the subconscious level and efforts to keep them repressed generally cause mental conflict. If severe enough, the conflict cannot remain repressed and sometimes erupts as criminal behavior.

Psychological explanations of criminal behavior can help us understand the motivation of individual criminals. However, no consistent relationship between personality type and criminal behavior has ever been demonstrated. These psychological theories, furthermore, have only limited value for explaining the incidence of crime or the variations in its rates. These aspects of deviance are better explained by sociology. Sociologists concentrate on the social causes of deviance, specifically, on the interaction between individuals in the context of a particular social structure. The Boston Tea Party is an illustration of the importance of this context. The "criminals" were protesting what they felt was an unfair tax imposed on them. We would distort much of their behavior if we looked only at the personalities of those involved and not at the role society played in causing the deviance.

Anomie Theory

Unlike the nonsociological approaches we have looked at so far, which take the existing social structure as a given, the sociological theory of deviance known as *anomie theory* gives an important place to society in the causation of deviance. Emile Durkheim, whose observations lie at the center of this sociological perspective on deviance, recognized that crime in particular is too complex and widespread to have its origins in particular individuals and their alleged abnormalities. (For a look at the incidence of reported crime in the United States, see Figure 4.2). In Durkheim's view, deviance occurs to the extent that society is in a state of *anomie*—that is, when social norms have broken down and individuals and groups are left with few constraints on their behavior.

Robert K. Merton (1968) modified Durkheim's concept of anomie and formulated a general theory of deviance based on it, using American society as a model. The theory rests on Merton's observation that certain social structures pressure some people to engage in deviant behavior (p. 186). He notes that economic success, as measured by material wealth, is the major *cultural goal* for which we are socialized. But although we may all want success, only some of us are given the tools—the *institutional means*, such as quality education, good jobs, and credit—to get it. Moreover,

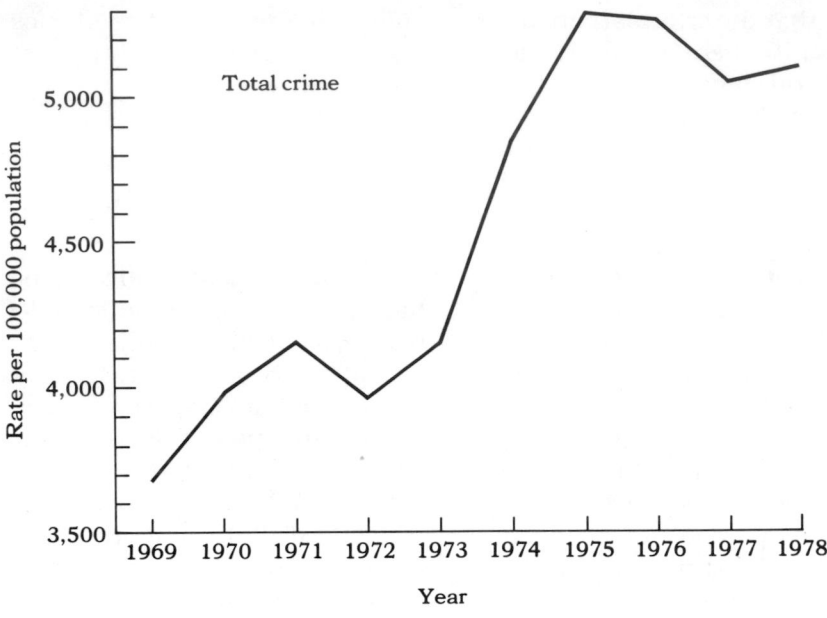

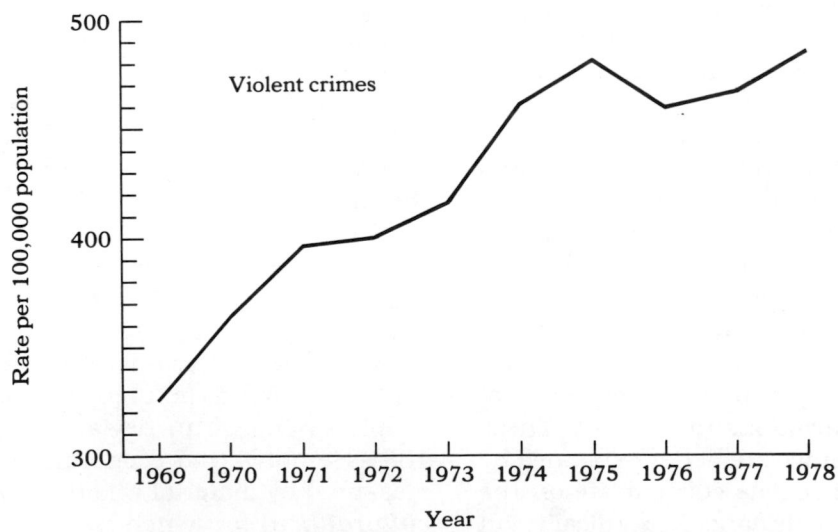

Figure 4.2 Reported Crime in the United States, 1969–1978

SOURCE: *U.S. Department of Justice, Federal Bureau of Investigation,* Crime in the United States *(Washington, DC: Government Printing Office, 1979).*

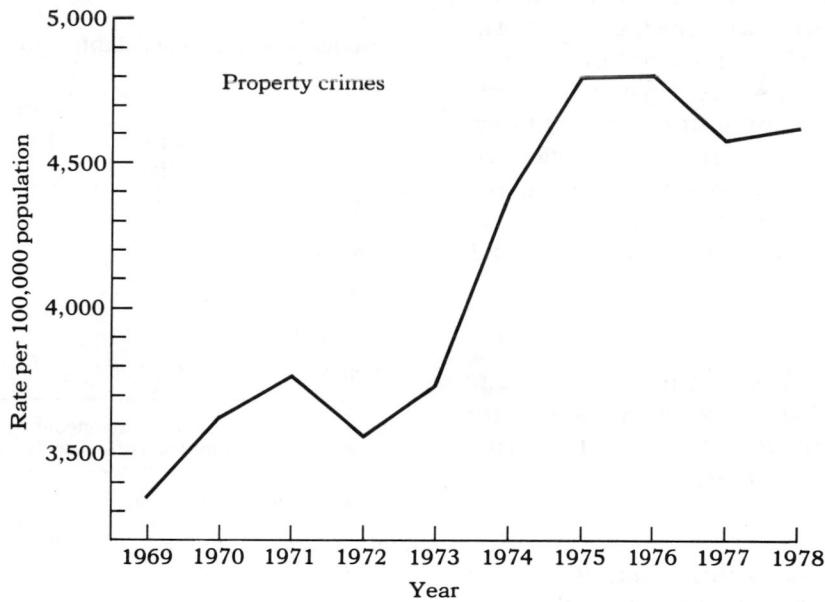

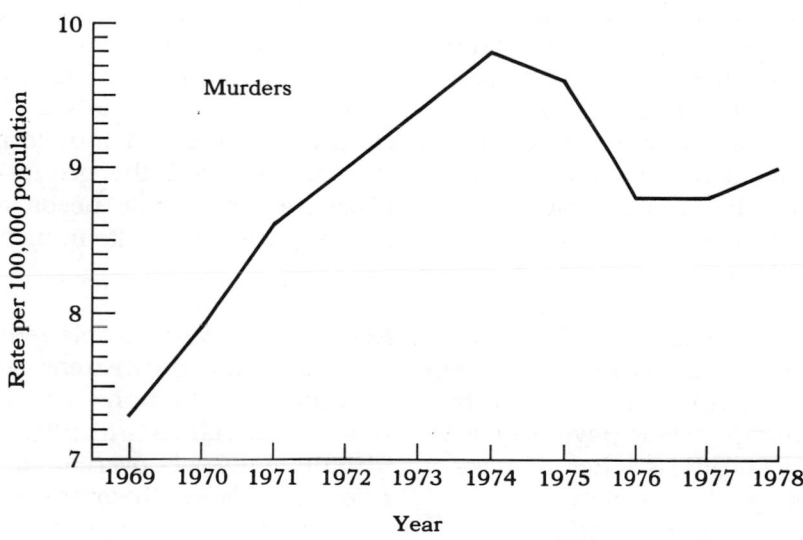

our culture emphasizes the goal to succeed much more than it stresses the "right" way of attaining it. Merton asked how individuals adapt to this discrepancy between means and goals and found in the answers the key to much of criminal behavior. He suggested that people respond in one of five ways to the discrepancy: conformity, innovation, ritualism, retreatism, and rebellion (see Table 4.2).

CONFORMITY Most Americans accept both the cultural goal of success and the approved means for reaching it; Merton calls that response **conformity.**

INNOVATION Many individuals accept the cultural goal but not the approved means of attaining it. They may respond with **innovation**—substituting an unorthodox means of achieving success. Most criminals take this route. They share the conformists' goal of economic success, but adopt illegal means. Innovators differ, however, in the norm-violating methods they use. Merton's sample innovator was Al Capone, who became a wealthy man as a result of his crimes (he even sent his son to Harvard), but drug pushers, prostitutes, "hit men," shoplifters, con artists, and the like are also innovators. And we should not neglect the more "respectable" innovators—corporate directors, for instance, who fix prices, violate antipollution laws, bribe foreign governments, evade paying taxes, and commit the countless other crimes—among the most costly to society.

In the view of Karl Marx and Friedrich Engels, our type of society encourages the criminal forms that Merton calls innovation (see The Economics of Crime). Ac-

Table 4.2 Deviance and Social Structure: Modes of Individual Adaptation

Modes of Adaptation	Culture Goals	Accepted Means for Attaining Them
Conformity	+	+
Innovation	+	−
Ritualism	−	+
Retreatism	−	−
Rebellion	±	±

+ indicates acceptance of goals or means; − indicates their rejection; ± signifies that prevailing goals and means were rejected, and new ones substituted.

SOURCE: Reprinted with permission of Macmillan Publishing Co., Inc. from Robert K. Merton, Social Theory and Social Structure (New York: Free Press, 1968, p. 194. Copyright © 1968, 1967 by Robert K. Merton.)

cording to Marx and Engels, the actions of people who live in capitalist societies are determined by their economic circumstances; thus people who cannot survive legally are forced into illegal acts. Also, the premium put on individuals in capitalist societies has often led individuals to place themselves above the group—that is, to place their economic needs above group norms—and this results in increased crime.

RITUALISM Most people tend to assume that all deviance threatens social norms, as innovators' actions do. But another form of deviance—*ritualism*—does not. **Ritualism** involves overconformity to petty rules and frequently arises when all hope of attaining economic success has faded. Having lost sight of the cultural goal, ritualists are really deviants, but we seldom label them as such because they appear to be conformists. You've met them: government bureaucrats who refuse to make exceptions to formal procedures no matter what the circumstances, office workers who violently claim "their" Xerox machine or who insist that documents be paper clipped in the upper left-hand corner only, for example.

The behavior of ritualists (which we find more annoying than anything else, as Merton points out) is an effective response to failure: rather than hope for an unattainable form of success, and therefore face constant disappointment, they scale their wishes down to an alternative they can control. But ritualism is also an alternative to social protest. It is a type of deviance that allows the social structure to continue as is. The two responses to social structure that involve a radical rejection of both cultural goals and approved methods for success—*retreatism* and *rebellion*—spark the strongest reactions.

RETREATISM Merton calls retreatists society's true aliens because **retreatism** is a rejection of approved goals and means that offers nothing in their place. Retreatists are the "burnouts"—the drug addicts, skid row alcoholics, and hoboes.

According to Merton, conventional society strongly condemns retreatist behavior. Conformists keep society going, but retreatists are social liabilities; innovators can be admired for their effort and ingenuity, but retreatists exhibit no such behavior; and ritualists conform to social mores, but retreatists pay no attention to them.

There have been several ethnographic studies of retreatist groups, in which researchers spent hours either interviewing or living with their subjects (Bahr 1973). One study of the elderly poor living in slum hotels (Stephens 1976) drew a picture of people who had little contact with (and even less trust of) others, who either did not work or worked in such low-status occupations as street peddling, and who desired nothing from the outside world.

REBELLION Unlike retreatism, **rebellion** involves the proposition of a new set of cultural goals and the institutional means of attaining them. This response is the only one of the five that is primarily oriented to perceived social—not individual—needs. Rebels use methods that vary from preaching their ideas, to peaceful mass demonstrations, to violence and destruction of property. Some rebels have become famous leaders of successful revolutions—Fidel Castro and Mahatma Gandhi, for example. Many more rebels have faded into oblivion after their attempts at revolution failed, and they turned to one of the other responses to the social structure.

Merton's scheme remains one valuable way of understanding the nature of deviance. While it was formulated on the basis of social and economic conditions that existed prior to World War II, it still has applicability today. Recently, some sociologists have attempted to extend it to today's economic structure (see Simon and Gagnon 1976).

Merton's theory shows us how deviance can be the normal product of the social structure rather than simply a creation of aberrant personalities. This emphasis on the role of the social structure in creating deviance is also apparent in another sociological approach to deviance, that of subculture theory.

THE ECONOMICS OF CRIME

Crime, despite the costs of controlling it, actually performs a positive economic function in society, as Karl Marx pointed out, somewhat tongue in cheek, over a century ago. "Crime," he wrote, "takes off the labour market a portion of the excess population, diminishes competition among the workers, and to a certain extent stops wages from falling below the minimum" (1956 [1867], p. 159). Indirectly, criminals support the apparatus of judges, lawyers, police, and others. Finally, they provide such goods and services as prostitution, illicit drugs, and certain kinds of gambling that, though illegal, are in great demand.

In short, crime is an industry and has a place in society's economic structure. This means that many individuals in legitimate businesses depend on a steady amount of crime for their own economic well being, including: the manufacturers and sellers of weapons, burglar alarms, and the like; police and private detectives; attorneys, judges, and their staffs; publishers of law books and printers of official forms; prison staffs; professors who teach and write about crime; as well as the actors, executives, technicians, and other people who produce television police dramas.

There is another economic aspect to crime in America; namely, that poor people are victims of violent crime to a far greater degree than those financially better off, while wealthy people are more likely to be the victims of property crime, as Figure 4.3 shows. If your family's income was under $3,000 in 1974, for instance, you would have been twice as likely to be raped, murdered, or assaulted than someone whose family income was over $25,000 that year. By the same token, your likelihood of having anything stolen would have only been two-thirds as great.

Deviant Subculture Explanations

In heterogeneous societies, such as our own, many subcultures exist as ongoing social entities. Because these subcultures are indeed cultures, people growing up in them experience a normal socialization to their special norms and values. Subcultural norms and values, however, can vary—sometimes substantially—from those of the dominant culture, as we saw in Chapter 2. This means that many individuals,

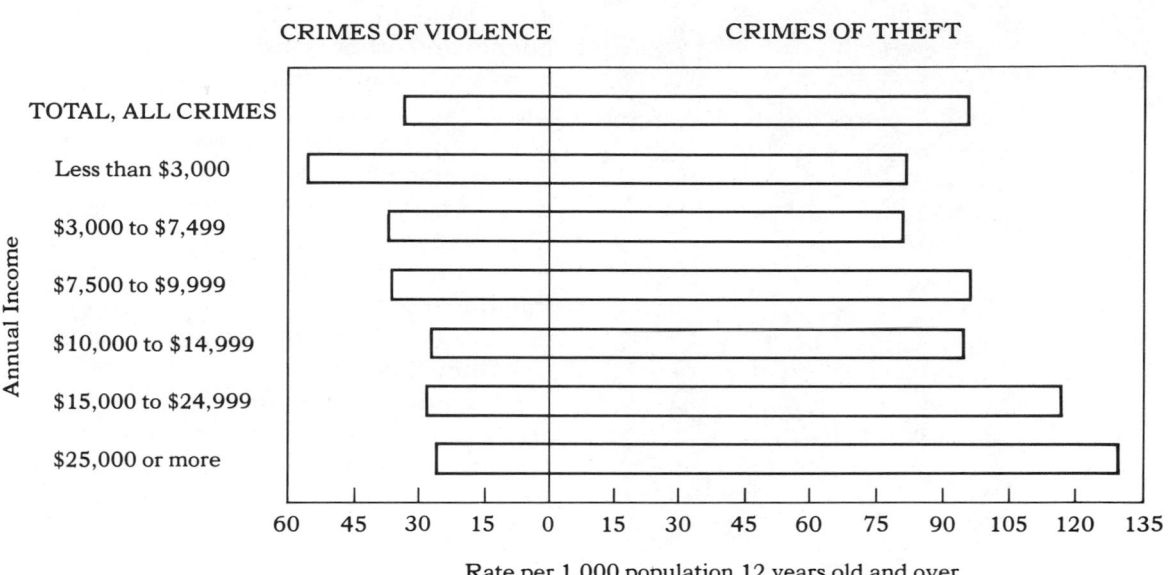

Figure 4.3 Personal Crimes of Violence and Theft in the United States, by Annual Family Income of Victims, 1974

SOURCE: U.S. Department of Commerce, Social Indicators: 1976 (Washington, DC: Government Printing Office, 1977, p. 228).

It is obvious that a wealthy person presents a much more desirable target to a thief than a poor person does (and that the best protection against robbery is having nothing to steal). But poor neighborhoods are often the most "dangerous" ones. Inner-city density, relaxed police protection, inability to leave these areas, and lack of many services (e.g., good lighting) that *might* reduce the likelihood of crimes help account for this relationship between poverty and victimization.

normally socialized into subcultures, have internalized norms and values often considered deviant—and sometimes criminal—by the dominant society. Many of the entirely normal behaviors of young males in the ghetto or barrio, for example, are seen as deviant by middle-class whites and the police. Sociologist Albert Cohen (1955) further elaborated the deviant subculture perspective in an influential study of juvenile delinquents. Cohen showed how lower-class males, because they were effective-

Fidel Castro only felt safe entering the city of Santa Clara after it was liberated by fellow rebel Che Guevara in 1959. Today Castro is a conformist. Do you get my meaning of "felt safe"?

inant society? According to Gresham Sykes and David Matza (1957), juvenile delinquents and other criminals reinterpret the norms of respectable society to protect themselves against the emotional hurt of not living up to them. Sykes and Matza term these redefinitions of deviant behavior to accord it dominant social norms **techniques of neutralization.** They identify five techniques: denying responsibility, denying the injury, denying the victim, condemning our condemners, and appealing to higher loyalties.

We can deny any responsibility for our crime by claiming we were driven to it: my poverty *made me* steal, or I killed in the heat of passion. There are many ways to deny any real injury: as car thieves, we were only "borrowing" autos that will be recovered anyway; as shoplifters, we refer to the large, impersonal department stores that will never miss the items, and, of course, there is always the insurance company that makes more money than it will lose.

There is no "victim" (denying the victim) if we can define the subject of our crime as a criminal. Thus we only rob store owners who overcharge, in an attempt to recover our "own" money, or we only rob those who are stupid to be walking around a certain part of town at night. And accused rapists often blame "loose women" for their acts, as you can see in Rape and Neutralization Techniques.

We can condemn our condemners by saying that all cops are brutal and corrupt, that the judge is "on the take," or that the entire legal apparatus only supports the interests of the rich. Finally, we can appeal to higher loyalties by saying that our gang war was fought as a "matter of honor" to avenge an insult to our group.

Besides gangs, other subcultures use

ly denied access to success and status by middle-class standards, sought status through accomplishments that were honored by the gang subculture and that were within their reach—stealing cars, winning drag races, caring the least about school grades, and so forth. Of course, some individuals find not only legitimate but also illegitimate avenues to success blocked (Cloward and Ohlin 1960).

How do members of deviant subcultures cope with the judgments of the dom-

the techniques of neutralization to justify their members' actions. Groups like homosexuals, winos, and Hare Krishnas often form deviant subcultures since they need to be part of a way of life (culture) that tells them their deviant behavior is justified. In the process, they often develop their own jargon, norms, territory (city blocks, gay bars), and styles of dress. With America's gay community making itself increasingly felt, sociologists have conducted a number of studies of its subculture (Blumstein and Schwartz 1975; Gagnon and Simon 1973).

Differential Association

In a more general way than the subcultural approach, Edwin H. Sutherland's *differential association* theory (1947) suggests that our own biological and psychological features have less to do with our tendency to commit crime than do the people we hang around with. Sutherland's theory begins with the assumption that criminal behavior is learned, just like other kinds of behavior. We get our basic social knowledge, including our knowledge about crime, while interacting with others, especially in intimate groups—most notably, our family and friendship groups.

There are two aspects to this learning. First, committing a successful crime requires that we learn certain skills—everything from how to pick a lock to how to put across a convincing alibi to the police—and our likelihood of learning these skills depends on whom we associate with. For instance, children growing up in an affluent suburb are not likely to have access to the finer points of mugging. However, we also learn something more basic—whether or not we are ready to use these skills. Sutherland disagrees with those who explain crime according to general needs (e.g., sex, power, money) and values (e.g., aggressiveness), for the very reason that they are general—they can be involved in both criminal *and* noncriminal behavior. Why, then, do some people learn to fulfill these needs in a criminal way? All of us encounter people who would never even think of violating major laws as well as those who would not hesitate to. Sutherland concludes that that choice depends on whom we associate with.

It is important to recognize, however, that our choice of associates is not unlimited or free. Associations can only form among people who have regular contact with each other. And a number of factors—including race, sex, education and income level, and age—go into determining who these people are. How likely, for example, is an inner-city ghetto youth to associate with a group of upper-middle-class suburban children? Or an upper-class youth to associate with working-class youth? For the most part, the wealthy associate with the wealthy, and the poor with the poor.

Sutherland's theory helps us explain the connection between poverty and a high crime rate among the poor because it shows how criminality can be transmitted. But perhaps more important in the link of poverty and crime is the fact that the wealthy and the poor have vastly different experiences with social norms. For the wealthy, conformity to the rules has brought material gains; their experience has been largely positive. But how well does conformity work for poor people? Obviously, it does not bring them much material gain, and so poverty can act as a spur to crime. Even so, many people who are economically well-off break the law, too.

RAPE AND NEUTRALIZATION TECHNIQUES

Techniques of neutralization are prominent in American society's treatment of rape. In court, rapists and their attorneys regularly deny the victim by claiming that she was responsible for the attack—that she was a "loose woman" or a prostitute; that she led her partner on or even that she really wanted to be raped. They reason that, once provoked, man's "natural animal urges" are uncontrollable. Put otherwise: *she* forced *him!* As absurd as these claims sound, judges and juries often accept them. In 1977, for instance, a Wisconsin judge dismissed a convicted rapist, saying that the man only reacted normally to a "permissive environment."

Data do not support these allegations. How can we agree that only loose women get raped when rape victims have ranged in age from under one year to over eighty, and have included nuns and young girls raped by their fathers or stepfathers? Yet, the neutralization technique remains a successful defense. Why?

Susan Brownmiller (1975) offers an explanation in *Against Our Will: Men, Women, and Rape.* She gathered a great deal of data from newspaper reports, government statistics, studies,

---

The differential association theory and Marx and Engel's discussion of crime and economy help explain the link between crime and poverty, but they aren't adequate by themselves to explain why the extent of criminality appears to vary so much by economic class. The reason why these explanations are not sufficient is that crime may appear to be mostly a lower-class phenomenon because of how crimes are defined and what types of people are most likely to be apprehended and charged with these violations. The importance of distinguishing between actual crimes committed and those that show up in the crime statistics was illuminated by a study of juvenile delinquents by Travis Hirschi (1969). When Hirschi asked juveniles from different classes whether or not they had ever engaged in delinquent acts, he found that middle-class youths reported that they had engaged in just as many delinquent acts as lower-class youths, but they were not as likely to be apprehended and charged for them.

Hirschi's study, which points out the significance of who is actually tagged as deviant, brings us to the final and most recently developed major sociological theory of deviance—labeling, which focuses on how people come to be labeled deviant and the effects these labels have on their

and from personal interviews with victims. She concluded that rape has an underlying structural cause in the basic relationship between men and women. In short, techniques of neutralization work in rape cases because of traditionally defined situations embedded in our sex roles and our culture. For the real issue in rape is power, not sexuality; and traditionally, men have had more power than women, so that rape reinforces the normative power relationships.

As a form of social control, rape forces women to restrict their movement to situations that involve their direct supervision by a man—whether husband or lover, father, or policeman. This limits their independent activity, keeping them the less powerful sex. Getting raped is the threatened punishment for violating this norm. The courts also sanction sexually deviant women by their reactions to them, saying that their punishment at the hands of the rapist was deserved. Brownmiller believes that the ultimate hope for substantially reducing the number of rapes is the power and independence offered women by the feminist movement, which will eventually change traditional definitions of male-female relationships.

subsequent careers (and not on the deviants themselves).

Labeling and Expectations of Deviants

Labeling theorists believe that an individual tagged with a deviant label is, in effect, assigned a new role. This occurs because once assigned a label, the individual is expected to behave in ways that are consistent with it. David R. Rosenhan (1973) and seven of his associates demonstrated this in a unique field experiment. Rosenhan and his colleagues each attempted to gain admittance to twelve psychiatric hospitals around the country by complaining that they were "hearing voices." Except for that piece of information and the false names and occupations they gave to disguise themselves, everything they told the hospitals about themselves was true. Even so, their complaint was enough to have them committed as "schizophrenic" (except for one associate who was tagged "manic depressive"). As soon as they were admitted, the experimenters acted as they normally did, which had always been defined as sane.

However, normal behavior was not

enough to get them reclassified. Not only did it take between seven and fifty-two days for the experimenters to win their release, but they were *never* seen to be sane at all by hospital personnel. They were let out as "schizophrenic in remission"—that is, still insane, just all right for now. While in the hospitals, all of their actions were apparently interpreted in light of the label. Rosenhan observes: "Once a person is designated abnormal, all of his other behaviors and characteristics are colored by that label. Indeed, the label is so powerful that many of the [phony patients'] normal behaviors were overlooked entirely or profoundly misinterpreted . . . The perception of his circumstances was shaped entirely by the diagnosis" (p. 252).

Here's an example: the experimenters took detailed notes of their experiences. At first, they did so secretly, for they were afraid it would make the hospital staff suspicious, as in fact it did make a number of patients. But the precaution was not necessary: doctors, nurses, and other members of the staff interpreted the notetaking as a symptom of "compulsive neurotic behavior." Nursing reports, for instance, contained entries that read: "Patient engages in writing behavior."

The experimenters' actions were interpreted in light of the physical context: since they had been admitted to a mental hospital, the patients must be crazy. Perceptions of the patients' actions were then based on that definition (insane)—not on the behavior itself.

SELF-FULFILLING PROPHECIES Presumably, the participants in the Rosenhan experiment returned to their normal lives with no ill effects from their diagnosis. But labeling theorists point out that labeling persons as deviant can become a "self-fulfilling prophecy." That is, people can conform to certain expectations we have of them merely because we predict they will. We saw one way this works in our discussion of socialization labels. We hear ourselves described in a certain way, internalize that description, and eventually try to live up to it, in a way similar to the development of our looking-glass self (Chapter 1).

Edwin Lemert (1972) tried to capture this aspect of labeling with the related concept of *secondary deviance*. **Secondary deviance** is deviant behavior generated in the labeled person solely by the fact of being labeled. Once people are socially identified as deviant, and accept the label as a self-identification, then their behavior is likely to change in response to restrictions imposed by the label. Others may interpret all the labeled individual's actions in light of the deviant identity (He didn't pick up the wrong hat by mistake, he did it because he's a thief). Also, when people encounter someone labeled deviant, they usually apply their own, informal sanctions, dramatically altering the deviant's life course in some cases. For example, many people are reluctant to hire exconvicts and former drug addicts because of their deviant labels. Or consider the film career of actor Lew Ayres, who made forty-eight movies between 1929 and 1941. After declaring himself a conscientious objector and refusing to fight in World War II, he was labeled a deviant and his career suffered. He found work in only eleven more films during the subsequent thirty years.

What we have said about the self-fulfilling prophecy and secondary deviance so far suggests that individuals labeled as de-

If people look deviant to us—whether that means "bad" or just "weird"—we expect them to act deviant. (Can you imagine this man as a nine-to-five executive?) This can become a self-fulfilling prophecy if the labeled person tries to live up to those expectations.

viant will simply conform to that label. One criticism that has been made of labeling theory, however, is that some individuals respond in a quite different way: they do their best to conform to social norms and attempt to "live down" the label. Labeling theory has also been criticized because it doesn't explain why people become deviants even when they go unrecognized and because it suggests that the labeling of deviance rests more on the setting than on the behavior, as in the Rosenhan experiment. However, despite these criticisms,

labeling theorists have shown us the great influence labeling has on how we act and how we perceive the actions of others.

LABELING AND SOCIAL CONTROL

The influence of deviance labeling on how we perceive each other makes it a potent weapon of social control. Two labels might refer to the same individuals but have very different implications for our reactions to them; compare, for instance, weird with eccentric, fat with overweight, or irresponsible with independent. We usually tolerate, or even enjoy an "eccentric," while avoiding anyone labeled "weird."

Labels can produce vastly different views of almost any action. If a group of Palestinian Arabs, for instance, hijack an airliner, most of the Western world will call them "terrorists." But the PLO and its allies would label them "freedom fighters." The two labels evoke very different images of the same individuals. Labeling in this case is a deliberate attempt to guide public opinion: we might sympathize with freedom fighters, but not with terrorists.

The manipulation of public opinion by labeling selected groups and individuals as deviants is a common tactic of governments and other organizations everywhere. By labeling efforts at change as the work of deviants, these organizations reinforce the status quo. They do so by undermining the legitimacy of the deviants' criticism of the status quo. Moreover, others joining the deviants must pay the price of social exclusion. The Soviets have used this principle to weaken the influence of some of their dissidents. The person is labeled "insane," not criminal, and sent to an asylum, not to prison. This prevents the dissident from being hailed as a "political prisoner." Moreover, it undermines the validity of the dissident's antigovernment acts and statements. Similarly, in the United States during the McCarthy period of the 1950s, thousands of people who had ever belonged to (or supported) a radical— or even very liberal—organization were labeled communists. At the time, this carried the connotation that the person was in some way actively working to overthrow the government of the United States. Many people thus labeled lost their jobs, their friends, and sometimes their spouses, and were prevented from obtaining any work in their professions. In addition, many forms of social criticism became suspect as communist inspired, thus stifling dissent and criticism.

The labeling of deviance is open to manipulation in two major ways: (1) by "selective enforcement" of who is actually labeled and (2) by the very definition of what acts constitute deviance. In this chapter, we have seen that only some of the behavior that is contrary to social norms is labeled deviant. What behavior, then, is most likely to be labeled as deviant? In the United States, it appears that the labeling process tends to be hardest on the actions of less powerful people (minorities and poor) and on perceived threats to the status quo (as in the case of civil rights fighters and antiwar demonstrators). A number of sociologists, for example, have found that juvenile offenses are far more likely to be entered in official police statistics if the offender is poor.

The composition of the prison population supports this contention. Prisoners are disproportionately poor and disproportionately black (American Friends Services Committee 1971; Chambliss and Seidman 1971). Similarly, the administrative rulings and legislation against crime in business tend to be lenient, favoring offenders of high social status. Business crimes include: embezzlement, misrepresentation in advertising, bribery, fraudulent appropriation of public funds, illegal tax exemptions, fee splitting, misrepresentation in the labeling and packaging of foods and drugs, and other illegal acts committed by people engaged in their legitimate occupations. Sanctions are often imposed by special federal agencies, and they usually entail injunctions to stop the illegal practice and sometimes a fine. But they rarely prescribe prison, and when they do, the convicts serve their brief sentence in minimum security prisons. Beyond that, our society spends much more time and energy prosecuting nonbusiness crimes.

In sum, a look inside a prison would not tell us as much about society's deviants themselves as about the official reaction to them. Before the police and courts take action, they must first perceive the violation as a threat to the social order as they define it. Thus the rape of a prostitute or a wave of burglaries in a housing project for the poor are not likely to receive as much attention as the mugging of a single business person or as the roamings of a group of black youths around an affluent white neighborhood.

More fundamentally, the very determination of what is a violation of law can be a politically loaded one. Many harmful actions never, or only belatedly, are defined as violations because of certain groups' power to enforce their private interests. For instance, although there were scores of attempts to pass stiff antistrip-mining legislation in Congress, they failed because of industry opposition. After many lost battles, a weakened bill was finally made law. Antipollution controls on cars were passed years after the health hazard of pollution was recognized. Even then, the auto makers continued to win delays in their implementation year after year.

Both the definition and selective enforcement of deviance, then, can be seen as open to political influence. This has led Robert Sommer (1976) to contend that it is impossible to separate the American le-

gal system from politics—although American society is not at all unique in this respect. Judges and parole boards are elected or appointed by elected officials, and they generally run for election under the auspices of a political party. The laws that define acts as criminal are made by elected officials, and an array of positions, such as that of federal prosecutor, are given as "spoils" to the party in power (Sommer 1976, pp. 82–83). Sommer's observation makes it easier for us to see many laws as norms developed by those who hold the reins of power, and not as eternal standards of right and wrong.

Of course, not everyone accepts the dominant standards of what is deviant and criminal. Opposition groups frequently use techniques of neutralization to justify their own deviance and to label their condemners as the real criminals. Consider, for instance, the justification for civil rights actions that Martin Luther King gave from his Birmingham jail cell, in answer to his critics:

> You deplore the demonstrations that are presently taking place in Birmingham [Alabama]. But I am sorry that your statement did not express a similar concern for the conditions that brought the demonstrations into being . . . it is unfortunate that so-called demonstrations are taking place in Birmingham at this time, but . . . it is even more unfortunate that the white power structure of this city left the Negro community with no other alternative (King 1969, p. 73).

The claim, then, is that the law perpetuated an evil much greater than its violation.

THE FUNCTIONS OF DEVIANCE

So far in this chapter, it may appear that deviance serves only negative functions for society and that it simply threatens the social order while conformity upholds it. But many sociologists have noticed that deviance serves some positive function as well, that it actually promotes social order. In fact, the three major sociological perspectives come together on one point—Durkheim (functionalist), Becker (symbolic interactionist), and Marx (conflict theorist) all recognize deviance as in some way basic to social control and normal society.

As early as 1895, Durkheim observed that deviance is a normal part of social life. In particular, he argued against the accepted view that crime results from individual or social "sickness." "In the first place," he said, "crime is normal because a society exempt from it is utterly impossible" (Durkheim 1964a [1895], p. 67). (The very existence of a norm makes its violation possible.) A crimeless society, moreover, would require that everyone have the same understanding of all social norms—and agree to follow them. As we have seen, norms by nature contain a certain amount of leeway for interpretation, and thus can never be uniformly adhered to. A crimeless society also requires that socialization have exactly the same effects on all of us, and as we learned in Chapter 1 this, too, is impossible. Durkheim therefore concludes that crime is inevitable in society because it "is bound up with the fundamental conditions of all social life" (1964a [1895], p. 70).

But Durkheim went beyond that to say that the existence of at least some crime is actually useful to society—a surprising statement at first. He said that the same conditions that allow crime to develop enables the genius and innovator to emerge. His example is Socrates, who was executed for "corrupting Athenian youth" with his teachings.

> According to Athenian law, Socrates was a criminal, and his condemnation was no more than just. However, his crime, namely, the independence of his thought, rendered a service not only to humanity but to his country. It served to prepare a new morality and faith which the Athenians needed, since the traditions by which they had lived until then were no longer in harmony with the conditions of life (Durkheim 1964a [1895], p. 71).

Nor is Socrates the only example. Galileo, Copernicus, and Columbus were all imprisoned for their "radical" views, and Karl Marx was forced to flee Germany for his life. Similarly, the leaders of great revolutions (Washington, Lenin, Gandhi, Bolivar, and others) were once called outlaws. All of them helped their societies adapt to changing circumstances. In a similar vein, Karl Marx wrote that the criminal interrupts the "monotony and security" of life in capitalist society, "protects it from stagnation, and brings forth that restless tension, that mobility of spirit without which the stimulus [for] competition itself would be blunted" (Marx 1956 [1867], p. 159).

Durkheim also recognized a social benefit in punishment—society's reaction to crime. Through punishing criminals, citizens have a chance to demonstrate their allegiance to society and show support for the violated norms. Without deviance, we would probably not be aware of this support. Conformist behavior, as we have seen, goes unnoticed. It is unlikely, for instance, that when dressing in the morning you say to yourself, "I'm now conforming to the norm that requires me to wear clothes in public." But you would surely become aware of your conformity if you observed someone else walking around nude. Then you might agree with Marx's statement that the criminal performs a "service" by arousing the public's moral sentiments.

At the same time, punishment may clarify a lack of support for certain norms, as shown in the efforts to decriminalize marijuana and in the numerous Supreme Court rulings that many laws are unconstitutional. For these rulings to occur, somebody had to break the law and be punished for it. In sum, without deviant behavior—in fact, without crime—society would undoubtedly become stagnant: deviance is often the one way to get rid of laws rendered obsolete by altered social conditions.

SUMMARY

Our reactions to "deviant" or "conformist" behavior are as essential to social life as the actions themselves. Conformity and deviance are not set categories of behavior; behavior takes on meaning only in relation to a particular society's norms. These norms, and therefore definitions of an act or person as deviant, vary greatly for different societies.

Conformity is not easily observable, precisely because it is so common—and so necessary for social life to proceed. Learning to conform—and to accept the social influence of particular organizations and individuals—is a basic lesson of socialization. Various studies have shown that group pressure and acceptance of the dictates of authority are important sources of our conformity.

Deviant behavior is as important to society as conformity. It is a major source of social evolution, providing alternative ways of acting. People have tried to explain deviance—and, in particular, crime—from several perspectives: the demonological and the classical (both nonscientific), the biological, the psychological, and the sociological. The sociological approach contains several different approaches. Merton's social structural approach explains crime in relation to cultural goals (accumulating wealth) and the accepted means for obtaining them. In general, people are conformists (accepting both goals and means); most criminals are innovators (still accepting the goals, but rejecting the means). Other types of adaptations are ritualism, retreatism, and rebellion. Subculture theories explain that criminal subcultures provide the individual with some justification for the criminal act. The theory of differential association holds that crime is learned behavior. Finally, labeling theorists emphasize the effects of labeling on creating and maintaining deviant behavior. People tend to conform to the labels we give them, making the labels self-fulfilling prophecies. In this way, labels act as efficient sources of social control.

Proponents of each of the three major sociological perspectives agree on one point—deviance is a product of society's basic and continuous social control operations.

Key Terms

deviance (p. 117)
conformity (p. 132)
innovation (p. 132)
ritualism (p. 132)
retreatism (p. 133)
rebellion (p. 133)
techniques of neutralization (p. 136)
labeling theory (p. 138)
secondary deviance (p. 140)

Review and Discussion Questions

1. Consider how you would have reacted if you were the "loner" in Asch's experiment, or if you were asked to administer the "shocks" in Milgram's experiment. How can you explain the actions of the actual subjects? How do people manifest this tendency in daily life?
2. Can you explain the so-called "bandwagon effect" in politics in terms of conformity and group pressure? What is the implication for our political process?
3. Try and imagine a society without deviance. How would it differ from our own? What would be missing? How would society suffer? How would it benefit? How would *your* life be different?
4. Are Soviet dissidents criminals or heroes? What makes them one or the other? Who decides? What does this mean for their treatment by the Soviet government and how Americans interpret that treatment?
5. Take some time to observe a deviant subculture—whether drunks, homosexuals, communists, "swingers," or others. What are some of their norms and behaviors that you find deviant? How do they justify their actions?

For Further Study

DEFINING THE DEVIANT Many of the scholarly works on deviance concern the ways that society defines some people and not others as deviant. Of all these works, Howard S. Becker's *Outsiders: Studies in the Sociology of Deviance* (New York: Free Press, 1963) stands out. Focusing on marijuana use, Becker presents the foundations of the labeling perspective. Another good book written from the symbolic interactionist perspective is Charles S. Suchar's *Perspectives on Social Deviation* (New York: Holt, Rinehart and Winston, 1977). Suchar surveys the way sociologists have come to view deviance, while weaving in his own theories throughout. Kai T. Erickson's *Wayward Puritans* (New York: Wiley, 1966) is a study of how New England Puritans defined people as permanently deviant, based on Calvinist doctrines. Erickson also provides much food for reflection on the way we determine who our deviants are.

DEVIANT SUBCULTURES Two good collections containing essays on a number of deviant subcultures are: Jack D. Douglas, ed., *Observations of Deviance* (New York: Random House, 1970); and Don Spiegel and Patricia Keith-Spiegel, eds., *Outsiders USA* (New York: Rinehart, 1973). An example of a deviant subculture all urbanites are familiar with can be found in Howard M. Bahr's *Skid Row* (New York: Oxford University Press, 1973). Bahr shows how the subjects of his New York City study reacted to losing all their ties with social groups and institutions. Perhaps the most powerful deviant subculture, however, is organized crime. This subculture supports the proposition that members' activities are, in fact, highly moral, and social ties among members are strong. See Francis A. J. Ianni, *A Family Business: Kinship and Social Control in Organized Crime* (New York: Sage, 1972).

SEXUAL DEVIANCE Until recently, virtually all forms of sexual deviance in the United States were considered disgusting, and almost nobody would devote a scientific career to understanding their causes. Today, however, there is a growing number of sociologists who specialize in human sexuality. Two of the more prominent ones are John H. Gagnon and William Simon, and they have edited a collection of writings on sexual deviance: *Sexual Deviance* (New York: Harper & Row, 1967). Another good volume that discusses such subjects as pornography, prostitution, homosexuality, and "kinky" sex is: Erich Goode and Richard Troiden, eds., *Sexual Deviance and Sexual Deviants* (New York: Morrow, 1974). A great deal of research has been aimed particularly at homosexuality. See: C. A. B. Warren, *Identity and Community in the Gay World* (New York: Wiley, 1974); and Alan P. Bell and Martin Weinberg, *Homosex-ualities: A Study of Diversity Among Men and Women* (New York: Simon & Schuster, 1978). A good article on lesbianism is S. Schaefer's "Sexual and Social Problems of Lesbians," *The Journal of Sex Research* **12** (Feb. 1976): 50–69. Finally, a personal account of maintaining a lesbian identity is: Kate Millet, *Flying* (New York: Ballantine, 1974).

PART TWO

Up to this point, we have seen how the individual is prepared for life in society: through learning the rules (socialization); the nature of these rules (culture, values, and norms); the way we organize our actions in various categories (roles and performances); and the ways people evaluate that behavior (deviance and conformity). With Part Two, we begin talking about how society is organized for social life. This requires an important abstraction. For although we have personal experience dealing with individuals, the nature of groups and other social structures is not as concrete. Yet these social structures influence us as much as the individuals with whom we come in daily contact. We will also examine the structural background—that is, apart from individual actions—for the dominance of some groups and individuals over others. Thus Part Two will demonstrate the immense impact social structures have in our lives, and give you the tools for analyzing it.

The Structure
of Society

Chapters 5 and 6 focus on the different forms in which
society is organized and its various structures. Chapter 5 lays
the foundation for moving from the individual to social level of
analysis, by showing the mechanisms of social organization.
Chapter 6 looks at social institutions. The basis of social
institutions and our perceptions of them are explored in
general, and three specific institutions—the family, religion,
and education—are looked at in more detail. Current
controversies surrounding these institutions are also
examined.

Chapters 7 and 8 look at the nature of inequality and why
we generally accept its existence. Chapter 7 offers a general
understanding of the social basis of inequality. It examines
actual inequality and explains the major theoretical
perspectives sociologists use to analyze it. Chapter 8, on the
other hand, focuses on specific inequalities based on race,
ethnic background, sex, and age. ■

CHAPTER FIVE
Social Organization

Social life, as we have seen in previous chapters, is *organized* life. Because of shared norms, roles, values, and beliefs, we interact in generally quite predictable ways, no matter how much we may think of ourselves as individualists. In his classic story, "Metamorphosis," Franz Kafka tried to indicate just how organized we are. Although the story's central character awakens one morning to discover that he has been transformed into a giant cockroach, he is more concerned that he has overslept and is late for work. The story can make us realize how much we conceptualize our waking life through social roles and obligations, so that almost nothing can *disorganize* our behavior.

The ways in which our interactions fall into regular patterns constitute society's *social organization*. Sociologists do not totally agree just what the term **social organization** should refer to, but we will use it to mean the patterned regularity of our social actions and beliefs. Norms, values, roles, and so on are its building blocks. In this chapter and the next, we'll look at the two main ways sociologists try to make sense of the relationships among these blocks. In this chapter, we'll look at **groups**—collections of people who share a common identity and interact with one another in a patterned way—and the relationships among them. And in the next chapter, we'll

look at *social institutions*—how societies ensure that essential and enduring social tasks are performed routinely.

THE NATURE OF GROUPS

The sociological understanding of the concept *group* is narrower than the common-sense definition of, simply, a number of people. For sociologists believe that all social groups must have two essential qualities: *patterned interaction*—that is, members must interact regularly and according to the same pattern of social organization (norms, roles, and so on)—and *consciousness*—that is, members must understand that they "belong together" in some way. Among the many social groups, then, are: your family, your sociology class, a picket line of striking workers, the congressional Black Caucus, the nuns in a convent, and the employees of an American Motors plant.

Aggregates and Categories

A social group can be distinguished from a simple social **aggregate**—a number of persons who happen to be in the same place at the same time but who don't share

Why aren't there any women in this group? There are probably no formal laws prohibiting them, but traditions and norms tend to restrict access to most "voluntary" groups—whether by sex, age, or other traits.

a common consciousness or interact regularly. A crowd observing a fire is an example of a social aggregate.

A social group can also be distinguished from a **social category**—a number of people who share a trait (hair color, age, or sex) that *we* (the observers) use to associate them with one another. Blondes, women, men, all people who live in small nations, everyone who has ever run for president—these are all examples of social categories.

Under certain circumstances, aggregates and members of categories can develop into groups. For example, Jeffrey Nash (1975) discovered that grouplike qualities developed among the regular passengers on Tulsa, Oklahoma, city buses. The riders interacted according to an extensive set of norms that prescribed everything from how to "hail" and wait for a bus, to where to sit, and the allowable topics of conversation. When the 1973 energy crisis brought many new riders, the "regulars" felt somehow invaded (consciousness) and viewed with amusement the behavior of the newcomers, which they considered deviant according to their group's norms.

Similarly, some elements of social categories have been known to develop consciousness and form groups. For example, until the development of the women's movement in the United States, almost no American women formed social groups based on sex. However, since the mid-1960s, more and more women have begun to vote similarly and work for the same causes—equal pay for women, abortion law reform, and the like. Not all American women support these issues, but among a great many of them a women's consciousness has certainly developed. This consciousness, plus their relationships with each other as women, allows us to consider women as a group.

GROUPS AND SOCIAL STRUCTURE

The patterned interaction that takes place within groups reflects an *internal social organization.* For example, the internal social organization of the family consists of several positions (mother, father, husband, wife, sister, brother, son, daughter) that involve role norms designed to accomplish group tasks: childbearing, child raising, "breadwinning," and many others. The rights and duties of the different family positions make some members dominant in relation to the others. For instance, a person busy with housework and child-rearing responsibilities usually cannot maintain a full-time job and thus is dependent on the major breadwinner.

Groups are not only internally structured but usually relate to other groups in patterned ways, as well. We do not just relate to one another as individuals, but as members of one or more social groups. And groups are related in rather formal ways. Think, for instance, of the relationship between the college athletic team and the coaches, and between these groups and the college administration. Or think of how a labor union local is related to other locals, to the national organization, to company officials, and to law-making bodies. The customary patterns of interaction within groups and between groups, evident in these relationships, constitute the *social structure* of a society.

These definitions might suggest a static, conflict-free social life. But just because groups operate in patterned ways does not mean that they work together harmoniously or that their internal relationships are without conflict. If society is to survive, there must be some shared meanings among groups, some meshing of their purposes, even if not always carried out voluntarily. But within these general confines, there obviously is conflict within and between many social groups.

Conflict occurs because the interests of groups clash and, as Georg Simmel noted (see page 26), because our personal interests may clash with those of the groups to which we belong. Businesses compete for economic markets, the Democratic and Republican parties fight over their political interests, and colleges compete for the same high school basketball player. We'll now look at a number of instances both of conflict between groups and harmonious relations between them. (For another conceptualization of social organization, see Territoriality.)

TYPES OF GROUPS

Sociologists classify groups in a variety of ways. Here, we'll consider some of the most important of these: in-groups and out-groups, interest groups, reference groups, and primary and secondary groups. Then,

TERRITORIALITY

Two sociologists, Stanford Lyman and Marvin Scott (1967) have given us another way of looking at social organization—*territoriality.* The concept of territoriality revolves around how rules for interaction are established for various spaces, based on who controls the space.

In *public territories,* for example, the state or social custom determines interaction norms. Thus, while everyone has free access to public territories, our freedom of action in them is not total, as there are social norms to follow. Restaurants, office buildings, and streetcorners are examples of public territories. In *home territories,* the participants have greater freedom of behavior and a feeling of intimacy and control. While there is no clear distinction between public and home territories—and, indeed, the same place may be used as both—individuals who regularly use certain territories may define them as their home and enforce that definition. Gay bars are home territories for homosexuals, even though they might simply be public bars in the daytime.

Interactional territories are still less clearly defined. They are, simply, any area where a social gathering may occur. Parties can mark off interactional territories. And though interactional territories exist only as long as the particular gathering, while they do, they maintain definite, though invisible boundaries. Finally, there are *body territories:* the space taken up by the human body. These territories are our

we'll take a more detailed look at what may be the most powerful type of group in modern society, the formal organization.

In-groups and Out-groups

The sense of belonging that is integral to group formation is only possible if the group has a *boundary*—a point at which "we" are separated from the "them" of other groups. In sociological terminology, the "we" is an *in-group* and the "they" is an *out-group.*

The boundaries that groups form around themselves vary in kind. Gaining membership in some groups is relatively difficult (e.g., the American Medical Association) and, for some, impossible (all-male executive clubs are closed to female executives; white-only country clubs are closed

most intimate, and we generally restrict the number of people who can "enter" this territory (e.g., move close to us or touch us) to a few.

The concept of territoriality alerts us to the boundaries that surround spaces, including the way "legitimate" users of these spaces respond to boundary violations. One such response, for example, would be the beating of a black who entered a tavern in certain white neighborhoods (or a white who entered one in certain black neighborhoods). Youth gangs often attack rival gang members who invade their "turf." The response to boundary violation need not be violent, however. You might just ignore or move away from a person who makes a pass at you (thus trying to enter your body territory). Similarly, if you're clearly unwanted at a party (interactional territory), people may ignore your comments. People may turn away or talk about people you don't know, professors may escalate their use of academic jargon in front of unwelcome students, or gays may affect a "swishy" manner to put off heterosexuals.

As you can see, territorial boundaries are often defined in terms of who has access to a particular territory. The concept of territoriality helps us see how small groups, by enforcing informal norms their members share, can exclude unwelcome newcomers from their territory. We can also see how minority groups—gays and young blacks, for example—feel that they can express their life-styles only if they segregate themselves in special home territories.

to blacks). The boundaries of these groups tend to be sharply defined. The boundaries of other groups, such as football fan clubs, are blurred, with persons moving in and out and no clear dividing line between those in and those out.

The consciousness of we-ness that group members have in common frequently develops over specific shared interests (e.g., to share knowledge about sociology, to sell the most automobiles, or to fulfill the church's aims). Whatever the group shares, its members see it as something unique, something that makes their group different from other groups. Muzafer Sherif and C. W. Sherif (1953) demonstrated this aspect of groups in a famous experiment in the 1950s at a summer camp for eleven-year-old boys. The experimenters arbitrarily divided the boys into two aggregates with separate living quarters. The boys from each set of cabins then had

Interest groups rely on a variety of methods to promote their members' interests. If they do not have large available funds or computer banks, they might take their case "to the streets."

to compete against each other in various athletic contests. It did not take long before the boys in each aggregate developed a sense of loyalty to the other boys in their set of cabins, which overrode any previous attachments to boys now in the other sets of cabins. In other words, the boys firmly established in-group and out-group boundaries on the basis of their separate living quarters. (However, this in-group versus out-group consciousness could be undermined with the appearance of a common goal. The experimenters manufactured a crisis in the camp by breaking the pipe which was the camp's only source of water, and both formerly antagonistic groups joined in to fix it cooperatively.)

Interest Groups

Every social group has interests in the sense that members share a common identity with some common goals, even if it is only as bridge players. That consciousness of we-ness is often just the members' understanding of their common interests or goal. Even the family is no exception—members usually share basic economic interests, concern for raising the children to adulthood, concern for the family's reputation (or name), and the common interests that come with sharing a residence.

Sociologists, however, usually reserve the term **interest group** for a group whose reason for existence is to promote its interests in competition with other groups, usually in the political arena. Lobbying groups, such as the National Rifle Association (NRA), are prime examples, as are trade associations such as the National Association of Manufacturers.

Reference Groups

Another important type of group is the *reference group.* Your **reference group** is the group you use to measure your own social standing or life course, whether or not you are actually a member of it. For instance, if after graduating from college you go to work in a corporation, you may evaluate your career in that organization not by how well your co-workers do but by the subsequent careers of your former classmates.

Sociologists also use the concept of reference group to refer to groups whose standards we use to judge our own behavior. Again, we needn't have any direct contact with members of that group. For instance, in the 1979 motion picture *Breaking Away,* an Indiana youth, while working and practicing to become a champion cyclist, develops a passion for Italian culture. (Italians are great cyclists). He begins speaking Italian, listening to and singing Italian opera, and adopting an array of Italian mannerisms—though he has never been to Italy or met any Italians.

Primary and Secondary Groups

Perhaps the most significant distinction to be made among groups is that between *primary* groups and *secondary* groups. Charles H. Cooley (1924), the social psychologist whose ideas about the origin of the self we discussed in Chapter 1, developed the concept of the primary group. A **primary group** is a group whose members interact with each other on a direct, face-to-face, and often long-lasting basis. The family is the classic example of a primary group, but small work groups, teenage gangs, and consciousness-raising groups (see Box: Consciousness-Raising Groups) are also primary groups. Size by itself is not a criterion of whether or not a group is primary, but there are obvious limits on how large a group can be for its members to still maintain primary relations.

A **secondary group,** by contrast, is a group whose members interact on a relatively impersonal basis (that is, mainly through specific roles), and whose relations with one another are frequently indirect and without strong emotional bonds. Examples of secondary groups are the corporation work team you may be part of, the political party to which you belong, and your sociology class.

Prior to industrialization, social life took place predominantly within primary groups, but in the industrialized countries of today, social life increasingly occurs within secondary groups. In the next section, we'll look at the most important type of secondary group, the *formal organization.*

FORMAL ORGANIZATIONS

The type of group that dominates modern life is the **formal organization:** a collection of interrrelated groups formed to accomplish a specific purpose and operating according to an explicit set of rules. In gen-

CONSCIOUSNESS-RAISING GROUPS

Today, many people are questioning the validity of traditional sex role behaviors. Social control, however—whether in the form of others' reactions or our own self-doubts—operates to inhibit us from actually asking those questions or testing alternative life-styles. According to Annette M. Brodsky (1973), small consciousness-raising (CR) groups have given many women the opportunity to explore such questions. (For a comparison, see Frank Reissman's [1977] account of his men's groups.) Brodsky studied groups involved with the women's movement but believes the principles can be applied to any therapy group.

A basic assumption in CR groups is that sex-linked behaviors and attitudes are social and not innate. While women have come to regard themselves as passive and conforming, as a result of their education and training, in the CR groups they are confronted by active women who are doing something about their present situations. All members are expected to be open to new perspectives about their roles.The CR group's primary structure—face-to-face interaction and open discussion of basic values—produces an intimacy that replaces the

eral, members of a formal organization relate to one another through organizational roles—boss, supervisor, client, shop steward, local president, teacher, bureau director—not as whole people. As this implies, norms are generally tighter in formal organizations than in other groups. In other words, the activities of a formal organization are *official*—clearly defined and tied to formal *offices* (positions, roles).

Formal organizations include major businesses, welfare agencies, armies, labor unions, schools, the FBI, and OPEC. They also include social and cultural groups, from the American Sociological Association to the Ku Klux Klan.

Types of Formal Organizations

Formal organizations serve many different purposes in many different environments. So it's not surprising that they vary. One of the most important ways in which formal organizations differ is in their form of recruiting new members and retaining old ones. We can distinguish three main

isolation and alienation from other women that often characterize female relationships in the society at large. The women in these groups share an understanding of what it's like to be a "woman in a man's world" and feel solidarity with each other (Brodsky 1973).

Women in CR groups explore their uniqueness apart from their roles and reveal taboo feelings (e.g., disliking child-rearing, wishing they had not married, being tired of gratifying the "male ego," and so on). In the group, women find that they are not alone in their doubts, and the combination of trust and closeness based on common problems is usually liberating. Some women have improved their marriages, divorced, returned to unfinished dissertations or college, and the like. Others—when faced with hostility outside the primary group—have left the group and returned to the traditional role. For those who remain, the group provides a cushion against the force of society's defining their behavior as deviant. Many group members even move from improving their personal condition to social action (organized protests, political lobbying, and so forth). Brodsky's study demonstrates the force that a primary group can have in mitigating social control.

types of formal organization according to this criterion: the coercive organization, the utilitarian organization, and the voluntary association (Etzioni 1961).

COERCIVE ORGANIZATIONS   Coercive organizations, as the term suggests, are organizations in which recruits have no choice about being members. A prison is a good example of a coercive organization. Other examples are the armed forces when a draft has been instituted and schools for most persons under the age of sixteen.

UTILITARIAN ORGANIZATIONS   Utilitarian organizations are organizations that provide some necessary practical benefit (hence the term *utilitarian*). Government departments and private enterprises are prime examples. People join these groups and conform to their rules because they need the money they pay in order to live.

VOLUNTARY ASSOCIATIONS Voluntary associations appeal to the recruits' good feelings or self-interests. Examples of voluntary associations include fan clubs, the

Ku Klux Klan, the PTA, and fraternities and sororities. These organizations vary in size from the handful of people in a neighborhood bridge club to the hundreds of thousands on the rolls of the Democratic party. Voluntary associations are most prominent at the community level—somewhere between the family and the "cold, cruel world." One student of communities has found fourteen different types of voluntary associations (see Table 5.1).

Voluntary associations are established to serve some particular interest of their members—that's why the members belong. The interest may be in playing poker, in aiding starving children overseas, or in changing local policy. The Rogers Park Community Council (RPCC) in Chicago, for example, was formed in 1962 when a group of homemakers and others decided to oppose developers who wanted to build high-rise apartment buildings on the neighborhood's beachfront. To awaken the city leaders to their demands—and to their power—the RPCC mobilized people in the community to send tiny bags of sand each day to Chicago's mayor, Richard Daley. Their action forced the city's politicians to guarantee the preservation of the beach. As a result, the RPCC has become a permanent watchdog and pressure group in the community's interests.

Americans in particular are great initiators and joiners of voluntary associations, and this tendency so impressed Alexis de Tocqueville (1805–1859), an early visitor to the United States, that he remarked in his classic work *Democracy in America* (1969 [1835]): "In every case, at the head of any new undertaking, where in France you would find the government or in England some territorial magnate, in the United States you are sure to find an association" (p. 513). From Tocqueville and later writers, the picture emerges of a nation filled with independent groups standing as collective forces for every conceivable interest. It is an exciting picture, and Tocqueville, for one, believed that these groups acted as the greatest possible defense of democracy because as long as they existed no tyrannical ruler could gain control of the nation.

Yet we must also be aware of the fact that the various voluntary groups are not equal in their power and may have little influence in comparison with government departments and large corporations. For example, the "independent Democrats" in Chicago's neighborhoods have, in the past, rarely triumphed over the organized "machine," and reform-oriented health-care groups have had little impact on policy compared to the American Medical Association. You might take a close look at the voluntary associations in your community and think about the power relations that really determine their effectiveness for you and the community. For example, you might consider the often limited funds of community groups compared with those of city governments, political parties, or real estate developers; the lack of time that can be invested by community workers who have other commitments, compared with their opponents who earn their living at these activities; and the fact that they are amateurs at what they are doing while the opposition is composed of professionals (see Helfgot 1974).

Authority and Compliance in Formal Organizations

In the several social groups to which we belong, we usually find people who issue

Table 5.1 Voluntary Community Associations

Type	Example
Community organization groups	Community Chest
Cultural groups	Drama groups
Economic groups	Chamber of Commerce
Education groups	PTA
Fraternal groups	Clubs and lodges
Groups for children and youth	Police Athletic League; gangs
Health groups	Community clinics
Housing groups	Homeowners' (or renters') associations
Intergroup relations groups	Ethnic clubs
Planning groups	Community councils
Political groups	Local party headquarters
Recreation groups	Neighborhood ball teams
Religious groups	Churches and synagogues
Welfare groups	Charities

SOURCE: *Ronald I. Warren,* The Community in America *(Chicago: Rand McNally, 1963, pp. 188–89).*

orders that we must obey. Our parents require us to attend boring family affairs or do household chores, politicians pass laws requiring us to pay taxes, and bosses give us certain jobs to do. When teachers assign papers, or the police shout "Halt!" we generally just do what is required of us. But why? How can we explain our obedience in the vast majority of cases?

Sociologists distinguish two bases for obedience: *power* and *authority.* **Power,** in a social relationship, is a general term referring to our ability to secure another's obedience. It can come from any source— a gun, a bribe, intimidation, control over a grade or over hiring and firing. We associate it with such words as *force* and *coercion.* **Authority,** on the other hand, is concerned with *legitimacy*—legal, moral,

religious, or whatever—to command behavior. It is not the same as raw power.

The distinction between power and authority can be seen in the abortion issue. Antiabortionists often defend their position on the basis of "the right to life." Obviously, the fetus has no power to prevent an abortion; but antiabortionists claim that the fetus's right to life, as a human being, rests on certain moral or religious principles. They thus claim the *authority* to act for the fetus and prevent abortion. However, they do not now have the *power* they need to do that.

The above example also illustrates a very important attribute of authority; namely, that it resides in the person who obeys, not the person who commands or has power. *Someone can have authority*

Is power or authority motivating these chain-gang prisoners to obey? Though the two often appear together, power is likely all the prisoners recognize. Is that a failure of the prisoners or the system?

only if another person recognizes it. Many people respond to the antiabortionists by saying, "Your morality and religion are not my morality and religion, so I do not recognize your authority." We recognize the clergy's right to tell us to say ten "Hail Marys" or to eat unleavened bread; we recognize the state's right to demand our service in the army or to require us to pay taxes. But without our recognition neither the church nor the state would have any authority over us. The state can still *force* our compliance (and authority and force often appear together), but we have learned that force alone cannot secure social control. Real social control resides in our own self-enforcement, or recognition of authority. Only by distinguishing between power and authority can we appreciate the *individual's* role in his or her obedience in groups. We must now try to understand the basis for the authority we give.

Max Weber (1946 [1927]) defined three types of authority, each with a different basis: *traditional, charismatic,* and *rational/legal authority* (see Table 5.2).

Table 5.2 Types of Authority

Type of Authority	Decisions Based on Answer to	Justification	Examples	Individual Examples
Traditional	What was done in the past?	Tradition	Family; religion	Parents; clergy
Charismatic	What does the leader say?	The leader's special gifts	Social movements; revolutions	Jesus; Mao; Gandhi; Martin Luther King
Rational/legal	What rules apply?	Rules	Government; businesses; science	Elected officials; doctors; "experts"

TRADITIONAL AUTHORITY Under systems of **traditional authority,** power is justified on the basis of its conforming to the way things have always been done. Although this basis is becoming less and less important to Americans, we still encounter it in the authority we give to the pope and to our grandparents, for instance. Even so, their authority has steadily declined, as indicated by the refusal of many American Catholics to accept the pope's restrictions on birth control and by our generally shabby treatment of the elderly. Traditional authority still moves us to fulfill family and holiday obligations and religious rituals, but we are challenging it in certain other areas. For instance, a husband's traditional authority over his wife's activities (working, driving, going out) has been breaking down. Changes in technology have also made traditional authority a problem in the work world: as a factory manager, would you continue with an inefficient production method just because your company had always done things that way? Or would you base your decision on another basis, one that considers levels of production, costs, and so on?

CHARISMATIC AUTHORITY In organization systems based on **charismatic authority,** legitimacy derives from the special personal qualities of an individual. *Charisma* literally means a "gift of grace," and charmismatic authority is based on that gift (as we see it). We consider the actions of charismatic individuals legitimate because of the sheer strength of their personalities. Hitler was a charismatic leader, as were Gandhi, Martin Luther King, Mao Tse-tung, Julius Caesar, Joan of Arc, and Malcolm X. (These examples might also indicate something about the charismatic leader—all of them, except Mao, met violent deaths.) Some charismatic leaders violate established norms and traditions, as these examples suggest; others, such as Winston Churchill and John F. Kennedy, remain within the general confines of the established order.

Because charismatic authority rests on the personal qualities of a single individual, and not on social norms, it threatens the world of routine. Otherwise conservative individuals have cast away their homes, jobs, and families to follow charismatic religious leaders. But by its nature, charismatic authority, at least in its original form, is short-lived. The charismatic leader can be silenced and, in any case, must eventually die, and the power structure he or she has built usually collapses. Nazi Germany surrendered and was partitioned after Hitler's death, for example, and King's Southern Christian Leadership Conference lost a good deal of its clout after his death.

If charismatic authority is going to survive in some form, it must be regulated somehow; for, since it is based on someone's personal qualities, it is essentially nontransferable. Weber (1946 [1922], p. 297) called this regulation the "routinization of charisma." Thus the Apostles routinized Jesus's authority, and Julius Caesar and Mao were succeeded by committees. The authority that belonged to a single individual is made the community's property, often in the form of social norms for living. So from Caesar came caesarism, from Christ came Christianity, and from Mao came Maoism. Routinization, however, also changes the basis of the authority. It can become traditional, shift from a nonrational basis to that of the third type of authority (rational/legal), or do both.

RATIONAL/LEGAL AUTHORITY **Rational/ legal authority** is based on rules. Under this type of authority, we obey people not because of their personal qualities or because they represent tradition, but because we recognize the legitimacy of the position they hold and because they follow the rules of conduct prescribed by that position. These rules may be set forth in the group's bylaws, in the laws of government, or in a constitution. We follow the rules and regulations because we believe in their rationality.

Rational/legal authority is the predominant type in the formal organization, but authority in any group is seldom just a single type. In the formal organization, procedures may be followed simply because that has always been the tradition of the company, or employees may work better for certain company officials because of their charisma. Sometimes, then, all three kinds of authority appear in the same situation. The trend in modern society, however, is toward rational/legal authority. And this type of authority underlies the hallmark of the modern formal organization—the *bureaucracy.*

Bureaucracy

A central characteristic of many formal organizations is that they are **bureaucratic**— that is, they operate according to defined rules and their authority structure is hierarchical and centralized.

WEBER'S ANALYSIS OF BUREAUCRACY The modern sociological understanding of bureaucracy, like that of types of authority, derives primarily from the writings of Max Weber (1946 [1922], pp. 196–244). Weber did not go around to all bureaucracies, jot down every aspect of their functioning, and call that massive collection of facts "bureaucracy." Instead, he tried to ferret out the essential features of this form of organization and then see how these features distinguished a bureaucracy from other organizational forms. He called this the "ideal type" of bureaucracy. The term may be unfamiliar but, in fact, you have used ideal types, even before you heard of Max Weber, when you used such concepts as "capitalism" and "democracy." As social scientists, we want to use our ideal types for analyzing behavior, although we should bear in mind that real bureaucracies (or capitalisms or democracies) will not conform completely to their ideal type.

Weber's ideal type of modern bureaucracy has five basic components. First, the activities that must be performed regularly to carry out the organization's task, be it building cars, distributing welfare checks, or even selling stolen merchandise, are *given out as permanent and official duties.* These duties are organized by formal rules and define the various roles in the organization—that is, individuals are held responsible for the activities assigned to their position and, of course, are thereby subject to sanctions, like firing, if they do not complete them satisfactorily. Through identification with the position, the individual learns to feel responsible for doing a good job (in other words, self-enforcement). In addition, from performing the same task over and over, the individual usually becomes good at it. This tendency and the dividing up of work jurisdictions has helped to create "specialists" for every task, which has become a distinctive feature of modern society. When my wife and I moved to Chicago, for example, we found an internist, neurologist, gynecologist, and endocrinologist easier to locate than a good general practitioner.

Bureaucratic organization's second characteristic is that it is *hierarchical;* in other words, "each lower office is under the control and supervision of a higher one" (Weber 1947 [1925], p. 331). That is, each official has the authority to issue orders to everybody under her or his supervision, but, at the same time, officials are also responsible for all the work done (or not done) in the offices they control. Thus, if

a worker in your department does something wrong, not only are you likely to reprimand the person but you're likely to be reprimanded as his or her supervisor as well. This hierarchical order of command can also be extended ridiculously, as pointed out in a television commercial for an air freight company. The commercial begins with a boss handing a package to an officer and snapping: "If this package isn't in Peoria by tomorrow morning, you're fired." The officer takes it to a lower official and says the same thing; the lower official gives it to his secretary and threatens her, and the secretary does the same to a clerk. Finally, the clerk takes the package to the freight company, and everybody's job is saved. The irony is that only the lowly clerk has the ability to get the job done—but after all, it was his specialty. (It is important to realize, however, that orders have to be consonant with organizational goals. Your instructor, for example, has the authority to "order" you to turn in your assignments but not to bring her or him a cup of coffee everyday). Figure 5.1 shows a hierarchical organization structure—the government bureaucracy for the Democratic People's Republic of (North) Korea. The chart shows that even the holders of the government's top offices are, in theory, accountable for their actions to everybody else.

Third, bureaucracies have a *system of definite but general norms* that are meant to be applied to *all* cases. These norms might, for example, specify filing papers in alphabetical order, counting money in a specific manner, not using company funds for illegal activities (like bribing government officials), or using only top-quality building material in construction. Bureaucratic norms are intended to assure that tasks will be done in a somewhat uniform way and that the number of organizational

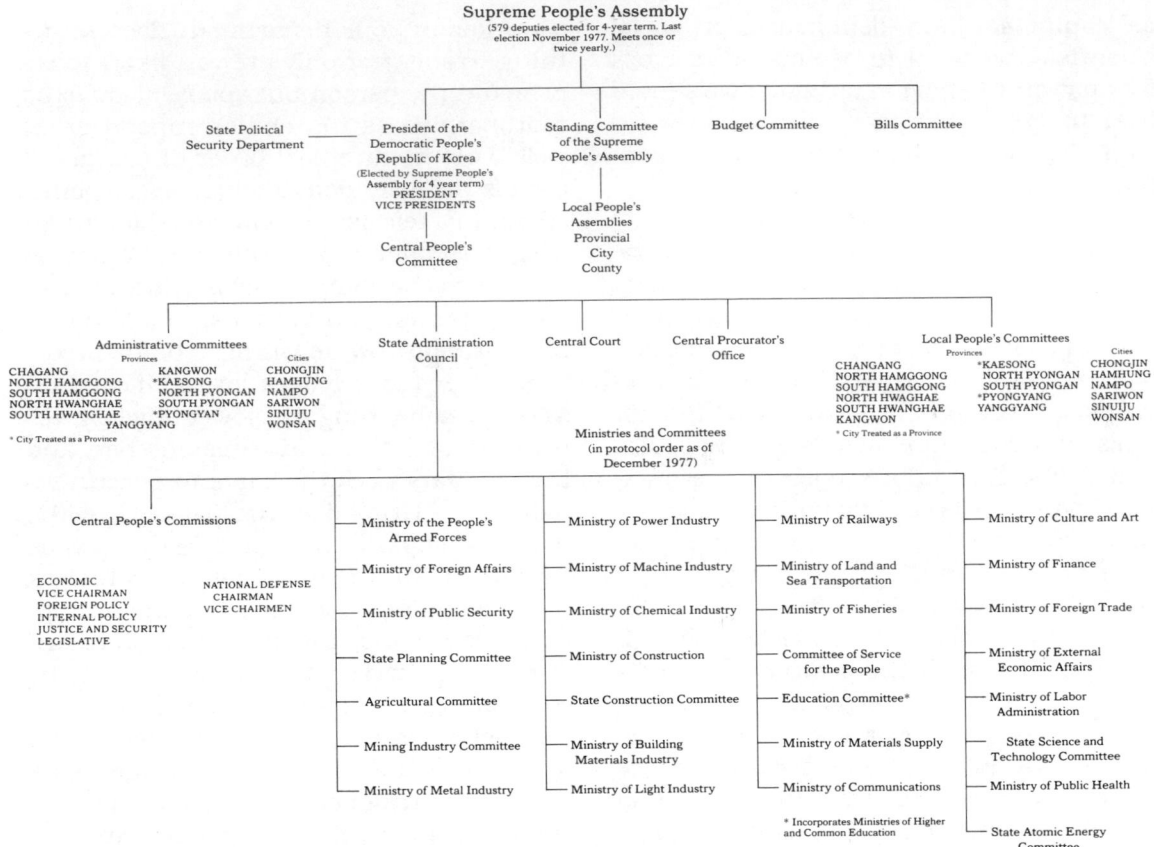

Figure 5.1 Structure of the Government of the Democratic People's Republic of Korea

SOURCE: *U.S. Central Intelligence Agency (Washington, DC: Document Expediting (DOCEX) Project, 1978).*

decisions made on the basis of personal feelings and interests will be minimal. The court system is a case in point. Although there are prejudiced decisions to be sure, a recent study of the cases of 1,522 juvenile offenders in a southeastern city showed that legal factors played a far more important role than prejudice in determining their outcome (Thomas and Cage 1977). The judges had to act in conformance with the rules of law. (But we also saw that

norms always leave some room for interpretation, so that even when followed in spirit there will usually be some deviation in practice.)

The fourth characteristic of bureaucracy is that officials are expected to discharge their duties *formally and impersonally.* This is one of the most important norms of bureaucratic organization. Like most people, you have probably complained about how some bureaucrat refused to treat you like a person. This impersonality *may* indeed hurt the quality of interaction in a society, but it also prevents officials from allowing their personal feelings to interfere with rational group norms. It assures that officials will not be easy or tough on particular customers on the basis of whether or not they like them or because the customer is black, female, Polish, or a relative.

The fifth characteristic of bureaucracy is closely related to the fourth: relations within the organization are to be conducted in the same formal and impersonal way as they are with outsiders. Emphasis is placed on technical expertise and efficiency, and these qualities are the basis of employment and movement of employees up the organizational ladder. Racial, religious, sexual, and other forms of discrimination are not allowed as criteria of selection for official posts, not because they are incompatible with social values but because they have nothing to do with technical ability.

BUREAUCRACY IN MODERN SOCIETY
How well does Weber's model mirror the contemporary reality of bureaucracy? Your experience with bureaucratic organization may have seemed quite negative—or at least aggravating. We are more likely to notice "bureaucratic bungling" and "bureaucratic red tape" than efficiency. And contemporary sociologists have shown how some types of inefficiency are built into the structure of bureaucracy. For example, two recent sociological studies (Heydebrand 1977; Goldman and Van Houten 1977) have demonstrated how officials at the top of organizational hierarchies may prevent the successful implementation of more efficient methods that threaten their own control within the organization.

But perhaps we complain so much about the bunglings of bureaucracy precisely because we expect it to be so efficient, because ordinarily bureaucracy, as Weber suggested, *is* more efficient than other forms of organizational structure. Charles Perrow (1979) even believes that other problems associated with bureaucracy—lack of individuality or creativity, concentration of power, and so on—as well as inefficiency are more the result of incomplete bureaucratization (e.g., people use the rules for personal power) than bureaucracy itself. In any case, without bureaucratic organization, how could we possibly coordinate the action of tens of thousands of people in the army, government, or university, to name just three examples?

One important aspect of contemporary bureaucracy that Weber did not foresee has been the emergence of primary groups in bureaucratic settings and the significance of these primary relations in determining the way bureaucratic organizations function. The image that Weber's model conjures up of each official being simply a functionary, following organizational rules in a machinelike manner, is a misleading one, as many social scientists have noted. Organizational employees have even developed their own rules outside of, and sometimes even contrary to, the bureaucratic structure.

An important series of field experiments that demonstrated the significance of primary groups in formal organizations was conducted by Fritz J. Roethlisberger and William J. Dickson (1939) at the Western Electric Company in the 1930s. In the Bank Wiring Room, for instance, where the workers were assigned to wire circuit boards and were paid according to the number of boards they wired, the researchers found

In theory, decision-making in bureaucracy is based on criteria of efficiency. But in practice officials may place their own interests above those of the organization and block changes that threaten their power.

that, contrary to expectation, the workers did not try to produce as many pieces as they possibly could. Instead, they developed a set of unofficial group norms that restricted output. The norms included a standard of what constituted a fair day's work, and work mates who did less work were sanctioned because they were, in effect, freeloading on the group's rate. And those who produced too much were also sanctioned since their higher productivity might encourage management to lower the piece rate for everyone.

With the exception of missing the significance of primary groups in secondary

settings, Weber's model of bureaucracy remains relatively accurate. In general, research continues to demonstrate its usefulness for understanding this dimension of formal organizations (see, for example, Mansfield 1973).

THE TRANSFORMATION OF GROUP RELATIONS

Since the birth of sociology as a special field of study in the nineteenth century, sociologists have remarked on the transformation occurring in Western society from predominantly primary group relationships to the predominantly secondary group relationships we associate with the urban, industrial order of modern society. Indeed, a central reason sociology arose at all as a separate discipline was to explain this and related changes. Sociologists have analyzed this transformation in various ways. The analysis we will consider here is that of the German social philosopher Ferdinand Toennies (1855–1936). After looking at his description, we will turn to the implications of this transformation for the individual and the nature of social control.

Gemeinschaft and Gesellschaft

Toennies (1957 [1887]) characterized the changes he saw happening around him in the late nineteenth century as a movement from a *gemeinschaft* ("community") type of society to a *gesellschaft* ("association") type. He defined a **gemeinschaft** type of society as a tightly knit community built around the principle of traditional authority. Gemeinschaft social relations are direct, face-to-face, and enduring—that is, they are predominantly those of the primary group. There is a sense of unity and social solidarity within the gemeinschaft society, and a feeling of loyalty to the group rather than individualism. "The theory of gemeinschaft," according to Toennies, "starts from the assumption of perfect unity of human wills" (1957 [1887], p. 37). Warmth and love permeate the atmosphere of the gemeinschaft, and this atmosphere nurtures strong feelings of compassion toward the underprivileged: "an instinctive and naive tenderness of the strong for the

weak, a desire to aid and protect" (p. 41). In addition, all of the members of the gemeinschaft provide mutual support for one another, so that personal insecurities are rare.

In a **gesellschaft** type of society, by contrast, calculation replaces custom. The fundamental principle is not that of the "natural will" but that of the "rational will"—the spirit of calculation. Individualism is valued over the group, and relationships among members of the gesellschaft are impersonal and superficial compared to those of the gemeinschaft. (See Table 5.3 for a summary of the characteristics of these two types of societies.)

The portrait Toennies draws of these two types of societies certainly makes the gemeinschaft the more attractive on first glance. But how accurate a picture of preindustrial village life is it? The evidence shows that Toennies ignored the brutality, ignorance, discrimination, and poverty that are often found in gemeinschaft societies. For instance, most of the black slaves brought to America were sold into slavery by other blacks; village officials on Java have sold their villages to plantation owners; the Kapauku Papuans, a New Guinea tribe, are more competitive than members of any modern capitalist nation; and the Yanomamo tribe is marked by a level of violence and distrust that members of few modern societies can possibly imagine. Toennies, displeased with the new urban and industrial Europe as it was developing, apparently romanticized the gemeinschaft much like the anthropologists Jessie Bernard (1973) describes:

When anthropologists looked at a community, they saw its culture as "a cup of life." Although it may have

Table 5.3 Gemeinschaft and Gesellschaft

Gemeinschaft	Gesellschaft
Traditional authority	Rational/legal authority
Closely knit groups	More impersonal
Primary relations	Secondary relations
Group needs dominate	Individual needs dominate
Past-oriented	Present- and future-oriented
Tradition determines right	Rationality—what "works"—determines right
Peopie interact on the basis of ascribed characteristics, tied to blood, religion, land, ethnicity, etc.	People interact on the basis of achieved characteristics, within particular social roles
Founded on ties of blood and traditional ties to the same territory	Founded on specific interests or purposes

been unintentional, they tended to project a kind of romanticism in their picture. When sociologists looked at the same people, they saw high infant mortality rates, disease and illness, malnutrition, poverty, exploitation, low life expectancy, and inefficiency in food production. They did not see a beautiful design . . . but hovels, poor tools, and low-yield strains of seeds. (p. 166)

What she calls "the mystique of gemeinschaft" does not go away. We see it whenever we turn on the television set and hear some commercial telling us about a product's "old-time" or "country" flavor.

If Toennies exaggerated the virtues of the gemeinschaft society, there arc also some limits to the extent to which ours has become a gesellschaft society. Primary groups such as families, friendship groups, and gangs still thrive. And, as we have seen, primary groups are also very evi-

dent, although not officially recognized, in many secondary settings. Nevertheless, the general trend delineated by Toennies is undeniable. Where does this increasing role played in our lives by large formal organizations leave the individual?

Groups and the Individual

As societies get larger, the impact that an individual acting alone can have becomes slight. (You would naturally expect 1 person out of 2,000 to matter more than 1 in 200,000,000.) This is especially true in the area of politics. For example, does writing to your representatives in Congress influence their actions? What changes can you bring about as an individual with a threat not to vote for a candidate unless she or he changes a position or with a $15 campaign contribution for a candidate? Perhaps more important, what impact do you have on who the opposing candidates are in the first place? If we don't have much impact, who does?

Students of politics used to look for an answer to this question in formal government structures. Political scientists and political sociologists today, however, see the answer in nongovernmental interest groups such as the oil companies, labor unions, and the National Rifle Association, to name only a few. These private, and often conflicting, interest groups influence the formal leaders, whose task is to respond to the pressure. One student of government sums up the relationship between government and interest groups in this way: "The legislature referees the group struggle, ratifies the victories of the successful coalitions, and records the terms of the surrenders, compromises, and conquests in the form of statutes" (Latham 1952, p. 35).

The political power of interest groups stems from their capacity to organize individuals and resources for a common cause. Otherwise powerless community members have formed organizations to stop high-rise development or the construction of expressways through their neighborhoods. Organizations like the National Association for the Advancement of Colored People (NAACP) and the National Organization of Women (NOW) have also given previously powerless people clout. But organization also helps the powerful retain their power. With their accumulated wealth, oil companies, for example, buy advertisements and affect the actions and opinions of millions of people. Furthermore, organizations can mobilize large numbers of votes. The National Rifle Association keeps a computerized file on all public officials, detailing their stances on gun control. Because its members vote ac-cording to this information, the NRA has maintained a strong influence on American politics. We may also believe in the legitimacy of these organizations and see them as far better equipped to advance our ends than we would be as individuals acting alone. All of this is not to say that we as individuals can have no effect on society but that, increasingly, the effects we are likely to have will tend to be as members of groups.

SOCIAL ORGANIZATION ON A WORLD SCALE

So far we've discussed groups and social organizations on the society level. But social organization also exists on a world scale. Just as individuals in a single society are linked together, there are links between individuals of different societies and between entire nations. Some linkage has always been evident, but only in recent years have we been able to talk about an "international society." For one thing, it is only recently that the majority of countries in the world have acknowledged each others' rights as nations. In the past, there were councils of European nations, alliances in the Far East, and so on. But the first real attempt to gather even all the uncolonized countries under a single structure did not come until after the First World War, when the League of Nations was established (1919). The League failed, but the attempt laid the foundation for the United Nations—whose membership continues to grow.

More than that, technological revolutions in the areas of communication and transportation have increased interactions among peoples of the world. These inter-

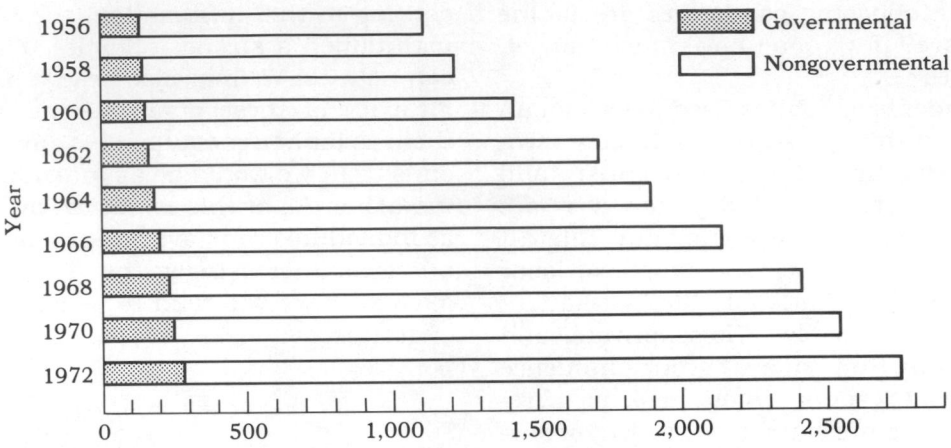

Figure 5.2 Growth of International Organizations, 1956–1972

SOURCE: Yearbook of International Organizations *(Brussels: Union of International Associations, 1973, p. 879).*

national interactions have given rise to groups on an international scale (see Figure 5.2). We have become fairly familiar with some international organizations over the years, largely because of their obvious impact on our lives. There are, for instance, the North Atlantic Treaty Organization (NATO) and the Warsaw Treaty Organization in Europe, grouping countries along ideological lines. There are regional organizations, including the Organization of American States (OAS), the Organization of African Unity (OAU), and the Association of Southeast Asian Nations (ASEAN). The Organization of Petroleum Exporting Countries (OPEC), based on economic ties, has become a worldwide force in recent years. By the year 2000, there may be as many as 1,215 international governmental organizations and up to 24,000 global nongovernmental organizations.

Bases of International Group Formation

As with groups within a single society, international organizations develop around the common interests of the participants. For example, the United States and most Western European nations banded together to form NATO (North Atlantic Treaty Organization) because of their common interest in defense against Communist countries. And the Communist countries of Eastern Europe banded together with the Soviet Union through the Warsaw Pact to defend themselves against NATO. However, some international groups are composed of segments (groups or individuals) of the nations involved. For instance, Socialist parties from all over the world hold joint conferences annually. Similarly, law-enforcement agencies have ties to Interpol, the international police organization.

The U.N. was founded in 1945 so that all nations could cooperate in the quest for world peace. . . .

OPEC was formed in 1960 to help oil producers secure their economic interests in competition with the West's; but its success was limited until 1973, when political events mobilized its members to take joint action.

The major bases on which international groups have formed are geographical ties; ties of heritage (racial, religious, and other); economic ties (trade, economic and technical aid, multinational corporate links, and tourism); and ideological bonds. The following discussion examines how groups emerge when these ties are energized by the nations' mutual interests.

Geographical Ties

Regional interests have often provided the basis for international groups. For instance, the Organization of African Unity (OAU) was formed when the increasing number of new countries in Africa recognized how little power they had compared with that of other nations. They felt that by presenting the world with an all-Africa position on certain issues—such as the Mideast, South Africa, and foreign aid—they would have greater clout than they each could muster individually. The European Economic Community (EEC), another geographical group, hopes to create a united Europe. Many of its programs involve trade and tariffs; but it has also made movement across member nations' borders easier, has created an investment bank for its members, and eventually hopes to standardize social security and wage rates in Europe. In 1979, the citizens of member states elected an all-European Congress.

Of course, conflict, as well as cooperation, occurs between neighboring nations. Israel and Syria, India and Pakistan, Vietnam and Cambodia, Iran and Iraq, China and the USSR, Somalia and Ethiopia—all "next-door neighbors"—have recently been at war with each other. Geographical closeness can often produce disputes, and closeness can intensify the differences between neighbors.

Ties of Heritage

When Irish Americans send funds to the IRA (Irish Republican Army), or when the entire Arab League supports Palestinian Arabs' shooting war with Israel, another basis of group formation is involved—common heritage. The historic English background, for instance, has been the primary basis of America's and Great Britain's special relationship. A common history as British colonies unites nations as diverse as Canada, Uganda, and India in the Commonwealth of Nations; the Catholic Church still commands worldwide allegiance; Jews unite behind Israel; and Islam draws Pakistan, Nigeria, Black Muslims in the United States, and others into the Arab cause.

Economic Ties

Often the relationships between countries have an economic basis, and international trade has often been the major source of contact and interaction between them. More than ever before, nations today are interdependent upon each other—for the energy we burn, for the food we live on, for the advanced technology we use, and even for the culture and entertainment that help fill our days.

Economic power has also been a source of international clout, and the hope of increasing it has caused nations—and cities—to band together. During the Middle Ages, for example, a number of cities from all parts of Europe united into the Hanseatic League. Their main interests of commerce and trade had been hampered by the restrictions of feudal kingdoms. Thus united, the cities pressed for and won independence from their national states. Subsequently, they became extremely powerful, forcing economic concessions from the kings and maintaining their own armies. More recently, we have the example of OPEC, which caused panic in the major industrialized nations when the member states agreed to fix prices and regulate the flow of crude oil to the United States, Western Europe, and Japan.

Ideological Bonds

You have probably read about the importance of ideology in shaping world history. Knights, royalty, and noblemen from all over Catholic Europe, for example, joined in the Crusades to capture the Holy Land during the Middle Ages. Today, ideology is important as a basis for both bringing nations together and driving them apart. Communist and capitalist nations now often face one another like Democrats and Republicans, each side with its own interests to defend. Of course, the composition of these allegiances often changes. In fact, the social organization of Europe—which is based on that opposition between capitalism and communism—has been threatened by the possibility of popularly elected communist governments in traditionally capitalist countries (particularly France and Italy). The growth in East Europe of Eurocommunism—the philosophy that each European Communist party should take positions on the basis of its own country's needs, rather than just follow Moscow's line—has caused similar changes.

A final example of nations joining together around a common ideology is the recent alliance of third world nations. Third world countries are characterized by poverty, powerlessness, and, generally, a nonwhite population; most were once colonies of European powers (Britan, France, Portugal, Spain, Holland, Belgium, and Italy). Few third world nations have industrialized to any significant extent, and, as a result, they have experienced foreign exploitation of their natural resources. In organizing as a group, they have promoted the position that, because of previous oppression, they are entitled to special economic and other aid from industrialized nations. They thereby hope to hold their own against the power of these industrialized nations. In the United Nations and at international conferences, for example, they have frequently presented the West with a united front, calling for aid and political actions such as pressuring South Africa to change its policices.

The term *third world* refers to the fact that these countries have not aligned themselves with either the capitalist West (the first world) or the Communist bloc (the second world). Thus a major weapon in their arsenal seems to be their ability to threaten both the United States and the Soviet Union with becoming allies of the other side. This new group should play an increasingly important world role in the coming years.

World Social Organization in the Future

The emergence of the third world organization demonstrates that the structure of global society does not stay the same. Nations in other categories may come to recognize their common interests and evolve into organized groups. Alliances among nations are continually dissolving and reforming with new participants.

Global problems are also beginning to spark countries to unite to combat them. We can observe international cooperation to fight ecological threats; in managing dwindling natural resources (especially among industrialized nations); in controlling rising populations (especially in poor nations); in producing more food; in stopping desertification (the spread of deserts); and in saving endangered wildlife.

Recently, an international commission headed by former West German Chancellor Willy Brandt recommended that all nations cooperate to implement emergency measures "to avert impending catastrophe" (Righter 1980). The emergency measures have four main objectives: promoting an efficient world food program; reaching agreements on energy supplies, conservation, and prices; initiating a massive transfer of money and other aid from the developed to the developing world; and reforming the international monetary system. The commission calls on the industrialized nations to spend approximately $5.1 billion each year, which is only 3 percent of the money spent on armaments in 1975.

The fight against international terrorism has also been the object of international cooperation in recent years. Almost no nations will give the terrorists refuge, but there is still resentment to the type of commando rescue raids staged by Israel in Uganda and West Germany in Somalia.

Of course, there are more positive reasons for global social organization. Many nations are jointly exploring outer space, the sea, and the continent of Antarctica. As part of that cooperation, they have taken steps to assure that the mineral and other riches they find will not be held by single countries. Finally, increasing affluence has enabled many individuals to visit foreign countries as tourists, and as tourism becomes more widespread, it can emerge as another basis for global organization.

SUMMARY

In looking at social organization, we have reached a new level of analysis from that of Chapters 1 through 4, which focused on the individual. More particularly, in this chapter, we looked at the nature of, and relations among, social groups—collections of people who share a common identity and interact with one another in a patterned way.

Groups differ from aggregates—a number of people in the same place at the same time—and from social categories—people who share a single trait. Groups, in the sociological sense, must have patterned interaction among their members and be conscious of themselves as a group.

Groups can be classified in a number of ways. Among the most important types of groups are in-groups and out-groups, interest groups (groups formed for the purpose of advancing their interests, usually political, in competition with other groups), reference groups (groups by which we measure our social standing), primary groups (groups in which members interact on a face-to-face basis) and secondary groups (groups whose members interact on a relatively impersonal basis).

The most powerful type of group in modern society is the formal organization—a collection of interrelated groups formed to accomplish specific purposes and operating according to an explicit set of rules. Formal organizations can be coercive, utilitarian, or voluntary.

In our examination of formal organizations we concentrated on two related subjects—the basis of our compliance in them and their generally bureaucratic structure. Following Max Weber, we distinguished power—the ability to force another to obey—from authority, which is the right to command. Authority can be based on past ways (traditional), legal rules (rational/legal), or the special qualities of an individual (charismatic authority), or, more usually, on some combination of the three. Rational/legal authority is the predominant type in formal organizations, and it provides the underpinnings for bureaucracy. According to Weber, the ideal type of bureaucracy has five characteristics: regularly performed tasks are considered permanent and official duties; the structure is hierarchical; a system of definite norms is applied to all cases; duties are discharged formally and impersonally; and hiring and promotion are also formal and impersonal. In general, there has been a trend in modern society from primary group relationships to relationships characteristic of bureaucratic formal organizations.

Social organization also exists among nations. International groups are formed on the basis of some common interest—geographical ties, ties of heritage, economic ties, and political ideology. Like groups within a given society, such international groups are subject to change.

Key Terms

social organization (p. 151)
group (p. 151)
aggregate (p. 151)
social category (p. 152)
interest group (p. 156)
reference group (p. 157)
primary group (p. 157)
secondary group (p. 157)
formal organization (p. 157)
power (p. 161)
authority (p. 161)
traditional authority (p. 163)
charismatic authority (p. 163)
rational/legal authority (p. 164)
bureaucratic organization (p. 164)
gemeinschaft (p. 169)
gesellschaft (p. 169)

Review and Discussion Questions

1. What large groups and organizations do you think make significant contributions to our society? What personal interests do they also serve? Could the same tasks be accomplished if the individual interests were not served? How do such organizations affect your life?
2. What are some of your in-groups and out-groups? How did you become an in-group member, and what prevents you from becoming an out-group member? And how do these groups set up boundaries to keep nonmembers out?
3. Although power and authority generally go together in practice, we can separate the two conceptually. Think of persons or agencies whose commands you obey. How much of that obedience rests on the person or agent's authority? How much on power?
4. Think of a bureaucracy with which you have dealt. How does it conform to Weber's ideal type of bureaucracy? Did you encounter any informality? How did you feel about your encounter?
5. How have international organizations altered the nature of world relationships over

the last five years? What changes are likely to occur in the next decade?

For Further Study

SOCIAL ORGANIZATION Because the study of social organization requires us to grasp the abstraction that bridges the individual and group spheres, it is sometimes too easy to restrict our study to such obvious organizations as bureaucracies and the like. A significant departure from this view is presented in Charles Perrow, *Complex Organizations* (Glenview, IL: Scott, Foresman, 1979). One of the first sociological essays to recognize the interaction between individual and group was Georg Simmel's "The Web of Group Affiliations," which you can find in Simmel, *Conflict and The Web of Group Affiliations* (New York: Free Press, 1955). With the deeper understanding of social organization that these books give you, you might want to look at Vincente Navarro, *Medicine under Capitalism* (New York: Prodist, 1977), a Marxist interpretation of health care that analyzes the health care system as an aspect of social organization.

FORMAL ORGANIZATIONS To gain a more detailed understanding of these concepts, a good place to start is with Max Weber's discussion of bureaucracy in *From Max Weber: Essays in Sociology* (New York: Oxford University Press, 1946, Chap. 8) and with Peter M. Blau's *Bureaucracy in Modern Society* (New York: Random House, 1956). Blau also conducted an excellent study of two particular bureaucracies in *Dynamics of Bureaucracy* (Chicago: University of Chicago Press, 1963). For a good reader, see: Eugene Kamenka and Martin Krygier, eds., *Bureaucracy* (New York: St. Martin's, 1979).

COMMUNITY Community can mean anything from "neighborhood" to what Toennies described as gemeinschaft. Jessie Bernard has examined all the major understandings of community, pointing out their contradictions and fallacies, in *The Sociology of Community* (Glenview, IL: Scott, Foresman, 1973). Of the several studies of urban communities, perhaps the best is Herbert J. Gans, *The Urban Villagers* (New York: Free Press, 1962). This is a study of Boston's West End just before it was demolished in urban renewal. E. Digby Baltzell, ed., *The Search for Community in Modern America* (New York: Harper & Row, 1968) is a short collection of articles on community. Finally, there are several good studies of "intentional communities"—communes and the like. For a discussion of the older communes (e.g., Oneida), see William M. Kephart, *Extraordinary Groups: The Sociology of Unconventional Life-Styles* (New York: St. Martin's, 1976). For an important survey of the contemporary commune experience, see Rosabeth Moss Kanter *Commitment and Community* (Cambridge, MA: Harvard University Press, 1972).

CHAPTER SIX

Social Institutions

I n order to survive, all societies, no matter what size, must carry out such tasks as production of food, regulation of sexual behavior, and education. And societies develop persistent patterns for doing these necessary tasks, complete with norms governing the relevant activities and established roles for their performance. Sociologists call these persisting patterns of expected behavior, which are built around enduring social needs, **social institutions.** The family, for example, is the social institution that regulates sexual behavior and serves the reproductive needs of society, and the economy is the social institution that serves the need for production of food and other commodities. Other prominent social institutions include the military, religion, education, and politics. Unlike social groups, then, institutions are not collections of people; rather, they are norms and roles, well established (or *institutionalized*) to serve enduring needs.

THE NATURE OF SOCIAL INSTITUTIONS

Social institutions provide a context for almost everything we do. We grow up in a family, probably have a religious identification, attend school, get married, spend years at an occupation in the "work world" or household, and live under a government we support by paying taxes and voting. In fact, we would be hard pressed to find many actions that do not take place within some institution. This context, like that of socialization discussed in Chapter 1, both enables us to live in society and controls us by limiting and organizing our behavior.

Social Institutions and Social Control

Social institutions enable us to survive because they provide regular patterns for fulfilling our needs. Without them, life would likely be quite haphazard and society would collapse. Be that as it may, when you were last at your job, you probably did not think, "Oh, yes, here I go serving society again!" More likely, you thought about your personal needs. For even at the individual level, we satisfy our needs through social institutions, which provide us with the economic, educational, and other rewards that keep us working. And usually we can only obtain these rewards through a social institution and not on our own.

But satisfying our needs through social institutions depends on our social control. Because fulfilling our needs appears to depend on our cooperation in social institutions, we are likely to believe that our own interests lie in preserving the status quo. Having a job, for instance, makes it less likely that we will rebel against the "system" because it occupies us for much of the day and gives us a stake in the system's survival (namely, our economic support).

That social institutions are important elements of social control does not mean, however, that they completely stifle conflict. Rather, they organize the conflict over the social needs they are designed to fulfill. Thus labor unions and management struggle in the economic institution for shares of the economic pie, and political parties vie for control over the reins of government. Social institutions keep these conflicts within certain boundaries, so that they rarely threaten the status quo. Louis M. Seagull (1977) observed this in the political institution when he compared the 1972 and 1976 American presidential elections. George McGovern's 1972 campaign, he says, threatened the nation's "dominant bourgeois values" of the "free" market system: "McGovern's proposal for an economic grant to every citizen, posed early in the campaign, violated the dominant ethos of the political culture which stressed competition for achievement. Similarly, the system of quotas for women, Blacks, and youth violated the same norm" (p. 91). Nixon's landslide victory over McGovern was a signal to all future candidates that challenging such basic norms in their campaigns would likely mean failure: "Thereafter the lesson for practical presidential politics became very clear. Serious candidates need to avoid proposals and appeals that are incompatible or inconsistent with the basic beliefs most Americans hold" (Seagull 1977, p. 91). The lesson was well

taken in 1976. None of the Democratic candidates seriously challenged the status quo, and Jimmy Carter moved out front by avoiding any specific issue positions, "instead striking symbolic appeals which resonated well with the religious character of the mainstream" (Seagull 1977, p. 92).

In short, because it is ordinarily *institutionalized*, political conflict is limited, and conflict kept within the political institution is not likely to pose a serious threat to the dominant interests in society.

Studying Social Institutions

As we have just seen, social institutions are not necessarily neutral in their consequences. Institutional norms are likely to benefit some people more than others. For example, family norms in many cultures place women and children in a subordinate position to men; our economic norms prescribe that executives are paid more than laborers; and our political norms discriminate against the young in terms of being elected to political office. When studying social institutions, then, we should keep the following three implications in mind:

First, being social, institutions are the product of human beings—they are not sacred. If people created them, people can certainly change them. Many people, however, tend to oppose any attempted change, and consider such attempts as an attack on the institution as a whole. For example, feminists who want equal pay for equal work are labeled "antifamily" or even "anti-God." If you want to observe this sacred treatment of a social institution, the next time you are with your parents (or co-workers or clergy), casually mention that you think we should change our economic system from a capitalist to socialist one. The answers you receive should indicate the extent to which people consider changing a major institution just "wrong."

Second, institutions are culture-bound—the particular form they take is tied to their sociocultural environment. We noticed this in Chapter 2, when we spoke about ethnocentrism. Most Americans profess a Judeo-Christian religion. This, however, does not mean that there is something wrong with all the Moslems in Egypt, or with the millions of pagans who live in the small villages of the third world.

Third, as elements of the same social structure, social institutions are linked to one another in many ways, and individuals and groups use the norms and values of one institution to support their position in another. A country going to war, for example, may claim to have "God on its side," thus enlisting the aid of the religious institution. Television programs portray the police, FBI agents, and politicians as heroes; and schools teach us to be patriotic Americans. Can you see the obstacles you would face if you tried to change even one of these institutions?

Despite the odds, however, Americans have raised significant challenges to each of the institutions—the family, religion, and education—we will be discussing in the rest of this chapter. We will see how each of these institutions is capable of being changed, how its forms vary from one culture to another, and some of the ways in which it is linked to other social institutions.

THE FAMILY

William Bascom (1969, p. 46) describes how members of the Yoruba tribe of what is now Nigeria were "deeply shocked" upon seeing a photograph of England's King George VI with his wife and two daughters captioned: "The King and His Family." The Yoruba could not believe that such an important man would have so small a family. It was not that the Yoruba were particularly fond of large families; it was that they understood a family to include all of one's blood relatives—although who actually lived together was another matter. Bascom reports that when he explained the Western understanding, the Yoruba "were highly amused by our idea of what constitutes a family" (p. 46).

Like most people, the Yoruba felt that they "knew" what a family is and would have no trouble recognizing one. What each culture knows, however, is a particular family form. Consider the following:

- Only 39 percent of the 139 societies studied by George P. Murdock (1949, p. 5) disapproved of premarital sex.
- Among the Nayar, husband and wife are ritually married at a young age and ritually divorced a few days later. After the divorce, the woman's ex-spouse visits her only occasionally, and she is free to take as many lovers as she wants; she can even bear legitimate offspring through them (Gough 1959).
- In one New Guinea tribe, mothers have no authority over sons who have reached the age of seven (Pospisil 1963, p. 41).
- Among the Trobriand Islanders, a child's maternal uncle (mother's brother) has the parental authority we associate with the father (Malinowski 1927).
- In half of the fourteen Caribbean societies studied by Goode (1960a), the majority of children were born outside of marriage.

No matter what form it takes, the family locates us in certain economic, ethnic, and other groups, and determines who our significant others will be.

Members of each of the societies referred to above have their own ideas of proper family practices. While these practices may seem bizarre to us, or even immoral, that is because we look at what "the family" is from our own, ethnocentric, perspective. In this section, we'll examine what is common to these practices that makes them all familial ones. Then, we'll look at the functions families perform and how we can make sense of the diversity of family patterns. Finally, we'll examine some of the major controversies surrounding the family in modern America.

What Is a Family?

A **family** is a group of two or more individuals who live together for an extended period of time; who are recognized by their society as bonded by marriage, blood relationship, or adoption; and who are responsible for the care of their offspring. This may seem a complicated definition compared to our common understanding of the family as mom, dad, and the kids, but it is necessary to incorporate the different forms of family life found around the world. In our lifetimes, we are likely to be members of two families: our **family of orientation** (the family into which we are born) and our **family of procreation** (the family we generate ourselves).

Whatever particular form it may take, however, the family is universal. Every society has some form of family life. The reason for the universality of the family lies in the crucial social functions it performs.

The Functions of the Family

The main functions that the family performs are reproduction, socialization and care of the young, regulation of sexual behavior, companionship, and transmission of social identity to the young.

The family is the arena for reproduction of the next generation—obviously a crucial social function if the society is going to survive. Reproduction can take place outside the family, of course, but our society and others make a distinction between *legitimate* children—those born through socially sanctioned unions—and *illegitimate* children—those born outside of marriage—and this distinction has significant consequences (see The Principle of Legitimacy).

In most societies, the family is primarily responsible for the physical care and socialization of the young. The family in almost every instance is expected to provide them with food, clothing, shelter, and health care. We discussed the family's role in socialization in Chapter 1, and need only add here that the trend in Western society has been for the school to take over more and more of this responsibility.

The norms of family formation and perpetuation regulate sexual behavior in all societies, limiting competition for sexual partners, and, in many instances, providing greater security for the offspring.

The family is also a source of companionship and emotional support for adults and children—another of its important social functions. For many Westerners in particular, it also serves as a refuge from the competitiveness and impersonality often found in the work world. Finally, it is through the family that we first gain our social identity. On the basis of our family of orientation, we belong to one or another ethnic group, religion, class, and culture.

When discussing the functions of the family, we should bear in mind three important cautions. First, the fact that the family performs many socially vital functions doesn't mean that it is the only social institution that could perform them. For instance, traditionally the family has served as the central unit of economic production, but this is no longer the case in industrial societies, as formal organizations have taken over this function.

We should also note that when we discuss the social functions of the family, this doesn't mean that the family is functional for all of society's members to an equal degree. In our society, being born out of wedlock still often means years of self-doubt, shame, and prejudice for the child, for instance. And because of the way in which social identity is transmitted through the family, many children are marked from birth as objects of ethnic, class, and religious prejudice.

Finally, we should note that there is more than one way for a family to carry out a function. For instance, the child-raising function that families are expected to perform may put an unequal burden on the woman, but that is only because of the way labor in the family has been traditionally organized, not because of the function it-

THE PRINCIPLE OF LEGITIMACY: FUNCTIONAL FOR WHOM?

Controlling reproduction has traditionally been a major family function; and, as a result, the family provides all children with a commonly recognized identity, regulates sexual behavior, and functions as a basic unit of social structure. Bronislaw Malinowski, a functionalist anthropologist, recognized this control in what he termed "the principle of legitimacy," which, in effect, states: "No child should be brought into the world without a man—and one man at that—assuming the role of sociological father . . . [and who] is the male link between the child and the rest of the community" (Malinowski 1974 [1930], p. 137).

But functionalist explanations of social institutions often fail to consider who benefits most from such social control; and however the principle of legitimacy functions, in this country at least, it also causes particular hardship among black, poor, and teenage mothers and their children. It is also, in many societies, one source of the father's power in the family.

In strictly biological terms, according to Malinowski, the father's task is merely "to impregnate the female and then to disappear. . . . Yet in all human societies the father is regarded by tradition as indispensable. The woman has to be married

self. It could just as well be the man who does most of this job. In the next section, we'll see how various are the ways in which families around the world are organized to carry out the functions we have been discussing.

Patterns of Family Organization

Sociologists and anthropologists have identified a number of principles of orga-

nization around which families vary. The most important of these principles are: the family form, the kind of marriage, the type of relationship among family members, the residence pattern, the form of authority, the rules of descent and inheritance, and the norms of mate selection:

1. Family forms
    Nuclear: husband, wife, and their dependent children
    Extended: more than one nuclear family, related by blood or marriage

before she is allowed to legitimately conceive" (1974 [1930], p. 137). Malinowski seems to suggest that this social rule—and not brute force or the like—gives the father power in the family; specifically, that the principle of legitimacy gives him control over the status of women and children. Indeed, he says, "an unmarried woman is under a ban, a fatherless child is a bastard." Do some women tend to violate this principle more often than others?

According to government studies in this country, yes. Black women, for instance, bore over half the illegitimate babies born in 1974—even though blacks accounted for only 16 percent of all live births. Poor women, regardless of race, are far more likely to bear illegitimate babies than nonpoor women (in one study, the likelihood was five times greater). Finally, illegitimacy is highest among the children of teenage mothers (U.S. Public Health Service 1976; 1975).

This is not to say that we must abolish the distinction between legitimate and illegitimate children before achieving social equality; in fact, many of our *reactions* to illegitimacy may be softening. The point is to recognize that the functions of any social institution are also mechanisms of social control, and that however they benefit society as a whole, they do not function equally for each and every individual in society.

2. Marriage forms
Monogamy: one man, one woman
Polygamy: multiple spouses
  Polygyny: one man, multiple women
  Polyandry: one woman, multiple men
3. Types of relationships
Affinal: linked by choice or selection
Consanguinal: linked by blood
4. Residence—where the family lives
Matrilocal: with the wife's parents
Patrilocal: with the husband's parents
Neolocal: separate from both sets of parents

5. Authority
Patriarchy: rule by husband
Matriarchy: rule by wife
Equalitarian: spouses share power and authority
6. Descent or inheritance
Patrilineal: traced through father's family only
Matrilineal: traced through mother's family only
Bilateral: traced through both parents' family lines
7. Mate selection forms

Endogamy: restricted to members of same group, such as social class or religion

Exogamy: required to marry people from outside such groups

FAMILY FORM   The family form prevalent in our society is the **nuclear family**—one set of parents and their dependent children. But there are also variations: one-parent families (divorced, widowed, or never married) and childless couples, for example. The nuclear unit, however, is normative.

The predominant family form throughout most of human history, and still common in many nations today, has been the **extended family,** which consists of more than one nuclear family, related to each other by blood or marriage. Some sociologists reserve the term for only those families in which three generations are present (children, their parents, and the parents' parents, usually). Other sociologists, however, also call families in which, say, the mother's or father's brother is living with the nuclear family an extended family.

KIND OF MARRIAGE   The second set of principles concerns the number of spouses. The basic distinction here is between *monogamy* and *polygamy.* **Monogamy** is the marriage of two people, one man and one woman, while **polygamy** is a general term referring to plural marriage. Although monogamy is a strictly prescribed norm in most industrialized societies, most preindustrial societies have allowed polygamy. Its most common form, **polygyny,** is the marriage of one man to more than one woman. Mormons in America practiced polygyny as late as 1890, when the federal government required them to abandon it as a condition of Utah's statehood. **Polyandry,** the marriage of one woman to more than one man, has been more rare; however, it was not uncommon among the polar Eskimos and ancient Spartans.

TYPES OF FAMILY RELATIONSHIP   Another set of principles concerns the type of relationship among family members. Most family members are related by blood—parent and child, and siblings (brothers and sisters). Their relationship is **consanguinal** and can never be broken; we simply cannot "divorce" our parents or siblings. The wife-husband relationship is unique in the family because it is **affinal,** or based on choice or selection. Our legal institution allows us to sever these affinal ties under many circumstances.

RESIDENCE PATTERNS   In our society, when young couples get married they generally set up their own households, independent of their parents'. This pattern of family location is termed **neolocality. Matrilocality,** residence with the wife's parents, and **patrilocality,** residence with the husband's parents, also occur in American society—but usually only as a transitional state until the young couple is financially able to run its own home.

FORMS OF AUTHORITY   The most common familial authority structure in the Judeo-Christian tradition has been **patriarchy.** Such a system gives the father wide-ranging power over most, if not all, aspects of family life and has enforced a traditionally male-dominated society. **Matriarchy,**

where authority is vested in the mother, is far less common in our society—indeed, in any society. We tend to expect it only when the male is absent or disabled. The impact of the feminist movement has helped to increase the number of **equalitarian** families, in which husband and wife wield equal control and authority over children and decision making. Even so, in most American families, husbands still make most major decisions, such as whether or not to move and what car to buy. In that respect, American society remains patriarchal.

RULES OF DESCENT AND INHERITANCE   Descent systems trace our "family tree" and usually govern the inheritance of property. **Patrilineal** descent traces descent only on the father's side of the family, while **matrilineal** descent only recognizes the mother's side. Westerners today, however, acknowledge their **bilateral descent**, which they trace through both sides. Vestiges of the patrilineal tradition remain, however, in our names. Russian patronyms and traditional Hebrew names are formed by adding the phrase "daughter/son of (the father)" to the child's given name. The same tradition persists in our exclusive use of the father's surname. Recent attempts to eliminate these vestiges have resulted in hyphenated names (Smith-Jones, for example) and the maintenance of separate surnames after marriage. However, it is not yet clear whether these practices will become widespread.

NORMS OF MATE SELECTION   Along with other aspects of marriage that we have covered, every society has norms regarding whom we may choose as a spouse. One universal norm is the *incest taboo*—the prohibition of sexual relations (and marriage) between members of the same nuclear family and sometimes between other close relatives as well.

The incest taboo is one form of **exogamy**—the requirement that we marry outside our own group. While in our society there are no restrictions other than the incest taboo on finding marriage partners among groups of which we are members, in other societies there are strict norms requiring that people choose their mate from outside given groups.

Until recently, interracial marriage was outlawed in many states, meaning that many Americans were required to marry within their own racial group. The requirement that we marry within our own group is known as **endogamy**. While endogamy is no longer required in our society, much of our behavior is endogamous nevertheless; for instance, Catholics are most likely to marry other Catholics and blacks other blacks. However, endogamy among many groups appears to be on the decline. For example, between 1960 and 1970, there was a 26 percent increase in the number of black-white marriages nationwide; if we exclude the South, the increase was 66 percent (Heer 1974). And the proportion of Jews marrying outside their religion jumped from one in fifty marriages at the beginning of this century to about one in twenty in 1960 and one in three today (National Jewish Population Study 1974).

The Changing American Family

In recent years, many commentators, noting the rising divorce rates in our country, changes in sex-role behavior (see Chapters 3 and 8), the decline in the socialization and economic functions that the family performs, and the relaxation of norms regulating sexual behavior, have suggested that the nuclear family is doomed. Given the many important functions it performs and the continued high rates of marriage, however, there is little likelihood that the nuclear family is actually dying out. But there are a number of indications that its character is undergoing some far-reaching changes. We can get some insight into the impetus for these changes by looking at the sexual revolution, the controversy over abortion, and the increased rate of divorce among Americans.

THE SEXUAL REVOLUTION John C. Messenger (1976), of the Kinsey Institute for Sex Research, studied sexuality in a rural Irish community and observes that: "Nudity is abhorred by the islanders . . . Only infants have their entire bodies sponged once a week, on Saturday night; children, adolescents, and adults, on the same night, wash only their faces, necks, lower arms, hands, lower legs, and feet . . . Even nudity of household pets can arouse anxiety . . . In some homes, dogs are whipped for licking their genitals" (p. 276).

Like this community, we, too, have norms that regulate our sexual expression—although not as extreme, of course. These norms distinguish heterosexual from homosexual sex, marital from nonmarital sex, "serious" sex from casual sex, and so on. The sanctions for the violation of sexual norms inlcude: gossip, guilt feelings, labeling (e.g., "tramp"), discrimination, violence, and legal sanctions such as jail terms and fines. Public nudity, homosexual sex, and nonmarital sex are outlawed in most jurisdictions; and extramarital sex is the

only ground for divorce accepted in all fifty states.

In recent decades, a sexual revolution appears to have been taking place in the United States, as many Americans have rebelled against the restriction of sex to marriage. Look around you: explicit mention of sex in advertising and song lyrics; more nudity, discussion of sex, and erotic content in the entertainment media; and the proliferation of sex education courses for young people—all reflect an increasingly open sexual atmosphere. Sexual attitudes have also changed, especially among young people, as you can see by comparing the results of two studies, fourteen years apart, at a small New York State college (Table 6.1). Not only were students in the later survey far more permissive sexually, but the difference in male and female attitudes had narrowed considerably (Perlman 1974). More permissive attitudes are also reflected in the growth in the number of "adult" bookstores operating openly, and in the growing public tolerance for people with nontraditional sexual lifestyles—"swingers" and homosexuals, for instance—although recent campaigns against gay rights buck this trend.

There are also indications that the sexual behavior of Americans is changing—not just attitudes. For example, in 1968, Robert R. Bell and J. B. Chaskes (1970) found a significant increase in the number of college women having premarital intercourse over college women a decade earlier. More significantly, they discovered that the increases were greatest for people who were not engaged, indicating that the decision to have intercourse had become less dependent on guarantees of marital commitment. In a 1970 survey at the University of Colorado, Gilbert Kaats and Keith E. Davis (1970) found that the reported pre-

Table 6.1 Sexual Attitudes at a Small New York State College, 1959 and 1973

Activity	*Percent Approving*			
	1959		*1973*	
	Female	*Male*	*Female*	*Male*
Petting—if engaged	94.1	95.2	96.7	96.7
Petting—if in love	91.4	93.7	97.1	97.9
Petting—if strong affection	81.3	86.8	97.5	91.1
Petting—if not particularly affectionate	28.9	43.9	74.1	75.9
Coitus—if engaged	74.3	78.3	96.7	95.0
Coitus—if in love	72.2	76.7	92.5	95.9
Coitus—if strong affection	49.7	60.3	95.8	92.1
Coitus—if not particularly affectionate	19.2	31.7	66.7	68.6
	N = 187	N = 189	N = 129	N = 113

SOURCE: Daniel Perlman, "*Self Esteem and Sexual Permissiveness,*" Journal of Marriage and the Family **36** (1974): 470–73. *Copyrighted 1974 by the National Council on Family Relations. Reprinted by permission.*

marital coital rate for females, 41 percent, was about double the rate reported in pre-1962 data. Conversely, males maintained the same 60 percent level found in earlier studies. Additional studies also show that changes in sexual behavior have been most dramatic among women (e.g., Gagnon 1977, pp. 182–84).

In sum, we can say that the sexual revolution appears to be a widespread phenomenon that challenges the traditional restriction of sexual relationships to marriage. Beyond that, premarital sex is increasing, sexual behavior is becoming detached from formal marital commitments, and the greatest changes have been occurring in female sexual behavior.

ABORTION ON DEMAND Accurate figures on the number of illegal abortions are impossible to obtain, but we know that over 1 million legal abortions are performed in the United States annually. In the debate over abortion, few people want to eliminate them entirely, particularly in cases where the mother's life is in danger. Current controversy in the United States, instead, concerns the legalization of abortion on demand: that is, abortion on a pregnant woman's request, because she has a right to control over her own body. The arguments in favor of abortion on demand appear to undermine traditional views of sexual behavior and the purpose of the family. To begin with, legal abortion makes it easier to reduce the possible consequences of premarital and extramarital sex. It also makes it possible for couples to remain childless even if methods of contraception fail. Finally, legal abortion on demand indicates that as a society we now see sexual relations as being independent of reproduction.

The abortion debate highlights the relationships among institutions. The ar-

Table 6.2 Contrasting Views of Marriage and Divorce

Marriage	Divorce
Marriage is a happy event	Divorce is a "tragedy"
Marriage is a sacrament	Divorce is a social problem
Marriage involves a celebration	Divorce is an adversary procedure
Family and friends come to your marriage	Lawyers come to your divorce
Marriage is (often) a religious ceremony	Divorce is a civil proceeding
People pay you when you get married (i.e., gifts)	You pay society to let you divorce

gument is over *legal* change, and it involves the courts and legislatures. *Political* candidates gain or lose votes because of their abortion stance. The *medical* institution must carry out the laws. Opposition to the use of welfare funds for abortions brings in the *economic* institution, while the *religious* institution plays a special role by providing antiabortionists with a powerful basis for their arguments.

The debate over abortion is entangled with many other family-related issues: congressional efforts to cut off Medicaid funds for abortions reflect attitudes about welfare and who should control its use; by making the option of voluntary childlessness more available, liberal abortion laws support the trend toward more individual freedom, particularly for women. The two sides in the abortion controversy each take a different position on who should control our behavior. Proponents of abortion on demand base their stance on their belief in a woman's right to choose; antiabortionists oppose that with their traditional beliefs of right and wrong.

In 1973, the Supreme Court ruled that criminal abortion statutes violate a woman's "constitutional right to privacy" *(Roe v. Wade)*. Antiabortionists' attempts to nullify that decision have been partially successful, and the debate continues. Nevertheless, it is likely that some form of legal abortion on demand is here to stay. The legal availability of abortion indicates that Americans' ideas about the family have changed considerably. The increase in divorces illustrates some parallel changes.

DIVORCE I was taught that when a married couple broke up it was a "shame." This sometimes meant that it was unfortunate that the two people had to go through such a painful experience, but it also meant that the divorced pair should be ashamed of themselves. Your early experiences may have been similar. Fear of this type of disapproval helped keep many unhappy couples together (see Table 6.2).

Divorce in the United States now, however, is at an all-time high. The adjusted divorce rate climbed at a slow pace between 1890 and the mid-1960s, with the exception of a brief period at the end of World War II; then an upward spiral began, as you can see in Figure 6.1. Thus, by 1977, there were over 8 million divorced Americans.

What are the reasons that are leading Americans in record numbers to divorce

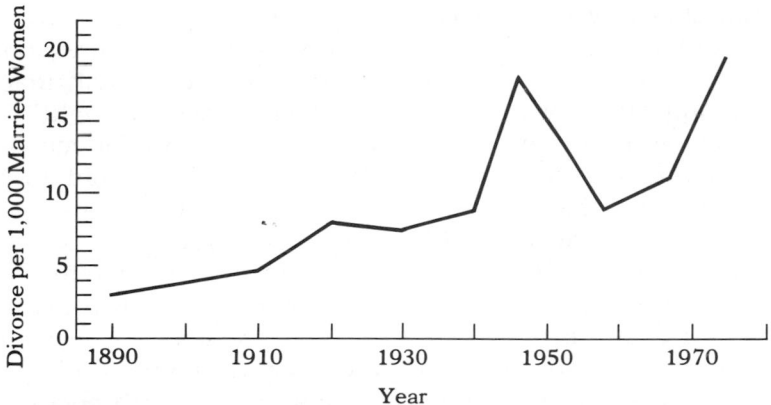

Figure 6.1 Adjusted Divorce Rate in the United States,
1890–1974

*The adjusted divorce rate measures the number of divorces granted in a given
year, per 1,000 married women (that is, women "eligible" for divorce).*

SOURCE: *U.S. Public Health Service,* One Hundred Years of Marriage and Divorce
Statistics: United States, 1867–1967 *(Washington, DC: Government Printing
Office, 1973) and U.S. Public Health Service, "Final Divorce Statistics, 1974,"*
Monthly Vital Statistics Report *(1976): 1–4.*

courts? Whereas high divorce rates in traditional ancient and Moslem societies were based on grounds of the inability to conceive or to have sons (and were therefore supportive of the view that marriage is primarily a means for reproducing the population), American couples are divorcing on more personal grounds. The courts, too, have responded to these arguments and will accept evidence of the couple's incompatibility as a reason to allow divorce— either as a legal ground for it, as an interpretation of the ground of cruelty, or in "no-fault" divorce. (Accepted in most states, no-fault divorce allows a couple to divorce for simply personal reasons without requiring an adversary court proceeding in which one of the spouses would be declared "guilty.")

The divorce rate can almost be taken as an index of dissatisfaction. Traditionally, poor people have divorced (and deserted) much more frequently than the middle class. Unemployment, few social rewards, and poverty in general have all contributed to unhappiness within their marriages. Recent increases in the divorce rate stem from the greater numbers of middle-class marriages that dissolved from the 1960s onward. The 1960s brought a good deal of social disruption, and they were followed by a general disenchantment with such major institutions as the political (Watergate), the police and FBI (allegations of illegal actions against Americans), and the economic (recession). Marriage, as a "sacred bond," does not seem so sacred at a time when so many other ties are wrenched.

Divorces are also responses to changed attitudes about the status of women. Marriages in the past often required the wife to accept a second-class status in the relationship, giving up any desires for a personal life outside the home. More and more people are challenging that arrangement, and increasing numbers of women are refusing to remain in marriages that so restrict them.

The point, then, appears to be not that more people today are necessarily any more unhappy in their marriages, as much as it is that fewer people today feel that society—and its institutions—have the authority to make them stick marriages out. This is not to say that marriage is a dying institution; in fact, marriage and remarriage are almost as popular as ever. What does appear to be eroding is the notion of having one spouse for life. To meet changes like this one, people are working out new forms of the old institution, which we will examine in the next section.

Alternatives to the Traditional Nuclear Family

We'll focus on alternatives to the nuclear family, not because all Americans live in one, but because the nuclear family is the ideal in our rapidly changing, mobile society, especially among the middle classes. Alternatives to the nuclear family vary to the extent that they seek to change that institution, but they all challenge certain aspects of it.

COHABITATION By *cohabitating*—living together without marrying—couples violate some important American nuclear family norms. Most obviously, they are breaking sexual mores, thereby challenging the social and cultural definition of marriage. If they have children out of wedlock, they are also defying the norms concerning legitimacy of offspring.

Many participants view cohabitation

as a temporary state, during which time they will get to know one another. Many of these couples eventually marry when they decide that they are "right" for each other, have the finances for marriage, or when they decide to have children. You can probably see some of the advantages this offers: couples will gain some knowledge of what to expect from each other, they will have an advance opportunity to try out solutions to such problems as how labor should be divided in the family, and they will less likely be surprised with sudden responsibilities or by the rigors of married life. A small number of couples view cohabitation as permanent and by doing so are trying to make a political statement about the marriage institution. In either case, cohabitating couples can be like married couples in every way, save their legal status. Studies have found that they tend to accept traditional sex-role patterns (Cole 1977), and some researchers suggest that cohabitating females carry a greater burden than their married sisters.

OPEN MARRIAGE Another suggestion for reform of the traditional patterns of the nuclear family is what Nena and George O'Neill (1972) call "open marriage." The O'Neills suggest that too many American marriages tend to be "closed," forcing individuals into stereotypical marital roles that do not allow much room for both partners to have careers and nurture children, for the cultivation of new friends and interests, and for the full expression of personality. The O'Neills' version of the open marriage, by contrast, is one in which the partners are each self-sufficient, bringing new input from their activities into the relationship, and in which partners pursue their activities more on the basis of per-

These single mothers—three out of 8.7 million in the United States—share a country house outside of San Francisco and provide their children as well as each other with emotional and other support.

ceived individual needs than on role requirements. Although open marriage challenges many marital norms, it does not necessarily include a *sexually* open marriage. According to the O'Neills, that is up to the individual needs of the pair (O'Neill and O'Neill 1972).

CONTRACT MARRIAGE Contract marriage has been proposed to reduce the trauma of divorce. Under this proposal, we would draw up and sign a contract before marriage that would be valid for, say, five years. After that time, the marriage would automatically expire unless we took action to renew the contract. In this respect, it is the reverse of traditional marriage, which automatically continues unless we take action to terminate it. Contract marriage might thus allow us to get out of bad marriages without feeling guilty because they would have a fixed termination point. Moreover, if we knew that our mate might let the contract expire, we would be less likely to take him or her for granted and would have to work at the marriage. Finally, the contract might also allow us to include specific clauses (concerning housework duties, for example) from the start.

COMMUNES There are also varying types of *communal* alternatives to the nuclear family that have been established or proposed. Some are small and have an anarchistic philosophy—that is, their members believe that family love and true fellowship are only possible when there are few social rules. You might recognize these as the "hippie" communes, which have grown in the United States since the mid-1960s. Other communes are large and highly organized. There are also many experimental communities, such as that of the Hari Krishnas, dedicated to a particular ideology or way of life. Different groups vary in how they constitute a family—that is, how they share property, child rearing, sex, and mutual responsibility. However, members of all of these groups attempt to live a life based on group ideals. Compared to the nuclear family, the commune offers its members the additional stimulation of many different "spouses," and it offers children more role models to choose from.

Even more than the other forms, communes require us to look at the family in a new way—much as the English were asking the Yoruba to do. You might find

the attempt difficult, as the current family institution is very much a part of our identity. However, the evidence of the preceding sections should make us wonder if such a basic rethinking—even if it is not reflected in basic changes—may be necessary for us to survive in the family of the future.

RELIGION

Like the family, *religion* is a social institution that often appears unquestionable to us and unsusceptible to change. Yet, clearly, religious beliefs differ from one group to another, religious doctrines are revised constantly, and patterns of religious affiliation are continually undergoing change. In approaching the study of religion, the sociologist does not question the truth of this or that religious doctrine but instead concentrates on how various peoples come to adhere to one faith or another, on what the secular functions of religion are, and on how to explain the patterns of religious belief. At least in this sense, then, most sociologists would agree with Marx's statement that "man makes religion, religion does not make man" (1956 [1844], p. 26).

Like the family, too, some form of religion is found in every society, but these forms are so diverse that it is difficult to derive a simple definition of what religion is. Some religions are based on a belief in a supreme god or a group of gods; others are based on a belief in impersonal, supernatural forces; while still others are built around an ideal way of life. What all religions do appear to share, however, is a concern with the **sacred**—awe-inspiring phenomena that are ultimately beyond our power to understand completely and set apart by religious beliefs. All religions, too, at least in the sociological view, are collective phenomena; religion is something shared among a community, not simply an individual's personal belief system. For our definition of religion we might thus adopt the one developed by Durkheim, whose writings on religion have set the tone for much of the sociological understanding of this institution. A **religion** "is a unified system of beliefs and practices relative to sacred things, that is to say, things set apart and forbidden—beliefs and practices which unite into one single moral community called a Church, all those who adhere to them" (1965 [1915], p. 62).

With this definition as a starting point, let's look at the major functions of religion, the elements of religious practice, and at how religious affiliation is related to secular beliefs and practices. As with the family, we will concentrate primarily on the United States in our investigation.

The Functions of Religion

As a social institution, religion performs many functions. Among these, three stand out as the most important: (1) it can calm us in times of anxiety, (2) it often enhances social cohesion, and (3) it frequently reinforces social norms.

Religion can calm us in times of anxiety because it offers us communal support and because it provides a way of interpreting unsettling experiences. The religious community may provide emotional support during periods of mourning, for instance, and religious practices may provide us with a way of overcoming the loss. At the level of belief, hard times may be easier to take if we believe in a life after death or

a final redemption, when all will be well. Religious rationalizations enable us to accept our inevitable failures and hardships. For instance, we might feel that although we have received no material reward for our actions, we have behaved in a good and moral way in the eyes of God (also see Lee and Clyde 1974).

Religion can also calm anxiety by providing answers to the unknown. In the opinion of Albert Einstein, this aspect of religion accounts for its origin:

> Now what are the feelings and needs that have led men to religious thought and belief? . . . With primitive man, it is above all fear that evokes religious notions—fear of hunger, wild beasts, sickness, death. Since at this state of existence understanding of casual connexions is usually poorly developed, the human mind creates for itself more or less analogous beings on whose wills and actions these fearful happenings depend (1949, p. 24).

In other words, Einstein supposed that primitive peoples believed these fearful things were caused by gods. From there, it was a short step to wondering whether the gods could be influenced by human actions. "Bribe" the gods with a sacrifice, and they may bring a good harvest or victory in war. Even today, many people feel that prayer and good deeds will help them gain eternal life. Without religion, how would we handle uncertainty?

Religion can also help bind members of a community together through shared beliefs and rituals, as Durkheim has pointed out. By placing the norms of a community in a sacred context, Durkheim argues, religion removes these norms from the realm of disagreement and dissension and thereby also promotes social solidarity.

A related function religion often performs is that of bolstering social norms and the status quo. The Bible tells us to obey the laws of the state ("Render unto Caesar that which is Caesar's"). Religion is often looked to as the legitimation for secular rule. Think of the "divine right of kings," for instance. Or consider President Eisenhower's statement that "our government makes no sense unless it is founded on a deeply felt religious faith—and I don't care what it is" (quoted in Ahlstrom 1978, p. 17). In the United States, where church and state are officially separate, religion is nevertheless quite prominent in government: the president is inaugurated by swearing on a Bible; Christmas is an official *national* holiday (and the nation has its own Christmas tree); Congress and political conventions open with a religious benediction; and religious principles have been the basis of "morals" legislation banning prostitution, gambling, and the sale of alcohol on Sundays.

In Marx's view, religion more specifically bolsters the status quo by mystifying the nature of oppression. In a famous passage, Marx terms religion "the opium of the people," saying that it provides people with a world of illusion that masks the true source of inequality and oppression. While there are many instances in which Marx's dictum appears to be borne out, scholars working even within the Marxist tradition now recognize that religious ideals can be, and often have been, interpreted to justify secular revolt rather than acceptance of the status quo. In 1978, for instance, the Shah of Iran was deposed after a long and autocratic rule, due in large part to the devotion of Iranians to a militant religious leader. (See Cargo Cults for a related instance.)

Religion and Society

The last two functions of religion we discussed—enhancement of social solidarity and reinforcement of social norms—suggest how closely entwined religious and secular society are. We can see this both in the influence secular considerations have on adoption of religious beliefs and in the effects of religious beliefs on social change.

Historical events show how influential social considerations can be in an individual's or a group's choice of religious affiliation. The following is just one example: during the seventh to tenth centuries, when the peoples of East Europe and Central Asia decided to abandon their pagan religions for a more "civilized" one, the choice usually involved a conflict between Christianity and Islam. The two religions were represented by powerful opposing states, who would send emissaries to argue the merits of their respective faiths. The religion a people selected determined their place in the conflict between these two states: those choosing Christianity became allies of the Byzantine Empire; converts to Islam were allied with the powerful Arabian Empire. The decision thus inevitably involved military and political considerations as well as religious ones. One kingdom that wished to remain neutral, Khazaria, did so by embracing Judaism.

The influence of religious belief on secular society is extensive. Most obviously, religious doctrine has spurred many social conflicts. In the past, full-scale religious, or "holy," wars were not that uncommon— the Crusades of the Middle Ages and the

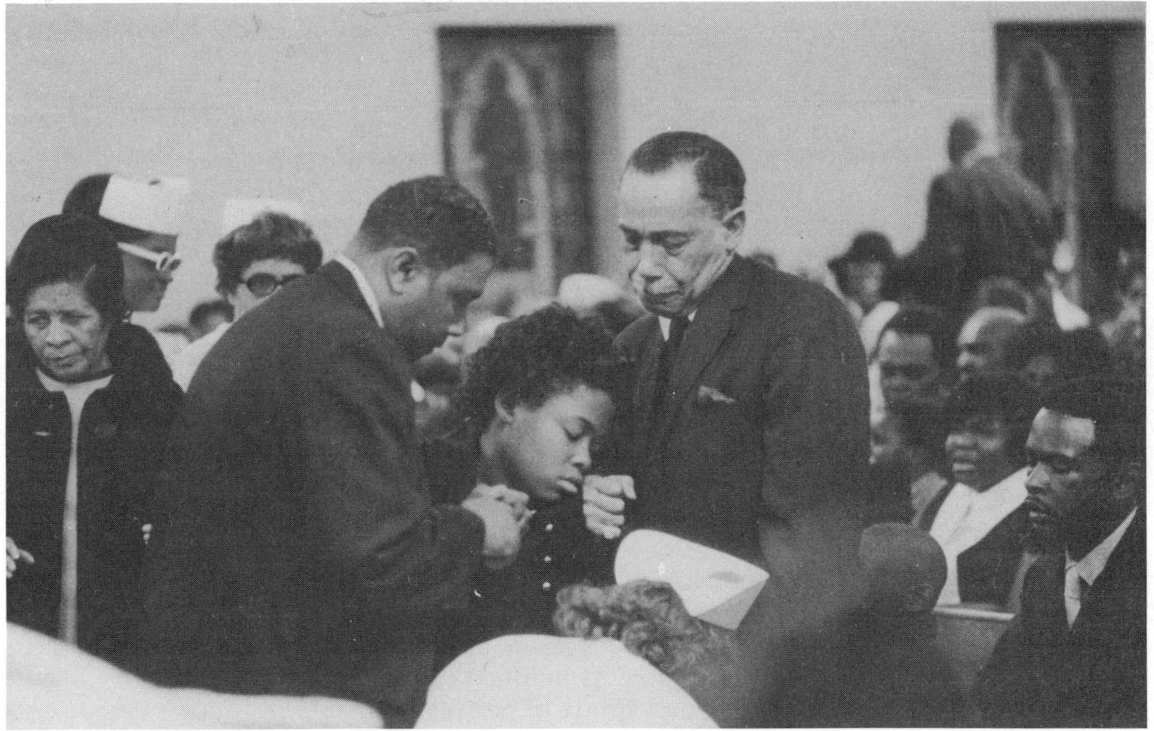

Not only different religions, but different rituals and patterns of worship characterize various social groups. How well would this Black Baptist funeral ease the grief of an upper-class, white Episcopalian family?

so-called "Peasant Wars" accompanying the Protestant Reformation are the best known. Today, however, religion still plays a role in conflicts, both within and between nations. India and Pakistan, for instance, were partitioned on the basis of religion, while religious beliefs lie behind some of the opposition to abortion on demand, gay rights, and women's rights in the United States.

THE PROTESTANT ETHIC Religious beliefs have also had more subtle, but perhaps more far-reaching, effects on secular society. The most important piece written

on this aspect of religion and society is Max Weber's *The Protestant Ethic and the Spirit of Capitalism* (1958 [1904]). Weber argued that Protestantism laid the groundwork for the development of modern capitalism. Protestantism, and in particular, Calvinism, did so, he says, by making success at business a religious act.

Calvinism includes a radical doctrine of salvation called *predestination*. It holds that God has chosen all human beings for either everlasting paradise or eternal damnation, and there is nothing any individual can do about it: "By the decree of God," so goes the Westminster Confession, ". . . some men and angels are predestined unto

CARGO CULTS

Conquering and colonizing peoples have often attempted to impose their national faiths on their new subjects. The Bible tells of efforts by Babylonians, Assyrians, and Romans to impose their religions on the Israelites; later, conquering Arabs won the entire Middle East for Islam; and more recently, Europeans have tried to convert their colonized subjects to Christianity. Sometimes these efforts have succeeded; sometimes not. On the island of New Guinea, members of *cargo cults* have developed their own alternative to the Protestantism brought by German and Dutch settlers. What do cargo cultists believe?

> The scene is a jungle airstrip high in the mountains of New Guinea. Nearby are thatch-roofed hangars, a radio shack, and a beacon tower made of bamboo. On the ground is an airplane made of sticks and leaves. The airstrip is manned twenty-four hours a day by a group of natives wearing nose ornaments and shell armbands. At night they keep a bonfire going to serve as a beacon. They are expecting the arrival of an important flight: cargo planes filled with canned food, clothing, portable radios, wrist watches, and motorcycles. The planes will be piloted by ancestors come back to life (Harris 1974, p. 133).

everlasting life, and others foreordained to everlasting death." We can be bad or good, attend church every day or never, repent all our sins or not, but nothing we did would have any bearing on our ultimate fate. As we might imagine, the absence of eternal rewards for the believers' actions would lead them to redouble their efforts for earthly rewards. But Calvinists also believe that while nothing we do will increase our stock in God's eyes, achieving worldly economic success is nevertheless a possible sign of election. Thus, Calvinists, out of religious anxiety, will strive for success in order to prove to themselves and others that they are among the elect, and hard work has become associated with piety and goodness.

As outsiders, we may find these actions a little odd, but we should be aware that the cult has been the focus of resistance against foreign domination.

Missionaries and other Europeans believed that they were spreading the Gospel and bringing civilization to "wild and immoral heathens." But they found that to attract converts, they often had to tempt the natives with gifts of food, steel tools, and so on—cargo. More cargo would follow, they said, only if the natives practiced the Protestant doctrine of hard work and simple lives. But when additional cargo was not forthcoming, some natives began working out their own explanation and formed the cargo cults.

Because native laborers unloaded many ships (later airplanes) containing supplies for the Europeans, they developed the theory that the Europeans were stealing their cargo. This led to two rebellions, which were easily put down; and deciding that further armed resistance was futile, the natives returned to the churches, appearing outwardly to be faithful Christians. But the cults flourished, and an ideology developed that ancestors would eventually bring the islanders the cargo, expel the Europeans, and usher in a life free of care.

Cargo cultists believe that the Europeans know the secret of cargo (for they regularly receive it), but instead of sharing that secret, they use it as a form of social control. They make receiving cargo conditional on the inhabitants living by the missionaries' words, working for the foreign bosses (plantation and mine owners), and doing as the authorities tell them. So the Protestant religious doctrine actually serves the colonizers' material interests.

Another important aspect of Calvinism is thriftiness and avoidance of worldly pleasures. To spend money on drinking, nice clothes, and other possessions is considered sinful. Wasting money, for instance, by buying more than you need, is also a sin. Besides that, Calvinists consider money made to be God's blessing; thus the only appropriate way to use it is to reinvest it in the business for the further glory of God.

Calvinists also believe that human beings face God alone. They are suspicious of other people because they might be among the damned. Thus the doctrine developed that it is only righteous for individuals to strive for their own success (as a sign of salvation). And if we want to ob-

Table 6.3 Distribution of Major World Religions

Total %	North America %	South America %	Europe %	Asia %	Africa %	Oceania* %
Roman Catholic 13.4	Roman Catholic 36.7	Roman Catholic 65.3	Roman Catholic 23.4	Hindu 19.5	Moslem 31.0	Protestant 57.7
Moslem 13.0	Protestant 26.2	Protestant 4.7	Protestant 13.6	Moslem 16.7	Protestant 14.9	Roman Catholic 19.8
Hindu 11.2	Jewish 1.7	Hindu .35	Eastern Orthodox 8.5	Buddhist 10.6	Roman Catholic 10.8	Hindu 2.2
Protestant 7.6	Eastern Orthodox 1.2	Jewish .24	Moslem 1.1	Confucian 7.0	Eastern Orthodox 3.3	Eastern Orthodox 1.8
Buddhist 6.1	Moslem .08	Eastern Orthodox .23	Jewish .54	Shinto 2.3	Hindu .21	Moslem .39
Confucian 4.0	Buddhist .05	Moslem .14	Hindu .04	Roman Catholic 2.1	Jewish .04	Jewish .33
Eastern Orthodox 2.0	Confucian .03	Buddhist .08	Buddhist .04	Protestant 1.5	Buddhist .002	Confucian .18
Shinto 1.3	Hindu .02	Shinto .04	Confucian .003	Taoist 1.3		Buddhist .09
Taoist .74	Shinto .02	Confucian .04	Zoroastrian .001	Jewish .14		
Jewish .34	Taoist .004	Taoist .005		Eastern Orthodox .08		
Zoroastrian .006		Zoroastrian .001		Zoroastrian .01		

*Includes Australia and New Zealand.
The percentages do not add up to 100 because many smaller religions and those people with no religious preference are not included.
SOURCE: Britannica Book of the Year 1979 (Chicago: Encyclopedia Britannica, 1979, p. 606). Reprinted by permission.

tain the limited resources available for success it is important to develop a spirit of competition.

This ethic, which glorifies hard work, economic success, and individual effort, has perhaps been developed furthest in the United States, and you might have recognized elements of what I called in Chapter 2 the American ideology in the Protestant ethic. The reason for this is that not only do Protestants share these values, but many American Catholics and Jews have come to share them as well, because of their membership in the culture.

Edward A. Tiryakian (1974) has traced a number of the United States' actions to the Protestant beliefs of its founders: winning the West, going to the moon, and helping to "modernize" less developed nations with Peace Corps volunteers are all expressions of a Protestant religious value of taming or cultivating wild and unknown areas.

Table 6.4 Religious Membership in the United States, 1978

Religion	Membership
Protestant	72,382,737
Roman Catholic	49,836,176
Jewish	5,775,935
Eastern Orthodox	3,752,525
Other (includes Buddhist, Muslim, Unitarian, etc.)	204,373

It is not easy to get accurate figures on church membership in the United States. For one thing, the official separation of church and state prevents the government from collecting such statistics. For another, there are over 200 religious bodies in the United States, which we generally group into five categories.

SOURCE: Yearbook of American and Canadian Churches, 1979 (Nashville, TN: Abingdon Press, 1979).

SECULAR CHARACTERISTICS OF RELIGIOUS GROUPS Weber's analysis of the connection between Protestantism and the origins of capitalism has stimulated many subsequent researchers to look for the social attributes of different religious group members. The most obvious of these attributes is the geographical concentration of members of the world's major religions. As we can see from Table 6.3, the major religions are distributed unevenly throughout the world. Judaism, for example, a major religion in the West, is not very prominent elsewhere, and Confucianism, although the fifth largest religion in the world, hardly exists at all outside of Asia.

Space doesn't allow us to detail world patterns more precisely, but we can examine the social characteristics of American religious groups more closely. If we look at the bare figures of Table 6.4, it seems quite simple: America is largely a Protestant society, with many Roman Catholics, and a few Jews and Orthodox Christians. But the figures are not really simple. To begin with, Protestantism is more a category than a real group, since it contains many different denominations (e.g., Baptist and Presbyterian). Moreover, the members of each denomination and religion tend to share a number of other social characteristics.

Most rural Americans are Protestant. Jews, and to a lesser extent, Catholics, are disproportionately concentrated in large cities, particularly in the Northeast and Midwest. About one-third of all American Jews live in the New York City area alone

(American Jewish Committee 1979). For the most part, Episcopalians and Unitarians are in the Northeast, Baptists in the South, and Methodists in the Midwest.

We can also associate certain nonreligious beliefs with each religion. Congregationalists, Unitarians, and Jews tend to be politically more liberal than members of other religious groups. Fundamentalists and Mormons tend to be politically more conservative, and we expect Black Muslims to favor the Arabs over the Israelis in the Middle East. Of course, these generalizations don't mean that every group member shares the opinion of the majority.

We can also go beyond geographical distribution and political preference, and look at the association of occupation and income with religious group membership. For example, in 1956, C. Wright Mills wrote a book describing the American "power elite"—major business executives, upper-class socialites, the very wealthy, lawmakers, and top military leaders—who he claims have the power and wealth to control all major decision making in the United States. Mills observed that this grouping of people was overwhelmingly Protestant—mainly Episcopalian (only 2 percent of the total American population is Episcopalian), and Presbyterian and Unitarian to a lesser extent. A study of Protestants that same year confirmed that some denominations drew their membership primarily from the rich while others did from the poor: 46 percent of the Episcopalians, 26 percent of the Presbyterians, 11 percent of the white Baptists, and 2 percent of the black Baptists had yearly incomes of $7,500 or more (Lazerwitz 1964).

Since the publication of Mills's *The Power Elite*, there have been many changes in the social and economic standing of the membership of various denominations. Between 1954 and 1964, American Catholics took proportionally more nonmanual jobs and performed much less manual labor than previously. The trend for Protestants as a whole was the opposite, and since the 1960s, Catholics have ranked higher than Protestants in average occupational level (Glenn and Hyland 1967). Non-Protestants have also increased their educational attainment relative to Protestants (for recent figures, see Figure 6.2). Moreover, there are more black Baptists, Roman Catholics, and Jews in Congress than twenty years ago, and since the publication of Mills's book, the United States has elected its first Catholic and southern Baptist presidents: John Kennedy and Jimmy Carter, respectively.

Despite these and other changes, however, Episcopalians, Presbyterians, and a few other Protestant religious groups are still overrepresented in America's power elite. Although Catholics have been gaining more prestigious jobs in recent years, compared with Protestants they have not obtained the decision-making jobs still controlled by the latter (Wilson 1978, p. 297). We will still not find proportionate numbers of Catholic, Baptist (white or black), or Jewish generals and admirals, heads of the largest corporations, socialites, bank presidents, and the like.

In our discussion of the social characteristics of religious group members, the only criterion of belonging to the group was self-report or official membership rolls. Religious experience obviously encompasses much more than these superficial associations. To understand more about the depths of religious sentiment in the United States will be our purpose in the next section.

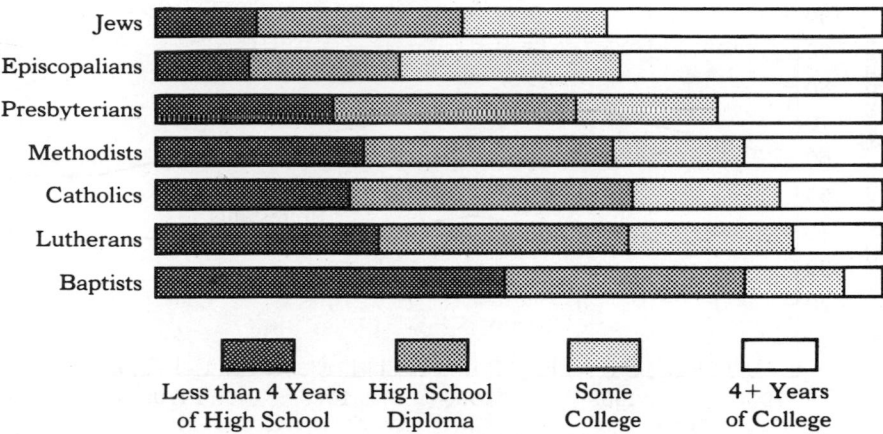

Figure 6.2 Religion and Educational Levels in the United States, 1978

SOURCE: National Data Program for the Social Sciences, Spring 1978 General Social Survey, July 1978 Codebook _(Chicago: National Opinion Research Center, 1978)._
Thanks to NORC staff for their aid.

Religiosity

What makes a person religious? The simplest view would hold that religiosity can be measured by church attendance and some formal affiliation. But what if a person attends all the time, yet thinks the church doctrine is silly and only goes because it looks good? Does a belief in God (or some sacred realm), then, make us religious? What about people who go to church each Sunday, but cheat their customers Monday through Friday? Are they religious? Finally, what about people who lead their lives according to high moral standards but do not go through formal religious rituals? Are they religious? If you find it difficult to answer these questions with a quick yes or no, you probably understand the religiosity issue's complexity. To try to make sense of this complexity, so-

ciologists of religion analyze religiosity by discussing three basic components: _ritual, belief,_ and _secular behavior._*

RITUAL In 1901, William James wrote that prayer is what distinguishes religious attachment from moral or ideological sentiment (1961 [1901], p. 361). While James's definition of religious attachment is not wholly adequate, we still can agree that praying is a uniquely religious phenomenon and the most obvious religious _ritual_—that is, prescribed religious ceremony. You probably know of other rituals, including religious holiday observances, special

---

*This is a more general presentation of Glock and Stark's five dimensions of religiosity (see Glock and Stark 1965; Stark and Glock 1970).

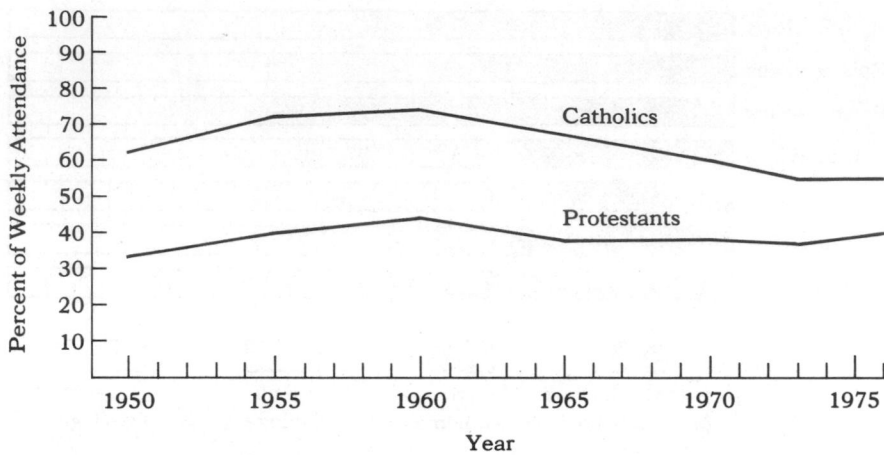

Figure 6.3   Church Attendance of American Christians, 1950–1976

SOURCE: *American Institute of Public Opinion*, The Gallup Poll: Public Opinion 1972–1977
(Wilmington, DE: Scholarly Resources, 1978) and The Gallup Poll: Public Opinion
1935–1971 *(New York: Random House, 1972).*

diets, and baptism. Both marriages and funerals are usually religious rituals also. These and other rituals symbolize the values behind them and remind us of our belief in those values. Rituals also enable us to submerge our individual selves within a larger group. This submission of the individual to the religious practice of the group has sometimes gone to the extreme of self-mutilation or even ritual suicide. Some years ago, for example, a number of Buddhist monks in Vietnam set themselves on fire to protest religious oppression.

Until recently, however, the percentage of professing American Christians—at least as measured by church attendance—has been declining. Figure 6.3 shows the trend in the church attendance of Catholics and Protestants over a twenty-six-year period,

from 1950 to 1976.* The drop in Protestant worship was relatively small, but the rate for Catholics—traditionally the group with the highest rate of church attendance—fell dramatically from 74 percent in 1959 to 55 percent in 1976. In a similar vein, less than half the Jews in Chicago belong to synagogues, which is a marked drop from traditional levels of synagogue membership (DeSantis and Benkin 1980). And studies have also reported declines in participation in many rituals other than church attendance (Saldahna et al. 1975; DeSantis and Benkin 1980). This trend seems to have reversed, however, as we shall see later.

BELIEF   Religiosity involves not simply conforming to formal ritual norms but also sharing religious *beliefs.* Every organized

*The figure shows the percentage of American Catholics and Protestants who responded yes to

the question: "Have you attended church within the past seven days?"

Festival of St. Anthony, New York City: Rituals advertise our religiosity—unlike beliefs, which others can't see, or moral behavior, which is easily overlooked in everyday life.

religion has some set of official beliefs, and these beliefs vary from one religion to the next: Christian doctrine holds that Jesus is the son of God; Jewish and Islamic scriptures say that there is only one divine being; Buddhist thought allows for no God at all; and Hindu theology contains many gods. And remember, these are only some of the major religions; there are countless more variations.

Sociologists' primary concern in understanding religious beliefs is not official doctrine, however, but what people actually believe. And the strength of American Christians' beliefs—like their rate of church attendance—has been declining. In 1952, for instance, 99 percent of the Protestants sampled said they believed in God. Further, 74 percent of the Protestants and 89 percent of the Catholics surveyed believed that Jesus is the son of God (Marty et al. 1968). By the time Rodney Stark and Charles Y. Glock conducted their extensive study of northern Californians in 1970, less than 75 percent of their Protestant subjects affirmed their belief in God. At the same time, only 69 percent of the Protestants and 86 percent of the Catholics asserted that Jesus is the son of God. Although the majority remain firm believers, we can see that a sizable minority of American Christians do not believe in the most basic teachings of Christian doctrine! And, as we might expect, even fewer respondents held many of the other beliefs we associate with Christianity. For example, only Baptists, as a whole, believed in the virgin birth of Jesus (Stark and Glock 1970).

Some researchers, however, have noted that the extent of belief has often fluctuated (down in the 1920s, up in the 1930s) in response to short-term events; and they caution that this downward trend may be such a response (Wilson 1978, p. 394). Thus the meaning of our findings on belief is not yet clear.

SECULAR BEHAVIOR How often have you heard somebody say something like this: "Well, I don't attend church or anything like that, and I can't say that I believe in God—but I consider myself a very religious person"? By religious, the person usually means "good" or "moral," and it is not rare to hear such a statement in American society.

Religion influences our behavior most obviously through ritual. Rituals are specific actions that remove us from our daily secular routines—we take time out to pray and celebrate holidays, for example. But we also expect religion to affect the way we conduct our life in general. Our Judeo-Christian heritage provides us with the Ten Commandments as guides: we do not expect a religious person to murder or steal, for instance. If the person does commit one of these acts, we may wonder about the depth of his or her religiousness.

In judging the degree of religious behavior among individuals, we must be careful not to let our culture's bias creep in as to what is "good." For instance, a former religious group in India, known as the Thugs, robbed and murdered the British rulers of that land, their Indian helpers, and wealthy travelers as sacrifices to the Hindu goddess Kali. We might not like to call that behavior religious, but it was part of the moral life prescribed by the Thugs's religion.

Religiosity, then, is a complex phenomenon, and its three dimensions must be taken together. To summarize, we can say that being religious entails certain beliefs and rituals prescribed by a religious group; this eliminates nonreligious philosophies that prescribe a moral way of life from our definition—for example, humanism and communism. Beyond that, we recognize that to be religious, we have to lead a moral life, as that life is defined by our religion's principles.

Recent Trends in American Religion

From our discussion of religion so far in this chapter, we might think that religion is on the wane in the United States. Indeed, religion did appear to be waning until the early 1970s, as membership and attendance declined from what it had been a decade earlier. As the seventies progressed, however, the decline in church attendance and membership in the major denominations slowed; and by 1976, according to a Gallup poll, the trend had reversed. At the same time, Americans seemed to be inundated by a number of *religious cults*—nontraditional and, in the eyes of most Americans, less legitimate religious organizations. Moonies, Jesus Freaks, and Hari Krishnas seem to be all over our major cities, on the streets and at the airports.

Cult members are highly visible because of their often strange appearance and actions. Hari Krishnas, heads shaven, dance and sing Indian music on streetcorners; Moonies often accost us, trying to sell flowers or candy for their "youth group." But religious cults did not become a national concern until the tragedy of the People's Temple in Jonestown, Guyana. There, nine hundred residents of the San Francisco Bay Area, headed by their leader and

"messiah," Jim Jones, were either killed or committed suicide because Jones commanded it. To be sure, Sun Myung Moon draws tens of thousands to his stadium rallies, but we must not get an exaggerated impression of the number of cult members. Although accurate membership figures are not available, the communal living arrangements of many groups, for instance, the Hari Krishnas, keep the number of devotees limited (Judah 1978).

We have also seen the proliferation of "born-again" Christians—Christians who claim a direct and personal encounter with the divine. Many are in mainline Christian churches, but others have joined together in Protestant fundamentalist sects. In general, they are not suspect in the eyes of most Americans; and in 1976, we even elected Jimmy Carter, one such individual, president. Thus the religious institution in America is undergoing some significant changes, and no clear trend is yet apparent.

EDUCATION

The individual's need for knowledge is universal; the institution of *education*—the formally organized transmission of knowledge—is not. In traditional societies, where social change is slow, primary socialization, plus some direct craft training, is enough to ensure the passage of skills from one generation to the next. Modern societies, however, demand that their citizens possess more general skills (like reading, writing, and arithmetic) and more specialized vocational training as well, and the institution of education was developed to fill these requirements. Like the other institutions we studied, then, the institution of education also changes in response to changing social conditions. In this section, we'll look at some of the changes and controversies in education in the United States.

The federal government estimates that anywhere from 63,959,000 to 78,681,000 Americans will be attending school in 1990 (U.S. Department of Commerce 1973). Going to school is now such a pervasive and widespread experience of ours that we find it difficult to imagine a time when only a few Americans were educated. But less than a century ago, education was almost exclusively the privilege of the sons (not daughters) of the elite. These children of privilege went to school to become cultured gentlemen and perhaps to learn professions like those of physician and lawyer. Other major occupations of the time—small businesses and simple factory work—were thought to require on-the-job training only.

Primarily as a result of the changes wrought by the industrial revolution, however, during the late nineteenth century and the first half of the twentieth, elite education became mass education. New industries required workers who could read and do simple math and who had acquired more specialized vocational skills. Partially to meet these needs, education was made compulsory for the young, and a public school system was created, which now consists of 15,750 school districts. These changes in schooling in America highlight the crucial social functions this institution performs in modern society.

Education's Functions

The primary function of formal education is to transmit culture from one generation to the next. This involves teaching the history, philosophy, language, and other things that make each particular culture unique. More specifically, though, the function of education is to train individuals for adult economic roles and to inculcate them with the values of the dominant culture. If you were to ask your classmates what they want most from their education, the majority would probably answer a "good job" or "rewarding career." And although this is not all that your education offers, it identifies education's basic function of training individuals for adult life, most obviously for an economic role. Schools prepare individuals for different roles in the labor force—laborer, executive, professional, and so on. From the early school years, students are placed by teachers and counselors in different classes on the basis of grades and subjective evaluations. Eventually, this leads to "college prep" or "commercial" curricula, or to vocational high schools. In the process, the schools make students aware of some role possibilities and lead them to reject others as beyond their reach or inappropriate, thus often reinforcing social inequalities, as we will see in the next section.

Our education also trains us to be loyal to the state and to share certain social values. This is done through history lessons, saluting the flag, even the patriotic songs that young students learn in music classes. Functionalists point out that education thus functions to increase group solidarity. And Randall Collins (1971) has commented that schools do a far better job in "inculcating unthinking political loyalty" than in teaching academic skills.

The educational institution also serves as the nation's largest child-care facility. Without mass education, we could hardly conceive of families with no parents at home during the day. Also, compulsory education keeps a certain percentage of potential workers off the labor market. Just imagine the profound unemployment problem if the millions of teenagers in school were competing for the already small number of jobs.

Finally, education, at least in the eyes of many Americans, is supposed to serve the cause of social justice. Many persons hoped that schools, by equalizing educational opportunity, would right racial and class injustices and sexual discrimination. However, as Christopher Jencks and his associates (1972) have pointed out, equalizing opportunity is not the same as equalizing results, in schooling or in incomes and jobs of school graduates. Thus, even if the schools did equalize opportunity, they could not fulfill these other equalizing functions attributed to them. And as we'll now see, American schools fall short of equalizing educational opportunity in the first place.

Education, Economics, and Equality

Sociologists have looked at education's impact on the individual in the light of two different models, the socialization and the allocation.

According to the *socialization model:* "Schools provide experiences which instill knowledge, skills, attitudes, and values in their students. These students then have a revised set of personal qualities enabling them to demand more from, and achieve more in, the role structure of modern society" (Meyer 1977, pp. 56–57). In other words, schools socialize us so that we can achieve better jobs and higher incomes. We gain these rewards, this model assumes, in proportion to what we have learned.

According to the *allocation model,* however, we are likely to be allocated our adult roles on the basis of years and types of education, apart from anything we learned. In the last section, we often referred to the socialization function. Here, however, the allocation model is more appropriate, because roles are allocated unequally—and not on the basis of free competition, as the socialization model would indicate. The school system helps reinforce inequality—thus helping those on top avoid competition—through a two-stage process. The first stage consists of the allocation of educational opportunities on the basis of socioeconomic background. For example, a study comparing the schools in low- and high-income areas of a Midwestern city found the educational facilities in the low-income communities to be inferior in every respect—deteriorating school buildings, substandard science equipment (or none at all), fewer medical facilities, and less-qualified teachers (and more "emergency" substitutes) compared to the schools in the high-income communities. Many of these schools also lacked lunchrooms, where poor students could have taken advantage of the city's free lunch program (Sexton 1964).

In other words, even though education is *public*, children will not be as likely to get a quality education unless their parents or guardians can afford to live in a high-income area. Patterns of residential segregation and income inequality mean that blacks and Latinos are the chief victims of this problem, and their needs have rarely been given priority by governments. So, writes E. Campbell: "Those whose nonschool environments are least equipped to provide or support meaningful educational experience are placed in schools that provide the least stimulating interpersonal en-

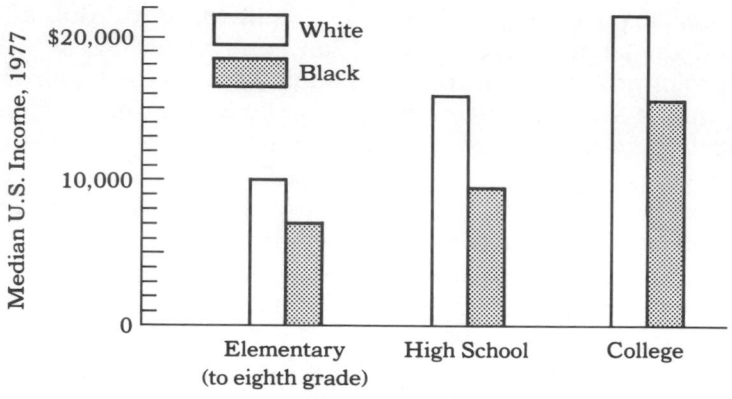

Figure 6.4   Education and Income in the United States, 1977

SOURCE: *U.S. Department of Commerce,* Money Income in 1977 of Families and Persons in the United States *(Washington, DC: Government Printing Office, 1979, Table 29).*

vironments for learning" (1969, p. 846). Thus the school offers unequal opportunities that reinforce inequality.

In the second stage of the filtering process, occupational roles are awarded on the basis of certificates of educational achievement, which are limited by the process's first stage. And that allocation of certificates strongly affects income, as Figure 6.4 shows. Each year, the high school dropout faces fewer and fewer job prospects, as the number of employers who hire individuals without high school diplomas shrinks; and those jobs that are available usually pay very little. However, a recent study of 947 males, drawn from a nationwide sample of youth originally surveyed in 1955, emphasizes that the number of years in school might have less effect on subsequent income than such qualitative factors as the school's prestige, teacher contact, high

school "tracking," and the science and math courses completed (Griffin and Alexander 1978).

There is little doubt that most Americans associate a good education with "the comfortable life" (Coleman and Rainwater 1978, p. 164). But the actual impact of education on subsequent income and social standing is not that clearcut. During the years 1938–1970, for example, educational requirements for jobs were consistently raised, even when such changes had little relevance to the demands of the job. This reduced the chances for mobility through educational achievement (Collins 1971). Perhaps more significant were the findings of Jencks and his colleagues that class and racial factors continue to significantly affect our adult social standing regardless of the extent and quality of our education (Jencks et al. 1972).

In short, many social factors prevent a simple translation of education into occupational achievement and income. But whereas education often impedes the achievement of equality by socializing us for unequal positions in life, it can also be a source of individual mobility, as the income figures show.

Contemporary Challenges to the Institution

Today, the educational system is facing many charges of bias and favoritism, which have forced increased public attention to school issues. Here, we'll consider three challenges to the present system of American education: the challenge of racial equality in educational opportunity, which includes the subject of busing; the challenge to reduce sexism in our schools; and the challenges facing higher education, including the commitment to mass higher education.

EQUAL EDUCATION Historically, the education of black Americans has constituted one of the clearest violations of the nation's stated value of equality for all citizens. Even after slavery was abolished, blacks were segregated—by law—in the poorest quality schools. In one southern town, blacks were given a "shell of a building" for a school, with no money allocated for furnishings, supplies, or fuel (Dollard 1937, p. 194). In some towns, no high school would admit blacks, making their secondary education difficult and expensive. Moreover, school terms were, by law, shorter for black children in the South. For instance, "During cotton-picking season every

member of the [black] family who is mature enough has to pick cotton and rural Negro children may not go to school until the picking is done" (Dollard 1937, p. 195).

In short, black children were given an inferior education, making it extremely difficult for them to break out of their low-status position. And this was not just true of the South, as similarly poor conditions characterized Northern schools as well.

In 1896, the U.S. Supreme Court upheld a state's right to legally segregate black and white children in schools. It did rule that the separate facilities should be equal, but as we just saw, they were not. But in 1954, the Court rejected the "separate but equal" doctrine, in the landmark *Brown* v. *Board of Education* decision. Said the justices:

> In these days, it is doubtful that any child may reasonably be expected to succeed in life if he is denied the opportunity of an education. Such an opportunity, where the state has undertaken to provide it, is a right which must be made available to all on equal terms. . . . To separate [children] from others of similar age and qualifications solely on the basis of their race generates a feeling of inferiority as to their status in the community that may affect their hearts and minds in a way unlikely ever to be undone. . . . Separate educational facilities are inherently unequal.

An attack on the inequities of our educational system accompanied the civil rights movement that blossomed in the aftermath of the Brown decision. Millions of dollars were appropriated for educational purposes, and a decade following the de-

Many angry white parents violently opposed court-ordered integration of their neighborhood schools. These buses needed a police escort in order to get their young black passengers safely to South Boston High School.

cision saw the emergence of "compensatory education programs," designed to make up for the inferior education blacks and other poor people had been offered.

At about the same time as these programs were established, the government commissioned sociologist James S. Coleman to assess the state of educational opportunities in the United States. Coleman surveyed about 600,000 public school students, their teachers, principals, and superintendents. The questionnaire asked students about their background and tested them for educational achievement (Coleman et al. 1966). Coleman and his col-

leagues discovered that on standardized achievement tests, blacks scored significantly lower than whites, and the differences grew with each year of school. And despite the Supreme Court's ruling, about 80 percent of all white students and 65 percent of all black students attended schools in which their own race constituted over 90 percent of the population. Finally, Coleman and his associates found that blacks scored higher on achievement tests when they had white classmates. This suggested to many legislators a solution to unequal education—busing.

Although the Supreme Court eliminated segregation by law, it did not prevent educational segregation that arose from other factors—from unequal wealth, discriminatory real estate practices, and the exodus of affluent (and other) whites from inner city to suburb, for example. It seemed to Coleman and to many others, then, that the only way to remedy school segregation was busing—physically moving students to create racial balance. Obviously, Americans are anything but agreed on this issue. Some people oppose busing because they are racists, others because they are ideological conservatives who see government interference as a violation of state and local rights. Still others argue that busing destroys the possibility of community control of schools, while some of busing's black opponents believe that black children should learn to appreciate their own culture and not look to white society for guidance.

Supporters of busing might agree with some of these criticisms, but they emphasize that we are faced with immediate and ongoing injustice, which demands some immediate solutions, even if they are not perfect. As the many public demonstrations over the issue indicate, the subject of busing arouses powerful emotions in partisans on both sides of the issue, and it is likely to remain a controversial subject for some time to come.

THE CHALLENGE TO REDUCE SEXISM IN SCHOOLS In Chapter 1, we looked at the school's role in socializing us, including the inculcation of what have become some of our basic values and orientations. With the emergence of the women's movement in recent years has come an awareness that schools traditionally have social-

ized children with *sexist* values—values that enforce the notion that women should have a subservient role in society.

Sexist values are transmitted in a variety of ways. Teachers, for instance, may bring traditional role expectations of girls and boys to the classroom, and students may take on these expectations as their own. Teachers of young students may talk about appropriate behavior for each sex and may also socialize passivity and dependence in girls, independence in boys. Consider, for example, the way a (male) kindergarten teacher reacted to two students who showed him their in-class carpentry, as recorded by Barbara G. Harrison (1973). To a girl: "These nails aren't hammered in far enough. . . . I'll do it for you." And to a boy: "These nails aren't hammered in far enough. . . . Take the hammer and pound them in all the way." In other words, the boy is taught to "pound" those nails—to do things himself. The girl learns she needs a man to do things for her.

Are such incidents trivial? By themselves they may be. But within the context of our entire school experience, they subtly reinforce certain images. The textbooks children read are a major part of their school experience, and extensive study has shown they perpetuate sex stereotypes. There are few female characters in the books, the main character is almost always male, and 80 percent of the pronouns refer to males—even animal characters are usually referred to as "he." The books generally show women and men in stereotyped roles—men in paying occupations, women as "mommies." Boys and men are portrayed as aggressive problem solvers, while girls and women are seen to just tag along or do housework *(Women on Words and Images 1975)*. In these books, "boys celebrate life by living it fully and reaching out to the world, and girls reach out to boys" (Harrison 1973, p. 38). English and history texts tend to ignore the contributions of women, while giving the impression that they have covered all the "important" material.

In high school, many of us receive sex-segregated career training that sends non-college-bound girls into home economics, cosmetology, or secretarial training and non-college-bound boys to industrial arts. Students headed for college often see the guidance counselor, who relies on standardized, but biased, tests, in giving advice. One of the tests, for example, suggests careers as dieticians, nurses, dental hygienists, and physical therapists for girls scoring high in the health professions; boys showing the same aptitude are expected to become physicians, dentists, and pharmacists (Walum 1977, pp. 56–77).

Feminists and others have challenged the educational system to eliminate sexism from its curriculum. There has been some progress: new readers attempt to portray males and females more equitably; court cases have dented the sex-segregated career tracking; and some private schools have made special efforts to eliminate sex bias. Most significant, however, has been the changing attitudes of teachers. Even so, nonsexist books are still a small minority, boys rarely take home economics, and most teachers still perpetuate the traditional attitudes. Young children get a very clear picture from the school system itself of which sex holds more power—even though that power is socially created and maintained. For although 88 percent of all elementary school teachers in the United States are women, 88 percent of the principals—their *superiors*—are men (Frazier and Sadlek 1973, p. 97). As we can see, sex bias enters education very subtly, which suggests that real change will not likely emanate from within the educational system, but through wider social change.

HIGHER EDUCATION IN THE UNITED STATES The mid-1960s was a time of social unrest on America's college campuses. Campus disturbances—beginning with the Free Speech Movement at Berkeley in 1964—were grabbing headlines across the nation and becoming associated in the public mind with the wider youth counter-culture. Students rioted, picketed, held sit-ins in administration offices, and played an active political role in the university.

The demonstrations often centered on the war in Indochina and, to a lesser extent, on racism—two broad social issues over which the university had little control. But the war was a catalyst for more immediate grievances: university expansion into surrounding, generally black and poor, communities was attacked; students demanded, sometimes successfully, that their schools stop engaging in military research; they won more say in curriculum matters and began publishing student evaluations of teachers and courses as guides; they got dress codes and the like abolished; and they questioned the "relevance" of a traditional liberal arts education.

Political activism virtually disappeared from campuses in the 1970s. Instead, universities faced a changed understanding of their purpose, for American higher education had become mass higher education. For years, student bodies consisted overwhelmingly of white males between the ages of eighteen and twenty-four, from middle- or upper-income families, and headed for professional or executive careers. Today, however, almost half of the enrolled students are women. The proportion of nonwhites enrolled for degrees tripled between 1960 and 1972. In colleges today are youths from poor families, low-income workers, homemakers, the elderly, members of the armed forces, and others. The number of older and part-time students is also increasing. In fact, the number of older students has been increasing at the same time that fewer new high school graduates are going on to college (Harris and Geede 1977, pp. 27–30).

Higher education in the United States has been made available to more Americans in recent years as a result of new community colleges, free or low tuition, federal and private aid, and less-structured programs. Continuing adult education, satellite campuses, and part-time education allow people to attend and still hold a job. However, it would be incorrect to think that this has made equality available. Students from prestigious universities still get much better paying jobs than students from junior colleges.

At the same time, there has been a decided shift toward career-oriented education. The idea of "knowledge for itself" is not very popular among today's students. A 1974 study of 157 two-year colleges found that the majority of students were studying occupational skills rather than taking programs that would lead to their entrance into a four-year school (Garland 1974). The same trend occurs in four-year colleges and universities. Almost two-thirds of a sample of first-year college students planned occupational majors in 1975 (Harris and Geede 1977, pp. 34–35). These figures represent a major social change with respect to higher education. Today's schools are attempting to more explicitly tie education to the economic institution than in the past. To a large extent, this change is due to America's economic situation and to the relative decline of the number of young people in the population.

SUMMARY

In order to carry out essential tasks, such as reproduction, all societies develop social institutions, including the family, religion, and education. These institutions are organized sets of norms and roles serving enduring social needs. They make social life possible, but they also act as powerful agents of social control. For this reason, we must understand that institutions are products of human beings, culture-bound, and linked to one another and that they can be changed.

In studying the family as a social institution, we looked at some of the principles of structure that sociologists have identified: those regulating the number of spouses; norms for relationships of family members; principles of residence patterns, authority, and descent systems; and norms for mate selection. All of these principles place clear social restraints on the way we must behave within a family.

Many Americans have challenged the traditional norms of the nuclear family in recent years by placing their personal needs over institutional restraints. The sexual revolution has brought changes in public morals, attitudes, and sexual behavior—especially among women and youth—which have allowed individuals to assert their own nonnormative sexuality. Divorces based on personal dissatisfaction have increased in number, and divorce laws have been liberalized. We also looked at emerging alternatives to the traditional nuclear family.

Like other institutions, religion serves

a number of personal and social functions (calming us in times of anxiety, bolstering social norms, and so on). And we saw that, as an institution, religion is rooted in the everyday world. This is evident in the uneven distribution of religions over areas and in social classes. Although once strict divisions have softened, we still associate religious groups with high or low status. In addition, we used Weber's theory of the Protestant ethic to see how even non-Protestant Americans share this social ethic of hard work, thrift, and individualism. We realized how complex religiosity is at the individual level, and we examined its three dimensions: ritual, belief, and secular behavior.

Finally, we focused on the institution of education—how in the United States, there has been a shift from elite to mass education, and how the institution functions to transmit the culture to new generations, serve social justice, and train individuals for adult life. We also looked at how education perpetuates social inequalities. In a two-stage process, individuals from lower-income families tend to be provided poorer quality educations, and then roles are awarded on the basis of educational achievement, placing the poor at a disadvantage. However, the challenges American education faces today all aim to equalize educational opportunities: by mandating racial equality, by reducing sexism, and by making higher education available to the mass of citizens.

Key Terms

social institutions (p. 181)
family (p. 184)
family of orientation (p. 185)
family of procreation (p. 185)
nuclear family (p. 188)
extended family (p. 188)
monogamy (p. 188)
polygamy (p. 188)
polygyny (p. 188)
polyandry (p. 188)
consanguinal (p. 188)
affinal (p. 188)
neolocality (p. 188)
matrilocality (p. 188)
patrilocality (p. 188)
patriarchy (p. 188)
matriarchy (p. 188)
equalitarian (p. 189)
patrilineal (p. 189)
matrilineal (p. 189)
bilateral descent (p. 189)
exogamy (p. 189)
endogamy (p. 189)
sacred (p. 196)
religion (p. 197)

Review and Discussion Questions

1. How have the major social institutions—either the ones discussed in this chapter or others—changed since your childhood? What brought these changes about? What form did resistance to these changes take? What do you foresee for the future?

2. Would you call most of the marriages you know of today "open marriages," in the O'Neills' sense of the phrase? Are today's marriages really more open than those of your parents' generation? How? Are communes, contract marriages, or other alternatives the wave of the future?

3. Some people say that the institution of marriage is dying out; others say that it is changing. How do you feel about marriage for yourself? What changes would you make in the traditional marriage contract?

4. What has your religious experience been like? How has it differed from that of your parents or from that of your friends? What personal decisions have you made about your religious practice?

5. Where have you encountered the reinforcement of traditional images of women and men by major institutions? Where did you

encounter these images in your schooling, in your family situation, or in religious doctrine and practice?

6. How well has American education served the cause of social justice? Should more be done to give blacks and other minorities equal educational opportunities? Should we pursue the goal of equality even if it hurts individual whites or males? If not, where do we draw the line?

For Further Study

THE FAMILY Sociological and popular literature abound with analyses of the family. For historical hindsight, see Philippe Ariès, *Centuries of Childhood: A Social History of Family Life* (New York: Vintage, 1962). Sociologist Jessie Bernard has applied her years of research on the family in two books that question some of our family institution's basic underpinnings: *The Future of Marriage* (New York: Bantam, 1973) and *The Future of Motherhood* (New York: Penguin, 1974). For discussions of alternatives to the nuclear family, see: Gordon Clanton and Chris Downing, eds., *Face to Face to Face* (New York: Dutton, 1975) and Roger Libby and Robert N. Whitehurst, eds., *Marriage and Alternatives* (Glenview, IL: Scott, Foresman, 1977).

RELIGION The two classic works in the sociology of religion are: Emile Durkheim, *The Elementary Forms of Religious Life* (New York: Free Press, 1965) and Max Weber, *Sociology of Religion* (Boston: Beacon, 1963). Durkheim studied the primitive religions of Australia, arguing that religion emanates from the same basic sentiments as society. Weber looked at both simple and complex religions and placed major religious concepts in a sociological perspective. A book of more contemporary essays supplements Durkheim's and Weber's basic perspectives: Charles Y. Glock and Phillip E. Hammond, eds., *Beyond the Classics? Essays in the Scientific Study of Religion* (New York: Harper & Row, 1973). Sydney E. Ahlstrom, *A Religious History of the American People* (New Haven, CT: Yale University Press, 1972) is the most comprehensive historical review of how religion developed in this country. There are also some fine collections of scholarly pieces on religion in America today, including the new religious cults, in: Charles Y. Glock and Robert N. Bellah, eds., *The New Religious Consciousness* (Berkeley: University of California Press, 1976); Jacob Needleman and George Baker, eds., *Understanding the New Religions* (New York: Seabury, 1978); and Irving Zaretsky and Mark P. Leone, eds., *Religious Movements in Contemporary America* (Princeton, N. J: Princeton University Press, 1978).

EDUCATION For additional evidence on education's ties with the economic and political institutions, see S. Bowles and H. Gintis, *Schooling in Capitalist America* (New York: Basic Books, 1976). Torsten Husen analyzes the school's problems as a social institution in Europe and America in *The School in Question: A Comparative Study of School and Its Future in Western Societies* (New York: Oxford University Press, 1979). Finally, there is a growing literature on sexism in schools, including: Nancy Frazier and Myra Sadlek, *Sexism in School and Society* (New York: Harper & Row, 1973); Judith Stacey, Susan Bereaud, and Joan Daniels, eds., *And Jill Came Tumbling After: Sexism in American Education* (New York: Dell, 1974); and in *Unlearning the Lie: Sexism in School* (New York: Morrow, 1973), Barbara G. Harrison has written about one private school's attempt to recognize and weed out sexism in its program.

CHAPTER SEVEN
Social Stratification

During our study of society in this book, we have continually encountered inequality as a basic fact of social life—from the unequal rewards people receive for playing different roles to unequal positions in bureaucratic organizations to inequality of educational opportunity. Moreover, we are aware of inequality in our daily lives—between parents and children, between teachers and students, between blacks and whites, between employers and employees, and in so many more cases. Sociologists try to make sense of these inequalities by analyzing their social bases, using the concept of *social stratification.* In this chapter, we'll look at the nature of social stratification, its importance, the form it takes in the United States, and groups that form around their unequal positions in society's stratification system.

WHAT IS SOCIAL STRATIFICATION?

Social stratification is the unequal distribution of valued resources among different categories of people in society. Writing in 1754, the French philosopher Jean Jacques Rousseau divided inequality into two types, physical and political:

I conceive that there are two kinds of inequality among the human species; one, which I call natural or physical, because it is established by nature, and consists in a difference of age, health, bodily strength, and the qualities of the mind or of the soul: and another, which may be called moral or political inequality, because it depends on a kind of convention, and is established, or at least authorized, by the consent of men. This latter consists of the different privileges some men enjoy to the prejudice of others; such as that of being more rich, more honoured, more powerful, or even in a position to exact obedience (Rousseau 1913 [1754], p. 160).

In studying social stratification, we are concerned with inequalities of the second type—inequalities created by society. If you object, however, that in a study of stratification, differences in "natural" abilities, like intelligence, must also be considered, you are correct. But as we will see in this chapter and the next, these natural abilities do not play as great a role in stratification as is popularly supposed. Furthermore, the significance given to differences in natural strengths or talents is purely social. In studying social stratification, sociologists therefore concentrate on the unequal privileges some people enjoy. These privileges, as sociologists today commonly conceive of them, consist of access to the scarce resources of property, social honor, and power.

Functions of Stratification

Most of us would agree that societies—even democratic and communist ones, with their ideologies of equality—are stratified. Some people in every society have greater access than do others to whatever that culture considers important. This apparent universality of social stratification has led some sociologists to argue that inequality is a functional necessity of society. The main arguments for this position are laid out in an influential article by Kingsley Davis and Wilbert Moore (Davis and Moore 1945). Every society, Davis and Moore argue, must fill a number of social positions to survive, and these positions are neither equal in their social value nor in their rewards for the individuals filling them. Society must therefore motivate sufficient individuals to fill all of them and perform the relevant tasks; moreover, it should motivate the ablest to fill the most important and difficult positions. All of this is accomplished through a system of differential rewards, which attract the most qualified persons for the most important positions. Stratification (inequality) is thereby functional, because it assures that the best qualified people will play these roles.

The Davis-Moore hypothesis of stratification's necessity has not gone unchallenged. Critics have noted that the hypothesis does not fit the social reality of stratification in a number of respects. For instance, there are many entertainers and movie stars in our society with incomes much greater than those of judges, senators, and the president of the United States, even though their social roles are obviously not as crucial to society. Nor does inherited wealth mesh well with the Davis-Moore hypothesis. Critics such as Melvin Tumin (1967) point out, furthermore, that inequality is actually dysfunctional in some important ways. It denies equal access to social positions, thereby keeping many talented individuals from reaching important positions. And inequality may lead to dissatisfaction and revolt among the have-nots, which undermines social stability. Finally, conflict theorists argue that the dominance of one social group over another—not social functions—is the key factor in explaining stratification. They view stratification as the outcome of social struggle between dominant groups that use their power to preserve the status quo and keep other groups out of the competition. In any case, it should be noted that even if we accept the Davis-Moore hypothesis, it does not justify the actual inequality found in a society. For even if we grant that the director of an automobile manufacturing company holds a more important position than a worker on the company's assembly line, that doesn't mean that the director deserves, or that society requires she or he receive, one hundred times the income of the line worker.

Types of Social Stratification

Sociologists make a distinction between two major types of stratification found in societies—*caste* and *class*—based on the possibility individuals have of moving between strata. Briefly, a **caste system** is one in which individuals are born into a specific social rank—their parents'—and can never leave it. Generally, caste members must also marry within their own caste, that is, marriage is endogamous. Caste status, then, is an *ascribed status,* outside of an individual's power to control (see Chapter 3). Nothing we do can change our caste status. The classic example of a caste society is India, where all contacts between people of different castes were rigidly regulated. Although the Indian caste system has been officially abolished, many caste practices continue. Another important example of a caste system is the historic relationship between whites and blacks in the United States. There was, and to some extent still is, a caste barrier that prevented blacks from reaching equality with whites.

In contrast to a caste society, a **class system** allows movement between strata. As a general rule, wealth is seen as the major determinant of class, although, as we will see, other factors are also involved. Class status is, at least to some extent, an *achieved status.* As we saw in Chapter 3, achieved statuses are earned—through business success, education, or some other activity. Achieved status can also be lost—if your business goes bankrupt, for example. The United States and other industrialized countries of the West are all fundamentally societies of the class type. We will focus on this type of stratification system in the remainder of this chapter.

During the 1940s and 1950s, many sociological studies were conducted of cities, towns, and villages, in part to try to understand social stratification in the United States. In an anecdote about one of these, one sociologist reported that he saw nine classes in the town he studied. This happened to be the hometown of novelist J.P. Marquand, who angrily countered that claim in his novel *Point of No Return.* Marquand replied that he had lived in the town all his life and had never seen any classes. Although the sociological term *stratification* is borrowed from geology, it lacks the tangible evidence of its geologic meaning—that is, of distinct layers of rock piled one atop another. To prove the existence of stratification, a geologist need only show a photograph of the walls of the Grand Canyon; everyone who looked would see the layers. Demonstrating the existence of social stratification, made up of "layers" of people piled one atop the other, is more difficult, especially in a class type of society. The reason for this is that class boundaries are blurred, while those of castes seldom are. Thus to some, stratification appears as a continuum rather than as a series of clearly delineated strata.

We will return to the issue of the discreteness of social classes later, but first we need to investigate the components of stratification.

DIMENSIONS OF STRATIFICATION

Two central figures continue to dominate our understanding of stratification—Karl Marx and Max Weber. Many sociologists treat Marx and Weber's theories on stratification as if they were in conflict with each other. To be sure, there are important differences between them, but both Marx and Weber believed power relationships to be the essence of social stratification. In this section, we'll concentrate on Weber's views, which provide us with the more detailed look at stratification. In the next section, on the discreteness of classes and on class consciousness, we'll concentrate on Marx.

Weber saw stratification in terms of the unequal distribution of power in society, and he identifies three dimensions of that distribution: property, prestige, and political power. Property, prestige, and political power can be thought of as social rewards, and the way they are distributed depends on the structure of the society.

The stratification of society along the dimensions of property, prestige, and political power isn't merely an academic fact, Weber emphasizes, but one that affects our life chances. By **life chances,** Weber means our opportunity to enjoy various goods, living conditions, and experiences. In this section, we'll examine each dimension of stratification—the unequal distribution of property, prestige, and political power in the United States—and the groups formed on the basis of their position along each dimension. Finally, in the coming pages, we'll see how closely property, prestige, and political power are linked to one another.

PROPERTY

In discussing property inequality, sociologists frequently make a distinction between annual income and wealth. *Annual income* is money received over a year's time (wages, salaries, rents, dividends, and the like) while *wealth* is the total monetary value of the property held (houses, cars, stocks, bonds, etc.). By practically any standard, inequality of both forms of property in the United States is considerable.

In terms of income, under a situation of complete equality, each fifth of the income-receiving population would gain one-fifth of the income. But, as you can see in

Table 7.1, this has not been the case in the United States today. In fact, the highest fifth of the population earns close to half of the nation's income, whereas the lowest fifth takes in only about a twentieth. Actual income inequalities are undoubtedly even greater than the figures indicate because they do not include fringe benefits, which go disproportionately to those with higher incomes. Those at the upper-income levels are more likely to receive liberal health and retirement programs, a free company car, maybe even free meals ("three martini lunches") and travel, for example (Miller and Roby 1970). In other words, the gulf separating the highest paid and lowest paid Americans is considerable. Furthermore, the extent of inequality by income fifths has changed little since the 1930s (Jencks and Riesman 1968). And taxation does little to reduce this inequality (see Table 7.2, p. 228).

In terms of wealth, the extent of inequality in America is even more dramatic. According to a comprehensive 1962 survey (Lampman 1962), still the most thorough conducted, the wealthiest fifth of the wealth-holding population held three-quarters of all personal wealth in the country, including all but 3 percent of the corporate stock. The top 5 percent of wealthholders alone held more than 50 percent of the nation's personal wealth that year. According to a 1974 study, the top 1 percent hold about a quarter of all wealth in the United States, and over half of all corporate stock (Smith and Franklin 1974). Most American families meanwhile own a car and perhaps a house, but beyond these items own little, particularly any sort of income-producing investments. Moreover, this picture of wealth inequality has remained fairly stable since 1945.

Stratification affects our play as well as our work, even what we drink. This happy man is having a great time singing "Drink! Drink! Drink!" in a Bavarian beer tent. And he is probably a clerk rather than an executive. . . .

While our serious and reserved wine taster is obviously of a "higher class."

Table 7.1 Income Inequality in the United States, 1947–1977

Percent Share of Aggregate Income

Year	Lowest Fifth	Second Fifth	Middle Fifth	Fourth Fifth	Highest Fifth
1978	3.8	9.7	16.5	24.9	45.2
1977	3.8	9.9	16.7	24.9	44.7
1976	3.9	9.9	16.7	24.9	44.5
1975	3.9	10.1	16.8	24.7	44.4
1974	3.8	10.1	16.9	24.8	44.4
1973	3.8	10.0	16.9	24.8	44.5
1972	3.7	10.0	16.9	24.7	44.8
1971	3.7	10.2	17.1	24.7	44.3
1970	3.6	10.3	17.2	24.7	44.1
1969	3.7	10.5	17.4	24.7	43.7
1968	3.8	10.7	17.4	24.7	43.5
1967	3.6	10.6	17.5	24.8	43.4
1966	3.8	10.7	17.5	24.7	43.4
1965	3.6	10.6	17.5	24.8	43.6
1964	3.4	10.4	17.3	24.8	44.1
1963	3.4	10.4	17.5	24.8	43.9
1962	3.4	10.4	17.5	24.8	43.9
1961	3.1	10.2	17.2	24.6	44.9
1960	3.2	10.6	17.6	24.7	44.0
1959	3.2	10.6	17.7	24.7	43.9
1958	3.3	10.8	17.9	24.8	43.3
1957	3.4	10.9	18.0	24.7	42.9
1956	3.4	10.8	17.7	24.5	43.5
1955	3.3	10.6	17.6	24.6	43.9
1954	3.1	10.4	17.5	24.7	44.4
1953	3.2	10.8	17.6	24.5	43.8
1952	3.5	10.9	17.3	24.1	44.3
1951	3.5	11.2	17.6	24.1	43.6
1950	3.1	10.6	17.3	24.1	44.9
1949	3.2	10.5	17.2	24.2	44.9
1948	3.5	10.8	17.2	23.9	44.7
1947	3.5	10.6	16.8	23.6	45.5

SOURCE: *U.S. Department of Commerce,* Current Population Survey: Consumer Income *(Washington, DC: Government Printing Office, 1977, Series P-60, No. 118, Table 13).*

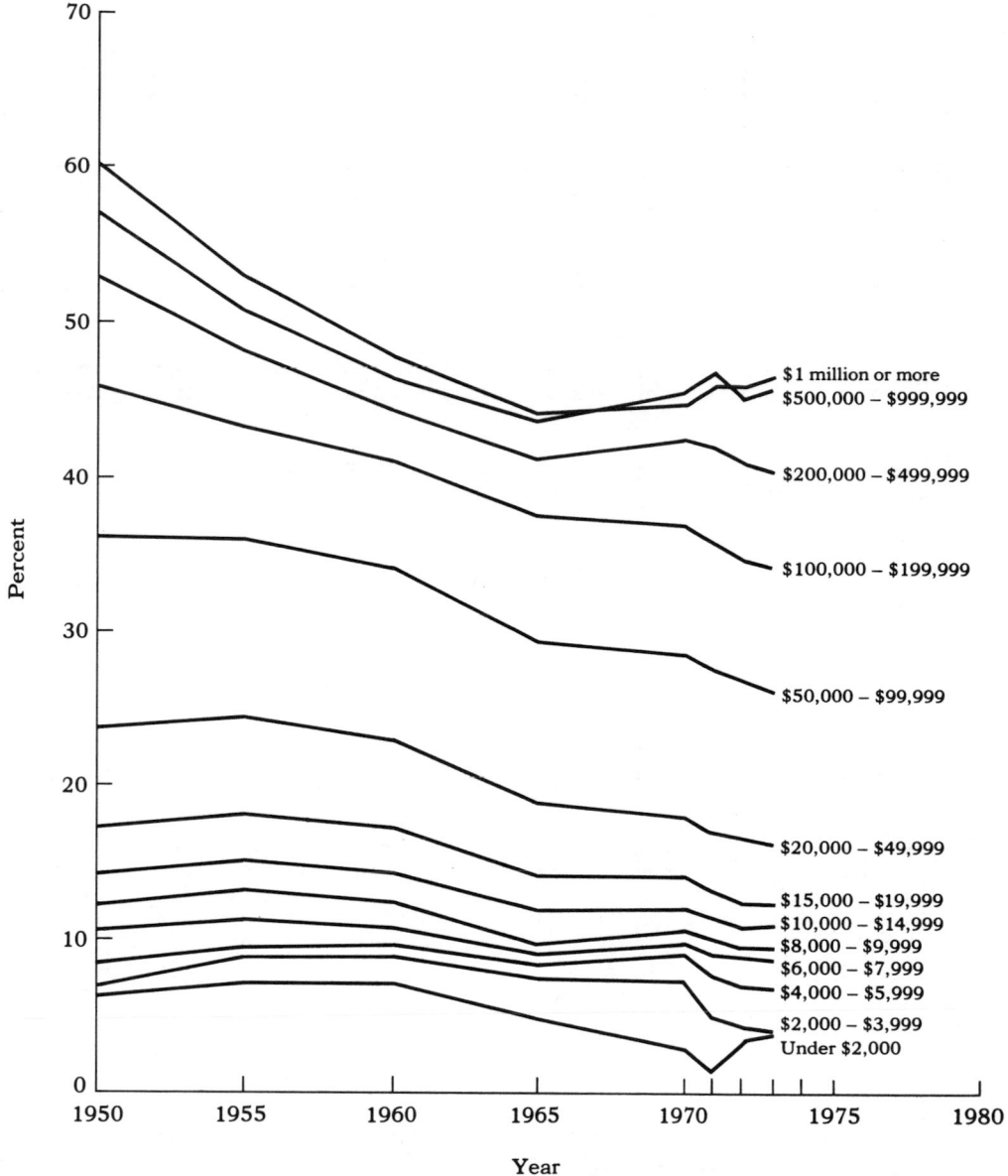

Figure 7.1 Average Individual Income Tax as Percent of Adjusted Gross Income in the United States, 1950–1973

SOURCE: U.S. Department of Commerce, Social Indicators: 1976 *(Washington, DC: Government Printing Office, 1977, Chart 12a).*

Table 7.2 Percent Share of Total Pretax and Posttax Income, Received by Each Tenth of Population, Selected Countries and Years, 1966–1973

Country and Year	Bottom Tenth	Ninth	Eighth	Seventh	Sixth	Fifth	Fourth	Third	Second	Top
Australia, 1966–67										
Pretax	2.1	4.5	6.2	7.3	8.3	9.5	10.9	12.5	15.1	23.8
Posttax	2.1	4.5	6.2	7.3	8.3	9.5	10.9	12.5	15.1	23.7
Canada, 1969										
Pretax	1.2	3.1	4.6	6.3	7.9	9.4	11.1	13.1	16.2	27.1
Posttax	1.5	3.5	5.1	6.7	8.2	9.7	11.2	13.1	15.9	25.1
France, 1970										
Pretax	1.5	2.8	4.2	5.7	7.1	8.7	10.4	12.6	16.0	31.0
Posttax	1.4	2.9	4.2	5.6	7.4	8.9	9.7	13.0	16.5	30.4
Germany (Fed. Rep.)										
Pretax	2.5	3.4	4.5	5.6	6.8	8.3	9.9	12.2	15.7	31.1
Posttax	2.8	3.7	4.6	5.7	6.8	8.2	9.8	12.1	15.8	30.3
Japan, 1969										
Pretax	2.9	4.7	5.8	6.8	7.7	8.6	9.7	11.3	13.9	28.6
Posttax	3.0	4.9	6.1	7.0	7.9	8.9	9.9	11.3	13.8	27.2
Netherlands, 1967										
Pretax	2.3	3.6	4.9	6.0	7.3	8.5	9.9	11.7	14.7	31.1
Posttax	2.6	3.9	5.2	6.4	7.6	8.8	10.3	12.4	15.2	27.7
Norway, 1970										
Pretax	1.7	3.2	4.9	6.7	8.2	9.8	11.3	13.3	16.4	24.5
Posttax	2.3	4.0	5.6	7.3	8.6	.2	11.7	13.0	15.1	22.2
Sweden, 1972										
Pretax	2.0	4.0	5.3	6.1	7.9	9.5	11.2	13.1	16.1	24.4
Posttax	2.2	4.4	5.9	7.2	8.5	10.0	11.5	13.3	15.7	21.3
United Kingdom, 1973										
Pretax	2.1	3.3	5.1	6.9	8.3	9.8	11.2	13.0	15.6	24.7
Posttax	2.5	3.8	5.5	7.1	8.5	9.9	11.1	12.8	15.2	23.5
United States, 1972										
Pretax	1.2	2.6	4.2	5.8	7.5	9.3	11.1	13.4	16.4	28.4
Posttax	1.5	3.0	4.5	6.2	7.8	9.5	11.3	13.4	16.3	26.6

SOURCE: *U.S. Department of Commerce, Social Indicators: 1976 (Washington, DC: Government Printing Office, 1977, Table 9/37).*

Property and Life Chances

The enormous differences in buying power, financial resources, and security that the above figures reflect clearly affect the life chances of American families in many ways. Below are just a few of the ways in which the distribution of life chances is based on economic condition.

For one, we saw in the last chapter the vastly unequal distribution of educational resources; namely, poor people have much less chance of getting a high-quality education than do rich people. The opportunity for health care also illustrates this inequality. Health care facilities in many poor neighborhoods are nonexistent or substandard. Physicians have been known to give poorer treatment to patients paying with Medicaid funds, while the on-again—off-again ban in many states on the use of such funds for abortions has deprived countless poor women of competent medical care in this area. Poor people suffer disproportionately from cardiovascular disorders, rheumatic fever, heart disease, diabetes, cancer, infant mortality, arthritis, sight impairment, and other medical problems (Hurley 1969, p. 132).

Poor people also have more problems with mental health than do persons of the middle and upper classes. Their physical environment does not provide the stimulation often required for mental health, and, because of often inadequate nutrition and prenatal care, they suffer higher rates of mental retardation (Hurley 1969). Two studies, ten years apart, both found that the poorer you are, the more likely you are to be defined as mentally ill, institutionalized, and kept in an institution. According to Jerome K. Meyers and Lee L. Bean (1968), the mental hospital staffs they studied tended to "give up" on the poorer patients, because they considered such patients "poorer risks" for release and knew that few poor patients could afford community and outside medical resources for maintaining care.

The poor also have unequal chances for adequate housing and protection from crime. They are victimized by criminals far more than the rich are, partly because they have to live in areas that receive comparatively little police protection. The poor also suffer most from absentee landlords, whose buildings are likely to violate safety codes, at least judging from my own year-long observation of Philadelphia's landlord-tenant court.

CLASS Weber calls people with similar life chances as determined by economics (the possession of goods and opportunities for income) a **class.** Class, then, is a phenomenon of a society's economic system. Note that, in Weber's sense, people in the same class situation don't necessarily form a group, or "community," with interaction among members and a common consciousness of interests (see Chapter 5). Weber does, however, see *class interests*—interests people share because of their economic position—as a potential, but not certain, base for collective action.

Frequently today, for instance, individuals in the same class situation act together to better their economic condition when that condition can be changed: unionization is one example, and communist revolutions are others. And people also act in accordance with their class interest to support the status quo. For instance, economist Robert L. Heilbroner (1966) has shown that the United States has the financial resources needed to eliminate poverty within its midst. He adds,

Land of opportunity? Children growing up in this affluent suburb will likely achieve their full potential. . .

however, that a major obstacle in doing so lies in the fact that the wealthiest groups have been able to influence laws and find loopholes in those passed (e.g., in inheritance and income tax laws) to protect their interests against those of the poor and middle-income groups (Heilbroner 1966, pp. 76–88). We'll return to the issues of class and class interest when we discuss Marx's views later.

POWER Social power is the ability to get your way in a social setting. It takes many forms. For example, society has given the police a type of power that gives them the right to order people about, to use firearms, and to arrest people. We stop when they shout "Halt!" There is also the power of large industries, such as General Motors: "Its budget is bigger than those of the three biggest states and bigger than all but two nations in the world . . . its enormous economic wealth has purchased the loyalty of congressmen, senators, and federal officials, and . . . its lobbyists can shape the tax laws, criminal laws, and economic policies of Washington" (Newfield and Greenfield 1972, p. 43).

Another type of power is the power to determine social goals and values. Religious leaders have this power, for example, Similarly, the small minority of American busineses that can afford to buy television time for advertising have the power to regulate the type of programs that we will see.

Power in contemporary societies is generally sanctioned by explicit rules (e.g., those that legitimate police use of weapons and allow large businesses to keep so much money). So we can understand why people would like to control the making and enforcement of those rules, whether for a bank or for the nation as a whole. Weber

. . . while millions of slum-dwelling Americans have limited opportunities for a good education, adequate health care, decent housing, or protection from crime.

called groups whose only purpose is to acquire such power **parties**. Parties vie for control of a situation, regardless of the content of the issue at hand. Although political parties are good examples of this type of group, they are not the only ones. Parties emerge whenever group action must be taken and, as is usually the case, people do not agree about what should be done or who should do it. Until recently, for example, whenever the College of Cardinals met to choose a Roman Catholic pope, the members grouped into parties, each party representing an important Italian family. In this context, we can think of parties as *factions*—organized collectives that act in a planned manner to influence group decisions. In any case, parties, by definition, will conflict for the power to impose their point of view, or simply their own candidate, on the entire group. Will Democrats or Republicans run the country? Will union

or management control wages? Who will set product safety standards, manufacturers or consumers? (Also see Popular Culture, High Culture, and Stratification on p. 233.)

Parties may form on the basis of, or represent, property and prestige interests, and they may recruit members from particular classes and status groups, but, as Weber points out, they don't *have* to represent these interests. For instance, in the American political process, political "pros" choose their party's candidates on the basis of how likely they are to get elected and this may not correspond to how well they represent the interests of, for example, the wealthiest party backers.

Finally, although wealth and power are generally related, they are not always. The *Chicago Sun-Times* columnist Mike Royko illustrated this in his biography of the former mayor of Chicago, Richard Daley. Daley started his political career at about the same time as former Chicago Alderman Thomas Keane started his: "Keane is considered to be second in party power, but it is a distant second. Keane wanted to be in the front, but he was distracted by a craving for personal wealth. You can't do both if the man you're chasing is concentrating only on power. Now Keane is rich, but too old ever to be the successor" (Royko 1971, p. 19). Meanwhile, Richard Daley concentrated on obtaining power and building a machine to maintain it. He thus became the last of the big-city "bosses" and one of the nation's most powerful Democrats. Several factors, including humble origins and his association with corruption, however, kept him relatively low on Weber's third dimension of stratification, prestige.

Prestige

The third dimension of stratification identified by Weber is prestige. *Prestige* is the esteem or social honor accorded a person or group in society. The term *status*, which we saw in Chapter 3 can be used to refer to a social position in general, is often used by sociologists to refer more specifically to a person's position in a prestige hierarchy.

Prestige, like property and power, can be thought of as a social reward, a recognition for our "good" performance in social roles. Like property and power, too, prestige is distributed unequally in American society. Judges are accorded more respect than machine operatives, for instance, and whites more than blacks. Because prestige is not granted equally, it appears to be in short supply, and for this reason people often struggle for the "amount" that is available. For instance, two people may

try to out-dress each other, or have the nicest lawn on the block, or compete to be considered the most intelligent or the best lover.

We constantly judge other people on the basis of their prestige. These evaluations may cause us to ignore certain people, or discriminate against them, or voluntarily segregate ourselves with others, or try to become part of that crowd. These judgments are also the source of the high interest in the lives of royalty, heiresses and heirs, and Hollywood actors and actresses. People follow the marriages and love affairs of these people with a passion, while ignoring the same events in the lives of people in their own neighborhood.

Our prestige judgments tell us to whom we should or should not (or need not!) listen. That is, we evaluate a person's characteristics to see whether it is worth our while to take the time and make the effort to listen. We determine that we can listen to our sociology instructor about social life, to Walter Cronkite about the day's news, or to an auto mechanic about our car, and receive a competent explanation. However, sometimes we inappropriately generalize our judgments: we expect a sociologist's statements about art, a physician's opinions about society, or the president's analysis of most things to be correct. For example, three social psychologists conducted a field experiment in which they found that pedestrians standing at a traffic signal were more likely to cross against the signal if they saw an individual they judged to be of high status crossing, than if someone they thought was of low status crossed (Lefkowitz et al. 1955).

We not only make prestige evaluations of others, we develop an awareness of our own standing in the eyes of others. Each of us internalizes a social definition of self

POPULAR CULTURE, HIGH CULTURE,
AND STRATIFICATION

According to sociologist Herbert Gans, "in heterogeneous societies, the struggles between diverse groups and aggregates over the allocation of resources and power are not limited to strictly economic and political issues, but also extend to cultural ones" (1974, p. 3). In fact, he says, there is a definite stratification system for cultural objects and events, composed of two main strata: popular culture (the lower) and high culture (the higher).

For the devotees of high culture, only such activities as attending museums, symphonies, art exhibits, and the like are truly cultured. For these people, such activities as watching television, reading popular novels, and so on are not at all cultured. The consumers of popular culture, however, are usually contemptuous of these people and their activities, which they consider dull. You have no doubt encountered both viewpoints. According to Gans, though, neither group is correct or incorrect. In fact, he believes that our position on this matter has a lot to do with various social traits, but especially with our social class. Thus most professionals, executives, and managers belong to one class of culture (upper-middle culture); members of the middle and lower-middle class belong to another (lower-middle culture); factory workers to another (lower culture), and the poor to quasi-folk lower culture.

Gans also notes that every item of culture carries certain educational requisites for its use—low for comic strips, high for the poetry of T.S. Eliot. Moreover, standards of taste are taught in the home and school, and our educational attainment—so closely tied to social class, as we saw in Chapter 6—is the best predictor of our cultural taste.

Gans concludes that the entire argument over what constitutes legitimate cultural pastimes—viewing abstract art or watching a television program, attending a symphony or listening to Johnny Cash—boils down to each group's attempt to impose its notion of the good life on everyone else. And in being assigned different values, each cultural activity becomes a source of social status, either high or low.

during the socialization process, and the combined reactions of others (who have experienced a similar socialization as members of the same society) reinforce our self-image throughout our lives. This self-image includes our status—whether economic, educational, political, or whatever—within the stratification system.

BASES OF PRESTIGE   There are numerous bases on which prestige is granted us, with occupation and income being among the most important. Occupational prestige and income often go together, especially in our culture where economic success is an important social value, but they don't have to. Gerhard Lenski (1966, p. 1), for instance, cites the example of Robert S. McNamara, who in 1960 left a $400,000-a-year post at Ford Motor Company to become President Kennedy's secretary of defense—at an annual salary of $25,000. Moving from Ford to the cabinet, McNamara traded a good deal of money for a lot of prestige. Researchers of occupational prestige have consistently found that Americans rank lower paying occupations like college professor, for example, higher in prestige than the better paying livelihoods of banker, building contractor, and board member of a large corporation (Hodge et al. 1964).

Extensive education is also accorded high prestige, as is intelligence. Our residence may also confer status, as may the way we speak and dress. We may be granted more prestige, for example, by appearing refined or keeping up with the latest fashions. We may also be granted some prestige for wearing a uniform, being at an important event, meeting a famous individual, or being good at something (sewing or playing tennis well, being able to drink more beer than all our friends, and so on).

STATUS GROUPS   When a number of people have roughly similar chances of getting what they want, on the basis of their prestige, they belong to the same **status group.** Nobel Prize winners and former astronauts compose status groups, for example. But American blacks and women may also be considered status groups, because the prestige they receive—or don't receive—affects their life chances.

Status groups often become identified with particular styles of life. For instance, you do not expect your instructors to talk in "street language" or to come to school looking unkempt. That behavior does not fit their status, and your reactions would let them know it.

Knowlege of the tendency of status to be associated with a style of life allows us the opportunity to try to manipulate the amount of prestige accorded us by trying to live the way high-status people do. People often hope to be granted prestige by their accumulating **status symbols**—things that indicate the possessor is worthy of respect because they are associated with high-status people (luxury cars, vintage wines, a yacht, and the like). Before the 1960s, for instance, many blacks tried to straighten their hair or lighten their skin and thus resemble the higher status whites; in fact, light-skinned blacks used to have high status within the American black community.

Even though we develop expectations about who is worthy of respect and the style of life they are likely to lead, we shouldn't lose sight of the true source of prestige. To a greater extent than wealth and power, our prestige depends on the social environment in which we find ourselves. The reason for this is that our prestige is not something intrinsically ours but instead is something granted us by others. Whereas wealth and power are largely independent of who recognizes our having them, our prestige depends entirely on whether those around us recognize it. For example, after World War II, a number of high-status Lithuanians emigrated to the United States when the Soviet Union took over their country. Upon arrival, however, these military officers, lawyers, teachers, politicians, and such found that their former status was not recognized here, and they had to adjust to menial positions (Benkin and DeSantis 1978). But we do not have to go from one society to another for the prestige accorded us to change; it can also change within a society, as the social environment changes. The prestige I had for being the best stickball player on the block does nothing for me when I am with other sociologists. Similarly, your instructors might have a great deal of prestige in the classroom, but when they drive home on traffic-jammed expressways, the other drivers don't pull over "for the professors"; they have to crawl along with everyone else.

While it is analytically useful to distinguish prestige from wealth and power, we should also appreciate how prestige is tied to other social rewards. If you remember how Protestantism related business success to God's approval, you can see why such success in itself often brings prestige as well as wealth in the United States. "Success" stories like those of Rockefeller, Kennedy, Getty, Vanderbilt, and Morgan have become part of our folklore. And it doesn't seem to matter how these men made their fortunes: many of them were

known as "robber barons" because of their ruthless and dishonest business practices, but they are granted high prestige nonetheless. In fact, even in preliterate societies, prestige seems to be closely related to an individual's economic productivity. In his study of the primitive hunting and gathering society of the Andaman Islanders, A.R. Radcliffe-Brown (1922) wrote that they give the greatest honor to the society's elders, who possess essential knowledge; people believed to have supernatural powers; and highly skilled hunters and warriors, because these categories of people are the most important to the group's economic system.

In prerevolutionary France, commoners who became wealthy enough tried to buy prestige by purchasing titles of nobility (e.g., duke, marquis). King Louis XIV saw a way to make additional money out of this market in titles: every time the French treasury ran short he declared all purchased titles void (Tocqueville 1955 [1856]). The king was right in his guess that people would buy the titles again, for it was their only chance to obtain that prestige. The fact that they could be declared void shows again that prestige depends ultimately on the honor others are willing to grant us and cannot be bought.

Prestige is also frequently associated with political power. This is apparent in the ability of "white-collar criminals," because of their prestige, to avoid harsh punishment. According to a government report (Anderson 1978), a poor black convicted of robbery has a 90 percent chance of being imprisoned, while white-collar embezzlers have but a 20 percent chance. And just as prestige can gain us political privileges, so political power can gain us prestige. Thus high government officials are granted more prestige in the United States than practically any other occupational group (Hodge et al. 1964).

This concludes our discussion of the three dimensions of stratification Weber identifies. Weber's conception of class, status, and party refines, and in some respects counters, the theories of class put forth by Karl Marx. Marx's theories, however, are still important in their own right because of their influence throughout the world and because they shed further light on the nature of stratification in modern society. Let's turn now to Marx's conceptions of class and class consciousness and see how applicable his theories are to the United States.

THE MARXIAN VIEW OF CLASS AND CLASS CONSCIOUSNESS

For Marx, the essence of social stratification in industrialized capitalist societies is *stratification by class.* By the term **class,** Marx means those people who are in fundamentally the same relationship to the means of production of a society. That is, in modern society at least, Marx believes the main determinant of a group's status and political power is its relationship to the means of production. He sees that throughout most of human history, some people owned or controlled the means of society's economic production while others did not, and because of this, masters and slaves, lords and serfs, capitalists and workers developed different, conflicting interests (see Who Wants Poverty?). The conflict between these collectivities, Marx argued, is the motive force of history.

In Marx's formulation, then, modern classes are antagonistic social groups that oppose each other in defense of their essential economic interests. The two main classes in capitalist society are the class of owners of the means of production—the **bourgeoisie**—and the working class—or **proletariat.** At the simplest level, industrialists want to get the most work out of their laborers for the smallest pay, and their workers want the highest wages they can get for the least work. Thus the very nature of capitalist economic production—where one class uses the other's labor for its own profit—is at the root of conflict between classes. It is essential to keep in mind, Marxist sociologists tell us, that the Marxian notion of class highlights certain relationships between individuals—specifically, those of dominance and subordination—and not their functional (occupational) roles (Kalleberg and Griffin 1980). In other words, a worker's actual "value" to society will not determine her or his life chances as much as the fact that workers neither control nor own the means of production.

So there are three important features to Marx's view of class. First, his definition does not allow us to see classes apart from class interests. Second, he defines classes in terms of economic *production* (owner, laborer), unlike Weber who sees them primarily in terms of *consumption* (behaviors, style of life). And third, he believes that history itself is primarily determined by the action of individuals pursuing class interests.

So far, our discussion hasn't made clear whether or not classes in the Marxian sense are groups or simply sociological categories. The reason for this is that Marx sometimes uses the term to refer to groups and other times to refer to categories. Thus he distinguishes between "objective class," which is a matter of economic fact, and "subjective class," which is not. Our objective class is our class membership that derives from our relation to the means of production—whether we are aware of that membership or not. But objective class membership is transformed into subjective class membership when members of the same class become aware of their common interests, that is, through *class consciousness.*

Class Consciousness

There are three main elements of class consciousness in the Marxian sense of the term. First, **class consciousness** includes the consciousness of kind that characterizes all sociological groups as opposed to just categories of people (Chapter 5). A second aspect of class consciousness is that the members of a subjective class will share a common and realistic perception of their class interests. Class consciousness was evident, for example, among members of the industrial union movement earlier in the century. Finally, the notion of class consciousness implies not only a common perspective, but organization for active defense of class interests as well. This defense might manifest itself as, for example, the lobbying efforts of organized labor and big business, each pursuing its own class interests by strikes, demonstrations, group support of political candidates, even revolutions.

Marx believed that class consciousness would increasingly develop among workers and eventually help to bring about a revolution to overthrow capitalism and usher in socialism. Obviously, such consciousness has not developed to a great extent in many Western societies. To explain discrepancies like this between what he saw to be in the best interests of workers and what they themselves saw as their interests, Marx developed the concept of false consciousness. **False consciousness** is a belief about our place in the world and our interests that is based on an illusory sense of objective reality. An unemployed white male worker who is laid off, for instance, might blame black and female laborers now entering the work force rather than an economic system that doesn't generate enough paying jobs for everyone to do. False consciousness can arise because between reality and our beliefs comes our interpretation of that reality and our relationship to it. For example, sociologists studying why people voted as they did in the 1940 presidential election found that people who identified themselves as "labor" tended to vote Democratic, and people whose self-image was "business" generally voted Republican (Lazarsfeld et al. 1948). Even if their objective economic circumstances did not conform to the self-image, people voted according to the way they saw themselves.

Throughout this book, we have seen that the way we interpret the world and ourselves is highly susceptible to influence of others. And in Marx's view also, the dominant ideas of an age are the ideas of its dominant class. For instance, in our society it is the group of capitalist owners who can afford to buy the most television time and other media advertising space and thereby exercise some control over the content of those media. It is also this group that can best afford to support a political candidate's expensive campaign. In short, this group controls the major sources of information and therefore has the most impact on our social ideology. Obviously, those in power aren't likely to use their con-

WHO WANTS POVERTY?

Why does poverty persist in the United States? Some people blame the poor for their own condition. Others inveigh against the capitalist system. But sociologist Herbert Gans (1977) suggests that poverty may persist because certain groups of people in society find it functional for them. If poverty were to suddenly disappear, their interests would suffer.

For instance, poverty serves four economic functions. First, it ensures that enough people will be desperate enough to do society's "dirty work"—jobs that are physically dirty or dangerous, or menial and undignified. If we did not have people who had no choice but to, for example, mop floors, we would have to offer very high wages to induce people to accept such work. Second, because the poor must accept menial labor, they provide certain services to the affluent, domestic help, for example. Poverty also "creates" certain occupations—social workers, criminologists (to a large extent), and welfare bureaucrats, to name three—and that's its third economic function. Poverty's fourth economic function is that it provides a market for otherwise unwanted goods, like secondhand clothing, day-old bread, and substandard apartment buildings.

Gans also notes some social functions that the poor perform. Their powerlessness enables authorities to tag them as deviants in order to bolster conventional norms. Attributing their condition to laziness, for example, justifies their poverty. ("If they would only work hard. . . .") This in turn reduces the

trol to spread subversive ideas and preach that it is in workers' true interests to overthrow them. Few writers, nevertheless, accept false consciousness as a completely adequate explanation of the relative absence of class conflict and class consciousness in the United States compared to Marx's predictions. In the next section we will consider how well developments in the United States fit the Marxian model and

some of the reasons why there has not been a proletarian revolution in our country.

Stratification and Class Conflict in the United States

To what extent does Marx's model of classes, class consciousness, and class conflict

moral pressure for government to eliminate poverty. Also, many people participate vicariously, through the poor, in uninhibited sexual and drug behavior—although as is viewing the poor as lazy, this, too, is a stereotype. Poor people also contribute positively to American culture, thus serving another social function. Blues, jazz, and country/western music, for instance, all originated among the poor.

The very existence of poor people also guarantees that most people will have someone toward whom they can feel socially superior. Furthermore, the "poverty market" has given many Americans the income that placed them in the middle class— landlords of slum housing, owners of currency exchanges, and pawnbrokers, for example. Finally, the poor, being powerless, are forced to absorb the cost of social change. *Their* neighborhoods are usually the ones destroyed to make room for expressways, for urban renewal (intended to lure the middle class back to the city), and for university expansion.

Gans is not saying that poverty is therefore a good thing. We might perform these functions in other ways. The point is that we cannot expect the groups who profit from poverty to eradicate it. These functions help explain our inability to eliminate poverty. Beyond that, Gans's analysis makes it clear that the poor are powerless and that other people—politicians, merchants, and so on—use them to make their lives easier. Poverty also bolsters the status quo by making the alternative to conformity look so unattractive.

---

apply to the United States? Many people would rightly point out that American society hardly resembles the capitalist society predicted by Marx—a society characterized by fierce class conflicts, deep gulfs between workers and owners, and highly developed class consciousness among workers. One reason that Marx's predictions have not come true is that the class structure has in some respects become more rather than less complicated since his day. Marx expected that the middle class would all but disappear as capitalist industrialization progressed. While he correctly foresaw the decline of small farmers, small entrepreneurs, and artisans, a new "middle class" of salaried managers, bureaucrats, professional, and technical workers has grown in its place (Giddens 1973; Dahrendorf 1959). These elements of the labor force can't be

Class conflict becomes particularly intense when the opposing classes are divided along ethnic, racial, or sexual lines as well as class lines. The United Farm Workers Union has successfully mobilized Mexican-American workers for prolonged labor actions.

neatly classified—or neatly classify themselves—as either proletarians or capitalists.

A second important reason that Marx's predictions have not come to pass is that he underestimated the pulls of competing group loyalties, some of which we will explore in the next chapter. Workers have been divided along ethnic, racial, nationalistic, and sexual lines, and sometimes these group loyalties have proved much stronger than class identification. For instance, consider the role that blacks have played in the white mind: "The existence of this large, easily identifiable, and exploited group has meant that every white American, even the lowest paid labourer, possesses a certain social prestige which raises him, at least in his own view, above the level of a proletarian" (Bottomore 1966, p. 54).

A third, and perhaps the most important, reason for Marx's misjudgment of the future is that he failed to see the important role of the widespread belief in America that by hard work and intelligence individuals can move up in the social order. Thus, contrary to Marx's prediction, most American workers feel satisfied, and not exploited, with their jobs, regardless of their objective circumstances (Wright and Hamilton 1978). American labor unions have been economic, not political, groups, seeking to better workers' conditions within the existing capitalist system. This belief in the impact of hard work and intelligence revolves around what we noted was a crucial factor distinguishing class from caste societies—movement between strata, or *social mobility.*

SOCIAL MOBILITY

Social mobility, quite simply, is movement from one social position to another. Obtaining a higher education, marrying someone of a higher or lower class than our own, getting a raise—these are only a few examples of social mobility.

Social mobility takes many different forms. It can be **horizontal,** involving movement from one position to another of the same rank (if a taxi driver becomes a waiter, for instance). When sociologists talk about social mobility, however, they usually mean **vertical** mobility—movement either upward or downward between ranks in a stratification system. Furthermore, sociologists make a distinction between *intergenerational* mobility, that is, a change in the status of a son or daughter compared to a parent, and *intragenerational* mobility—a change of status for an individual within her or his own lifetime.

When we think of social mobility, we usually think of *upward* mobility, and talk of "success," realizing the "American dream," and so on. These concepts are ob-

viously not rigorous, but we probably agree that they represent some mix of prestigious occupation, education, and relatively high income. How do people achieve "success" in this broad way in America? Here, we'll first look at the avenues of mobility open to us and then, more narrowly, at how much economic and occupational mobility there actually is in the United States.

Avenues of Mobility

The most obvious way to be upwardly mobile is to change jobs, and statistics show that many Americans do just that. We are more likely to change jobs the younger we are (see Figure 7.2). Young people are still testing their likes and dislikes and are not attached to a career and the benefits that attachment brings (e.g., seniority rights). Generally, we are more likely to leave our jobs if we have not invested a great deal of time, money, education, training, or the like in them (Sommers and Eck 1977). Males change jobs more frequently than females do, two reasons being that women have fewer job alternatives and get fewer offers of higher pay than men do. Farm laborers also have few job alternatives, and thus they change jobs less often than nonfarm laborers do.

Not all occupational change is change for the better; however, the social mobility that results from increased education generally is, as we saw in Chapter 6. In light of that discussion, it should not surprise us that poor children start out with less chance of getting to college than middle-class children do. In fact, a recent study in Michigan found that high school dropouts are overwhelmingly poor and that 70 percent come from homes headed by a dropout

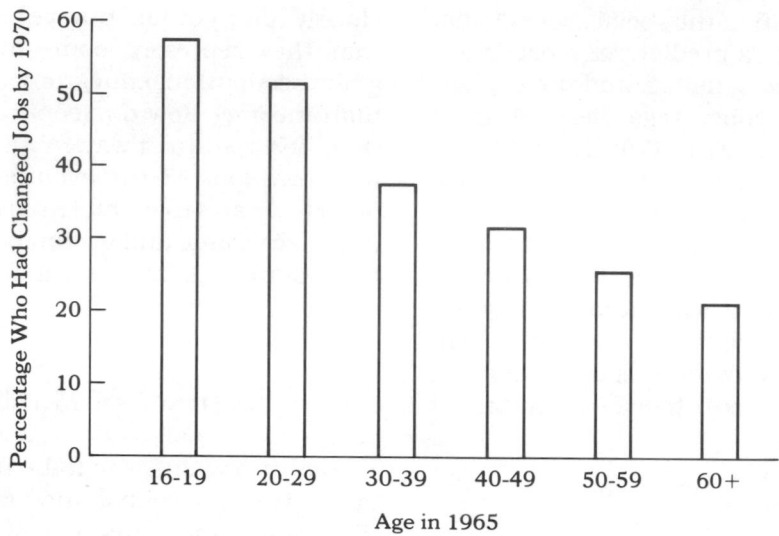

Figure 7.2 Occupational Mobility of American Males, 1970

SOURCE: *Dixie Sommers and Alan Eck. "Occupational Mobility in the American Labor Force,"* Monthly Labor Review *(Jan. 1977): 5.*

(Krauss 1976, p. 131). For those with little hope of achieving success through conformity to social norms, a number have attempted—and some attained—upward mobility through crime (as we saw in the discussion of Merton's concept of innovation in Chapter 4).

What about upward mobility through starting your own business? This is still an ideal for many an American worker. However:

> with the growth of large-scale organizations in all parts of American society, small-business ownership has lost some of its meaning, though its ideological appeal has not necessarily been weakened thereby. Many persons still cherish the idea of success achieved through individual effort,

> though their own careers show little evidence that "private enterprise" has had much significance for them personally. Mobile persons in the white-collar occupations are mobile in a bureaucracy. (Lipset and Bendix 1959, p. 173)

While some individuals eventually make a fortune through starting a small business, most such attempts end in failure. When the effort is moderately successful, furthermore, the owner may simply use it as a stepping-stone to a salaried manager's position (Featherman and Hauser 1977, pp. 88–97; Curtis and Jackson 1977, pp. 45–52). In short, occupational success will most likely come from working within a large enterprise.

So far, we've concentrated on avenues of individual mobility—an individual moving from one category to another. However, there is another type of mobility that sometimes occurs—a change in the social definition or rewards of a whole category. Examples include the higher prestige rankings of scientists in the 1960s compared to a similar survey done in 1947 (Hodge et al. 1964) and the consistent increase in unskilled blue-collar wages compared to those earned in low-skill white-collar occupations (U.S. Department of Labor 1978). Only this latter type of mobility alters the nature of the stratification system itself. Individual movement within the system, no matter how dramatic, does not change the system itself. As we'll see, there continues to be considerable individual mobility in the United States, but the extent of stratification has hardly changed at all over recent decades.

The Extent of Mobility

Americans have a definite ideology about mobility—specifically, that everyone should have equal opportunity to move freely among strata according to their talents and that the American dream of well being should be open to all. Certain factors may indicate that ours is becoming a more open society. The American economy is generally characterized by growth, and many Americans enjoy the world's highest standard of living, as well as ever new technological advances for leisure items (e.g., video tape machines for the home). Moreover, increased industrialization creates increased job mobility and a decline in the influence of ascription in determining status. Increased automobile ownership and the percentage of Americans attending college also seem to indicate mobility. Sociologists have

also documented some mobility from manual to nonmanual occupations in the United States (Lipset and Bendix 1959; Lenski 1966). Recent census statistics note a growth in the number of white-collar workers—from 33 percent of the work force in 1950 to 40 percent in 1974—many of whom come from blue-collar families (Krauss 1976, p. 449).

Throughout the twentieth century, however, there has been essentially no change in our chances to significantly increase our status: that is, the odds are still against lower status individuals improving their position relative to higher status persons (Featherman and Hauser 1977, pp. 169–70). We saw earlier that the patterns of income and wealth distribution haven't changed substantially in recent decades, and the same can also be said for the rate of occupational mobility. While there is some minor variation from decade to decade and from study to study over the past century, only about 35 percent of manual workers' sons have moved into white-collar positions each generation, while—and this is the darker side of the mobility picture— about 25 percent of the sons of white-collar workers have ended up in blue-collar jobs (Thernstrom 1973). This means that for considerably more than half of all male workers there is no intergenerational mobility at all between blue-collar and white-collar occupations.

In considering the above figures, it is important to also note that considerable evidence suggests that the move from blue- to white-collar occupations frequently does not represent an increase in status or wealth (see Table 7.3). Such mobility is generally into the lower white-collar occupations (e.g., clerical)—high-status white-collar jobs tend to go to people whose origins are white collar. And an overwhelm-

Table 7.3 Wages for Unskilled Blue-Collar and White-Collar Workers, 1977

Area	Wages, Percent Increase in 1 Year	
	Office Clerical Workers	Unskilled Plant Workers
Chattanooga, TN	6.9	8.3
Chicago, IL	8.0	10.4
Cincinnati, OH	6.8	8.7
Green Bay, WI	7.1	8.4
Greensboro—Winston-Salem—High Point, NC	8.6	10.6
Greenville—Spartanburg, SC	7.7	7.8
New York, NY	5.8	7.3
Northeast Pennsylvania	7.4	8.8
Paterson—Clifton—Passaic, NJ	6.6	8.5
Trenton, NJ	6.7	8.5

SOURCE: U.S. Department of Labor, Occupational Earnings and Wage Trends in Metropolitan Areas, 1977 (Washington, DC: Government Printing Office, 1978, Summary 78–2).

ing number of people questioned in a study conducted in Boston and Kansas City stated that they no longer perceived any status difference between white- and blue-collar workers (Coleman and Rainwater 1978).

We have seen that there is considerable movement between strata over relatively short distances but not much of the rags-to-riches variety. The extent of mobility is apparently still enough to sustain the belief shared by most Americans that by intelligence and hard work, they—or their children—can share fully in society's fruits. For this reason many people tend to see their class position as a matter of their own responsibility and to see their personal interests as lying in doing well within the existing stratification system rather than in changing it. After all, most people re-

ceive *some* rewards for their efforts, while rebellion involves the risk of poverty, social ostracism, the loss of potential for future "success," and perhaps even death.

SUMMARY

Inequality seems a basic fact of social life. Although some inequalities can be attributed to "natural" differences in ability, others stem from the unequal distribution of social rewards. Society's stratification system sets the criteria for the distribution of property, prestige, and power. By so doing, the stratification system unequally affects our life chances—for health care, mental health, education, housing, and so forth.

Although many Americans with lower socioeconomic backgrounds have been able to gain the trappings of middle-class life in recent decades, the basic stratification structure—including significant inequality—has remained unchanged.

But people do not simply accept such judgments; they will generally try to improve their social position. If they change positions—up, down, or horizontally, they are socially mobile. As a reward for "proper" behavior, social mobility is a form of social control. The most common avenues of mobility in America—occupational mobility, education, and self-employment—are not as open as they might appear. Although there is some mobility in America, there is little movement into the elite positions.

Max Weber identifies three dimensions of stratification: property, prestige, and political power. These dimensions are independent as abstractions, but in reality they are closely related to one another. John Glenn's prestige as a hero helped get him a senate seat, for example. According to Weber, classes, parties, and status groups each contain people who share both similar behavior and chances for success in life, because of their common property, power, or prestige.

Karl Marx defined class in terms of relationship to the means of production. In capitalist society the bourgeoisie own the means of production, the proletariat does not and has to work for the bourgeoisie. Marx believed that conflict between the two classes would one day bring a socialist revolution. He also spoke of class consciousness, whereby members of class recognize their essential common interests and formulate a plan of action in pursuit of them. But he also noted that class consciousness might not develop because members of a class may accept a view of their own interests based on a misperception of reality; this is false consciousness. Finally, we looked at mobility rates in the United States and found some significant movement between strata, but little overall change in the stratification of the population.

Key Terms

social stratification (p. 221)
caste system (p. 223)
class system (p. 223)
life chances (p. 224)
class (Weber) (p. 229)
parties (p. 231)
status group (p. 234)
status symbols (p. 234)
class (Marx) (p. 236)
bourgeoisie (p. 236)
proletariat (p. 236)
class consciousness (p. 237)
false consciousness (p. 237)
social mobility (p. 241)
horizontal social mobility (p. 241)
vertical social mobility (p. 241)

Review and Discussion Questions

1. What people command your attention on a range of subjects merely because of their high status with regard to you? And how do the reactions of others help determine your own status?
2. How good are your own life chances, and what has helped determine them? What avenues of mobility have you contemplated?
3. Give some instances where wealth, power, and prestige are intertwined in a real situation.
4. In what ways can you apply Marx's theory of class and class consciousness to contemporary America? Why or why not will there likely be a socialist revolution in the United States?
5. How does false consciousness among working-class whites and blacks serve the economic interests of the capitalist class?
6. How does the nature of society and the stratification system make it dangerous and risky to try and change your economic position by attempting to change that system?

For Further Study

COMMUNITY STUDIES Several of the studies of individual communities in America still provide insights into stratification here, despite their age. The first major study of this type was Robert and Helen Lynd's *Middletown* (New York: Harcourt, Brace & World, 1929). Another important contribution is the "Yankee City" series, based on research conducted by W. Lloyd Warner and his associates; see, for example, W. Lloyd Warner and P. S. Lunt, *The Status System of a Modern Community* (New Haven, CT: Yale University Press, 1942). August Hollingshed developed an operational definition of classes, still used by sociologists and nonsociologists alike, in *Elmtown's Youth* (New York: Wiley, 1949). Finally, Arthur Vidich and Joseph Bensman, in *Small Town in Mass Society* (Princeton, NJ: Princeton University Press, 1958), look at the pressures for change on one such community stratification system.

OTHER STUDIES OF CLASS IN AMERICA No one has so thoroughly described the American upper class as has E. Digby Baltzell. From an upper-class Philadelphia family, Baltzell has critically, yet sympathetically, analyzed the formation and deterioration of upper-class norms in *Philadelphia Gentlemen: The Making of a National Upper Class* (New York: Free Press,

1958) and *The Protestant Establishment: Aristocracy and Caste in America* (New York: Vintage, 1964). For a perspective on the class system that considers its impact on all of us, see: Richard Sennett and Jonathan Cobb, *The Hidden Injuries of Class* (New York: Knopf, 1972).

POVERTY IN AMERICA   The clearest and most incisive work on American poverty remains Michael Harrington's *The Other America: Poverty in the United States* (Baltimore: Penguin, 1962). From his perspective as a socialist and social reformer, Harrington explains how American society can support a large number of its citizens with the highest standard of living ever known, while at the same time allowing millions of its citizens to live in degrading conditions. A more recent discussion, which considers specifically the role of ideology in maintaining poverty, is Joe Feagin's *Subordinating the Poor* (Englewood Cliffs, NJ: Prentice-Hall, 1975). In *The Stigma of Poverty: A Critique of Poverty Theories and Policies* (New York: Pergamon, 1977), Chaim Waxman explains the persistence of poverty in America from an interactionist perspective. Finally, there is an excellent reader on poverty, with articles written from a radical perspective: Pamela Roby, ed., *The Poverty Establishment* (Englewood Cliffs, NJ: Prentice-Hall, 1974). All of these works point to the structural causes of poverty, so we do not mistakenly look at the individual poor for the reasons.

GENERAL DATA   Students who would like raw data on income levels, status, and mobility in the United States can find them in a number of publications put out by the government. Periodic reports published by the U.S. Bureau of the Census and the U.S. Bureau of Labor Statistics are useful, as are the *Current Population Survey* and *Occupational Changes in a Generation*. These publications are available to the public, either through libraries or through the Government Printing Office.

CHAPTER EIGHT

Race, Ethnic, Sex, and Age Stratification

Chapter 7 gave us a general view of society's stratification system; in Chapter 8 we'll take a closer look at some examples of social stratification: stratification by race and ethnicity, sex, and age. These are generally ascribed statuses. We do not choose the ethnic group into which we're born and obviously have no control over our race, age, or, except by radical physical change, sex. Stratification on the basis of these ascribed traits seems to contradict Americans' belief in equal opportunity. Denying a person decent employment, equal pay for equal work, equal access to education, and so forth on the basis of race, ethnic background, sex, or age has been increasingly challenged as unfair in recent decades. Organizations have sprung up to promote the rights of women, blacks, ethnic minorities, old people, and children. But prejudice and discrimination persist nonetheless, as we'll see. In this chapter, we want to explore the nature of these types of stratification and some of the controversies surrounding them. We'll look at the history of inequality, at the relations between racial and ethnic groups, the sexes, and age groups, and at current trends in stratification. We'll begin by considering racial and ethnic stratification, and then take up sex and age stratification.

RACE AND ETHNIC STRATIFICATION

Race and Ethnic Group Defined

At first glance, race appears to be a fairly simple concept to explain. Technically, it's a biological category, referring to patterns of gene concentration responsible for physical traits (e.g., skin color, hair texture, eye slant, and lip thickness). But as soon as we try to apply this concept we run into problems, for there is no such thing as a pure race. There has been so much mixture of populations and, within a population, so much variety, that there is no consensus among scientists about where one "race" ends and another begins. Given this confusion and the many evils done in the name of race, some scientists have even abandoned the concept altogether.

Race is still an important and useful sociological concept, however. The reason for this is that many persons believe, and act on their belief, that associated with the innate physical traits by which they recognize the people of each race are certain innate behavioral characteristics. In this, sociological, sense, then, a **race** is a category of persons whom others define as sharing similar innate physical characteristics.

If a race is identified by shared physical characteristics of its members, an *ethnic group*, as we noted in Chapter 2, is identified by its members' shared *cultural* characteristics. An essential element of an ethnic group is that its members share a consciousness of being part of a distinct group. This group consciousness can develop around, among others, members' common territory, religion, or language. Thus persons of the same race can form an ethnic group if they share a group consciousness and common culture.

From our discussion so far, we might think that we can "join" an ethnic group by, say, converting to Judaism or moving to Greece and learning the language and customs. But people would not likely accept us as a Jew or a Greek because we would lack blood ties with the group, and many people consider ethnicity to be a matter of culture developed around a common descent. This is so much the case, as we'll see, that there is a common misconception that the cultural similarities of an ethnic group are biologically inherited.

Some ethnic groups form and persist as a matter of choice. The Amish, a tightly knit endogamous religious group, is one example. Other groups develop out of a shared predicament. In either case, the group's social situation heavily influences the way its culture actually develops. According to William L. Yancey and his associates (1976), for instance, even if immigrants (including southerners who moved to northern cities, for example, as well as those from abroad) share a similar culture, they do not simply transplant it from, say, Poland to the United States. Rather, social factors in their new country help form their ethnicity. These factors include economic conditions, employment possibilities, educational opportunities, residential concentration, city size, and so on. A study of Chicago's Italians, for example, concluded that "community and group consciousness among southern Italians in the United States did not cross the Atlantic, but developed in the new homeland" in reponse to residential and occupational concentration in Chicago (Nelli 1970, p. 5).

In this chapter, our primary concern will be with ethnic groups and races in so far as they form *minorities*. A **minority** is a group within a larger society that, because of its physical or cultural characteristics, is denied equal participation in the life of that society. The dominant group in societies in which minorities are present is sometimes termed a *majority*, but to avoid confusion, we'll simply use the term *dominant group*. Note that the term minority does not refer to the relative size of the group's population. A racial or ethnic minority can form the numerical majority in a society; think, for instance, of South Africa, where a tiny white elite rules a numerically far larger black minority.

Prejudice and Discrimination

The unequal treatment of minorities in a society—discrimination—stems from prejudice. **Prejudice** is an inflexible, hostile belief about the members of a particular group. Prejudice is often based on **stereotypes**—distorted portraits of supposed group characteristics used to interpret the actions of all members of the group.

For an illustration of stereotyping, consider the "Amos and Andy" show, an extremely popular comedy about blacks that ran for years on both radio and tele-

In the Republic of South Africa rigid segregation—eventually to result in separate, but dependent, black "homelands"—undergirds the internationally condemned apartheid policy. The homelands established to date have proven to be economically and politically nonviable.

vision. It was about the "antics" of a few black characters: Kingfish—lazy, scheming, and dishonest (he never worked and was always tricking Andy out of his money); Andy—a well-meaning man, but gullible and not very bright; Lightning—a slow-witted and unbelievably slow-moving janitor); Sapphire—Kingfish's domineering wife, always after her husband to get a job, and always failing; and Amos—the brightest (and, on the TV show, the lightest skinned) black, a cab driver, whose warnings to Andy about being cheated always have no effect.

Some blacks feel that the show reflected the ways black people managed to survive in the ghetto but, whether it did or not, it provided white Americans with a certain picture of black life. What conclusions were we likely to draw about blacks from the show? Blacks are generally unintelligent (e.g., Andy and Lightning); when they have something on the ball (Amos), they work hard, but have less effect on other blacks than people like the Kingfish do. Kingfish exploits his own people, is under the thumb of his wife, and hates to work. If we then believe that all blacks are like these characters, we would have formed stereotypes of blacks.

Stereotypes are usually distorted versions of characteristics some members of a group share. But they implicitly assign the same traits to all members of a group, while ignoring the variations—*all* Asians are crafty, *all* Jews are money grubbing, *all* women are dependent, and so on. What might *seem* like harmless "ethnic" jokes (where an ethnic group is the butt) actually reinforce popular stereotypes, implying that certain ethnics are, for example, stupid. Besides being insulting, such stereotypes are harmful because some people act as if they were real.

Behind many, but not all, stereotypes (such as the one discussed in Race and Intelligence, on p. 253) lies a belief that cultural characteristics are genetically based. Particularly in the past, this confusion was often expressed by using the term *race* to refer to ethnic groups. Researching old government reports and other documents, Ronald M. Pavalko (1977) found how integral this confusion has been in American history. In 1894, a group of prominent, upper-class Americans (all white Anglo-Saxon Protestants) founded the Immigration Restriction League, seeking to ban all further immigration from southern and eastern Europe. One of its founders put the matter bluntly: "The question before us is therefore, a race question. Slav, Italian, Jew, not discouraged by the problem of maintaining high standards of living with many children, are replacing native Americans" (quoted in Pavalko 1977, p. 5). The statement is erroneous in light of our definition of ethnicity, but it was used to place distance between old-stock Americans and the new immigrants. In a 1911 hearing before the U.S. House Committee on Immigration, one congressman stated that

"the Southern Italian is not a 'white man,' nor is the Syrian." Elsewhere, Greeks are described as a "commercial race," and in 1912, a writer noted that "the willing Slav" and "submissive Lithuanian" replaced "white men" at manual labor (quoted in Pavalko 1977, p. 10). In general, the immigrants were stereotyped as being by nature lazy, unintelligent, criminal, and tending to have too many children.

Donald L. Noel (1968) suggests that we can largely explain these evaluations by a deeply ingrained ethnocentrism—that is, the tendency to value another group's characteristics less than those of our own (see Chapter 2). And it is true that a minority group's reception in America has largely depended on its resemblance to the dominant WASP (white Anglo-Saxon Protestant) group, as we will see further on. Moreover, this particular version of ethnocentrism is not restricted to the dominant group. Immigrants socialized into American society have generally adopted the WASP standard of values when viewing other minority groups—and to some extent even when evaluating their own group (Lenski 1966, p. 398). Indeed, immigrant parents and others often teach their children not to be "different" from other Americans, because that difference may cause other Americans to look down upon them and deprive them of equal opportunities (Novak 1972; Benkin 1978).

Leaving the explanation of prejudice simply at the level of ethnocentrism, however, ignores how useful stereotypes can be in justifying **discrimination**—the actual behavior of denying access to social rewards to persons simply on the basis of their group membership. Andrew Greeley (1976) and Michael Novak (1972) have shown how Irish and Slavic Catholics are stereotyped as superstitious and unintel-

RACE AND INTELLIGENCE

Is there any necessary relationship between a person's race and how intelligent he or she is? Put another way: Are white people inherently more intelligent than blacks? As far as we know, there is no such link, and the belief that there is rests on prejudice, not fact. Yet, some people subscribe to that belief, and the educational status of blacks is generally lower than that of whites. In 1978, for instance, 16 percent of the black population over sixteen had not finished high school and only 18 percent had attended some college, while only 7.2 percent of the whites had less than an elementary education and about 30 percent had gone to college (Brown 1979, p. 55). But although people often associate intelligence with educational attainment, Chapter 6 pointed out that the relationship is a weak one.

Black-white differences in IQ scores seem to confirm the prejudice. In particular, in the first wide-scale IQ testing of adults after World War I, white soldiers scored higher than black ones. More detailed analysis, however, pointed to social origins for the disparity. Northern blacks, for instance, scored higher than whites from the Deep South—which is not to say that Northerners are more intelligent than people from the South. If those who constructed the tests were Northern whites, for instance, they would ask different questions than either blacks or Southerners would. In other words, IQ tests do not measure pure intelligence for they reflect the social bias of the testmakers. In any case, research has related all these differences to varying socialization, which both race and religion affect (Hunt 1969).

Despite the evidence to the contrary, the myth that race determines intelligence persists among many people, which has led Ronald J. Samuda (1975) to suggest that IQ tests are an active form of discrimination. In the late 1960s, some studies purported to support a link between intelligence and race, arguing that the IQ differences have remained stable in spite of changed social conditions (see, for example, Jensen 1969). But these researchers have never explained the supposed link between race and intelligence.

ligent and thereby kept out of important positions in the academic world. In South Africa, many whites claim that "their" black Africans are incapable of handling independence and of running their own affairs. Although evidence from other African nations disputes the claim, the prejudice allows the whites to feel justified in maintaining their virtual monopoly of social rewards.

Prejudice and discrimination are often mutually reinforcing for the dominant groups. Prejudice has justified discrimination in the form of segregation in housing or schools, unequal pay for the same work, and the like, all the way to placement in concentration camps. But such discrimination also reinforces prejudices to justify future discrimination. Returning to the South African example, if we object that blacks certainly are capable of running their own affairs, we might get the response: "Don't be absurd; you can see that they have never *shown* themselves capable. We whites, on the other hand, are quite experienced at it."

In the next section, we will see ample examples of prejudice and different forms of discrimination.

Ethnic and Racial Stratification in the United States

In this section, we'll look at the history of white ethnic relations in the United States and at the present extent of stratification among white ethnic groups. Then we'll turn to the development and present extent of racial stratification in America.

WHITE ETHNIC GROUPS Although no cleavages within white America are nearly so large as that between blacks and whites, the white immigrants who came to this country over the past two centuries were definitely stratified.

THE IMMIGRANT PAST The earliest white immigrants to the newly formed United States—mostly Protestant and northwest European—were very similar in religion, culture, and often language to the white Protestants already here from colonial times. But the immigrants who dominated successive periods of American history resembled these early settlers less and less. The first real conflict came with the Irish in the 1840s, since their Catholicism awakened the anti-Catholic sentiment that was part of the English Protestant tradition, and touched off waves of reaction ranging from prejudice to violence. In Philadelphia in 1846, for example, after a number of deadly raids on the immigrants in the city's Kensington section, thousands of Irish Catholics fled "the city of brotherly love" in panic. The next immigrants were the Germans, whose "different language, separate communal life, and freer ideas on temperance and sabbath observance brought them into conflict with the Anglo-Saxon bearers of Puritan and Evangelical traditions" (Gordon 1964, p. 92).

Although we should not underestimate the hostility they faced, both of these northern European groups were accepted more readily than the next wave of immigrants, from southern and eastern Europe. Mostly Catholic and Jewish, the new immigrants differed greatly in their histories and backgrounds from the northern Europeans who preceded them. The differences were great enough for many Americans to declare that these Poles, Italians, Greeks, and such would be incapable of

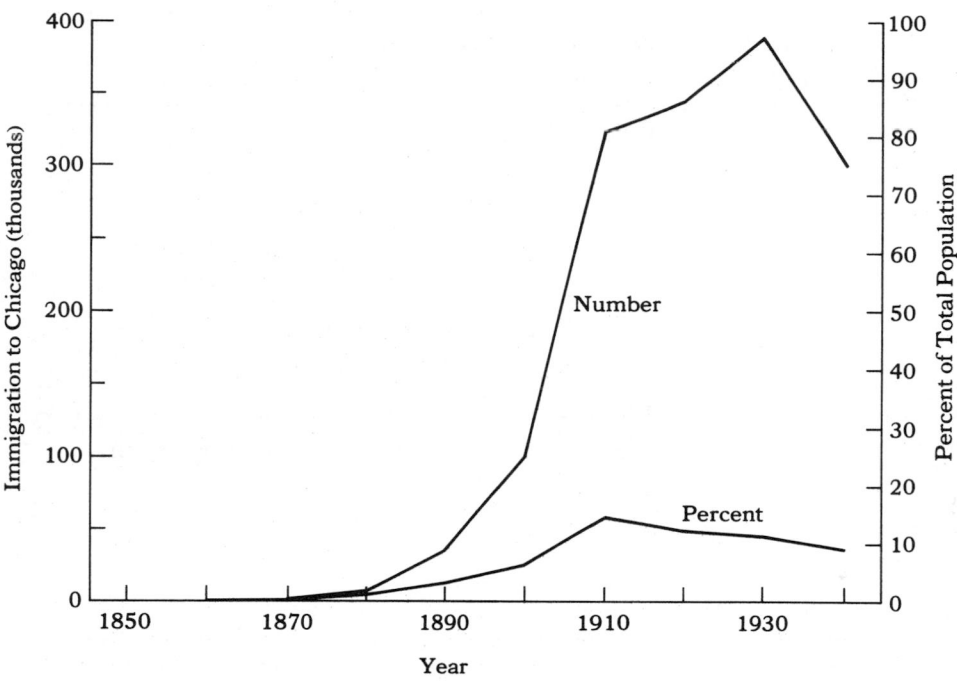

Figure 8.1 Immigration to Chicago from Southern, Eastern, and Southeastern Europe, 1850–1940

Bohemia, Czechoslovakia, and Hungary were considered to be central European, and immigrants from there were not included in the totals.

SOURCE: The People of Chicago (Chicago: Department of Development and Planning, 1976).

handling American democracy. Their large numbers probably fueled the opposition (see Figure 8.1). These immigrants had to contend with mob violence (see Table 8.1 on anti-Italian violence), open discrimination, and attacks in the press, Congress, and other institutions of American life. In the early 1920s, they were even subject to Justice Department raids (called "Palmer raids" after the Attorney General, A. Mitchell Palmer). Working with local police, Justice Department officials swooped down on immigrant neighborhoods at night and ab-

ducted and deported many immigrants as "subversives."

Sentiment against these immigrants ran so high that Congress eventually placed severe restrictions on further immigration from southern and eastern Europe (1921 and 1924). It was the first time that the United States closed its doors to white immigrants.

WHITE ETHNIC GROUP STRATIFICATION TODAY Despite this history of prejudice

Table 8.1 Mob Violence Against Italian Americans

Date	Place	Casualties
Dec. 1874	Buena Vista, PA	4 killed
Mar. 1886	Vicksburg, MS	1 lynched
Apr. 1891	New Orleans, LA	11 lynched
Jul. 1893	Denver, CO	1 lynched
Mar. 1894	Altoona, PA	200 wounded and/or exiled
Mar. 1896	Walsenberg, CO	6 lynched
Nov. 1896	Hahnville, LA	3 lynched
July 1899	Tallulah, MS	5 lynched
July 1901	Erwin, MS	5 lynched, 1 wounded
Nov. 1901	Marian, NC	2 killed, 5 wounded
Sept. 1910	Tampa, FL	2 lynched
Oct. 1914	Willisville, IL	1 shot
June 1915	Johnson City, IL	1 lynched

SOURCE: *Luciano J. Iorizzo, "The Padrone and Immigrant Distribution," in S. M. Tomasi and H. M. Engel, eds.,* The Italian Experience in the United States *(Staten Island, NY: Center for Migration Studies, 1970, pp. 50–51).*

and discrimination, white ethnic groups have managed, on the whole, to gain a relatively equal share of social resources. Reliable figures on the various white ethnic groups are sparse (for instance, government figures do not necessarily include grandchildren of immigrants, and the Constitution forbids government agencies from asking people their religion). Nevertheless, a number of studies concur that while ethnic groups differ in their incomes from one another, overall their incomes don't differ markedly from the population as a whole. Andrew Greeley (1975) found the following average family incomes:

Jews	$13,340
Irish Catholics	12,426
Italian Catholics	11,748
German Catholics	11,632
Polish Catholics	11,298
Slavic Catholics	10,826
German Protestants	9,758

According to the government, the national average was $13,772 that year.

In terms of occupational characteristics, Catholic ethnics seem to be the backbone of our skilled labor force (Novak 1972; Glazer and Moynihan 1963, pp. 205–07). In particular, Thomas Sowell (1978, p. 217) found a large number of German, Polish, Irish, and Italian Americans in manual trades. Jews, on the other hand, are found more often in businesses and professions, and tend to be bunched overwhelmingly in middle-class occupations, especially as middle-class managers or proprietors in retail and wholesale trade and manufacturing (Gordon 1964; Rosenberg and Howe

1974). Despite these individual variations, the mobility rates of white ethnic groups are comparable to those of the population as a whole, although control of banking and large industries is still in the hands of WASPs.

NONWHITES White ethnic groups in America have faced substantial prejudice and discrimination, but their experiences and those of nonwhite Americans have been qualitatively different.

For one thing, all white ethnics share the host population's race. We can see the importance of this in the treatment of Asian immigrants. Asian immigrants in the nineteenth century faced shootings and other random violence in the West, and were even more set upon than their European counterparts back East. They gravitated to segregated "Chinatowns" and "Little Tokyos" soon after arriving and largely remained there, although many Japanese did try small-scale farming in the West. The racist treatment of Japanese Americans culminated in the mass arrest and "internment" of Americans of Japanese ancestry during World War II.

In addition to the racial prejudice and types of discrimination we have been discussing, blacks faced a more extreme form of discrimination than that known by either Asian or white ethnic groups: namely, a system of formal racial stratification.

RACE AND CASTE Many societies in the past—and even some today—have been strictly and formally stratified by racial criteria. The Union of South Africa's apartheid system is the most notorious instance today. In that nation, whites live by one set of norms, blacks by another, and "col-

oreds" (mixed race) by a third. Moreover, the black population receives very few social rewards. Blacks and whites are separated into special districts to maintain white dominance. Blacks are assigned to small, poor areas, and whites control the rest of the country.

The South African system follows the stratification pattern John Dollard (1937) identifies as a combination of class and caste. That is, there is a *racial caste system*, where mobility is not possible; and there are separate *class systems* within those castes. So, blacks can compete among themselves for property, prestige, and political power, but they cannot compete with whites.

Dollard's study of the combination of racial caste and class systems wasn't made in South Africa, however, but in the American South during the late 1930s. And in America, blacks have traditionally formed a racial caste, first as slaves, and later as restricted by formal segregation laws in the South and by informal but often as effective policies in the North.

This caste heritage of blacks helps explain the fact that while the lot of most white immigrants improved after a generation or two, blacks have, until recently, largely remained at the same level. The National Advisory Commission on Civil Disorders (the Kerner Commission), appointed by President Johnson in 1967 to investigate the causes of racial tension and urban riots, comments:

Racial discrimination is undoubtedly [a] major reason why the Negro has been unable to escape from poverty. The structure of discrimination has persistently narrowed his opportunities and restricted his prospects. Well before the high tide of immigration from overseas, Negroes were already relegated to the poorly paid, low status occupations. . . . Upon the arrival of the immigrants, the Negroes were dislodged from the few urban occupations they had dominated. . . . European immigrants, too, suffered from discrimination, but never was it so pervasive. The prejudice against color in America has formed a bar to advancement unlike any other (Kerner Commission 1968, pp. 278–79).

This is not to say that all whites are better off than all blacks. But it does mean that if we go through the poorest areas of any city, we will find black people living in almost all of them; upwardly mobile blacks move into white neighborhoods, not the other way around. It means that we are more likely to see a higher percentage of black workers than white at low-paying, low-skills jobs—or at the unemployment office. And it also means that the most run down of city schools with the least educational facilities are likely to contain more black than white children. This is all reflected in the basic statistics of racial stratification, which we'll now examine.

INEQUALITY IN BLACK AND WHITE According to the 1960 census, for instance, the median income for white males was nearly *twice* that for black males. And in the late 1960s, fully 40.6 percent of all nonwhite Americans (most of whom are black) lived below the "poverty level" defined by the Social Security Administration, compared with 11.9 percent of the nation's whites (Kerner Commission 1968, p. 258).

Since the 1960s, the position of blacks relative to whites has improved somewhat, but great disparities remain. The unemployment rate of blacks continues to be over twice that of whites: 12.4 percent compared with 6.1 in January 1980 (U.S. Department of Labor 1980). The disparity is even greater between black and white youth: 34.3 percent for blacks, 13.9 for whites (U.S. Department of Labor 1980). Even when educational difference is controlled for, the rate of black unemployment exceeds that of whites among those with more than eight years of schooling (Michelotti 1978, p. 55). Moreover, blacks who are able to find jobs are paid, on the average, less than whites. In terms of average median weekly earnings blacks made only 70 percent as much as whites in 1967, and the percentage had only risen to 80 by 1978 (U.S. Department of Labor 1978).

Occupation and education are closely related to income, and here, too, there is ample evidence of racial stratification. Figure 8.2 shows larger proportions of whites than blacks in more prestigious professions. For example, 14.3 percent of white males in the labor force are professional and technical workers (upper middle occupational group), while only 6.5 percent of black males are (notice the difference, however, among females). In short, a greater proportion of blacks than whites are confined to low-paying semi- and low-skilled jobs. And instability, low prestige, and little or no chance for meaningful advancement often characterized such jobs (Kerner Commission 1968, pp. 253–54).

Since the early 1960s, blacks have also become a more serious political force than they had been in previous years. The civil rights movement mobilized millions of Americans to make their feelings about racial discrimination known to lawmakers.

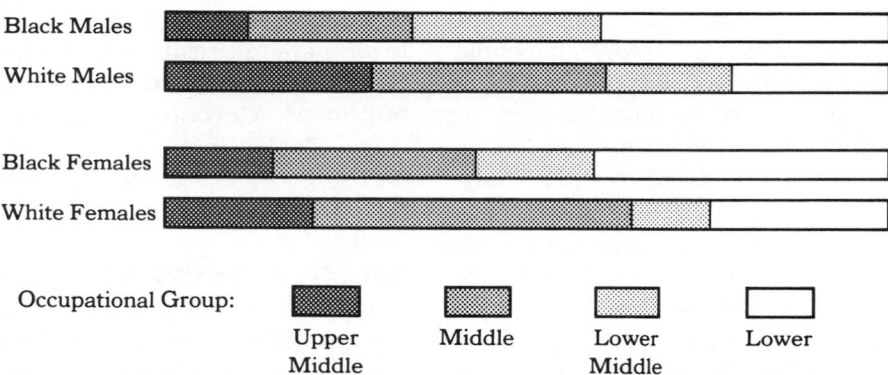

Figure 8.2 Occupation Status of Whites and Blacks, Sixteen and Older, in the United States, 1976

SOURCE: *U.S. Department of Labor, Bureau of Labor Statistics.* Work Experience of the Population, 1976 *(Washington, DC: Government Printing Office, Special Labor Force Report 201, 1977).*

Another demonstration of black power was urban rioting. Race rioting is not new. There were a number of big city race riots during World War II, for example, most notably in Los Angeles, New York City (Harlem), and Detroit, but none had the impact the series of race riots in the 1960s did. The riots of the 1960s did indeed make many white people aware of the conditions blacks had been facing—and black people knew it. I was living in Philadelphia a few years after a major race riot there. When it appeared that blacks might riot again, both the governor of Pennsylvania and the mayor of Philadelphia acted quickly to enact programs to satisfy many black demands. I remember talking with some members of the black community who were particularly impressed at the government's speed—after years of inaction—at the threat of unrest.

Blacks have gained another and potentially more lasting source of power as well. For one thing, they have become the most populous minority group—in some cases, the majority—in most large cities. Between 1950 and 1966, black population grew twice as fast as white in metropolitan areas (Kerner Commission 1968, p. 250). In many cities this increase has been translated into political power through the election of black mayors and congressional representatives, as well as more black control at the ward level. Blacks now compete with whites for many resources and social services: jobs, education, housing, political power, even control of organized crime. While the fact that blacks are in the running at all is an advance, equality is still far off. A 1974 study in Chicago, for instance, found that the increased number of black decision makers has not brought an overall shift in racial power relations (Baron 1975). The same study also notes that although increased black union membership has brought some increased power, blacks have not won equal representation within the unions.

Congress, the Supreme Court, government agencies, and the American people as a whole have at long last removed the most obnoxious and obvious barriers to racial equality. And there are fewer Lester Maddoxes swinging ax handles rather than admit blacks to their chicken restaurants than there were in the past; and even George Wallace, who once cried "segregation forever!" now agrees that racial integration is a good thing (*Chicago Sun-Times* 8 December 1978). But the goal of racial equality still remains barred by complex, more subtle forms of discrimination. Blacks are not alone in suffering this ingrained form of discrimination. Other groups—most prominently women—are similarly treated, as we will see later in the chapter. Before turning to sex stratification, however, we should look at the central ideas that inform ethnic and racial relations in the United States.

Ideologies of Assimilation

All of us in the United States are either immigrants or their descendants. Even if our family came over on the *Mayflower*, they immigrated. As we could expect, therefore, our understanding of what an "American" is has changed over the years, as immigrants from different parts of the world have become Americans. They learned to speak American English; joined American, not ethnic, clubs (e.g., unions, friendship groups); intermarried, and so forth. They started eating "American" foods—even if that now includes spaghetti, Polish sausage, lox and bagels, and the like. We call the process by which such a group or individual is integrated with the culture and society of the host country **assimilation** (becoming alike). Americans have held three general ideologies of what that process should produce in their own country. Milton M. Gordon (1964) has identified these ideologies as: *Anglo-conformity, the melting pot,* and *cultural pluralism.*

ANGLO-CONFORMITY The central assumptions of the Anglo-conformity ideology are the superiority of English institutions (as modified by the American Revolution) and the desirability of maintaining them. Thus all immigrants are expected to shed their ethnic cultural practices and adopt American/English characteristics. At least in its more moderate form, this ideology has dominated Americans' thinking about assimilation throughout their history, according to Gordon, who quotes an 1848 description of our ethnicity:

> The people of the United States, considered as a whole, are composed of immigrants and their descendants from almost every [European] country. The principal portion of them, however, derive their origin from the British nation . . . the English, the Scotch, and the Irish. The English language is almost wholly used; the English manners, modified to be sure, predominate, and the spirit of English liberty and enterprise animates the energies of the whole people. (p. 95)

Since white Anglo-Saxon Protestants controlled the largest industries and political power, early immigrants adopted this ideology as they were socialized into the society.

Some Americans would have all ethnics adopt an "English" way of life; others envision a new American type coming from the mixture of so many groups; still others see ethnics assimilating the dominant culture's major norms while maintaining certain aspects of ethnicity.

In its most obnoxious versions, Anglo-conformity involves bigoted notions of Nordic superiority. This concept refers to the *peoples* of northern Europe, but it became a racial concept. As such, it had wide currency in both Europe and America until the downfall of the Nazis. A more moderate Anglo-conformity has taken the form of people favoring immigration from northern or western Europe because those immigrants are "more like us."

Anglo-conformity has also been the ideological force behind a number of "Native American" movements, which sought to end all future immigration and which brought about the 1921–1929 laws restricting immigration from southern and eastern Europe and from Asia. This restrictive policy was reaffirmed in 1952, by the McCarran-Walter Act. The recurring waves of anti-Semitism and of Ku Klux Klan activity are also symptoms of Anglo-conformity.

THE MELTING POT A second ideology of assimilation is that of the melting pot. According to this set of ideas, the various ethnic groups in the United States are blended together (as if melted together in a giant pot) to form a new and distinct American type. There is an implicit assumption in this that each culture has something to contribute.

The melting pot idea was first explicitly stated as such in Israel Zangwill's 1908 play, *The Melting Pot.* In the play, one character says:

> America is God's crucible, the great
> Melting Pot where all races of
> Europe are melting and re-forming!
> Here you stand, good folk, think I,
> when I see them at Ellis Island [the
> point of entry for immigrants in New
> York's harbor], here you stand in
> your fifty groups, with your fifty
> languages and histories, and your
> fifty blood hatreds and rivalries. But
> you won't be long like that,
> brothers, for these are the fires of
> God you've come to—these are the
> fires of God. A fig for your feuds and
> vendettas! Germans and
> Frenchmen, Irishmen and
> Englishmen, Jews and Russians—
> into the Crucible with you all! God
> is making the American. (1909,
> p. 37)

Actually, the melting pot idea has always been basic to America's self-image. It was a source of pride to Americans that theirs was a "new nation" forged out of the immigrating people. This remained an unstated assumption, however, as long as the immigrants were all of northern European stock. It was only asserted as an American value when people began trying to keep other immigrants "out of the pot."

Has the melting pot ideology become reality? There is little doubt that the great majority of Americans conform to a general way of life, and a number of community studies suggest that class has replaced ethnicity as a basis for people's interests (Gans 1962; Fried 1974; Yancey et al. 1976). Moreover, the mass media bring a common cultural message into every home, and in so doing weaken ethnic barriers. But ethnic groups have not merged into a new American type.

Immigrants to the United States have made invaluable contributions to their new society, but they have not altered the fundamentally Anglo-Saxon character of its basic institutions. To be successful as Americans, they had to join economic, political, and cultural organizations that were essentially Anglo-Saxon (Benkin 1978). For some people, the melting pot ideology was indistinguishable from that of Anglo-conformity. As Gordon states: "Entrance . . . into the social structures of the existing white Protestant society . . . has not led to the creation of new structures, new institutional forms, and a new sense of identity which draws impartially from all sources, but rather to immersion in a subsocietal network of groups and institutions which was already fixed . . . with an Anglo-Saxon, general Protestant stamp" (p. 127).

In short, all ethnic groups have had to come to terms with a dominant, largely WASP, American culture.

CULTURAL PLURALISM According to the ideology of cultural pluralism, ethnic groups would share the same institutions (schools, political administrations, and the like) but retain other distinctive cultural practices. Cultural pluralism is based on the assumption that *any* culture benefits from the input offered by a variety of subcultures. And this is not a one-time contribution, as the melting pot theorists held. Instead, we expect thriving subcultures to continually provide unique perspectives for the entire society.

Cultural pluralism, unlike the other two ideologies, legitimates ethnic differences—they are not "supposed" to go away but rather remain as part of American society. In practice, moreover, pluralism has defined the legitimate areas of ethnic expression. What are some of these areas? They include religious practices, ethnic foods, national festivals, and so on. And it has also been legitimate for ethnics to lobby for the interests of their ethnic homeland as long as those interests do not conflict with American interests: American Jews lobby for Israel; Greek Americans lobbied for an arms embargo against Turkey when that nation invaded Greek-dominated Cyprus; Lithuanians have helped keep the United States from recognizing the Soviet Union's control of their homeland.

For a time, it appeared that American pluralism could not be a reality, and that ethnic differences would be erased under the impact of assimilation. By the 1950s, many people thought they were witnessing the end of European ethnicity in America, at least in the middle classes.

They were wrong. Although a number of ethnic traits were invariably lost in the transition from immigrant to native American, we can easily observe the ethnic groups around us. The late 1960s and 1970s, for example, saw an increased demand for ethnic studies (Levine and Herman 1971, p. 272), and politicians began paying more attention to the "ethnic vote." With the growth of black power in the 1960s came a growth in ethnic consciousness among whites, as well. One reason for this was that white ethnics were indiscriminately classified as "white racists," and

asserting their ethnicity appeared to give them a legitimate basis for claiming that their own interests (often economic) were being hurt.

The essential contribution of the ideology of pluralism to American society is that rather than promoting the elimination of all ethnic distinctions for fear of the conflict they may cause, it promotes their acceptance, thus recognizing that diversity and even conflict are legitimate features of American life.

SEX STRATIFICATION

In every society, women and men are expected to play different roles. In Chapter 3, we touched on these sex-role differences in our own society. Difference alone, however, doesn't necessarily mean inequality. Yet in every known society, there has also been an unequal distribution of property, prestige, and power on the basis of sex. Moreover, while men and women are more equal in some societies than in others, women are generally subordinated in almost every society. People throughout the industrialized world have challenged the subordination of women in recent years, perhaps nowhere more vocally than in the United States. In this section, we will look at some explanations of sexual inequality, some ways in which sex stratification is perpetuated, and at the progress toward its elimination.

Explanations of Sex-Role Stratification

Sociologists—and others—have made many attempts to explain sex-role differentiation and stratification. In one of the more absurd attempts by a scientist, Herbert Spencer (1820–1903) asserted that the individual woman's development in the womb is arrested in order to reserve her "vital power" for reproduction. As a result, he adds, women lack: "those two facilities, intellectual and emotional, which are the latest products of human evolution—the power of abstract reasoning and . . . the sentiment of justice—the sentiment that regulates conduct irrespective of personal attachments and the likes or dislikes felt for individuals" (1961 [1874], pp. 341–42). Spencer assumed that male dominance is justified, and he believes that all inequalities—including sexual ones—are the product of natural law; specifically, that of "survival of the fittest."

More recently, some sociologists have explained sex-role differentiation as society's way of handling natural differences between the sexes: "Sex roles may be seen as the social accommodation and elaboration on the basic differences in the behavioral predisposition of males and females" (Udry 1974, pp. 48–49). Although this seems less offensive than Spencer's explanation, it still gives us the impression that sex-role behaviors are necessarily functional. For although in hunting-gathering societies, for example, long periods of pregnancy and the child's helplessness kept females from obtaining social power through their participation in hunts (Friedl 1975, pp. 31–32), and made her (and her child's) dependence on a man "functional," this is no longer the case in most of the world. Yet, sex-stereotyped behavior persists. Beyond that, any "natural" predisposition for men or women to excel at particular tasks has been exaggerated by social customs. Functional explanations, furthermore, don't help us much in understanding why men's tasks, no matter what they are, are considered in every society more valuable than women's.

Theorists associated more with the conflict than the functional orientation in sociology have also attempted to explain the origins of and reasons for sex stratification. These theorists emphasize the historically unequal relationships between men and women and point to the conflicting interests involved. Some have traced the subordination of women to the male's greater physical strength, to the fear of rape, or to the male's wish to establish paternity and perpetuate his family line. Many ingenious theories have been proposed (e.g., Engels 1972 [1902]), but none is completely satisfactory.

Whatever its origins, we can say with some confidence that sex stratification today is culturally imposed and perpetuated. As Simone de Beauvoir has said, with reference to women: "One is not born a woman. No biological, psychological, or economic fate determines the figure that the human female presents in society; it is civilization as a whole that produces this creature" (1952, p. 249). The point is that sex roles are not natural but social. We learn them through an intensive process, *gender identification*, as part of our socialization. We will now see how that process works and how it contributes to inequality between the sexes.

Gender Identification

In Chapter 1, we learned how socialization assures that most people will control their own behavior and that developing a self-

"One is not born a woman . . . it is civilization as a whole that produces this creature." We learn the image of our sexual selves we must present.

And like other learned behavior and attitudes, that can change.

concept through interaction with others is an essential part of the process. If you take a moment to think about your own self, you may immediately recognize that your gender is its most basic characteristic, the result of gender's primary place in our socialization. One sociologist has commented that the ideas we internalize during socialization are so "intense and striking, or subtle and pervasive . . . that to violate them as adults is difficult, uncomfortable, improbable, and in some cases, psychologically impossible" (Walum 1977, p. 37).

It is amazing how early gender socialization begins. We know that many hospitals immediate label newborn infants by wrapping them in either male (blue) or female (pink) blankets. Moreover, our parents stereotype us from birth, as we saw in Chapter 1 when parents described their female and male babies differently. A group of researchers has even found that parents apply the same "female" and "male" adjectives to newborns of the same size, shape, and the like (Rubin et al. 1974). It would be a mistake to think that we consider infants to be genderless.

Those babies are at the initial point of learning what their own sex is and the cultural characteristics associated with it. This is called **gender identification**. Through gender identification, we learn how boys and girls are "supposed to" behave and internalize male or female responses as part of our personality. The aim of gender socialization and the result of gender identification is to prepare us for filling adult gender roles. The next sections describe the sex roles and their role in stratification.

WOMAN'S ROLE In our society, females traditionally have been trained to play a

nurturing role—that is, to provide love, support, and comfort to others (particularly husband and children), while asserting as few individual needs as possible. And if they work, they are more likely to be a nurse than a doctor, an elementary school teacher than a principal, a helping secretary than an ordering boss—all nurturant roles.

Boys and girls learn from a number of sources that females are properly passive, dull, deceitful, unintelligent, and timid. We can look at the toys children receive. Boys get trucks, Erector Sets or building blocks, and sports equipment—things to make or do things with. Girls are more likely to get toys like dolls, which encourage more passive play. Girls are supposed to play quietly and stay neat and clean; on the other hand, "boys will be boys," and they are given much more freedom of movement. In Chapter 6, we saw that children's books are another source of these messages about proper sex roles. One study of prize-winning books found that women were stereotyped by their relationship to a man (e.g., the president's wife, but never the president) (Weitzman et al. 1972). The feminist group Women on Words and Images (1975) conducted a survey of about 3,000 stories in more than 100 elementary school readers and found the following proportions:*

Male to female biographies 6:1
Male folk or fantasy to female folk or fantasy stories 4:1
Male adults to female adults as main characters in stories 3:1
Male-centered to female-centered stories 5:2

---

*Adapted from *Dick and Jane as Victims*, p. 10; expanded 1975 edition, Women on Words & Images, P.O. Box 2163, Princeton, NJ 08540.

Male animal to female animal stories	2:1

Obviously, schoolbooks project an image of men as the main doers in the world.

The negative images of women are a form of **sexism**—prejudice or discrimination on the basis of sex. Television shows provide plentiful examples of sexist stereotypes, from women's roles in the serials to the presentation of men as the major source of wisdom and aid on commercials (whether it is fixing our car, our dishwasher, or our aching head). But J. Bergman (1974) has even found the "progressive" program "Sesame Street" to be sexist. Girls tag along after boys, and all women are mothers, wearing aprons and making tortillas. So, the show teaches the subservient female role as well as reading.

In addition to these images of how men and women should and do behave, in most American families children have front-row seats to sexual stratification. In the nuclear family, children observe two primary roles—mom and dad—one of which is accorded more prestige and authority. Either alone or with his wife "helping out," the man is most likely the family's basic source of income and thereby the likely holder of economic power. And while about half of all American children now have mothers in the labor force, one-fifth of these working mothers have only part-time jobs compared to one-tenth of working males (U.S. Department of Labor 1978a).

If you are like a lot of students, you might be thinking: "Wait a minute, I know some women who don't act that way" or "That's the way it used to be." You are seeing that people deviate from roles and that role definitions may change over time. But despite many important changes, Americans continue to associate a number

of personality traits with being "feminine"; some are: passive and dependent, easily influenced, overly emotional, not "having a head for business," and lacking self-confidence. Women are expected to be sweet, not aggressive. As the nursery rhyme tells us, girls are "sugar and spice and everything nice." Many women do possess these traits—but many do not. And we know from our discussion of race that stereotyping can have dangerous consequences.

Other, more positive traits ascribed to women include tact, gentleness, neatness, an appreciation of art, and intensity in personal relationships (Rosenkrantz et al. 1968). But Mary Wollstonecraft (1759–1797), perhaps the first feminist author in modern times, takes a dim view even of these traditional compliments paid to woman's character. She wrote:

> My own sex, I hope, will excuse me, if I treat them like rational creatures, instead of flattering their *fascinating* graces, and viewing them as if they were in a state of perpetual childhood, unable to stand alone . . . I wish to persuade women to endeavor to acquire strength, both of mind and body, and to convince them that the soft phrases, susceptibility of heart, delicacy of sentiment, and refinement of taste, are almost synonymous with epithets of weakness, and that those beings who are only the objects of pity and that kind of love, which have been termed its sister, will soon become objects of contempt. (1975 [1792], pp. 81–82)

Not only do women learn to excel at activities that will not bring them much social power or put them in competition with men, but they are complimented for doing so. Because we come to see our own value in the way we play our major roles, women effectively are induced to value their powerlessness.

A number of studies support Wollstonecraft's assertions. In one such study (Broverman et al. 1970), researchers asked practicing mental health clinicians (psychologists, psychiatrists, and psychiatric social workers) to complete a sex-role questionnaire listing thirty-eight personality or behavioral traits. One group of clinicians was asked to describe a mature, healthy, and competent man; another group was asked to describe a mature, healthy, and competent woman; and a third group was asked to describe a mature, healthy, and competent adult. Both male and female subjects described a healthy *man* and a healthy *adult* almost identically—dominant, independent, objective. But they only considered a woman mentally healthy if she behaved in ways considered *unhealthy* and *immature* in our culture—emotional, conceited, and submissive. This puts women in a bind: they can either be healthy adults, and in conflict with their feminine role requirements, or be healthy women, and violate cultural standards of maturity.

MAN'S ROLE   As a rule of thumb, we can derive the traits associated with the male sex role by taking the opposite of the traits traditionally associated with the female role. So, instead of passive, men are expected to be aggressive; instead of being emotional, they are supposed to be rational; instead of tactful, they're supposed to be blunt; and so on. Barbara S. David and Robert Brannon (1976) have suggested that there are four "dimensions" to the traditional male sex role:

> *No Sissy Stuff:* Avoid anything vaguely feminine.
> *The Big Wheel:* Demonstrate success, status, and power.
> *The Sturdy Oak:* Be tough, confident, and self-reliant.
> *Give 'Em Hell:* Have an aura of aggression, violence, and daring.

Whereas little girls learn how to behave, little boys typically learn how *not* to behave—specifically, not doing anything that women do. Knitting is an obvious example; but having a soft and gentle voice, painting, an interest in poetry, and even liking some foods can also stigmatize as feminine. (Salads, for instance, are sometimes thought of as "women's food"—"real men" eat big steaks, as we know from the "steak sauce" advertisements.) Moreover, people often frown upon men who display emotion and intimacy.

We also learn that "real men" are successful, primarily at business, but in other areas as well. Men are supposed to know how to fix things and how to solve problems. They are supposed to be "Sturdy Oaks" by always being "cool," sure of themselves, and capable of strong and independent action. In other words, they should act like Robert Redford, Humphrey Bogart, Paul Newman, and Clint Eastwood. Finally, men are supposed to fight aggressively—in business, in love, in sports, and so forth.

Surrounded by these images of what constitutes manliness, a young boy will likely learn to value himself in terms of achievement. Praise and rewards are his whenever he proves his superiority over another boy. Think, for instance, of the interest paid to winning in school athletics.

Even fighting, though normatively wrong, can be a source of prestige from both parents and peers—as long as he wins, of course, In fact, it would be downright *unmanly* to run away from a fight.

The result of this socialization for the adult male is that he is likely to see his value in terms of power and success. Trying to be the best at *anything*—the biggest eater, the hardest drinker, or the best lover she ever had—is part of the American male's search for selfhood. As a result, he is likely to see himself as a "doer."

The fact that traits we consider masculine are generally the preferred ones in American society has led many people to conclude that the system of sex roles has only benefited men. In terms of power and social rewards, this is largely the case. But researchers also attribute higher death rates, heart attacks, high blood pressure, and such to the role's demands. Also, Herb Goldberg (1976) and Mirra Komarovsky (1976) have pointed out the contradictory demands (role conflicts) American men confront. The traditional norm of male dominance, for example, contradicts our general norms of equality, as well as newer norms concerning sexual equality.

The impact of this sex-role socialization has been to perpetuate the division of most Americans into two distinct sex strata, with the male generally dominant and the female submissive. The roles give women and men different sets of ideal behavior to strive for, and conforming to these ideals brings men power and wealth relative to women. But, we might rightly ask, how have these ideals held up under the impact of contemporary changes? Let's now look at what impact the growing consciousness of the subordination of women has had on sex stratification.

Persistence and Change in Sex Stratification

In recent years, we have witnessed some changes in the system of sex stratification; but at the same time, the roles have acted to blunt the impact of more egalitarian views. Take, for example, the situation of women who move into high-level professional and administrative careers. To be sure, there has been change in this area, but tradition limits such change. Two researchers (Wolman and Frank 1972) have studied such women, finding that they face a "catch-22" in which any responses they give are labeled deviant by their male colleages: "If she acted friendly, she was thought to be flirting. If she apologized for alienating the group she was seen as a submissive woman taking her place. . . . If she asked for help, she earned a "needy" female label. If she became angry . . . she was seen as competitive in a bitchy, unfeminine way" (p. 8).

Rosabeth M. Kanter (1977) explains such responses to token female executives (*token* meaning that a small number are allowed to gain important positions to give the illusion of equality). In the large industrial corporation she studied, male executives outnumbered their female counterparts by ten or twelve to one in the various work groups. Because the women were few in number, they were highly visible and under excessive scrutiny, their differences from men were exaggerated, and their attributes were distorted to fit female stereotypes. As a result, their male colleagues reacted to each of them as if they were a mother, seductress, pet, or iron maiden.

The "mother" found her male peers constantly bringing her their troubles, expecting comfort, as they assumed that all women were good listeners. All the actions of the "seductress," such as having lunch with a male colleague, were given sexual connotations. The "pet" was "adopted by the male group as a cute, amusing little thing" and was never taken seriously. Because the men assumed she was incapable of doing much, they made a patronizing fuss over anything she did well. Still, such demonstrations of competence did not change their view of her. The woman who successfully avoided (or resisted) being pigeonholed in one of these three ways was dubbed an "iron maiden"—a "bitch." Because she refused the submissive roles offered her, she was viewed with suspicion and hostility (Kanter 1977, pp. 981–84). In other words, Kanter notes that *any* behaviors of "token women" will be defined by their male colleagues to fit the subordinate role they expect women to play. So we can see how a conservative majority will discourage nontraditional behavior through social pressure. (See Spangler, Gordon, and Pipkin [1978] for a test of Kanter's hypothesis at two law schools, which confirmed its validity.)

The fact that we can talk about women executives at all indicates some change, however. We also read in Chapter 6 that women today comprise almost half of the college population, and there is evidence (Van Dusen and Sheldon 1976) to suggest a decline in the stereotyping of occupations by sex (e.g., nurse, truck driver, and so on), although much still exists. Also, women today have less tendency to play down their competencies when interacting with men than their sisters did in the past (Dean et al. 1975).

In comparison to these and other changes in women's behavior, men's behavior has been slower to change. Certain-

ly, men's greater power and higher prestige made change *seem* unnecessary to them. Nevertheless there are some indications of movement on the part of men toward more equality. The image of the absent father, who only sees his children for a short time in the evening and maybe at dinner, for instance, seems less and less to reflect reality. Fathers are beginning to take a more active role in rearing their children. At the same time, there has been a general trend toward more "role sharing" between spouses—that is, sharing work roles and decision making, as well as parenting roles. As a whole, American marriages have become more egalitarian and less patriarchal in recent years (Giele 1975). These changes in role behavior are important and should not be ignored.

Neither should the changes we've been discussing be overestimated; they are as yet only a trend toward more equality, not equality itself. Most females today, regardless of their ability, are still relegated to jobs that bring them less wealth, prestige, and power than males gain. Figure 8.3, for example, shows that median weekly earnings for women, over a ten-year period, have been substantially lower than those of men—from 61 to 63 percent lower.

We should also recognize that many men benefit from the inferior status of women and aren't likely to readily give up their superior position. For instance, if women were encouraged equally with men to choose careers, men would face more competition for work. What's more, a man has a good deal in a wife—everyone should have one: she cleans up after him, takes care of the "little" chores, and comforts him (see Syfers 1973). Equality, then, threatens many vested interests—men would lose their disproportionate control over social resources and women would lose their near

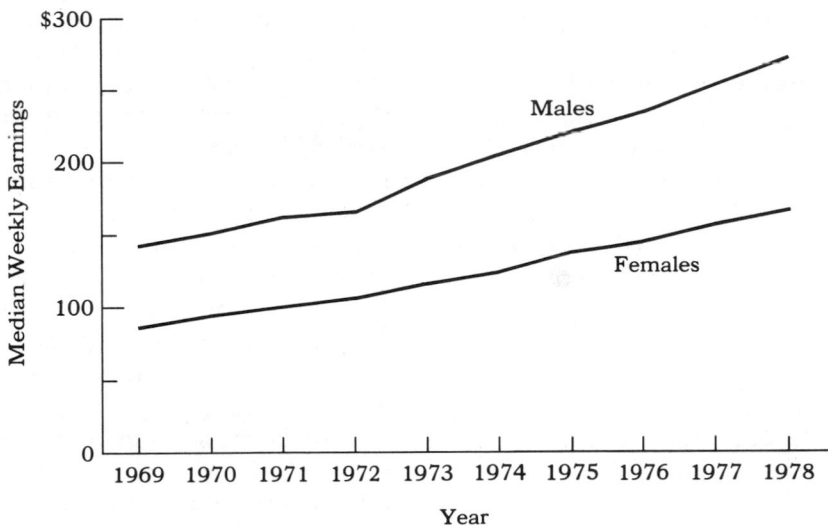

Figure 8.3 Median Weekly Earnings of Males and Females in the United States, 1969–1978

SOURCE: U.S. Department of Labor, "Survey Shows Weekly and Hourly Earnings for Major Groups of Workers," USDL 78–842, 1978.

monopoly of nurturance functions and the security that their traditional role has brought them. (Remember what Mary Wollstonecraft had to say about those "privileges.") **Institutionalized sexism**—sexism that pervades our customary ways of life—which we have reviewed in the last pages, is responsible for maintaining the inequality, even while allowing several specific changes.

Institutional—and thereby ingrained—sexism is a major concern of the women's liberation, or feminist, movement. More than equal pay for equal work—although that is an important goal, too—feminists seek a change in our ideology about the relationship between women and men, so that both sexes can compete on an equal basis and both can provide nurturance. Perhaps the extensiveness of these changes

helps account for the hostility the movement has encountered—from women and men alike. We'll briefly come back to feminism in Chapter 10, but right now, we'll look at another important type of stratification—age stratification.

AGE STRATIFICATION

"Of all the class struggles in modern societies, the most underrated may prove to be those between *age classes*," writes Gerhard Lenski (1966, p. 426) in his study of stratification. Although most if not all people may agree, we tend to exclude stratification by age from our understanding of inequality. Yet age is a universal basis of institutionalized inequality, if only in the denial of certain rights and privileges to the very young.

In this chapter, we'll be discussing three broad age classes, or age strata: youth (those aged sixteen to twenty-four), middle age (those aged twenty-five to sixty-four) and old age (those aged sixty-five and over). A fourth stratum, childhood, is also important, but space doesn't allow a full treatment.

Characteristics of Age Stratification

Age strata can be conveniently distinguished by the social roles people are expected to play in them. To oversimplify, youths generally occupy the roles of student and job trainee, middle-aged people generally have established work roles, and elderly people are frequently retired. Age is in fact a major criterion for entering and leaving social roles. We have to reach an "age of consent" before we can *legally* marry or have sex, we must leave our work role by age seventy now, we have to be at least thirty-five to become president, and so on.

Age strata can also be recognized by the interests their members share. During the 1960s, for example, many young people banded together to protest the war in Indochina fought by soliders of their age group. Likewise, the elderly have successfully fought to raise the mandatory retirement age from sixty-five to seventy. And recently in Chicago, as elsewhere, adults have acted as a group to raise the drinking age, because they felt that youths abused the privilege.

While persons in the same age stratum sometimes take collective action in defense of their interests as an age group, it is important to note that members of every age stratum are vulnerable to many cross-cutting allegiances—that is, to pulls to act in accordance with the norms of their class, race, ethnic group, sex, and so forth. In addition, age strata suffer from continuous membership change. Unlike other forms of stratification, our mobility out of an age stratum is universal and inevitable. This fact of aging limits the possibilities for the development of group cohesion within an age stratum.

Another characteristic of the broad age strata we have identified is that much of our social experience is likely to occur with others of the same stratum. A number of sociologists have noted that we spend considerably more time with our age peers than people did in the past. That is, our society is more *age segregated* than it used to be. In the extended families of the past, people interacted daily with grandparents, cousins, and many people of varying ages. Living in nuclear families, we tend not to have much contact with people of other ages; and fewer children in a family also reduces the age range. Most of our socialization (outside of the family) is from our peers—whether in a child's play group, a fraternity, at work, playing tennis, or at a "Golden Age" club.

Dimensions of Age Stratification

Age groupings in our society are not just relatively separate but, as pointed out, unequal. We find people stratified by age on each of Weber's three dimensions—property, power, and prestige. Let's look at age stratification in the United States along each of these dimensions.

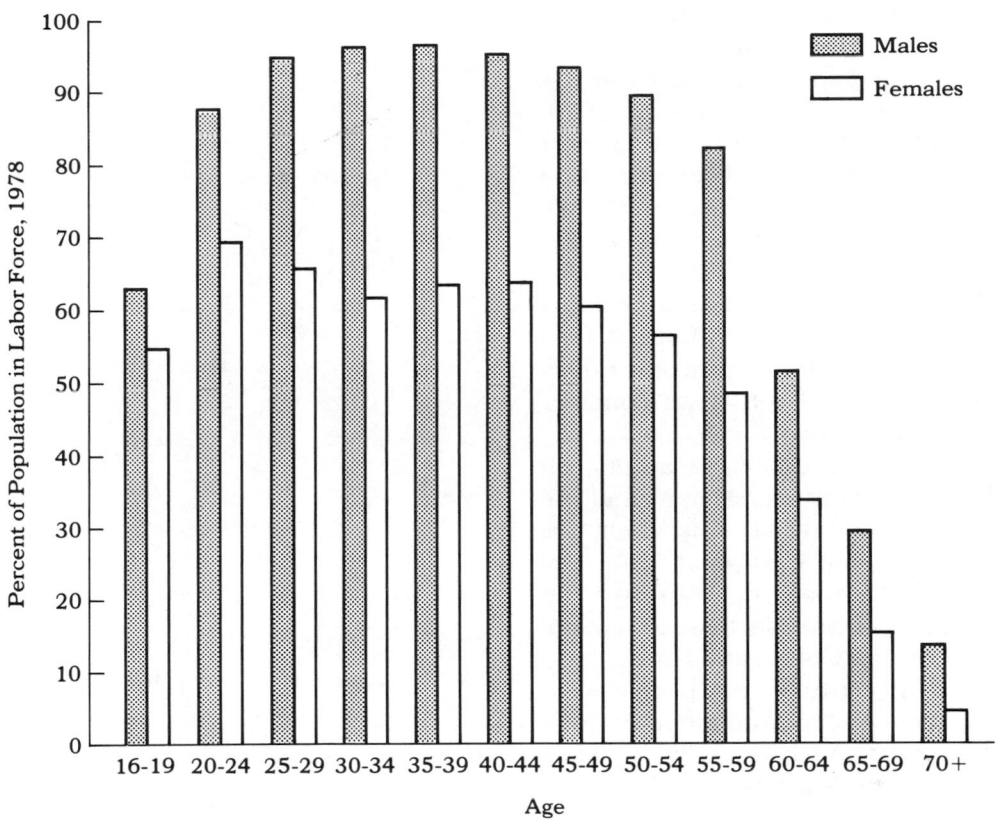

Figure 8.4 Age and the Labor Force in the United States, 1978

SOURCE: *U.S. Department of Labor*, Employment and Unemployment during 1979: An Analysis, *Special Labor Force Report 34, 1980, Table 3.*

AGE AND ECONOMIC RESOURCES Of our three age strata, only one—middle-aged adults—has a solid position in the American economic structure (see Figure 8.4). The reason for this is that our society is structured so that youth and the elderly are discouraged from working (by mandatory schooling and retirement, for instance).

Among those in the labor force, middle-aged persons also tend to receive the most income. Using census data in a study of male income, Roy Kass (1977) shows that highest earners at any given time tend to be between the ages of thirty-five and forty-four. In 1970, for instance, the median yearly income of these men was $9,133. Men aged forty-five to fifty-four earned $8,842; those aged twenty-five to thirty-four earned $7,914; and those aged fifty-five to sixty-four earned $7,293. But males aged twenty to twenty-four earned only $3,653, and those aged fourteen to nineteen earned even less—$904.

Comparisons of the weekly income of youth and adults using more recent data indicate that the gap separating these age strata is enlarging. From 1967 to 1978, median earnings increased by 7.6 percent annually for men twenty-five years and over, 7.5 percent for women that age. By contrast, in the sixteen-to-twenty-four-year age bracket, the rise was only 5.7 percent for men and 6.0 percent for women (U.S. Department of Labor 1978). As we can see from Figure 8.5, the income difference is considerable even if we consider only full-time workers.

Compared to middle-aged adults, elderly people and youth hold marginal positions in the economy—that is, their *recognized* value is not that great, and they do not *seem* to be that important in it. In many societies of the past—such as the ancient Danes and Goths, and Hindus into the nineteenth century—old people were regularly killed as "unproductive" drains on the economy. A good many societies have also killed their infants—another unproductive class—in times of famine (e.g., Australian aborigines), or when found to be defective and therefore burdens on the group (e.g., the ancient Spartans). While our society doesn't allow such slaughter, the young and the elderly do often suffer from their marginal economic position.

YOUTH Many young people play no substantial role in economic production, and their only legitimate work role is that of student (high school or college), from which they derive no income. Those youths in the labor market are often treated as second-class workers. Child labor laws—originally passed to protect children from exploitation by their parents and other adults—prohibit even many eighteen-year-olds from

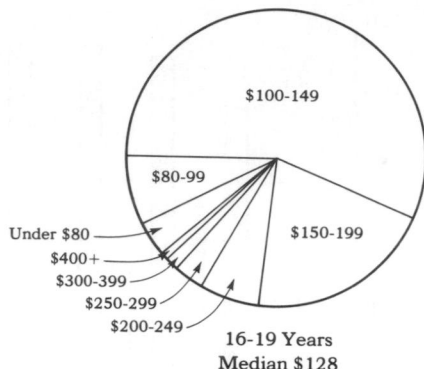

16-19 Years
Median $128

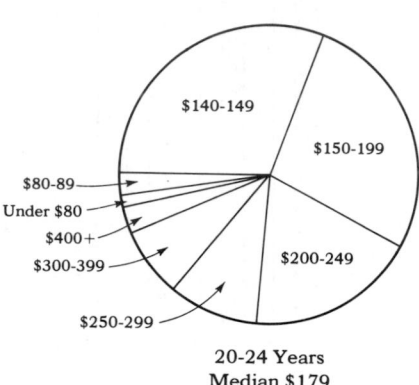

20-24 Years
Median $179

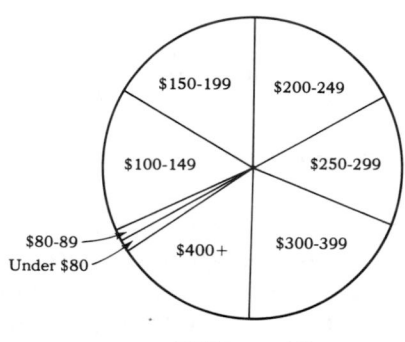

25 Years and Over
Median $246

Figure 8.5 Weekly Earnings by Age in the United States, 1978

SOURCE: U.S. Department of Labor, "Survey Shows Weekly and Hourly Earnings for Major Groups of Workers," USDL 78–842, 1978.

equal employment with the rest of society: they may be prevented from working certain times of the day or be restricted in the number of hours they can work. Furthermore, youths—because of their age or because of the jobs they are likely to get (e.g., working at a drug store or McDonald's)—are often *legally* paid below the minimum wage (Nelson and Levy 1977). Finally, workers between sixteen and nineteen years of age are heavily concentrated in wholesale and retail trades (U.S. Department of Labor 1980a), which means that they have virtually no place in most sectors of the economy.

Edgar Z. Friedenberg (1963, pp. 5–7) has observed that the economic position of adolescents is a contradictory one, and his analysis can be generalized to include all youth. On the one hand, juvenile delinquency, schooling, and caretaking are a tremendous drain on the economy, a drain accepted "on the assumption that youth must be drawn into the social order if the social order is to continue." On the other hand, we know from our study of socialization that the process of drawing people into the social order is most easily accomplished when the person being socialized is relatively powerless before the agents of socialization—thus, adult society has an interest in keeping youth economically dependent. We can imagine how difficult it would be to socialize *independent* youths. In addition, more and more businesses depend on revenues from the "youth market" for their profits and, by extension, on the dependency of youth. "Big business and industry are interested in seeing that [their] tastes become fads and in selling [them] specialized junk that a more mature taste would reject" (Friedenberg 1963, p. 7). Rather than bringing independence, young people's money ties them to their depend-

ent social role. Labor unions share that interest, as they want to keep any "extra" workers out of the labor market. If unemployment is bad now, imagine how much worse it would be if there were millions more young people looking for work.

THE ELDERLY Like youth, the elderly have been relegated to a second-class position in the economy. But whereas young people generally have caretakers to support them, many old people receive little or no help. Social Security payments are inadequate for many; they were never intended to be more than a supplement to pension income and savings, which don't exist for a great many people.

The major reason for relative poverty among the elderly, as we mentioned above, is lack of paying work. The elderly face many obstacles in finding and retaining jobs. They may not be physically able to perform some work, and they face widespread discrimination by employers who are certain they cannot and believe it is more profitable to train and retain younger workers. Elderly people, like youth, face an odd partnership of business and most organized labor, with both groups wanting to force out older workers to make room for younger ones in an economic system that can only absorb so many workers. The result has been mandatory retirement rules in many companies, formerly at age sixty-five and now at age seventy. And this phenomenon is a global one (see Worldwide Age Stratification).

There are some signs of change, however. More people are coming to appreciate "the valuable contributions of older workers and . . . the waste caused by arbitrary compulsory retirement based on age" (Nelson and Levy 1977, p. 4). The increased

WORLDWIDE AGE STRATIFICATION

The social problems of the elderly are not restricted to the United States, but are a worldwide phenomenon. In 1976, for example, researchers found that elderly Britons were more likely than others to be living in decaying urban areas, often without indoor toilets or baths. The elderly of Iran's cities have the lowest income of any population group. And two-thirds of the aged in Madras, India, live in slum huts or one-room hovels. But it is not only in cities that the elderly sit at the bottom of the stratification ladder. In rural areas, according to United Nations researchers, young people are migrating to cities in large numbers, often leaving the aged without "traditional resources and social support" (Hancock 1979).

It's true that rich and poor, male and female alike grow old and face certain common hardships, but most of the world's elderly were poor all their lives. For most people around the world, old age takes away their single salable commodity—their labor. Women also suffer disproportionately from aging. First of all, women live longer than men (an average of ten years longer in many industrialized nations) and marry at a younger age than men do. Thus many of the elderly are widows. Also, they

use of the term **ageism** to refer to prejudice and discrimination against people because of age may signify that we are becoming more aware of the problems of the elderly. Many states and the federal government have either raised the age of mandatory retirement from sixty-five to seventy, or have outlawed the practice altogether. Does the passage of such legislation indicate that the political power of the elderly is growing? Increasing numbers of elderly persons in the American population—the result of medical advances and demographic changes—as well as the emergence of an "age consciousness" might indicate that it is. Even so, we should look more closely at what the relationship is between age and the unequal distribution of power in American society.

Political Power and Age

While the middle-aged control most of the strings of political power in our society, the elderly wield more power than youth. To be sure, the elderly have often been without advocates for their special interests, but that has changed. A general awareness in society of their problems, human rights movements for other minorities, and im-

generally earn less than men do during their working lives, so they receive much smaller pensions.

For the poor, women, and ethnic minorities, old age completes a life of poverty and/or powerlessness. But almost all old people, regardless of their past, have moved from a postiion where others depended on their productivity to one where they must rely on that of others. Moreover, today's youth tends to be better educated than previous generations and to have less reason to look to the elderly as sources of traditional wisdom.

Throughout much of the third world in particular, there are practically no government programs for aiding the poor. Thus, says Simone de Beauvoir (1972), "Society cares about the individual only insofar as he is profitable." But will the growing number of elderly add to the aged's political power? Perhaps; but according to one view, the small number of political activists among the aged in the West might very well be "drowned out by the clatter of advertising men homing in on a new market. But commercials that explain to retirees the best times to telephone out-of-town relatives are not of the slightest value to the weak, the crushed, the desperately poor, and the powerless who make up the vast majority of the old today, and who do not retire to a place in the sun" (Hancock 1979).

proved leadership have brought political action on a number of "elderly" issues. There are, of course, a large number of elderly poor—as there are many poor people of all ages—but their problems are being addressed.

One reason some of the problems of the elderly are being addressed may be the fact that many top political leaders in the United States and other nations have held power past age sixty. This is not to say that we have a *gerontocracy*, or rule by the elderly (although your own experiences may tell you otherwise). Another reason for attention to issues of the elderly is politicians' awareness of their relatively high voter participation rate (Verba and Nie 1972). Youngest voters (eighteen to twenty-one), on the other hand, participate the least in elections, and people under age eighteen are not allowed to participate at all.

It is quite clear that the control of younger people by their elders has been a basic condition of life in most, if not all, societies. We observed the extent of this power imbalance in our study of socialization, especially in the family. Compulsory schooling and the growing necessity of a college education for career success have substantially lengthened the period of the young's dependence. This was not

advocates. Youth has had few opportunities to get redress of grievances through normal political channels. This may be one reason young voters often support more "extremist" candidates, regardless of political ideology. In 1968, for example, young people heavily supported *both* right-wing candidate George Wallace and Eugene McCarthy, whose views were to the left of political center. Four years later, the left-leaning George McGovern found his strongest support among youth (Seagull 1977, p. 25).

Age and Prestige

The unequal distribution of prestige to age strata is more complex than that of wealth or power. Is the United States a "youth-oriented" society? Do people hold a special reverence and respect for old people? We often hear these assertions made, and there is some truth to them. But emphasizing them obscures the fact that in terms of *prestige*—as with wealth and power—the position of these two age groups in modern industrial society is marginal.

Older persons in our society command a certain respect because of the "credits" they have accumulated over the years—work experience, personal accomplishments, knowledge of the past, and so on. But it is in the technologically most primitive societies that old people receive the most social honor. For instance, the Andaman Islanders, a simple hunting and gathering society, value old people as individuals with extraordinary skills and powers (Radcliffe-Brown 1922). Then there are gerontocracies, as exist among Australian aborigines, where the elderly are held in awe by the rest of the tribe.

The 1970s saw the emergence of what we can call "grey consciousness." Many elderly people formed interest groups, like the Grey Panthers; governments started providing more aid for senior citizens; and younger people became more aware of the plight of the elderly. Yet, the problems persist.

the case in the past, at least for males, as boys in their early teens often secured their economic independence through work.

Within the political system itself, rules of seniority restrict young politicians from occupying many positions of real power. There are occasional exceptions, such as John Kennedy; but even this "young" president was forty-two when elected. Thus few political leaders are likely to share the interests of young people and act as their

If advanced years are an asset in technologically primitive societies, however, they are often a liability in industrialized ones. As we age, we must forfeit those major social roles that were the basis of a lifetime of self-evaluation. Although retirement from employment is supposed to be a "reward" for years of service and may be pleasurable, it usually involves a loss of prestige. In our society, most prestige goes to income earners, and people generally feel that a career of leisure (play) characterizes the socially immature (children) or socially obsolete.

Old people also lose their equally essential domestic roles. Children grow up and leave home; the house itself becomes too large and expensive and is often sold (which also takes the full-time homemaker's role away); and a spouse may die. Some people might expect the role of grandparent to provide sufficient domestic gratification. A number of studies, however, have indicated that most aged get little satisfaction from interaction with young visitors (Rosow 1967; Rosenberg 1970; Hochschild 1973).

In *The Coming of Age*, Simone de Beauvoir (1972) wonders if old people are even considered human beings by the rest of society. If that sounds a bit ridiculous, try to imagine a person being deprived of her or his social roles and activities. What would make that person like the rest of us? Ask yourself, too, if you consider an old person's complaints as legitimate as you do those of other people. Another way we deny old people's humanity is by viewing them as sexless creatures. We often deny that an old person should even think about sex too much (denying an emotional aspect of the person), and we might consider them "dirty" (deviant) if they do. But studies show that old people are physiologically able to enjoy sex if they want to (Butler and Lewis 1976)—all the obstacles are social.

As we have seen throughout our look at age stratification, young people, too, are treated as second-class citizens. Society prevents them from assuming the major roles that would allow them the same level of prestige as that granted the middle-aged. We can see this in the amount of regulation and control young people are subject to (school and schoolwork, motion picture ratings, child labor laws, sex and marriage restrictions, and much more)—control any adult would find an unacceptable denial of human rights. Moreover, even the young adult—and certainly other youths—are considered incapable of taking care of themselves. Of course, children *are* incapable of taking care of themselves, but historical evidence suggests that we prolong the transition to adult status much longer than necessary (Aries 1962).

The extension of voting and some other rights to eighteen-year-olds may indicate some improvement in prestige, but youths continue to be considered immature. For young people and the elderly alike, then, we have observed a situation in which they are faced with life conditions generally inferior to those of middle-aged adults. We have also observed change and conflict, and perhaps a more hopeful future for at least some of them.

SUMMARY

We have looked at stratification based on the ascribed statuses of ethnicity, race, sex, and age. Many people feel that a person's race, ethnicity, sex, and age determine his or her behavior. In believing this, they attribute the same trait(s) to all members of a group, while ignoring the variations among them. This stereotyping is especially harmful because many people act as if the stereotypes were real. People often use stereotypes to justify their prejudice, or inflexible, hostile attitudes toward members of particular groups. Discrimination occurs when people act on their prejudice or otherwise deny persons of these groups social rewards merely on the basis of their group membership.

Looking at the consequent stratification of people by ethnic group, race, sex, and age, we saw much statistical evidence that American society contains deep cleavages in terms of property, power, and prestige that tend to keep blacks, women, youth, and the elderly at the bottom of the stratification system.

To be sure, there has been a great deal of conflict and controversy, especially in recent years, over these inequalities, and there has been some improvement in the underprivileged groups' conditions. Even so, the existing ethnic, racial, sexual, and age stratification systems are rooted in our common socialization, and social institutions are structured to reinforce them. Although they have been significant, the social movements for equal rights have only begun making headway on this deeper and more subtle level.

Key Terms

race (p. 249)
minority (p. 250)
prejudice (p. 250)
stereotypes (p. 250)
discrimination (p. 252)
assimilation (p. 260)
gender identification (p. 266)
sexism (p. 267)
institutionalized sexism (p. 271)
ageism (p. 276)

Review and Discussion Questions

1. To what extent does a racial caste system still exist in the United States today? How does this differ from the stratification of white ethnic groups?
2. Equality for all is a cherished American principle, yet we have seen that inequality between white and black Americans persists. Why, despite that principle and many changes in the law, does prejudice and discrimination remain a part of the American scene?
3. What stereotyped female attributes can you recognize in Spencer's explanation of male/female differences? What are their implications for woman's "proper" role?
4. What changes have you noticed away from sex-stereotyped behavior and how have they affected the system of sex stratification? Who stands to lose (wealth, power, and/or prestige) from this?
5. What benefits would men receive from changing their sex-role behavior in ways that would in effect reduce the amount of power they have in relation to that of women?
6. Are there any likely bases on which the elderly can build prestige in contemporary society? How might society improve their economic conditions?

For Further Study

ETHNIC STUDIES There have been many pieces written which examine specific ethnic groups in American society. A sampling would include: Irving Howe, *World of Our Fathers* (New York: Simon & Schuster, 1976) (about American Jews); Helena Z. Lopata, *Polish Americans: Status Competition in an Ethnic Community* (Englewood Cliffs, NJ: Prentice-Hall, 1976); Joseph Lopreato, *Italian Americans* (New York: Random House, 1970); and Stanford Lyman, *Chinese Americans* (New York: Random House, 1974). For a comprehensive study of ethnic relations around the world, see: Chester L. Hunt and Lewis Walker, *Ethnic Dynamics: Patterns of Intergroup Relations in Various Societies* (Homewood, IL: Dorsey, 1974).

ASSIMILATION The majority of American sociologists and nonsociologists alike take an ethnic group's assimilation largely for granted. Although some assimilation almost always occurs, the process is seldom a smooth one. See: Andrew M. Greeley, *The American Catholic: A Social Portrait* (New York: Basic Books, 1977); Michael Novak, *The Rise of the Unmeltable Ethnics* (New York: Macmillan, 1972); and L. Paul Metzger, "American Sociology and Black Assimilation: Conflicting Perspectives," *American Journal of Sociology* **76** (Nov. 1971): 627–47.

BLACK AMERICANS Many white Americans—and not a few blacks—have a difficult time conceptualizing black demands outside of the moderate, assimilationist perspective; but there is a more radical understanding of the situation; see: Stokely Carmichael and Charles V. Hamilton, *Black Power* (New York: Random House, 1976). For an account of a group that faces both racial and sexual discrimination, see: Gerta Lerner, *Black Women in White America* (New York: Pantheon, 1972). Also see the excellent collection of articles on the black family: Robert Staples, ed., *The Black Family* (Belmont, CA: Wadsworth, 1978).

THE SECOND SEX In 1949, Simone de Beauvoir wrote the premier feminist book of recent times, *The Second Sex* (New York: Bantam, 1961). It is an exhaustive and lucid review of the denigration of women in Western history. Despite its age, the book is still of great value today. The subjugation of women by the medical and legal institutions is discussed in: Phyllis Chesler, *Women and Madness* (Garden City, NY: Doubleday, 1972); and Karen DeCrow, *Sexist Justice* (New York: Random House, 1974). In *Women and Equality: Changing Patterns in American Culture* (New York: Oxford University Press, 1978), William H. Chafe explores the development of and change in the sex roles of American women. Finally, a number of good readers have appeared in recent years on women, including Marcia Millman and Rosabeth Moss Kanter, eds., *Another Voice: Feminist Perspectives on Social Life and Social Science* (Garden City, NY: Doubleday, 1975).

THE ELDERLY An extensive literature on aging in America has emerged in the past decade. Again, we can turn to Simone de Beauvoir for a comprehensive review of Western society's treatment of its elderly: *The Coming of Age* (New York: Warner, 1973). Sharon R. Curtin, *Nobody Ever Died of Old Age* (Boston: Little, Brown, 1972), critiques aging in the United States and its consequences for the elderly. Some good readers on the topic also are available; see, for instance: Cary S. Kart and Barbara B. Manard, eds., *Aging in America* (Port Washington, NY: Alfred, 1976); and Jill Quadagno, ed., *Aging, the Individual and Society* (New York: St. Martin's, 1980).

PART THREE

By now, we have a solid understanding of society's building blocks and how they work, both as controlling elements in our lives and as forces that make social life possible. In Part Three, we will apply this understanding to the various processes of social change.

Chapter 9 examines the way social structures can deteriorate, as well as how they stay together. In doing so, it presents the important concepts of alienation and anomie, which refer to different aspects of the breakdown in the power of norms to command us. We will also look at the concept of social solidarity and how people have tried to explain the phenomenon of social structures remaining whole despite daily conflicts.

Chapter 10 covers collective behavior and social movements. Collective behavior does not refer simply to the behavior of people in a group, but to the special ways that people act as a group—in crowds, audiences, and mobs—in reaction to fads and crazes. While liberating us from normal constraints, being in a crowd also leaves us vulnerable to manipulation by individual leaders. Social movements can be considered a form of collective behavior, but they are less fleeting than other forms. Individuals in a social movement act in concert to promote specific interests over a prolonged period.

The Dynamism
of Society

Social movements also have a more lasting impact on society as a whole.

Chapter 11 is concerned specifically with processes of social change. First, we'll look at various sociological perspectives on change. We will consider the inevitability of change, its irreversibility once a fact, and tendencies of certain groups to resist change. We will then examine the various sources of social change. Several governments, particularly that of the United States, have institutionalized small changes (e.g., in elections) to prevent more radical change from occurring. Technological advances are increasingly an important source of social change, and we will examine that relationship. Also, we will see how changes in population bring about social change—not all of it for the better, and we'll analyze some of the social problems associated with population change and how we might solve them. Finally, we will note the increasing urbanization of our world (not just the industrialized West).

We should be aware that the type of analysis we will be carrying out in Part Three is essential for the sociological imagination, for it enables us to go beyond our own problems—or the problems of any individual, for that matter—to consider the overarching patterns that lie behind all individual problems. ▪

CHAPTER NINE
Social Disorganization and Solidarity

Throughout the preceding four chapters we have been looking at various aspects of social organization. In this chapter, we are going to look not at how social life is organized, but at how, once organized, it can become disorganized. This chapter will focus on two important concepts of social disorganization: *alienation*—the feeling of separation from the world, other people, and ourselves—and *anomie*—the social condition of normlessness. We will also look at their opposite, *social solidarity.*

SOCIAL DISORGANIZATION

Social organization operates according to a set of rules that govern our interactions with one another and the interactions among groups in society. What happens when these rules begin to break down? That is, what happens when conditions change so that the rules no longer regulate social life as effectively as before or when people no longer see these rules as legitimate? Sociologists call this condition **social disorganization:** the disruption of a preexisting social organization in such a way that previously normal social control breaks down.

Many sociologists have used the term *social disorganization* in a way that im-plies it is something "bad" or to be corrected. But we needn't hope that social disorganization would never occur in our society or group. If, for instance, the disorganization involves liberating our country from foreign oppressors, we may very well hope it occurs; but if, on the other hand, an economic depression disrupts the pattern of our interactions, we're likely to look at the situation quite differently. Similarly, we are likely to view social disorganization differently depending on how it affects our own social position. If we are union organizers, we undoubtedly would look with favor at growing disaffection with working conditions among employees of a plant we are trying to organize. But if we are the plant's owners or managers, obviously we will look at the slowdowns and inefficiencies which are likely to accompany the disaffection in quite a different light. That is, how we look at social disorganization depends on the results it has.

Social disorganization can be caused by any type of change in existing conditions. In Chapter 11, we will look at the nature of social change in general and at some of the main causes of change in modern society. In this chapter, however, we will concentrate on the deterioration or breakdown of the power of society's rules to command our assent, either because we don't accept them as our own (alienation) or because they are not clear (anomie). Finally, we will look at the nature of *social solidarity*—our willingness to cooperate with one another and follow the rules of society—which keeps society intact.

Alienation

Like *culture, class,* and so many other terms, the meaning that *alienation* has for sociologists and other social scientists differs from the meaning it has in ordinary usage. We might, for example, read an article in *Time* about "alienated youth" or hear a news commentator talk about "the alienated American voter." While we could get a general idea of alienation's effects from such discussions, the concept of **alienation** is much richer than these usages suggest. In its essence: "The word 'alienation' implies an intense separation—from objects in a world; from other people; and from ideas about the world held by other people" (Horowitz 1972, p. 557).

We can be alienated from our parents, our religion, or our government, for example. Normatively, these are individuals and institutions that we should identify with. For that reason, alienation can create intense strain and tension, both individually and socially. Evidently, we feel we should bridge that separation when it exists.

The concept of alienation has gone through many changes in meaning, particularly in the last century. To appreciate the concept's usefulness, we need to know what some of these meanings have been. We'll start by looking at the ideas of the most important writer on alienation, Karl Marx, and then turn to contemporary meanings of the term.

Karl Marx: Alienated Labor

"Alienated Labor" (Marx 1963 [1844], pp. 120–34) contains Marx's theory of alienation. Marx believed that conditions of modern capitalist production alienate workers from their work and the economic system as a whole. One of those conditions is *advanced technology.* Whereas the independent artisans of preindustrial times owned and controlled their own tools, modern workers do not. Today, only corporations and other businesses can afford the cost of controlling the large and expensive equipment needed for modern industrial production. Unlike a hammer, drill, or other hand tool, modern machinery—a blast furnace, for example—requires many operators. Also, the tools appear to control those who use them, by determining the pace of modern labor. An auto worker, for instance, must work at the assembly line's pace (although we should note that it's the people in the front office, not machines, that determine the speed at which the assembly line moves). Because of this, Marx said, modern workers lose their freedom and feel powerless before the machine—a feeling that the expense of the machine reinforces because it suggests they can never achieve more control.

The *division of labor* and increased specialization in production also make factory work seem meaningless. A job's meaning was clear, for example, when a worker made an entire product. If asked what he or she was doing, the quick response would be: "I'm making a pair of shoes (or a jacket or whatever)." But if the same worker is turning three screws on door after door on an assembly line, could he or she say, "I'm making a car"? Although it may be necessary for modern production efficiency,

According to Marx, conditions of labor under capitalism produce intense feelings of meaninglessness and powerlessness, which alienate workers from the world around them, other people, and even themselves.

specialization separates each worker from the entire process. Marx recognizes that it is easy for people to feel alienated from something that they have to spend many hours doing and that yields little satisfaction in return.

Marx saw the private ownership of the means of production, however, as the fundamental source of alienated labor. What workers produce is not considered their own but the employer's property. Once a product leaves their hands, workers lose the little control over it they had. The employer determines not only whether to produce it but also its disposal (how to market

it, what price to set for it) regardless of the worker's desires. As a result, their product appears to be an alien thing with power over them. For instance, if the product sells, the worker can expect continued work and wages; if not, it might be disastrous for the worker's economic well-being. Besides that, the profitability of the product will also influence the employer's decision to, for example, build a new plant, buy more machinery, hire or fire workers, or close down the operation. And even though these decisions have a great impact on their lives, individual workers have no say in them.

Marx's unique contribution, however, has been his concept of *self-alienation.* In "Alienated Labor," he noted that our labor—and therefore we ourselves—becomes a commodity: our price, like that of other commodities, is set by the impersonal laws that determine the cost of replacing us with someone who would perform the same task. And, in some ways, we *feel* like we are treated as things. On the job market, we recognize the truth of the cliché that "everyone has his or her price." Marx also noted that we cannot gain our livelihood voluntarily but must do the bidding of our employers, which may make us feel like someone else's tool. Workers separate—or alienate—what they recognize as human in themselves from the production of commodities. Consider that people often take jobs they find boring or below their intelligence, and persist at them. All the time, however, they might think: "I'm not stupid but I do this because I have to make a living." If this has ever happened to you, then you were alienating your self from your labor.

Some people have criticized Marx for implying that only greed and the struggle for profits control business decisions and that workers in capitalist society are motivated only by their economic self-interest (see Marx 1963 [1844], p. 121). This view is too simplistic because it doesn't take into account the ties of loyalty some workers, especially those with some minimal authority, feel toward their tasks and the enterprises for which they labor, and it doesn't consider the power of workers, through unions and legislative efforts, to restrict the owners' power to command their workers. Moreover, although Marx once did admit that those who control industry might be alienated, he did not consider it important: "The possessing class and the proletarian class express the same human alienation. But the former is satisfied with its situation, feels itself well-established in it, recognizes this self-alienation as *its own power*. . . . The latter feels itself crushed by this self-alienation, sees in it its own impotence and the reality of an inhuman situation" (1956 [1845], p. 231).

Since the time of Marx, however, the managerial stratum and white-collar strata generally have grown considerably, meaning that we must examine the extent of alienation not just among the industrial working class but among these other workers as well. Erich Fromm (1955), for one, wrote about alienation among managers. Like industrial workers, they deal with impersonal giants—not giant machines, however, but giant competing enterprises, national and international markets, consuming populations, unions, and a government with a multitude of business regulations and agencies. Together, these giants determine the manager's life as much as machines determine the worker's. For white-collar workers, their personal traits (e.g., a salesperson's ability to convince a customer, to speak well, to exercise firmness with a complaining customer, and so on) all become part of the company's means of production. These workers turn their very intimate features into tools under someone else's (the employer's) control.

There have been a number of good empirical studies of alienation in the United States. Robert Blauner's 1964 study is one (see Testing the Theory of Alienation, p. 290). Blauner conceptualizes four dimensions of alienation, to find that although not all blue-collar workers are alienated, modern technology does tend to alienate workers, confirming Marx's theory in that respect. In another study, Melvin Kohn (1976) sampled 3,101 males working at various jobs, finding support for Marx's contention that modern workers are alienated. He differs from Marx, however, in his finding that control over the work process, not the product, is the crucial factor in the extent of alienation. Like Marx's other work we have reviewed, his theory of alienation needs to be revised in some respects. But his theory contains some unique insights into the way human behavior is structured by competition in modern capitalist society.

Contemporary Meanings of Alienation

Since Marx's time, the concept of alienation has undergone many changes and is now used in a number of different senses. The most important change from Marx's conception is that among American social scientists, alienation tends to be interpreted almost exclusively as a matter of personal feeling. Whereas Marx believes that workers under capitalism were alienated

Alienated people often feel powerless, especially compared to big business, organized labor, and other established special interest groups. Some hope to have an impact by demonstrating publicly, but this often only confirms their powerlessness—as it did for these anti-nuclear demonstrators when the power plant they protested against was built anyway.

whether they personally felt themselves to be or not, writers outside the Marxist tradition tend to call alienation only that which is consciously experienced as such.

In the social-psychological sense in which the term is used today, Melvin Seeman (1959) has identified five main usages of the term: powerlessness, meaninglessness, normlessness, isolation, and self-estrangement.

POWERLESSNESS The interpretation of alienation as powerlessness is perhaps the

closest to the Marxist sense of the term and the most frequently employed. People are alienated in this sense when they feel that what they do has little or no effect on the forces that shape their lives. This type of alienation is not uncommon when people feel that who they vote for makes no difference in determining the actual policies to be carried out. Below are a number of voter comments collected after the 1959 mayoralty contest between John F. Collins and John E. Powers in Boston. How many of these complaints remain common today?

TESTING THE THEORY OF ALIENATION

Over the years, Marx's theory of alienation has been a valuable sociological tool, even though Marx never actually tested his theory. But how well does his theory apply to contemporary American workers? To find out, sociologist Robert Blauner (1964) surveyed blue-collar workers in the automobile, chemical, textile, and printing industries to see if they *felt* alienated (that is, he did not directly test the relationship between alienation and social structure).

Blauner first conceptualized four dimensions of alienation: powerlessness, meaninglessness, social alienation (feeling isolated from other workers), and self-estrangement. To measure powerlessness, he asked workers if their job made them work too fast and if they could try out their own ideas. For meaninglessness, he asked about the worker's product— what it was and how it was used. For social alienation, workers were asked to rate their company's and job's importance. And self-estrangement was measured by asking workers if their job was too simple for them.

Blauner did not find all blue-collar workers alienated, but he did find that modern technology tends to alienate them, confirming Marx's theory in that respect. Technology reduces their control; machines determine job pace; workers neither own nor control their tools; and the division of labor in factories keeps workers from seeing how their particular task

"Collins is the lesser of two evils."
"Neither candidate appealed to me."
"Voting wouldn't do any good."
". . . both no good."
"I don't like the caliber of the candidates."
"I think they're all the same. It doesn't matter who you vote for."
"I guess they're all a little crooked."
"Talks too much, does very little."
"Collins is for Collins."
"Too much of a politician, commitments to groups."
"His connection with big business. He wasn't doing his own talking."
"I felt he made deals with backers of the campaign."
"No concrete platform; too evasive."
"He had a lot of phony talk."

(Levin 1960, p. 59)

Politically alienated people feel that they are not part of the political process and that a small group of powerful people (mostly

relates to the finished product. But Blauner also believes that the nature of each specific industry can greatly reduce the amount of worker alienation.

Workers producing unique products in the printing industry, for instance, feel less alienated than those working on standardized products (e.g., automobiles). Printers also experience less alienation because they work on large parts of the product. Craft workers generally experience less alienation than do workers in flourishing industries. Finally, alienation is lower for those who work in groups than for solitary workers.

Blauner found that auto workers experienced the most alienation, chemical workers the next highest, textile workers next, and printers the least. Moreover, 69 percent of the auto workers said they'd choose a different trade if they could begin life anew; 58 percent of the chemical workers and 54 percent of the textile workers thought so, too; but only 36 percent of the printers would choose another trade.

People have criticized Blauner's methodology (he used an old questionnaire and assistants did most of the interviewing). Indeed, he might have gotten more precise measures. Even so, the study does yield insight into the nature of alienation in modern industry, including the ways that production can be organized to reduce worker alienation. It also shows that theories, even those derived without empirical data, can be important tools for sociological research and analysis.

politicians, big business, and the media) controls elections and government policy. In response to this alienation, many people withdraw, as low voter turnouts testify. Other people try to overcome these feelings through political activism, ranging from backing "independent" candidates to political reform to revolution (Schwartz 1973, p. 159).

Feelings of powerlessness frequently stem from other aspects of modern society as well. The price of food and other necessities keeps rising no matter what we do; the media show us world events that occur as if we did not exist; government offices are unresponsive to our requests. And we can do little, personally, about taxes, crime, pollution, or any number of things. As far back as 1903, Georg Simmel (1950, pp. 409–24) observed that many urban dwellers respond to this sense of powerlessness by withdrawing and living as virtual strangers from their surroundings. Other people have withdrawn into suburbs, where they have little contact with other people. But, in an analysis of a number of studies of labor in Ohio and Sweden, Seeman (1966) concludes that people can overcome feelings of powerlessness and alienation by belonging to groups and exercising some control through them.

MEANINGLESSNESS This type of alienation involves people's inability to make sense of the world or their place in it. As a result, it is difficult if not impossible to determine appropriate courses of effective action. Instead, such alienated persons might launch misplaced attacks on social groups that, in reality, are not responsible for the real problems. Racial and religious prejudice are examples: Jews, for instance, or blacks may be attacked as scapegoats for economic hardship or lack of social mobility.

NORMLESSNESS When used in this context, the concept of alienation generally refers to the feeling that we can realistically hope to reach socially desired goals only by violating social norms. If you remember our discussion of Merton's theory of deviance in Chapter 4, you will see that this usage of alienation is directly related to his analysis.

In our society, poverty is one source of this type of alienation. Poor people generally want the same things out of life as middle-class persons do (Coward et al. 1974), but they lack the socially approved means of obtaining them. As a result they may become alienated. The alienated poor may respond to their alienation with passivity and withdrawal. They may instead protest or reject the norms of the society that has rejected them and form protest organizations, riot, or resort to crime. Minorities may feel alienated, even if they are not poor. For example, women who try to make headway in a career, only to be blocked by prejudiced males in more powerful positions, may experience a similar type of alienation.

ISOLATION The fourth type of alienation refers to the sense of separateness that comes from not sharing the dominant values of the culture. The typical example of this type of alienation is the intellectual who feels cut off from the surrounding society and culture because she or he holds an unorthodox set of values. But intellectuals aren't the only ones who can be alienated in this sense. Herbert Gans (1974, pp. 106–7), for example, has written about this type of alienation among manual workers, who are affected by middle-class-oriented television news programs and manifestations of "high" culture. The stories and issues presented in the news often have little meaning for blue-collar life. Furthermore, in the media, academia, and even government, we are ordinarily presented with a white, often Protestant, middle-class image of America. People not of that group might very well experience alienation.

SELF-ESTRANGEMENT The final type of alienation is self-estrangement. We saw some examples of this type in our discussion of Marx's concept of alienation. Another instance is what Ernest Schachtel (1961) has termed "alienated identity," which comes from being identified by, and identifying ourselves with, official papers and numbers. For example, if your college is like many others, your identity for them is your nine-digit Social Security number; you hand a traffic cop your identity in the form of a driver's license; your passport is your identity that allows you to leave and reenter this country. Psychoanalysts have reported how using these badges—and they are necessary for life in a large society—can estrange us from ourselves and lead us to see ourselves in terms of these bureaucratic devices.

While these types of alienation can be logically distinguished, in reality they often appear blended together. Now we're going to look at *anomie,* a second form of social disorganization that can induce alienation.

ANOMIE

With alienation, we have been talking mainly about people's feelings and reactions to certain social situations; *anomie,* however, is entirely a product of the social structure. Individuals can be alienated, but only societies can be anomic. Another word for anomie is normlessness; more particularly: **anomie** is a state of society in which major norms are either unclear or missing. When a country is occupied by an invading army, for example, all citizens face a choice: should they obey the invader's law and just go about their business, or should they break the law (kill, steal, sabotage, and so on) and try to liberate their nation? We might have personal feelings about which is the right course to follow, but there is no clear social norm to guide us. Proof of that is the fact that large numbers of people in this situation have

chosen each alternative. The situation is anomic.

Anomie rarely characterizes an entire society; it is generally confined to a segment of it. During New York City's blackout in 1977, for example, many people started rioting. Stores were looted and vandalized, and entire city blocks were gutted. In the abnormal situation, where the possibility of detection and arrest was small, the rioters recognized no proscriptive norm against stealing. For them, the situation was anomic. But the rioting was confined to the city's poorest sections. Other New Yorkers stayed calm, and some even helped direct traffic since the traffic lights were out, too. The norm to be followed was clear throughout most of the city.

If you were to object, however, that not everyone in Harlem and other poor areas rioted, you would be correct; most people did not. Your observation would, in fact, underscore that the situation was anomic; if everyone had rioted, we could say that they were following a clear norm. This was not the case, and people had to decide whether to follow the norm to obey the law or follow the immediate communal norm to riot.

An anomic situation also exists when there is a conflict between cultural goals and the social norms for attaining them. This is the situation that underlies the type of alienation Seeman calls normlessness. Under anomic conditions, Robert K. Merton writes, cultural values may even drive people to violate specific norms (1968, p. 216). Lower-class as well as middle-class Americans learn to value economic success and high social status, for example. But what do people do when, despite their hard effort, they do not attain these goals? They may turn to crime, look for substitute satisfaction in alcohol or in having many children, or they may simply work even harder. The point again is that they have no single clear norm to follow: should they follow the norm that dictates that they should be successful, or should they follow the norm that dictates that they should only strive for goals in culturally approved of ways?

As we might gather from these examples of conflicting norms, anomie is not uncommon in our society. A society, or a segment of it (e.g., group, institution, community), is anomic as long as the normative conflict remains unresolved and the normative structure remains unclear. Alan Roberts and Milton Rokeach (1956) have formulated five indicators of anomie from their studies of anomie, authoritarianism, and prejudice.

1. Leaders do not care about the people's needs.
2. People feel that little can be done, socially, in their orderless society.
3. The personal goals of individuals seem to be receding rather than being realized.
4. There is a general sense of futility.
5. People feel they cannot trust their personal associations for support.

How many of these do you recognize in your society?

To learn more about the nature of anomie, we are now going to look at the theories of Emile Durkheim. Although the term *anomie* was used in writings on law and theology in the sixteenth and seventeenth centuries, it then meant "lawless behavior" rather than normlessness. Its contemporary meaning, which we have been discussing here, was developed by Durkheim in the late nineteenth century.

Emile Durkheim and Anomie

For Durkheim, anomie's essential characteristic is lack of regulation. In anomic societies, the breakdown in norms erodes the usual limits and restraints on individual behavior. Durkheim believed that such restraint is necessary for individuals and for social stability. Because our needs go beyond those necessary for physical survival, he reasons, there is no limit to them: "Irrespective of any external regulatory force, our capacity for feeling is in itself an insatiable and bottomless abyss" (1951 [1897], p. 247). The problem with unlimited desires is that they cannot be satisfied. Unsatisfied, they may torment us and lead to social chaos. Only society can provide the necessary regulatory force to restrain these desires.

This is all certainly true, but we shouldn't therefore necessarily conclude that all anomie is "bad" and all restraints "good." To even begin to make such judgments, we need to know how much and what kind of restraint. Social restraints may preserve us from harm but they may also preserve our inequality. Durkheim's analysis seems to leave out questions of legitimately challenging the restraints. He says these social restraints impose a "common interest" over our quest for individual ones; for instance, we will often keep working at a hateful and low-paying job because it is what we are supposed to do. But we have seen that apparently "common" interests tend to benefit some at the expense of others. Thus, in the long run, anomie might even prove beneficial: disregarding certain social restraints, deprived persons might struggle to obtain equality. The discontent caused by the unmet needs might spur a population to depose a dictatorial or corrupt government. Whether the ultimate results are good or not, however, anomie itself produces a strain in society, as elements of social organization (norms, roles, institutions) disintegrate.

Durkheim first observed anomie in social crises, when a society failed to provide basic necessities, leading people to question its restraints. When a country is invaded, its government has failed to adequately defend its citizens; in economic depressions, a society has failed to adequately feed its citizens. Durkheim noted, however, that in such circumstances, neither the physical danger nor poverty in itself produces anomie. It is the crisis situation itself—the disruption that forces people to find new norms for living—that causes anomie. Durkheim demonstrated this by pointing to anomie in crises with constructive outcomes: the unifications of Germany and of Italy (Durkheim 1951 [1897], pp. 241–44). Similarly, even though the 1920s in the United States was a time of swift economic growth and the emergence of the nation as a world power, it was also a decade of high anomie, as traditional restraints on drinking, entertainment, and the activities of youth broke down in large segments of the middle class.

Anomie is not restricted to these rare phenomena, however; it can become a normal state of affairs. Durkheim argued that, in the economic sphere at least, anomie has become normal in modern society, as the traditional restraints on economic relations and personal ambition break down:

> From top to bottom of the ladder, greed is aroused without knowing where to find ultimate foothold. Nothing can calm it, since its goal is far beyond all it can attain. Reality seems valueless by comparison with the dreams of fevered imaginations; reality is therefore abandoned . . . A thirst arises for novelties, unfamiliar pleasures, nameless sensations, all of which lose their savor once known. . . . The whole fever subsides and the sterility of all the tumult is apparent, and it is seen that all these new sensations in their infinite quantity cannot form a solid foundation of happiness to support one during days of trial. (1951 [1897], p. 256)

Sebastian de Grazia (1948) has refined Durkheim's theory of anomie by distinguishing between **simple anomie,** in which there is a conflict between the directives of the norms we are supposed to follow, and **acute anomie,** in which we have no authoritative norms to follow.

Simple Anomie

If you are like most people, you have probably found out that adult life often requires that you violate one norm in order to act in accordance with another. We may have learned not to cause other people harm, for example, but the norms of business life might require us to hurt a competitor, possibly driving him or her out of business. We have all learned that we should tell the truth, but a "little fib" such as "I have a headache" might be necessary to tactfully break an unwanted engagement or refuse a date. Moreover, a politician who did not lie about possible achievements would seem pretty weak compared with other politicians and their campaign promises. You

*Alienation implies an intense separation from objects, ideas, and other people. Anomie is
a state of society where major norms are either missing or unclear.*

can probably think of other examples. In each case, there is a conflict between the rules of conduct we are expected to follow.

Ordinarily, these deviant acts—and when normative standards conflict, we must deviate from at least one of them—cause us some discomfort; but we justify our acts on the basis of the standard we follow, which we believe takes precedence (e.g., business success as a value, not wanting to hurt somebody's feelings). It is only when there is no clear overriding norm to resolve the conflict that the situation is truly anomic. This situation is most likely to occur around times of social change and disruptions of normal social life.

The Vietnam War brought an anomic period for the American middle class. Although its children had learned that breaking the law was morally wrong—and often feared doing so—many of them wondered if fighting in a war they believed unjust was worse. The dilemma became critical when they had to choose between going to war and resisting. Some people served, but others resisted by burning their draft cards, deserting, or hiding out. In this situation there was no consensus on how to resolve the conflict. And even now, although public opinion tends to support the protestors' conclusions about the war itself, their guilt has not been officially absolved (no president has granted complete amnesty).

Another example of simple anomie involves the conflict between religious beliefs and modern social mores in the industrialized world. At one time, we could clearly distinguish between "right" and "wrong" by seeing what the Bible or our clergy had to say. But with the process of secularization, which has characterized development throughout the twentieth century, people increasingly want answers that can be justified logically. It's unlikely that you would simply accept the Bible's pronouncement about how to conduct your business affairs, for example. But religion has remained a moral force to some extent. That is why people still question premarital sex, birth control and abortion, and other such practices on religious grounds, even though these practices are becoming normal. Actions of peers and secular standards often conflict with religious beliefs, and people become unsure of what is right; even the law is unclear and changing. The situation is anomic.

In the above examples, we have a problem resolving the conflict between norms. In these instances, and in other instances of simple anomie, people are confused about which way to turn, but they have a way to turn. As we'll now see, this is not the case in instances of acute anomie, which is why it is so much more volatile.

Acute Anomie

Whereas simple anomie is a product of conflicting normative systems, acute anomie results from the *disintegration* of a normative structure. Because people cannot bear the anxiety of living without a normative structure for long, the response to acute anomie is often a radical one. For example, during the early 1960s American blacks at first turned to the federal government and moderate black leaders to attain their civil rights. As the decade wore on, however, black faith in moderate leaders and in the willingness or ability of the government to bring about racial equality eroded considerably. Having lost faith in the normative system by which they had been living, many blacks became part of a militant black-power movement. Some groups preached racial separation, others advanced communistic or socialistic ideologies, but all supported norms aimed at forcing equal treatment.

The populations of Eastern Europe after World War II also experienced acute anomie. The governments of the region had either been soundly defeated by the Germans, or had capitulated; in any case, they lost their authority. For as long as six years, the populations had to live under an often brutal military administration. During that time, traditional norms were of little value in satisfying basic needs. Thus the liberating Russian armies were able to step into the vacuum created by the disintegration of the traditional normative structure. To be sure, their military might was an important factor, but they were also welcomed by many Europeans tired of the anomic years. In his novel *The Painted Bird*, Jerzy Kosinski describes such a situation in the life of a young Polish boy. Sent for protection to the countryside from Warsaw at the war's outbreak, he soon finds that all he had learned in the city is inapplicable in the countryside. Unfortunately, he is repelled by the brutality of the

HOW ANOMIC ARE WE?

Is American society anomic? We often hear people complain that it is; specifically, that family bonds are weaker, the economy's failing, politicians no longer respond to people's needs, tradition and religion have lost their hold, and so on. Such complaints may or may not reflect reality, but they are often based on random observations and personal feelings of the moment. Sociologist Leo Srole has attempted to measure anomie in a scientific way.

Srole constructed a list of nine statements designed to indicate how people feel about their society—its institutions and its people. (Because anomie is a condition of social structure, the answers only indicate perceived anomie.) Researchers at the National Opinion Research Center (NORC) asked scientifically chosen samples of Americans in 1974 and 1976 if they agreed with the statements (see Table 9.1).

The NORC findings show that a majority of Americans expect little from their interpersonal relationships, feel that their government is generally unresponsive to their needs, and believe that their condition will continue to deteriorate (statements 1 to 4). A large minority is generally pessimistic about the society's future (statements 5 to 7). There is, however, still a general consensus that, despite all these problems, there is more to life than money (statements 8 to 9).

The agreement with broad social values, shown by the lack of agreement with the last two of Srole's statements, plus the absence of any significant desire to change the social structures, which so many in the sample indicated, makes it clear that anomie need not involve a loosening of the social control we internalized during and after our socialization. We can also see that social control does not even depend on our satisfaction with social institutions as they are.

peasants' norms and by their own victimization. At the end, he becomes strongly attracted to the Red Army, which was able to defeat the Nazis, and, by extension, to their doctrine of communism.

Probably the clearest case of acute an-

omie in modern times is that of Germany between the two world wars. Germany's crushing defeat in World War I greatly compromised its traditional values, and by the Germans' own norms, the nation was humiliated. The kaiser fled, a revolution oc-

Table 9.1   How Anomic Are We?

Statements	Percent Agreeing	
	1974	1976
1. These days a person really doesn't know whom he can count on.	75.7	75.6
2. Most public officials (people in public office) are not really interested in the problems of the average man.	65.7	66.7
3. In spite of what some people say, the lot (situation, condition) of the average man is getting worse, not better.	61.2	60.6
4. Most people don't really care what happens to the next fellow.	59.3	59.3
5. Nowadays, a person has to pretty much live for today and let tomorrow take care of itself.	44.0	47.0
6. You sometimes can't help wondering whether anything is worthwhile anymore.	43.6	40.4
7. It's hardly fair to bring a child into the world with the way things look for the future.	36.8	43.1
8. Next to health, money is the most important thing in life.	28.8	33.6
9. To make money, there are no right and wrong ways anymore, only easy and hard ways.	21.5	27.0

SOURCE: U.S. Department of Commerce, Social Indicators: 1976 (Washington, DC: Government Printing Office, 1977, Table 11/19).

curred, and the governments of the period failed to win widespread allegiance. Economically, inflation was astronomically high, and unemployment was substantial and persistent. Youth was especially alienated, and many segments of the population feared a deep depression and a Communist revolution. In short, for the average citizen traditional norms appeared to provide little protection against social chaos. In this situation of acute anomie, only the National Socialists seemed to be able to whip up a sense of German pride, to stand up to foreign countries, and to offer the population an ideology of secure beliefs and hope—the hope of military glory.

These concepts of types of anomie and our earlier discussion of alienation help us understand why German youth joined the Nazi party and why people today in our own society join totalitarian organizations. In 1941, Erich Fromm, then a refugee from the Nazi regime, wrote a book analyzing the rise of Hitler. Fromm explains Hitler's success by the German populace's desire to escape from alienation, or what sociologists like De Grazia and Durkheim would call a desire to escape from anomic conditions. As a result of individuals being thrown back on their own resources by the breakdown of the old order, there arose, says Fromm, a "craving to belong"—to escape from aloneness, to "escape from freedom," to use his title. Nazism not only offered many of them membership in a collective, but also a release from the anxiety of living without a clear system of beliefs.

But we can recognize this same craving today. Not long ago, it was demonstrated quite starkly by the People's Temple. This was a religious group whose members left their homes in the city for a life together under authoritarian rule in the jungles of Guyana. The enterprise ended with a mass suicide-murder of the 900 members.

A number of religious cults—the Moonies, Jesus Freaks, Hari Krishnas, and others—have been attracting more and more young Americans to their groups, as we read in Chapter 6. The cults offer members a clear ideology and belongingness in a community—something many cannot get in the modern society—but also strict regimentation, authoritarian rule, and absolute adherence to religious principles.

Modern Western society is a complex of large, often impersonal, entities and a host of competing belief systems. As such, alienation and anomie are general conditions of our lives. In these circumstances, it may seem that society rarely stays together at all. But, of course, we know that it does. We have seen how societies fall apart, but now we want to know why they stay intact. This is the study of *social solidarity*.

SOCIAL SOLIDARITY

At the outset of our study, we saw that we never encounter society as a thing itself, but only through the individuals who are its members—in casual interactions, in groups, and in institutions. The idea of social solidarity implies that these individuals feel that a common bond exists linking them with each other, as representatives of the whole group. As an American, for example, you have probably been proud when other Americans landed on the moon, were victorious in war, or won Olympic gold medals. To that extent, you felt they represented you. Beyond feeling, solidarity also implies how society's members will behave with each other. This implication finds its reality in the norms we follow and reciprocal roles we take, our institutional memberships, the common criteria we use to judge status, our sense of shared identity that derives from our socialization, and other dimensions of social life. Finally, we should note the interplay between social solidarity and social organizations. Through our feeling of solidarity, we create and recreate social organization. And our participation in the social organization gives rise to our sense of solidarity.

Two Views of Social Solidarity

Social scientists, social philosophers, and people in general have taken two viewpoints of social solidarity, based on the different ways they understand the nature of society. From the *atomistic* perspective, the individual appears as society's basic unit, while from the *collectivist* perspective, the social structure appears as the basic unit.

THE ATOMISTIC VIEW People who take the atomistic view perceive society as the result of many preexisting individuals joining together. Of course, they note, in coming together, people give up some individual freedoms, such as living without social norms. (Recall our account in the prologue of Thomas Hobbes, whose ideas provide a prime example of atomistic thinking.) To account for people giving up their freedoms, atomists have offered various explanations of what they receive in return.

Philosopher Jean Jacques Rousseau (1913 [1754] wrote that people exchange some freedom for the benefits of joint effort in, for example, capturing animals for food. The *social contract*, as Rousseau calls the exchange agreement, is society's foundation. People form society on the basis of their individual self-interests, and self-interest is what holds society together. The implications of this view of social solidarity are so great that they underlie entire theories in the various social sciences. Adam Smith's economic theory, for example, which is the theoretical foundation of modern capitalism, presumes that the economy is the work of many individuals acting separately. Smith holds that if everyone just pursued their individual interests to the

fullest, an "invisible hand" would direct them all to social ends (Smith 1961 [1776]). Among sociologists, Harold Garfinkel's theory of ethnomethodology proposes that individuals create social structures through their everyday interactions.

The atomistic view rests on the assumption that society is nothing more than the sum of its parts (individuals). Certainly, individuals are essential to society, but throughout this book we have seen evidence of so much more in society that is not reducible to atomized individuals: norms, values, roles, institutions, ideologies, symbols, collective goals. There is obviously very little that is "individual" in goals like social prestige.

THE COLLECTIVIST VIEW Adherents to the collectivist view perceive the group as society's original unit, with individuals emerging from it. Charles H. Cooley's (1924) concept of the looking-glass self (see Chapter 1) illustrates how individuals cannot exist without society. Most of the writers we have discussed in this book—and most sociologists as a whole—are collectivists. Those who take the collectivist view see society as more than just its members; it includes a structure of social relations, too. They view collective restraints as necessary checks (social controls) to keep one individual's freedom from interfering with another's.

The collectivist view shows us the essential role that social structures play in our lives, especially in the formation of our personalities. It also shows us that these personalities only emerge from interaction, and that individuality continues to develop within social limits. This is Durkheim's perspective throughout his writings on social solidarity. Since he is the most important writer on social solidarity in the sociological tradition, we should look at his views in some detail.

Durkheim's Theory of Solidarity

Durkheim set out his influential theory of social solidarity in *The Division of Labor in Society*, where he delineates two types of solidarity—*mechanical* and *organic solidarity*. Durkheim's typology parallels Toennies' gemeinschaft-gesellschaft distinction (see Chapter 5). Just as all societies contain some gemeinschaft relations and some gesellschaft relations, so, too, each society has both mechanical and organic solidarity but in different proportions. And just as Toennies sees the industrial revolution as changing relations from gemeinschaft to gesellschaft, so Durkheim sees the basis of solidarity changing from mechanical to organic.

MECHANICAL SOLIDARITY According to Durkheim, **mechanical solidarity** is solidarity based on similarity, and it is therefore prominent in societies with a homogeneous population where people share a common religion, customs, and attitudes. Durkheim terms the sum of all these similarities the **collective conscience:** all the beliefs and sentiments "common to average citizens of the same society" (Durkheim 1964 [1893], p. 79).

The collective conscience demands a high degree of conformity, and violations of collective norms are punished harshly. If I break into your house and steal your stereo set, I have not only harmed you, but have also, in effect, told society that it has no authority to tell me what I cannot do (specifically, that I cannot steal). For that reason—and not for your personal sake— a society with mechanical solidarity must punish me firmly, and it must do so publicly, so all can see that a person cannot violate the collective conscience and get away with it.

Mechanical solidarity also assumes a high degree of consensus about right and wrong, so that norm violations outrage every individual. As societies become more complex, however, disagreements become more common. For one thing, people immigrate from elsewhere, bringing their own ideas of morality, which challenge the previously unquestioned collective conscience. Moreover, a greater diversity of economic and other types of interest means that a smaller proportion of people are likely to share the same moral outrage over any given act of deviance. We can imagine, then, that violations of the old morality would increase, and that society would never reassert its authority. Its stability would be threatened, unless another basis for solidarity were developed as well (Durkheim 1964 [1893], pp. 147–99). That other basis is *organic solidarity.*

ORGANIC SOLIDARITY The collective conscience only unites people on the basis of likeness, and it cannot bind anyone to the group who does not share its beliefs. But **organic solidarity** holds people together because they are dissimilar and mutually dependent on each other (Durkheim 1964 [1893], pp. 111–32). In this respect, the division of labor serves as an important basis of solidarity. As a farmer, I need you in the city to manufacture the machines I use and to buy the food I produce. Likewise, you need me as a source of food—even if our urban and rural values conflict.

Of course, heterogeneous societies, with a great deal of organic solidarity, do not find consensus for harsh punishments in order to reassert the collective conscience. Even the assassinations of such popular leaders in the United States as Robert Kennedy and Martin Luther King, Jr., did not cause enough moral outrage to have the convicted slayers executed. We see crime not as a challenge to society but as offenses against individuals. Even so, attempts to reassert mechanical solidarity may be seen in the agitation by many Americans to reinstitute the death penalty.

Although Durkheim was a functionalist, he admits the importance of conflict within heterogeneous populations. Beyond that, he stresses that societies institutionalize conflicts—through the economic market, politics, the courts, and so on. Durkheim's theory of solidarity thereby becomes a theory of social control, as well. In simpler societies, social control is exercised through a well-defined moral structure with harsh sanctions for violators. In more complex societies, social control is effected by getting us to see a personal advantage in conforming (see Chapter 4). In either case, it seems to work.

While Durkheim's theory of solidarity has had great influence on subsequent social thinkers, on one point in particular his theory has been challenged. Durkheim posited that primitive societies were characterized by repressive laws aimed at punishing (harming) the wrongdoer. Similarly, advanced societies pass laws intended to restore equity (e.g., repay someone who has been swindled and the like), and are not so much concerned with punishment. Durkheim then associated the first type of law with mechanical solidarity and the second

legal structure with organic solidarity. Robert A. Nisbet (1974, pp. 128–32), however, notes that anthropological and other evidence casts doubt on that association. Public law in primitive societies was not penal but more like today's "tort law." In fact, many of the offenses we punish today—theft, trespass, even murder—were once considered private matters, to be settled between the offender's and injured party's families. In addition, modern societies have witnessed an increased amount of repressive law, as centralized authority has replaced kinship ties. However, we must note a modern tendency away from overtly punitive acts such as capital punishment and any "cruel and unusual" punishment.

Although Durkheim, perhaps recognizing this problem, never returned to the specific distinction between mechanical and organic solidarity after writing the *Division of Labor*, he continued to explore the relationships between social solidarity (structure) and individual behavior. His study of suicide demonstrates how a practice considered purely "individual" is rooted in social structure.

SOLIDARITY AND SUICIDE If you are like many people, you probably think that anybody who commits suicide is mentally disturbed. But that generalization only holds true for a minority of suicides. As Durkheim showed, the incidence of suicides in a population depends on the extent of social solidarity. As we know, that relationship involves conflicting sets of demands, one set concerning our personal lives and another concerning our lives as society members. Should I use my gas-guzzling car or take the bus? Should I buy the less expensive Philippine-made sweater or buy

American? Should I have an affair or be faithful to my spouse? In these and many other choices, we generally act in accordance with social norms, even if we give up some personal pleasure in doing so.

Apart from our immediate interests, including our fear of sanctions, we conform because we feel obligated to follow group norms. Durkheim notes that this obligation extends to the belief that we should be "worthwhile" individuals—either to society as a whole or to particular individuals such as our children or our coworkers. As a result, our social self considers our death a loss to society. If we are thus integrated with society, we will not kill ourselves and rob it of this resource. But certain conditions weaken that integration.

Durkheim's findings show that suicides are higher among unmarried and childless men, a fact which recent studies show still holds true today (Glick and Norton 1971). These men have fewer responsibilities and emotional bonds to tie them to society than married men do. Married men can see that others depend on them and therefore are less likely to be absorbed solely with their personal interests. Besides the family, almost any other group we join (clubs, trade associations, and so on) makes us feel to some extent part of the collective. But when ties are weak, persons may not recognize any binding obligations over personal interest. If suicide seems preferable to life, there are no ties to restrain them. Durkheim (1951 [1897], pp. 208–10) termed suicide under these conditions **egoistic suicide,** and its incidence increases as people no longer feel tied to, or part of, society.

But we should not get the impression that less solidarity simply means more suicide and vice versa. For Durkheim encountered high suicide rates in some European military societies with high solidarity. "Disgraced" members (who showed cowardice, were gravely insulted, or lost a love) often took their own lives. This led Durkheim to conclude that too much social integration leaves us without a sense of individual worth. We make no distinction between personal and group interests, and if we fail to live up to group ideals, we are left with nothing to keep us alive. The traditional Japanese samurai practice of *hara-kiri* is an example of suicide under these circumstances. Durkheim (1951 [1897], pp. 217–40) called this type of suicide **altruistic suicide.** In some ancient societies (and in some preliterate ones until recently), old people would kill themselves when they thought they had become a drain on the group—for them, killing themselves meant fulfilling their social obligations.

Durkheim also identified a third type of suicide, which arises under conditions of anomie. An anomic society, as we saw earlier in the chapter, has lost the power to support and guide the individual. It is normless and has little ability to confirm the value of individuals, throwing them back on their own resources. Like egoistic suicide, **anomic suicide** occurs when people no longer feel tied to society. Anomic suicide differs, however, because the problem is not the individual's lack of social attachments, but society's inability to provide any coherent and practical guides for conduct. Take, for example, the high number of suicides among college students— now a national concern, as suicide is one of the leading causes of death for this group. Indeed, students are separated from family, community, and old peer group ties—especially if they attend school away from home. Their new social environment

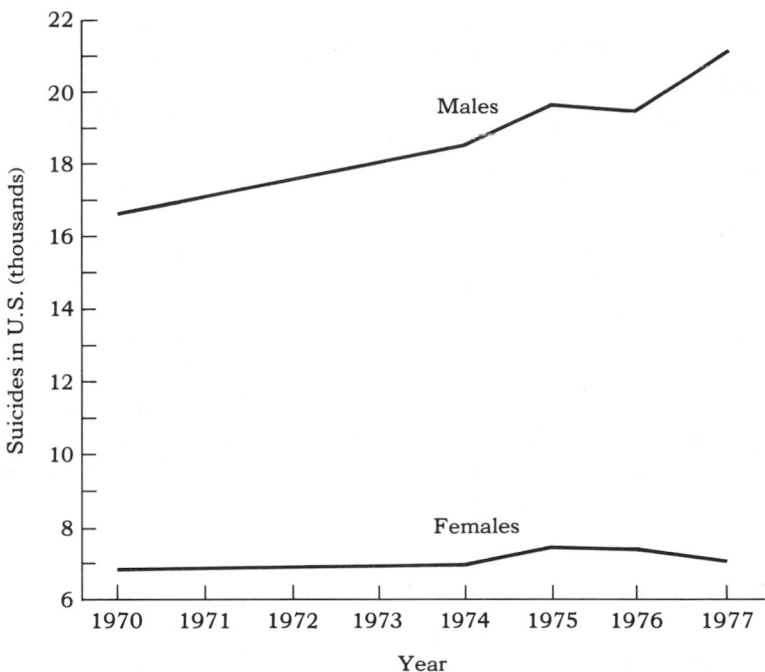

Figure 9.1 Female and Male Suicides in the United States, 1970–1977

SOURCE: *U.S. Department of Commerce,* Statistical Abstract of the United States, *1979 (Washington, DC: Government Printing Office, 1979, p. 182).*

at school cannot easily provide those clear and practical guides that they once received from the family, community, and peer groups.

As we noted, Durkheim found that men in general commit suicide more often than women do. The contemporary United States also bears this out. Considering that the number of men and women in the population is roughly equal, Figure 9.1 graphically demonstrates this difference. In fact, in the 1970 1977 period, suicides among men increased 26.9 percent, but the increase was only 10.5 percent for women.

The dilemma we face with anomic and egoistic suicides is one that has been cropping up throughout the book: do we solve the problem of people's link with society by reasserting the old values (collective conscience) or by changing them? In fact, this is a crucial question in many public debates. Challenges to affirmative action ("reverse discrimination"), new forms of families, defendants' and gay rights, and others are often based on the premise that we have gone "too far" in the direction of civil liberties. And many people decry the loss or absence of "community." We each have political and personal stances, but Durkheim's analysis suggests that we cannot simply reinstitute a collective conscience without destroying modern society or degenerating into totalitarianism.

SOCIAL CONFLICT AND SOLIDARITY

In the 1967 film *The Dirty Dozen*, twelve hardened convicts, condemned to die, are taken from death row during World War II for a special "suicide raid" into German territory. At one point during their training, an argument breaks out between the men and their commander: he orders them to shave and they refuse. When asked by another officer what he wants done about the act of defiance, the commander replies that he just wants to keep a conflict alive. Although the training is proceeding well, he feels that the men lack solidarity; they have not developed identity as a unit. The argument marks the first sign of mutual interest among the men, and when the training is over, the men emerge as a group. The point is that conflict with an outsider is their source of solidarity.

In stable societies—like our own—coalitions of people are forming and dissolving all the time: farmworkers and Eastern liberals face teamsters and growers in a battle for control of migrant farm work; coalitions of businesses otherwise in competition with each other unite against government reforms, unions, and consumer pressure; unions and manufacturers work together to restrict foreign imports; and you can probably think of many more. In all these cases, the unified parties had at other times opposed each other. Far from constituting a threat to social stability and solidarity, such conflicts and coalitions may help hold society together: "A society . . . which is ridden by a dozen oppositions along lines running in every direction may actually be in less danger of being torn with violence or falling to pieces than one split along just one line" (Edward Ross, quoted in Coser 1956, p. 76).

Durkheim rightly asserted that society cannot rest on individual interests, which are subject to frequent fluctuations and are often based on the way people feel at one time. But we also know how important those interests are to the individuals. Therefore we cannot accept the collectivists' tendency to ignore these interests. But we can agree that social solidarity will exist to the extent that individual interests are also group interests—whether society is that group, or those twelve men in *The Dirty Dozen* are. Sharing interests with others becomes the basis for acting in concert. Moreover, as we do, we develop interests in maintaining the group—from the power it gives us to the emotional ties we develop. This suggests that social solidarity becomes real as individuals pursue their concrete interests—not simply as they find themselves linked by abstract social values.

SUMMARY

There are two types of social disorganization: alienation and anomie, both products of social structure. Alienation refers to the fact that some people feel separated from society, its members, its values, and themselves. Alienation may involve feelings of powerlessness, meaninglessness, normlessness, isolation, and/or self-estrangement. Marx links alienation to the nature of modern labor in capitalist society. Workers feel powerless before the advanced technology; the division of labor prevents them from seeing a finished product as giving their labor meaning, and property institu-

Conflict can provide group members with a common goal and clarify the group's identity.

tions rob them of any control over how that product is manufactured or eventually disposed of. Marx's major contribution is in noting that workers become detached from their own selves as they come to feel more and more like commodities.

Anomie refers to a relative normlessness, where society has lost the power to offer its members guides for conduct. Society may offer no clear means of resolving the ever-present norm conflicts (simple anomie), or the belief system might disintegrate altogether (acute anomie). To Durkheim, this means that people lack external regulations for their behavior and desires. Without these limits, personal

satisfaction is impossible, and we would be led to despair of our present condition—whatever it might be. Anomie may result from the disruptions brought on by social crises or from the normal workings of social institutions.

In contrast to disorganization, we looked at the sources of social solidarity. Adherents to the atomistic view of solidarity believe personal interests tie us together, and that society is nothing more than the sum of its individual members. Adherents to the collectivist view take the opposite perspective. Although the latter view emphasizes our social origins and how much our actions are institutionalized, it may lead us to assume, falsely, that people simply adapt to these structures.

Durkheim identifies two types of solidarity—mechanical, based on likeness, and organic, based on differences. Although all societies contain both types, mechanical solidarity is characteristic of preindustrial societies (gemeinschafts), and organic solidarity of modern ones (gesellschafts). As societies develop, the collective conscience of mechanical solidarity is challenged by outsiders who enter the society and by the conflicts that result from competing social interests. But, as the division of labor develops, it serves as an important basis of solidarity, binding the now different people to the group through their interdependence with one another.

Finally, Durkheim relates the possible consequences of solidarity or its lack to suicide. Rather than an individual phenomenon, suicide demonstrates our social ties. If the ties are too weak, we might commit egoistic suicide, as we no longer see any obligation to stay alive. But if the ties are too strong, we may take our own life when we fail to meet our social obligations (altruistic suicide). Regardless of personal circumstances, our ties with each other will be weak if the society is anomic, giving rise to anomic suicide.

Key Terms

social disorganization (p. 285)
alienation (p. 286)
anomie (p. 293)
simple anomie (p. 295)
acute anomie (p. 295)
mechanical solidarity (p. 302)
collective conscience (p. 302)
organic solidarity (p. 302)
egoistic suicide (p. 304)
altruistic suicide (p. 304)
anomic suicide (p. 304)

Review and Discussion Questions

1. Marx focuses his theory of alienation on the industrial working class. However, do you see evidence of alienation, in the Marxian sense, in any other realm of American society?
2. It's commonly held that alienation is not that uncommon in the United States today. Since we expect that people will attempt to counteract alienation, have you witnessed any attempts of what Fromm would call "escapes from freedom"? Think, in particular, of political trends and events.
3. Changing notions of traditional sex-role behavior can produce some anomie (remember, anomie itself is neither good nor bad). Have you experienced this anomie (on a date, for instance, or when addressing someone), and how did you decide on the "proper" action?
4. How would an atomist and a collectivist alternatively view the complaint that some people have of "too much government"?
5. Within your own society, when have you witnessed harsh punishments applied as an expression of moral outrage? When have you personally felt outraged and wished such a punishment had been applied?

For Further Study

ALIENATION Anyone wishing to read extensively about alienation has a large number of works from which to choose. You could examine the two empirical studies by Robert Blauner (1964) and Melvin Kohn (1976) already mentioned, which examine the relationship between alienation and work. Also of interest is David P. Claerbaut, *Black Student Alienation* (San Francisco: R&E Research, 1978). If you want a more general look at alienation, you can find a thorough historical analysis in Joachim Israel, *Alienation: From Marx to Modern Sociology* (Boston: Allyn and Bacon, 1971). One of the best collections of readings on alienation is Eric Josephson and Mary Josephson, eds., *Man Alone: Alienation in Modern Society* (New York: Dell, 1962), which includes Marx's "Alienated Labor" discussion.

ANOMIE The classic sociological discussions of the concept of anomie are, of course, the works cited for Durkheim, and Robert K. Merton's *Social Theory and Social Structure* (New York: Free Press, 1968). A good effort at reformulating Merton's concept to fit a modern context can be found in William Simon and John H. Gagnon, "The Anomie of Affluence," *American Journal of Sociology* **82** (Sept. 1976): 356–78. One of the rare attempts to study anomie empirically is W. H. Form's "The Social Construction of Anomie: A Four-Nation Study of Industrial Workers," *American Journal of Sociology* 80 (May 1975): 1165–91. Finally, there is a good collection of articles that explore both anomie and alienation in Simon Marcson, ed., *Automation, Alienation, and Anomie* (New York: Harper & Row, 1970).

EMILE DURKHEIM Probably no individual has done more for the study of social structure than Emile Durkheim. Many of his writings are easily available and are often required reading in theory courses. Recently, a number of good books on Durkheim's work have appeared. See, in particular: Steven Lukes, *Emile Durkheim: His Life Work: A Historical and Critical Study* (New York: Harper & Row, 1972); and Robert A. Nisbet, *The Sociology of Emile Durkheim* (New York: Oxford University Press, 1974).

CHAPTER TEN

Collective Behavior and Social Movements

In most of the preceding chapters we concentrated on the organized behavior that takes place in groups and formal organizations. In this chapter, we will examine the generally less organized behavior of persons who are not so bound together by rules, by consciousness of themselves as a unity, and by long-term interactions. We are going to look, in other words, at what sociologists call *collective behavior.*

WHAT IS COLLECTIVE BEHAVIOR?

Logically, we might think that the term *collective behavior* should apply to all our discussions of groups and institutions in this book. Traditionally, however, sociologists have reserved the term for behavior that is relatively transient and spontaneous, and not like the routine behavior of established groups. **Collective behavior,** then, is the relatively transient, similar, or related behavior of a number of people. The people who engage in it can be either physically near to one another or spread over a wide area with no direct contact.

Collective behavior can take many different forms. It includes the disco fad, witch hunts, the behavior of crowds trying to escape a theater fire or trying to get good seats at a sold-out performance, the shifting public opinions about the job the president is doing, the storming of the Bastille, and the activities of feminists in support of sexual equality. In this chapter, we will look at the three basic types of collective behavior. First, we will look at the behavior of *diffuse collectivities* (that is, similar behavior or expressed attitudes of persons who have little or no direct contact with one another). Such behavior includes fashions, fads, crazes, and public opinion. Next, we'll study crowd behavior (a crowd being an unorganized collection of people at the same place at the same time). This type of behavior includes the behavior of theater audiences, lynch mobs, and rioters, among others. In the final part of the chapter, we will concentrate on *social movements* (concerted efforts by large numbers of people over a period of time to effect or block social change).

DIFFUSE COLLECTIVITIES

Diffuse collectivities, as we just noted, are collectivities whose members share similar behavior or expressed attitudes but who usually have little or no direct contact with one another. There are two general kinds of behavior associated with diffuse collectivities, one involving fads, fashions, and crazes, and the other involving public opinion.

Fads, Fashions, and Crazes

Fads, fashions, and crazes all involve a relatively brief period of great, seemingly irrational, popularity of a particular activity or item. Many are relatively harmless, such as the fad of roller-skating among young people; others are more serious, such as the witch crazes that swept through Europe in the Middle Ages.

FADS AND FASHIONS Fads are behaviors that are widely engaged in for a brief time and then decline abruptly in popularity. Wearing mood rings, collecting pet rocks, and running nude in public places (streaking) came and went in quick succession in recent years. Most everyone considers such practices trivial, but we should note that activities that some people take very seriously, such as transcendental meditation and left-wing politics, have also been fads for others.

Fashions are similar styles of appearance (e.g., dress, hairdos, furniture, or other items) chosen by large numbers of people at a given time. In Western society, fashions are manipulated by the "fashion industry," which encourages regular style changes to keep consumption high. For a while, mini-skirts were in fashion, then came long skirts, and, most recently, the fashionable length is somewhere between the two. Men's fashions once featured only white shirts, black and brown pants, and jackets. They seem quite dull, compared to today's colorful male fashions. Other recent fashions have included hot pants,

Nehru jackets, the "natural look," the heavily made-up look, white nails (polish), dark red nails, and crew cuts.

As you have probably experienced, being in fashion and following the latest fad has important implications for how you appear to others. First of all, it can mean the difference between being "in" or being "out of it." If we are slow in adopting a new fashion or fad, we appear dull; as we will if we continue with one after its popularity has faded. (What, for instance, would you think of a "streaker" today?) Fashions can also symbolize rebellion or discontent, as long hair did on men in the 1960s. Additionally, people can often gain social prestige for being the first to adopt practices that become fads.

All the while, the succession of fads and fashions benefits the industries that promote them and, depending on how we look at it, provides society with diversity, or gets us to waste our money.

CRAZES Crazes are both more volatile and more intense than either fashions or fads, and their consequences are often more severe. Seventeenth-century Holland's industry was greatly neglected during that country's tulip craze; in that craze, people invested—and many lost—fortunes in tulip bulbs that might cost as much as a house (Mackay 1962 [1841])! A more notorious example of a craze is the great witch craze of the Middle Ages, in which thousands of women, and some men, were denounced as witches and burned. According to Marvin Harris (1974, pp. 225—40), this mania, far from being spontaneous, was actually a well-organized series of events calculated to bring people closer to the church at a time when its authority was under attack.

As we can imagine, fads, fashions, and

A fad may involve an entire way of life. From punk rock music came new and different fashions in dress, attitudes, values, styles of speech and art, and other "New Wave" elements.

crazes can seem all-important to their participants. Yet, when they are over, the objects and activities associated with them decline sharply in value. They can appear silly or worthless, and their immense popularity is derided as "faddish." There is another form of collective value-setting that is generally more constant and that often involves reasoned discussion and debate—*public opinion.*

Public Opinion

A **public** is a collection of people who share an interest in and express their attitudes about a given issue. The members of a public don't have to be, and usually aren't, in close physical proximity to one another. As we might suppose, **public opinion** is the sum of views expressed by a public on a given issue. Members of a public feel affected by the same event or situation, they can make their feelings known, and they are therefore treated as a collective.

Publics can express their opinions in many different ways. They may write letters to the editors of newspapers or to their representatives in Congress. They may express their opinions in the voting booth, and they may "vote with their feet" by, for instance, refusing to buy products that do not meet their standards. And, they can register their concerns about an issue or a candidate's statements through public opinion polls.

The great Danish philosopher Søren Kierkegaard once paid tribute to the power of public opinion when he wrote that "twenty-five signatures make the most frightful stupidity" legitimate, more so than the considered statement of one brilliant individual (1962 [1847], p. 79). Governments, corporations, and individuals can often effectively ignore public opinion when no view clearly predominates, but when one view is plainly dominant, public opinion can have great power. We saw in Chapter 4, in Solomon Asch's experiments, the power that nearly unanimous opinion can have in swaying the views of others, even against their own better judgment. The heavy reliance on public opinion polls by modern business, government, and politicians testifies to its power. Businesses use polls to "test the market" for a product; on the basis of those surveys they will decide whether to market a product, where to market it, and how to advertise and sell it. Government leaders and politicians also use polls to determine public attitudes toward particular programs. When campaigning for election, politicians often alter their platforms to float with the tides of public opinion.

To make the point clearer, consider the following. In 1978, Californians were asked to vote on a referendum that called for massive cuts in state property taxes. A good many politicians, led by Governor Jerry Brown, passionately opposed the measure because it would reduce funds available for social programs. But, after voters overwhelmingly approved the tax cut, many of the same politicians, passionately led by Governor Brown again, did an about-face and became some of its most avid supporters. Brown became a self-appointed national spokesman *for* the cause. As opinion polls across the nation indicated strong voter sentiment for similar tax cuts, reducing taxes became the dominant theme in almost every politician's election campaign and legislative stance. It is a rare politician who does not try to mirror the prevailing public opinion in his or her public statements (Mayhew 1977).

The importance of public opinion has led individuals and groups to try to steer the direction it takes through the use of *propaganda.* **Propaganda** is the manipulation of ideas through an appeal to people's emotions and prejudices. We easily recognize propaganda in totalitarian states, such as Nazi Germany and Soviet Russia, and it certainly is pervasive in such states. However, it is quite common in democratic nations as well, whether it is used by ambitious politicians or in commercial advertising.

Historian Richard M. Freeland (1974) has written about one important instance of such an attempt to manipulate public opinion in the late 1940s. Immediately following World War II, the former allies, the United States and the Soviet Union, began struggling for political and economic control in Europe. To further American aims in this conflict, the Truman administration planned a massive foreign aid program for European countries. However, the American public still viewed the two nations as allies, and the isolationist Congress refused to pass the necessary legislation. Because he did not have the power to change the legislators' votes, President Truman decided to "change their minds" by trying to change public opinion. Thus the government began emphasizing the "communist menace" to the West. In a famous speech, known as the Truman Doctrine, Truman spoke of an immediate Soviet threat to Greece and Turkey, so that voting against his aid bill would appear contrary to American interests. The public response was overwhelmingly favorable to Truman, and a number of aid bills passed. The anticommunist gambit has been used time and again by politicians such as Joseph McCarthy and Richard Nixon during the 1950s. Propaganda will undoubtedly always be part of society, but it is most dangerous when the public's access to information is limited by government censorship or business control of the mass media (Reasons 1974).

The various forms of collective behavior we have looked at so far are generally diffused over a wide area and can exist apart from any specific event. Another category of collective behavior, *crowd behavior*, involves collectivities whose members have physically come together, usually for a specific reason.

CROWDS

A **crowd** is an unorganized collection of people who have temporarily assembled together at the same time. Members of a crowd ordinarily share a common perception (a crime was committed, the police are beating someone up, the theater is on fire, and so on). There tends to be little social organization in crowds and the norms that do emerge tend to be simple. Crowd behavior is uninstitutionalized and often unpredictable compared to behavior in established groups and formal organizations. One of the reasons for this is that individual members may feel protected by their anonymity in a crowd and commit acts that they would not consider doing by themselves, such as lynching someone or throwing a rock through a store window.

Because crowds have been responsible for many brutal, unjust, and, from the outsider's viewpoint, stupid acts, they have often been analyzed as fundamentally irrational. In Gustave Le Bon's classic book,

The Crowd, we read: "The arguments [that crowds] employ and those which are capable of influencing them are, from a logical point of view, of such an inferior kind that it is only by way of analogy that they can be described as reasoning" (1960 [1895], p. 65). The idea that a reasonable person could be part of a lynch mob or pogrom (anti-Jewish riot) is not a very comfortable one. But the characterization of crowds as irrational is not very helpful because it obscures the fact that crowd *behavior* is often very rational—although it may often be based on irrational and/or incorrect assumptions. Thus, if we *believe* that a person has murdered, it might seem rational to lynch that person if the legal authorities will not do the job. If we *believe* that Jews are responsible for our economic hardships, it might seem rational to riot against them. The behavior will achieve our goals if our assumptions are correct. Of course, our assumptions may be false, but anti-Semitism and other faulty assumptions are frequently not the invention of the crowd acting upon them.

There are three points to keep in mind when analyzing crowds. First, we must understand that participants in crowd behavior will probably interpret their actions differently than we will. Second, we should be aware that crowds are very vulnerable to manipulation. Finally, to properly understand the essence of crowd behaviors, we must leave aside our prejudices about the content of the crowd's actions.

Types of Crowds

We can distinguish two broad types of crowds, *audiences* and what Herbert Blumer (1951) has called *active crowds.*

In December 1979 gunmen assassinated Dr. Mohammed Moffateh, Dean of Teheran University's theology department and one of Ayatollah Khoumeini's most influential followers. Thousands of faithful crowded the inner courtyard of the Great Mosque in Quom, as his coffin was carried above the heads of the crowd.

AUDIENCES An **audience** is a crowd that assembles to witness an event. The event can be planned (e.g., a play or concert) or unplanned (a fire or a car accident). In any major city, you can find audiences gathered around construction sites watching work on new buildings. Because an audience's purpose is so limited and passive and its life so brief, its members' interaction with each other is likely to be minimal. Little social organization will be apparent, and the audience will be unlikely to violate established social norms.

Audiences are generally aware of the norms associated with each event; for instance, that people watch a movie or listen to a classical concert in silence; that they yell during a rock concert or baseball game. Other norms prescribe the manner of response (polite applause or cheers), whether we can eat during the event, or that we should stand during the "seventh inning stretch." But since an audience is still a crowd, nonnormative behavior may be allowed. For instance, smoking dope is almost normative at many rock concerts, and sports audiences think nothing of the terrible verbal abuse they inflict on players.

ACTIVE CROWDS *Active crowds* are collective responses to particular events; that is, they are crowds engaged in getting something done. Compared to audiences, active crowds tend to have a more developed social organization. They often form in order to accomplish tasks that members feel society's institutions are incapable of. Lynch mobs, for instance, have secured what they felt was justice—the execution of a "guilty" party—when they thought the legal process inadequate. Civil rights and antiwar protestors engaged in collective civil disobedience to change government policy, when they found the courts and legislatures unwilling to do so. And through looting, urban rioters often "redistribute" income to the poor, which the economic system won't do.

Audiences can easily become active crowds when triggered by some event. Early in this century, for example, Parisian audiences, outraged by the innovative music of Igor Stravinsky and films of Luis Buñuel, rampaged against the performing musicians and the theaters. Events that pose a direct threat to the audience, such as a fire in the theater, can cause panic and transform an audience into an active crowd. Panic is, in fact, one form of collective behavior that occurs with some frequency in active crowds. Let's now look at it and then at two other important behavior patterns of active crowds—mob actions and riots.

PANICS A **panic** is a collectivity's hasty, fearful, and unorganized reaction to a perceived direct threat. One of the most notorious panics occurred in Chicago's Iroquois Theater in 1903. A vaudeville audience panicked when someone cried "Fire!" The audience rushed for the exits, most of which were unmarked and difficult or impossible to get through. Comedian Eddie Foy, who was on the stage, described the scene on the balcony stairs:

> Here most of the dead were trampled or smothered, though many jumped or fell over the balustrade to the floor of the foyer. In places on the stairways, particularly where a turn caused a jam, bodies were piled seven or eight feet deep. . . . An occasional living person was found in the heaps, but most of these were terribly injured. The heel prints on the dead faces mutely testified to the cruel fact that human animals stricken by terror are as mad and ruthless as stampeding cattle. Many bodies had the clothes torn from them, and some had the flesh trodden from their bones (Foy and Harlow 1928, pp. 285–86).

The fire itself did little damage, but the panic killed 602 persons.

The precipitating event does not have to result in panic, but in this case it did. Why? We can identify four conditions of a panic (Janis et al. 1964, p. 120): (1) people feel threatened by something (e.g., a fire), (2) escape routes are very limited, (3) escape routes are blocked (in the Iroquois case, by the many people trying to escape), and (4) there is a lack of communication between front and rear. The first three conditions indicate that there will be conflict over the scarce exits; panics are less likely when there are few people in a theater or when the exits are plentiful. The fourth condition suggests that the crowd acted irrationally and that if everybody had only remained calm nobody would have been hurt. But the people in the theater did not know that—how could they? From their individual points of view, their actions were the only rational response, especially once the panic had begun.

What happened at the Iroquois was an *escape panic*. Another type of panic is an *acquisitive panic*, when people panic to get things. Hoarding is one example. When Americans were told of coming beef, coffee, and toilet paper shortages, some consumers panicked and emptied store shelves. Hoarded meat would rot in some people's refrigerators while others went without. Here the basic conflict is between the large number of people who desperately feel they must have a small number of goods.

MOB ACTIONS AND RIOTS A **mob** is an emotionally aroused crowd whose members are ready to engage in violent action. Mobs frequently have a leader or leaders and often act as a unit. A **riot** is general public violence generated by a mob.

Mobs often have a clearly defined and limited goal but underlying it can be much broader aims. Consider lynch mobs, for example. They might act on the clear goal of punishing an alleged lawbreaker. Although lynchings have taken place throughout the United States, they were concentrated in the Deep South (see Table 10.1). Moreover, of the 4,951 persons lynched between 1882 and 1927, 70 percent were blacks, most of whom were lynched for alleged offenses against whites (White 1969 [1928]). In other words, the underlying goal of most lynch mobs has been to maintain white supremacy. Likewise, college students in the 1960s rioted to protest the draft and the Vietnam War, but they were also asserting their independence from adult authorities and attempting to obtain increased civil rights.

Unlike panics, mob actions and riots are often rooted in social discontent. Rioting crowds typically act out of a general resentment or anger with social conditions: poverty, government's refusal to help, discrimination, low prestige, and so on. Although political agitators may be present at the onset of a riot, they cannot *cause* one to occur if the resentment is not already present.

In the United States, the most extensive riots in recent history were the ghetto riots of the late 1960s. These riots had enough impact to lead President Lyndon Johnson to empanel a commission to investigate them. The Kerner Commission (1968), as the panel is known, found that the riots were generated by a tense social atmosphere, not specific incidents. The riots were generally preceded by a *series* of incidents over weeks or months. In the twenty-four riots studied, the commission found the following "prior incidents" that led up to the violence:

1. Police actions: 40 percent.[*] These were alleged police brutality, unfair arrests, harassment, or racial abuses. They were the final incident in twelve riots.
2. Protest activities: 22 percent. These were black demonstrations, rallies, and protest meetings. They were the final incident in five riots.
3. White racist activities: 17 percent. These were cross burnings, harassment of black college students, the killing of blacks by white groups.

---

[*]*The percentages do not total 100 because some incidents overlapped categories.*

Table 10.1 Lynchings in the United States, 1882–1927

State	Total	Whites	Blacks
Mississippi	561	44	517
Georgia	549	39	510
Texas	534	164	370
Louisiana	409	62	347
Alabama	356	52	304
Arkansas	313	69	244
Florida	275	28	247
Tennessee	268	55	213
Kentucky	233	79	154
South Carolina	174	9	165
Oklahoma	141	97	44
Missouri	117	51	66
Virginia	109	24	85
North Carolina	100	20	80
Montana	89	87	2
Colorado	68	64	4
Nebraska	58	55	3
Kansas	55	36	19
West Virginia	54	21	33
Indiana	52	41	11
California	50	48	2
Wyoming	41	37	4
New Mexico	38	35	3
North and South Dakota	35	34	1
Illinois	32	13	19
Arizona	31	31	0
Washington	28	27	1
Maryland	27	2	25
Ohio	26	11	15
Idaho	21	21	0
Oregon	20	19	1
Iowa	18	17	1

Table 10.1   Lynchings in the United States, 1882–1927 *(continued)*

State	Total	Whites	Blacks
Not specified	16	15	1
Minnesota	9	5	4
Michigan	8	7	1
Pennsylvania	8	2	6
Utah	8	6	2
Nevada	6	6	0
Wisconsin	6	6	0
New York	3	2	1
Connecticut	1	1	0
Delaware	1	0	1
Maine	1	1	0
New Jersey	1	0	1
Massachusetts	0	0	0
New Hampshire	0	0	0
Rhode Island	0	0	0
Vermont	0	0	0
Totals	4,951	1,438	3,513

SOURCE: *Walter White,* Rope and Faggot *(New York: Arno, 1969 [1928], pp. 234–36).*

4. Previous disorders in the same city: 16 percent. These were both major and minor racial confrontations.
5. Official city actions: 14 percent. These were actually often inactions, for example, a lack of inner-city summer recreation funds; also, failure to allow black groups adequate opportunity to speak at official hearings.
6. Administration of justice: 9 percent. These were discriminatory court rulings and procedures.
7. Disorders in other cities: 5 percent. These were learned about through media coverage and subsequent rumors. They were the final incident in five riots.

The commission recognized, however, that the incidents themselves did not cause the violence but only brought the underlying grievances to flash point. (See The Riot Process, pp. 322–23.) And although there was no pattern to the violence, the commission did find that the violence generally broke out at times when many people were on the street anyway (usually at night). In other words, in those instances, audiences were transformed into active crowds. Finally, control was established through the use of the local police force, outside force (e.g., federal troops), negotiations between community and city representatives, and on-the-street persuasion efforts by "counter-rioters" (Kerner Commission 1968, pp. 120–27). As we saw in our discussion of ethnic stratification, the black riots of the 1960s helped draw much attention and some funds to black urban communities but they did little to change the overall patterns of racial inequality and discrimination.

Theories of Crowd Behavior

Crowd behavior such as the 1967 ghetto riots has been explained in many different ways. In the past, the theorist who set the tone for studies of crowds was Gustave Le Bon who, as we saw, characterizes crowds as irrational. Le Bon argues that, in a crowd, the aggregate of individuals is transformed into a psychological unity, which he calls a "collective mind." In crowds, Le Bon believes, individuals lose much of their capacity for reason and self-control and become highly susceptible to suggestion. Moods, ideas, and attitudes are communicated by contagion within the crowd, and the crowd acts more or less as a unity.

With this background, we can now turn to some more recent general theories of crowd behavior, the *emergent norm theory* and the *value-added theory*.

EMERGENT NORM THEORY The emergent norm theory of Ralph Turner and Lewis Killian (1972) focuses, as its name suggests, on norms. Specifically, it holds that

crowd behavior is a response to situations in which norms are unclear and that it is through the actions of crowd members that new norms emerge. We can see the emergence of norms in three general types of crowd situations.

Some active-crowd situations initially lack norms, as the Iroquois Theater panic did. In this situation, the collective norm that emerged was to rush to the exits. We can see that fire drills are designed to provide appropriate norms ahead of time and thereby avoid panics. In other situations, people feel that existing norms are inadequate and create their own. Members of lynch mobs, for instance, believe that legal norms will not secure justice in some cases; so they turn to the alternative norms of lynching. Finally, there are situations that involve gross violations of strongly held values. When Nazis rallied in Chicago, for instance—and their ideology obviously offends basic social values—a large counterdemonstration formed. Several groups had unsuccessfully tried in court to have the rally stopped. Since the court refused, on the basis of the First Amendment, counterdemonstrators came and shouted down the Nazi speakers.

The emergent norm theory shows us that crowd behavior is not unregulated but operates according to norms. The conformity we see in the behavior of crowds, Turner and Killian argue, is conformity to these norms. Unlike Le Bon, these theorists assert that crowd members are not all alike and have different feelings about and understandings of the situation. Individuals follow the norms not because they merge into a collective mind but because they may fear the ridicule, hostility, and perhaps even the physical power of other members of the crowd. In contrast to Le Bon, then, Turner and Killian show us that crowd be-

THE RIOT PROCESS

In its final report to the president, the Kerner Commission concludes that we can best understand the 1965–1967 riots of urban blacks in light of a two-step *riot process* 1968, pp. 116–27). For in each of the twenty-four riots examined, the triggering incident was relatively trivial compared with the violence that followed. Besides, such incidents occurred rather frequently in the ghettos, and thus could not have caused the riots alone. Rather, an "increasingly disturbed atmosphere" lay behind the riots. In short, the failure of social institutions (political, economic, and so on) paved the way for this form of collective behavior as an alternative to them.

Thus none of the riots would have occurred were it not for a "reservoir of grievances" within the black community. The exact grievances varied from city to city, but they generally included discrimination, poor living conditions, and frustration with the lack of change. Municipal inaction generally intensified these complaints. This accumulation of grievances was the first step in the riot process. But, according to the commission, it took specific events—which it terms prior incidents—to reinforce the community's sense of shared frustration.

havior is similar to other social action and can be analyzed using familiar sociological concepts.

VALUE-ADDED THEORY In Neil J. Smelser's (1963) value-added theory, collective behavior is also seen as a form of social action that redefines norms for behavior. Smelser is an economist as well as a sociologist, and his "value-added" concept is an economic one. Consider automobile production: iron ore must be mined, then turned into steel, the steel must be shaped into car parts, the parts put together, the car painted, and then finally shipped to the dealer. Each step adds some value to the product and further defines its character. Likewise, Smelser argues that there are parts to a collective behavior incident, each of which adds something to it and defines its character. These parts are: structural conduciveness, structural strain, growth of a generalized belief, a precipitating factor, mobilization for action, and type of social control. To understand this scheme, let's apply it to what the government's Walker Commission labeled a "police riot"

The number of prior incidents preceding a riot varied and occurred over a period of weeks or months. There were at least three in most cities where rioting occurred; some cities had more (there were ten in Houston, for example, over a five-month period). Prior incidents included: white racist activity (e.g., there were fifteen cross burnings in one northern city), smaller disorders, official city actions—including unequal treatment of blacks and whites, and police actions.

The triggering incident (step two) typically occurred within a few hours before the riot's outbreak. Such incidents most often involved some police action (as in Newark, where a black cab driver was injured by police in the heart of a black neighborhood). Black protest rallies and media coverage of riots in other cities were also cited as triggering events.

The commission emphasizes that not all blacks participated in the disorders—but all blacks shared one or more of the accumulated grievances. Also, some of the rioters participated purely for material gain and did not respond to the incidents and grievances. But the long list of deep-seated social problems was the common background in all the riots.

at the 1968 Democratic National Convention in Chicago. In that incident, hundreds of people, many of whom were not taking part in the protest demonstrations, were assaulted and jailed by the police.

Structural conduciveness underlies all collective behavior incidents. In this case, the Chicago police were trained to respond violently to social disturbances. We can speculate that if they had been trained in nonviolent methods (such as persuasion), the riot might not have occurred. But that is not enough to produce a riot; there must be a *structural strain* in

addition. This consists of the tense and uncomfortable feelings that the participants have. The appearance of many Vietnam War protestors, hippies, and radicals in Chicago to loudly protest the convention's actions in nominating Hubert Humphrey for president, created a strain for the police, who viewed such people as unpatriotic and "un-American." They undoubtedly would not have rioted against a similar gathering of born-again Christians or antiabortion protesters.

Many *generalized beliefs* spread throughout Chicago. It was rumored that the young people were intent on overthrowing the American government, destroying the Democratic party, and introducing LSD into Chicago's water supply. There were two *precipitating factors* that triggered the riots: one was the protesters' attempts to sleep in the public parks, which was against the law; the other was their attempt to march beyond the police barricades. However, people had broken the law in Chicago before without creating a police riot. The riot occurred because the police reacted to the event within the context of the other factors. That is, given the conduciveness, strain, and growth of generalized beliefs, it was not likely that they would respond calmly.

The police were largely *mobilized for action* before the incident. It was their responsibility to guard the convention. Beyond that, the department easily alerted police from other areas as they were required. How did other social control agencies react? Was the *type of social control* of the police action supportive or repressive? The major reaction was supportive: other police agencies assisted the Chicago police, the mayor supported their actions, the protesters were jailed, and the Justice Department instituted a major trial against their leaders. The media, however, also an agent of social control, condemned the police, as did a federal investigating commission, but these condemnations have not kept the Chicago police from rioting, albeit on a much smaller scale, against members of the city's Latino community since then.

So far, we have been looking at the kinds of behavior engaged in by various types of collectivities. Now, however, we want to shift our focus and concentrate on the aggregate of individuals who engage in particular types of collective behavior in the course of their participation in a social movement.

SOCIAL MOVEMENTS

At the outset of the chapter, we defined a **social movement** as a concerted effort by a large number of people over an extended period of time to effect (or block) social change. The behavior in which members of social movements engage often includes many of the forms of collective behavior we have already covered, such as riots, mob action, public opinion, and even fads and fashions. What links these behaviors together in the case of social movements is that they are performed by the same or associated individuals who share a roughly common goal of social change. We should note, however, that members of a social movement, while they may share an interest in, say, reforming environmental protection laws or bringing about a revolution, may also have quite different ideas on how to go about making this change and in what, exactly, the change should consist.

The Genesis of Social Movements

What gives rise to social movements? To some, social movements appear to arise out of the personal inadequacies of their members—poverty, personal failure, psychological or moral defects, and the like. According to Eric Hoffer (1951), for example, social movements contain poor people, misfits, outcasts, minorities, adolescents, the ambitious, "those in the grip of some vice or obsession," the impotent, the inordinately selfish, the bored, and the sinful.

In the past two decades Americans have supported many causes through social movements—equal rights for blacks, women, gays, and other minorities; saving the environment and wildlife; and halting abortions. What all the participants had in common was a belief that they could not achieve their goals through normal political channels.

"They see their lives and the present spoiled beyond remedy and they are ready to waste and wreck both" (p. 30). While it is true that individuals join social movements for a wide variety of reasons, including, sometimes, hopes of overcoming personal inadequacies, such an explanation doesn't tell us why collective movements arise, and why they arise when they do, and furthermore it presents a misleading picture of who the actual participants in social movements tend to be. Among sociologists, two

alternative theories of the origins of social movements have gained prominence, although neither one of these alternatives is completely adequate either. Let's look at these alternative theories.

DEPRIVATION One theory centers around the assumption that a social movement arises out of a *consciousness of deprivation,* or of unmet needs, on the part of its members. Various Americans, for instance, expressed a sense of deprivation through many social movements: the abolitionists for freedom for the slaves, the suffragists for women's right to vote, and the union movement to gain the right to bargain collectively, to name a few.

The significant question, however, is under what conditions does this sense of deprivation lead to the development of a social movement. One important factor clearly involves what Smelser terms "structural conduciveness." There must be sufficient social disorganization in the society to allow a social movement to take root. For instance, the American labor movement did not grow because workers were poor—that had always been the case—but because changing conditions of production did away with the old employer-employee relationship while throwing large numbers of discontented workers together. Another important structural factor is that socially approved avenues for gaining social resources must be effectively closed to the deprived population. A third important factor is that people must share an ideology (what Smelser calls a "generalized belief") that provides them with a target for their activity and a sense that they are entitled to more than they actually get; we have discussed this issue of legitimacy in previous chapters.

But even when these conditions are conducive to the development of a social movement, one does not always arise. After all, throughout history, whole classes of people have suffered from deprivation but not revolted. In Smelser's terms, how much "structural strain" is necessary before people revolt? Some people might suggest that people will mobilize when they are denied life's basic necessities (absolute deprivation) or when they *feel* considerably deprived compared to other groups in the so-ciety (relative deprivation). But there are too many counterexamples to make these answers adequate ones. James C. Davies (1969) offers a more sophisticated version of the deprivation theory by suggesting that the development of social movements depends on the relationship between the people's expectation of their future and their actual reality. If we have always been poor, for instance, and there is nothing to suggest that our condition will change, then we are not likely to rebel as long as we get the little bit that we expect. But when our condition begins to improve, our expectations of being satisfied increase as well. Then, if conditions suddenly change for the worse, we will find the "gap" between our now higher expectations of satisfaction and what we actually receive intolerable, and we will be prone to rebellion. Davies' model seems to fit some instances, like the French Revolution, rather well; but it fails to explain why people didn't rebel in other situations in which the gap would seem to have been just as intolerable.

In recent years, sociologists have developed an alternative explanation of the genesis of social movements, the resource mobilization theory, which deemphasizes the role of deprivation as the crucial factor.

RESOURCE MOBILIZATION At the heart of this approach is its concept of resource. Resources can be material (e.g., jobs, money, property) or nonmaterial (e.g., authority, moral commitment, trust). We are always using resources in our everyday lives, and we normally try and manage them to our greatest benefit. If you get a traffic ticket, for example, you might draw on your political connections (a resource) and ask a politician to "fix" it for you, rather than depleting your monetary resources by paying the fine. Or you may invest your cash in a college education, which will generate additional resources for you. Anthony Oberschall (1973) notes that, as in these examples, resources are essentially used in exchange for something else.

Social movements *mobilize* their members' resources—that is, they assemble and invest those resources for group goals. The National Organization for Women, for example, has mobilized its money and influence to help pass the Equal Rights Amendment to the Constitution. NOW has, for example, attempted to convince organizations to hold their conventions only in states where the Equal Rights Amendment has passed (see Feminism and Resource Mobilization).

According to the resource mobilization view, whether a social movement is able to develop often depends more on how well the movement is able to marshall resources than on the extent of popular grievances. Plenty of deprivation and "structural strain" always exist, these theorists argue, so to explain the rise of social movements we need to look and see whether there are sufficient funds, access to the media and other groups, and effective leaders to build the movement (McCarthy and Zald 1977).

Both the deprivation and resource mobilization theories have much to offer us in understanding social movements. Rather than seeing them as opposing theories, however, we might more fruitfully view them as complementary. The deprivation theory shows us the importance of grievances in the generation of social movements, while the resource mobilization theory makes us realize that unless those grievances are effectively channeled and organized, a social movement will have little impact or even fail to be born. Neither theory is complete or provides an adequate explanation of social movements. One reason for this is that social movements are so diverse. It is to this diversity that we now turn.

Types of Social Movements

Turner and Killian (1972) distinguish three general types of social movements: value-oriented, power-oriented, and participation-oriented. *Value-oriented movements* are movements in which participants seek changes that benefit a particular group and justify their demands on the basis of some widely shared social value. The present antiabortion movement, for instance, justifies its members' political claims on the fetus's "right to life." *Power-oriented movements* are aimed at gaining power for movement leaders; the Nazi movement in Germany, for example. The main attraction that *participation-oriented movements* have is the joy of being involved in them; they are not really concerned with ends. The Yippie movement of the 1960s is an example of a participation-oriented movement.

Of course, movements are rarely one type exclusively, although we can often speak of dominant trends. For example, the current feminist movement is value-oriented in that it seeks to improve conditions for women and does so on the basis of all Americans deserving equal rights. On the other hand, it offers women a new lifestyle outside the confines of the traditional female role and is thus participation-oriented as well (Carden 1978). McCarthyism in the 1950s was essentially a power-oriented movement for politicians, who exploited the climate it created to win elections, but other people saw it in terms of

FEMINISM AND RESOURCE MOBILIZATION

Why do people join particular social movements? Maren Lockwood Carden (1978) has applied the resource mobilization approach to answer this question in regard to the contemporary American feminist movement. She collected her data through in-depth interviews with moderate and radical feminists, was a participant-observer at feminist meetings and conferences, and conducted a content analysis of written material by feminist groups.

She first identifies several personal motives that her subjects had for joining the movement, including: companionship of like-minded women; the challenge, interest, and "fun" of demonstrations, committee work, writing, preparing legal cases, and dealing with the press; and the relief of getting out of the house. Through the movement, they can satisfy these various needs (satisfaction denied them by the traditional female role) in a range of activities—community organization, leadership training, legal research, running for office, canvassing for candidates, and social services.

Beyond that, Carden notes the impact of the collective goal in feminist ideology. All in the movement, she reports, are committed to the goal of achieving equal rights and greater autonomy for women. Initially, many women were attracted to the ideology out of personal dissatisfaction, such as dissatisfaction with some aspect of the female role, discrimination at work, frustration in the homemaker/mother job, and the like. Feminism provided a perspective whereby they could reconceptualize their problem and better invest their resources in solving it. "Intellectually and emotionally they

---

a social value, anticommunism. What we see as a movement's goals, then, may be a matter of whom we talk to.

Social movements can also be usefully distinguished on the basis of their relationship to social change. There are four important types: reactionary, reform, revolutionary, and utopian.

REACTIONARY MOVEMENTS Reactionary movements are movements aimed at blocking or reversing social changes. The prime example of a reactionary movement is the Nazi movement in Germany. Among the goals of the Nazis was a return to authoritarian rule, a return to pre-World War I prestige, and, at least rhetorically, pro-

became convinced that the traditional interpretation of woman's role is 'wrong' and that the role should be greatly expanded" (Carden 1978, p. 185). That is, time and talent (resources) should be used to work for change in the role, instead of using them to adjust personal behavior. And, once involved in the movement, the members obtain satisfaction from working together for their common cause.

Carden also explains why the movement's structure—that of many groups instead of a few centralized ones—is particularly appropriate for feminists. For one thing, women are not a homogeneous group—not in their status (political, economic, ethnic, or otherwise), nor in their belief of how to achieve their goal (e.g., should feminists work within the political system or strive for a restructuring of that system?). Also, large, centralized organizations tend to assign specialized roles, hire professionals for specific tasks, and so on, thus failing to satisfy a good number of the women attracted to the movement. Moreover, there would be more fights over methods and ultimate aims, all of which would expend a great deal of the movement's potential resources without coming any closer to equality. Given the movement's present structure, each member can involve herself in whichever activity she is most competent at doing, that is, where her resources are most valuable.

Thus, besides shedding light on why people join social movements, this study demonstrates how movement structures can develop in response to the resources members have to offer. Moreover, we can see how, by working together in a movement, individuals can reduce the control that certain social structures have over the way we behave.

tection of small businesses against more competitive larger firms. Other examples of reactionary movements include the Ku Klux Klan and the John Birch Society.

REFORM MOVEMENTS Reform movements are movements whose aim is to change some particular aspect of social life rather than the basic structure of the distribution of power. Reform movements have been especially plentiful in the United States, and they have been responsible for many changes from which we benefit today, including the vote for women, the establishment of hygiene requirements for

Reform movements aim to change some aspect of social life without altering the basic structure that distributes power.

food processing, and the regulation of pollution. Political reform (local and national), prison reform, reform of the living conditions of black people, consumer reforms, antipoverty reforms—all have had broad support in the United States. Social reformers often do battle with powerful groups (e.g., government and big business), and we often look at crusaders like Ralph Nader, who has spearheaded attempts to institute consumer-protection reforms, as minor folk heroes. But as important as the changes have been, social reformers tend to support the basic social structure of the society, which has given rise to the ills they see in need of correction. Prison reformers try to make treatment of inmates more "humane" and less brutal, for example, but they do not challenge society's use of prisons. Other reformers have tried to help the poor by giving them money and

sometimes vocational training without making them competitors for middle-class jobs, and thereby have left unquestioned the system of stratification. And few consumer groups challenge the economic system whose ills they fight.

While many reform campaigns in America have been at least partially successful, these movements have often run into problems, particularly when confronting vested interests. The attempts to clean up city halls since the turn of the century provide an example. Upper-class reformers often lead these crusades against "machine" politics, sometimes with allies in the press. They may have eliminated most open forms of corruption (New York's "boss" used to divide graft money on the steps of city hall!) but they are no match for the political "pros" in the long run. (If there are fewer machines today than in former years, it is due more to the emergence of the civil service and federal programs [e.g., welfare], economic changes, changes in the city's population composition, and the like, than to the efforts of reformers.) Philadelphia's experience is typical.

When reform candidates defeated that city's Republican machine in the 1881 elections, reformers thought their job was done and went home. The political pros remained, however, and, back in power four years later, were even stronger. But when a group of Democratic reformers unseated the Republican machine for good in 1951, there was some real reform: crooked politicians were thrown out, a civil service system replaced patronage, blacks were finally hired at city hall, and so on. At the same time, however, Democratic political pros and their party were gaining tremendous power in city hall and among the people. Soon, a Democratic machine ran Philadelphia, and, like the Republican one, it was corrupt. Not only were the upper-class reformers inexperienced at politics, but they weren't in touch with what the people wanted either. In contrast, political machines have built their strength on the public services and favors they can give or withhold from citizens (Guinther 1976).

Thus, since social reform movements don't challenge the basic distribution of power, the reforms they are able to effect are likely to be only those that dominant groups in society are willing to accept. Gabriel Kolko (1963) recognizes this limit in America's Progressive movement early in this century. He argues that the movement operated on the assumption that the general welfare would be best served by satisfying the concrete needs of business (pp. 2–3). Any actual reforms (e.g., of working conditions, pricing of goods, health standards for food processors, and the like),

were usually instituted by the dominant businesses that were to be regulated. They heard enough grumbling to convince them that some form of business regulation was inevitable; they therefore sought to control and limit that change as much as they could. They monopolized positions on the government's regulatory agencies and, by allowing minor changes, legitimated their powerful positions (p. 280). In instances like this, partial reforms are often instituted to drain the social movement of much of its driving force.

We now see that social reform movements, if channeled skillfully by people in power, can actually strengthen the latter's positions. Such channeling thus becomes an important form of conflict management. However, this type of manipulation of social movements is less likely to occur when the movements are revolutionary in character.

REVOLUTIONARY MOVEMENTS   We Americans constantly hear the word *revolution* in our lives, especially in advertisements. We're told about a "revolutionary" refrigerator that makes its own ice, "revolutions" in hair-dryer design, sugarless gum, and so much more. It's a good advertising gimmick, but, in truth, a *revolution* is a kind of collective action, often violent in nature, which, unlike the development of ice-making refrigerators, is aimed at overthrowing the existing power structure.

According to Claude Welch, Jr., and Mavis B. Taintor (1972), political revolutions replace old leaders with new ones, open access to political power to groups previously denied it, and expand political participation, which legitimates a new power structure. The American Revolution replaced King George III with a president and Congress, made most adult white males, regardless of lineage, eligible for these positions, and gave them the right to vote. Together with the Constitution, this method of leadership selection legitimated the American political system, which has gone virtually unchallenged subsequently. True social revolutions, we should note, go beyond a mere change in leadership and have a profound effect on the life of the people. Many so-called "palace revolutions" in Asia and Latin America are not true revolutions because they only replace one group of leaders with another.

Revolutionary movements are movements that aim to bring about a social revolution. Their social organization consists mainly of leaders, factions, and goals. History always remembers the most important leaders, at least those who were successful—Lenin in Russia, Mao in China, Nasser in Egypt, and so on. However, revolutionary movements in a country are rarely composed of just one group. Besides Lenin's Bolsheviks, for instance, the Constitutional Democrats, Socialist Revolutionaries, and Mensheviks were also prominent in the Russian Revolution. After a successful revolution, the various factions often fall out over whose specific goals to institute. In Russia, the Bolsheviks won that factional conflict, with their goals of a communist society, redistribution of land and wealth, full equality, and so on. Until the revolution is successful, the factions usually stay together—no matter how opposed they really are. Iran's 1979 revolution succeeded through a coalition of radical Marxists, ultraconservative fundamentalist Moslems, and many groups in between. What was their common interest? It was every revolution's main goal—seizing state power.

CLASSICAL AND MODERN REVOLUTIONS Most revolutions have tended toward one of two ideal types—the classical or the modern (Huntington 1968). The essential difference between the two is that *classical revolutionaries* attempt to seize the central reins of power (e.g., national government, army) and only then try to win over the population, while *modern revolutionaries* attempt to build a popular base and wage a protracted, popular war.

A classical revolution is like a game of chess in which, to win, all you have to do is to corner your opponent's king. Its leaders take the capital city first and only later establish their rule in the rest of the country. The French Revolution was won in Paris, the Russian Revolution in Moscow and St. Petersburg (now Leningrad). Classical revolutions are often brief, too. The 1903 war of liberation from Columbia waged by Panama, with substantial American help, lasted less than a day, and the Russian Revolution lasted only ten days.

Modern revolutionaries, on the other hand, spend years among the people, establishing control of the countryside. They have to. Their task requires that they not only take power but be seen as legitimate as well, and they are often fighting a strong and well-supplied professional army. Mao Tse Tung's strategy of revolution was the "people's war"—the mobilization of a hostile population against the ruling group (Johnson 1969, pp. 34–35). In this way, according to Mao, government repression increases revolutionary hostility, rather than overpowering it. In contrast to the sequence in classical revolutions, taking the capital city is the last act of a modern revolution. The National Liberation Front, for instance, had already won when they marched into Saigon (now Ho Chi Minh

City). It would be a mistake, however, to conclude that modern revolutionaries simply carry out the "will of the people" and that they never impose their own ideas. Fidel Castro tells us as much in a 1967 speech: "Whoever stops to wait for ideas to triumph among the majority of the masses before initiating revolutionary action will never be a revolutionary. . . . Humanity will, of course, change; human society will, of course, continue to develop—in spite of human beings and the errors of human beings. But that is not a revolutionary attitude" (1969, p. 146). Castro and other revolutionaries have seen their movements as agents of change. It should not surprise us, therefore, that following most revolutions, whether modern or classical, intense power struggles occur in the form of factional violence, civil war, or reigns of terror.

Many classical revolutions were sparked by single events: for example, disaster in World War I ignited revolutionary activity in Russia and Germany; the storming of the Bastille did likewise in France. These events cannot "cause" a revolution, but they are signals that the old regime can no longer defend itself. The long-standing grievances that have been building for years create revolutionary situations. Take France in 1789—few personal freedoms, a corrupt and dictatorial church, great poverty, landless peasants, and a rising middle class denied both prestige and a say in running the country. Similarly, the revolutions that broke up the Austro-Hungarian Empire in 1918 were the product of long-standing ethnic tensions. Only the empire's military forces had kept these ethnic groups together under a unified administration, and when those military forces were defeated, there was nothing to enforce obedience. And although the empire was divided among several independent states (see Figure 10.1), this division was made along political rather than ethnic lines. So underlying ethnic tensions have remained a constant potential source of revolutionary activity in eastern Europe (Burks 1961).

RECRUITMENT TO REVOLUTIONARY MOVEMENTS To win converts and justify their often illegal actions, revolutionaries more than activists in other social movements must have a coherent ideology that they can communicate. It might be embodied in revolutionary slogans like "No taxation without representation," or "Liberty, Equality, Fraternity," or "Power to the people." These slogans neatly provide an organizing principle for a host of grievances and suggest the appropriate goal to work for. In modern revolutions particularly, a persuasive ideology is essential because the revolutionary movement relies on convincing a population that it is right rather than simply taking over the reigns of government. It is also essential because the mass media keeps the movement in the public eye, constantly forcing its members to justify themselves.

Even with an appealing ideology, recruiting committed members to revolutionary or other radical movements is seldom easy because of the significant risks membership often entails. Students of radical social movements have observed that these movements often secure a member's commitment through what Luther P. Gerlach and Virginia H. Hine (1970, pp. 142–58) call *bridge-burning acts*. By performing such acts, members "burn their bridges" back to the existing order. They thus develop a strong interest in seeing the radical movement triumph, for it is their

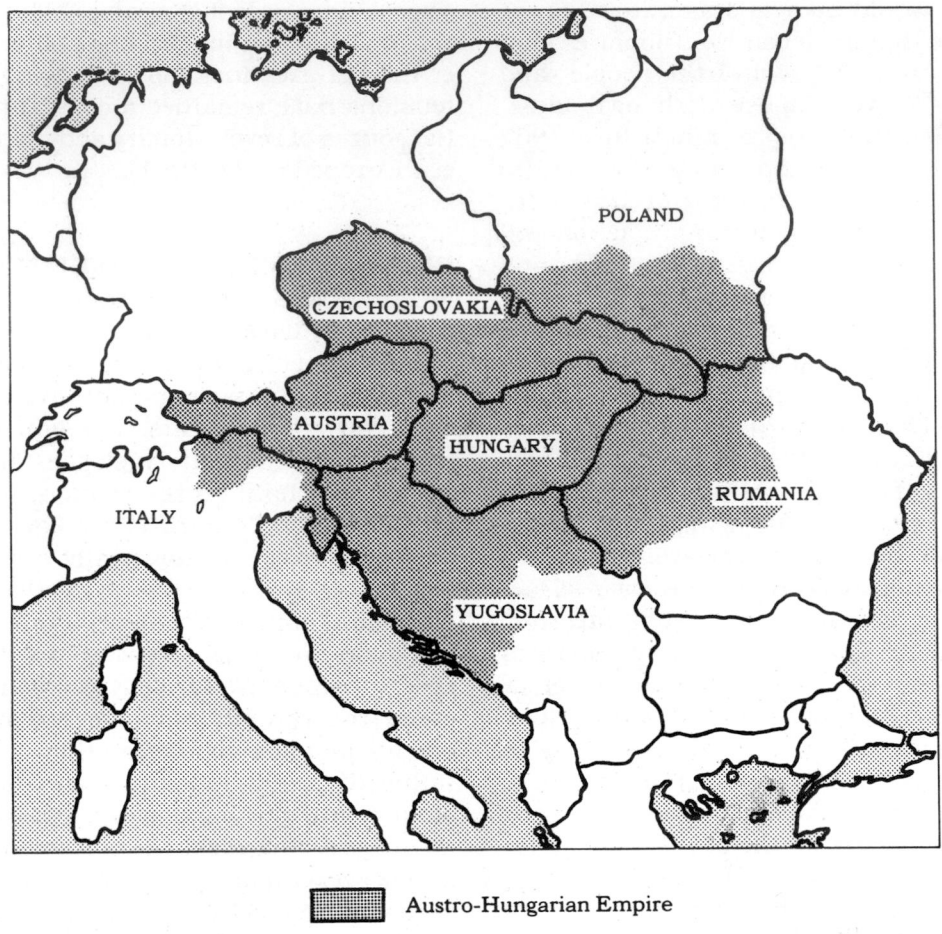

Austro-Hungarian Empire

Figure 10.1 Countries Created by Revolutions in the Austro-Hungarian Empire, 1918

chance for a new legitimacy. These acts might be illegal ones, labeling the member as a criminal, but they symbolize identity with the radical group. Gerlach and Hine note about the Black Power movement, for instance, that: "Repeatedly, in published statements and during the interviews we conducted, participants explained that the 'baptism in blackness,' the surge of pride

in being black, occurred at the very moment of confrontation with the representatives of the white power structure" (1970, p. 143).

Bridge-burning acts do not have to be illegal or even immoral, and they do not have to involve a politically radical group. Upon entering certain Jesus Freak communes, for instance, members relinquish their "worldly" names for a group name and must later marry whomever the leader chooses for them. In doing so, they symbolically abandon their past lives and personal aspirations and place all their hope in the commune. This strengthens their commitment to the group.

Because people are generally not ready to commit such drastic acts right away, a series of lesser actions often precedes them. Each successive act will be a little more drastic than the one before, until the person is prepared to take the final step and remove herself or himself from the mainstream of society. Two social psychologists have demonstrated in laboratory experiments that subjects will, in fact, agree to grant larger and larger favors if the size of each is slowly increased (Freedman and Fraser 1966). In this way, many young people became more involved in the anti-Vietnam War movement. A person might first have been asked to attend a demonstration—a good thing if she or he opposed the war. Then the person might have been asked to help out at a rally or at a fundraising meeting. The next step might be putting up antiwar posters, then organizing a rally. And after this series of actions, the person might have been ready to participate in an illegal sit-in, or destroy draft records, or do something else that might land her or him in jail. At that point, the only chance to save face would appear to be for the movement to succeed, proving the actions necessary and right. (Note, however, that each act does not *have to* lead to a more drastic one.)

The final type of social movement we will consider, the utopian, also involves a high degree of commitment from its members, but for somewhat different reasons. Unlike revolutionary movements, utopian movements are not likely to involve a violent confrontation with the power structure, yet they require complete dedication to a new society on the part of their members.

UTOPIAN MOVEMENTS Most of us associate the word *utopia* with ideals and idealists and with an environment that could never exist. But firm believers have attempted to make the impossible a reality by building their own communities from scratch. The English Puritans, a seventeenth-century religious movement, for instance, were utopians. Their members were persecuted and had the unpleasant choice of accepting the persecution or abandoning their religion to escape it. True, they could have tried revolution, but they had neither the power nor the popular support needed for success. Reacting to this no-win situation, they chose to leave England and start a totally new society, and what better place to do so than in the "uncivilized" New World? All of us studied these utopians as the Pilgrims. And utopians they were: their aim was to build "God's city" on earth.

Another important group of utopians built the Israeli *kibbutzim*, or collective farming villages, and, to a large extent, the nation of Israel, too:

> The kibbutz grew out of the desire
> of a group of young, turn-of-the-
> century, Eastern European Jewish
> intellectuals to found a new and
> democratic society in what was then
> Palestine. They had experienced the
> dying years of the Russian Czarist
> regime, with its brutal anti-
> Semitism, and were fired by the
> Zionist dream for Israel; they
> wanted a society free of the
> prejudice that closed the world they

had left behind, dedicated to full social and political equality. (Rabkin and Rabkin 1969, p. 40)

Many of these pioneers had previously dedicated themselves to socialism and revolution in Eastern Europe. But after repeated failures, capped with anti-Semitism within the revolutionary movement itself and a general disregard for their own group's demands, they turned to this radical alternative.

There have also been less dramatic (and often less successful) attempts to establish utopias, many in nineteenth-century America. Most of the new American societies were bold experiments in communal living based on a religious and/or communistic philosophy. According to Rosabeth M. Kanter, "property was jointly owned and shared, goods equally distributed to all members, and private property abolished" (Kanter 1970) in the most successful groups. All successful groups required members to sign over their financial resources to the community when they entered. The leader of one utopia, New Harmony, even burned the contribution record book.

As it happened, most of the communities eventually disbanded for economic reasons; but two—Amana and Oneida—eventually developed successful corporations, as you might recognize from their names. These utopias were not only radical in their economics, however. For one thing, the Oneidans had their own doctrine of sin (Perfectionism), which held that Christ had already returned to earth, meaning that humans had been freed of the original sin and could be sinless, given the proper environment. They also abolished marriage and the nuclear family and forbade monogamy, which they considered a form

of private property. In all these utopias, children were raised communally as the group's offspring (Kephart 1976).

The Fate of Social Movements

Social movements, like all forms of collective behavior, are transient by nature. After their rise in popularity, they become routinized and eventually decline. This routinization can happen in several, often interrelated ways. First, formal organizations spring up from within the movement, and norms and roles within the movement become established. In most movement organizations, a hierarchical division of labor appears, with an elite of policy makers at the top, organizational functionaries below them, and the mass of participants at the bottom. In the life course of social movements, even ones based on egalitarian and democratic principles, decision-making power and control of the movement's resources tend to become concentrated among an elite. Robert Michels (1962 [1911]) called this tendency of not just social movement organizations but all organizations, the "iron law of oligarchy," *oligarchy* meaning rule by the few. Michels noted that the policy-making elite tends to become more conservative as it concentrates the organization's control in its hands, and that, further, it may lose touch with the real interests of the organization's members. This tendency has been seen in movement organizations of many types, a recent example being the history of the National Welfare Rights Organization (Piven and Cloward 1977). We should be careful, however, to recognize that Michels's "law" does not always hold and that he is speaking of organizations, not movements as a whole.

The word utopia *means "no place" in Greek, and many people believe that utopias cannot work. But the youths on this New Mexico commune—like others before them—are trying to make their utopia a reality.*

Nevertheless, as we noted earlier in the chapter, a movement in which discontent isn't effectively challenged and organized is likely to make little or no headway.

Second, social movements become routinized through their very successes. The most obvious instances are those in which a revolutionary movement is successful and its participants become society's new rulers and institutionalize their policies. Even partial successes, however, can lead to the decline of a social movement through institutionalization. A case in point is the American industrial union movement. The original organizers were by and large left-wing radicals, and their aims were often revolutionary. In a mass movement, workers were able to gain legitimation for the right to strike and to engage in collective bargaining. This has enabled many industrial workers to win much higher wages and better working conditions than they might otherwise have received. But after these official sanctions and gains, the movement itself began to fall apart, and union organizations were all that remained. The revolutionary leaders were replaced by reformers and bureaucrats. In their success, industrial unions have generally accepted the unequal worker-management relationship and, in some cases, even support business interests against those of other workers (examples have involved coal miners and farmworkers, as well as black workers). Of course, not all members of the industrial union movement lost interest in more radical solutions, and they fought on, but the movement itself was by this time nearly dead.

The fact that a social movement dies or becomes institutionalized doesn't mean, however, that it was futile. In the course of its lifetime, it can cause considerable social change, the subject of the next chapter.

SUMMARY

Collective behavior is relatively transient, similar, or related behavior of a number of people. In this chapter, we looked at the behavior of diffuse collectivities, of crowds, and of social movements.

Diffuse collectivities are collectivities whose members share similar behavior or expressed opinions, but who usually are not assembled in one place. One set of behaviors characteristic of diffuse collectivities are fads, fashions, and crazes—all of which involve an object's or an activity's brief and intense popularity followed by its abrupt decline. An increasingly important form of diffuse collectivity behavior is public opinion, the sum of views expressed by a public on a given issue. Public opinion polls are used by business and political leaders in decision making, and public opinion can be—and has been—manipulated for personal ends.

Crowd behavior involves an unorganized collection of people who have temporarily assembled together at the same time, usually with a common focus. Crowds are uninstitutionalized and vulnerable to manipulation, but not necessarily irrational. An audience is a passive crowd that assembles to witness an event (e.g., a play or fire) and nothing more. But if the audience feels threatened by something (a fire in the theater), for example, it can become an active crowd. Crowd behavior includes panics, mob action, and riots.

We examined two theories of crowd behavior. The emergent norm theory holds that a crowd redefines norms in situations when they are unclear, and it emphasizes the regulating norms that emerge. The value-added theory posits six necessary steps: structural conduciveness, structural strain, a generalized belief, a precipitating incident, mobilization for action, and a type of social control.

A social movement is a concerted effort by a large number of people over an extended period of time to effect or block social change. Of the two leading theories of the development of social movements, one emphasizes the importance of long-standing discontent and the other the importance of a movement's capacity to mobilize material and nonmaterial resources on its behalf.

We looked at four main types of social movements. The aim of reactionary movements is to halt or reverse social change; the goal of reform movements is to alter only certain aspects of society, while the aim of revolutionary movements is to replace the current structure of power with a new one. Finally, the aim of utopian movements is not to overthrow existing structures but to create a new society outside of the confines of the old. Typically, social movements become routinized over time and decay. Formal organizations appear and gain power in the movement, and the structure of power within these organizations tends to become oligarchic. If successful, social movements become institutionalized by, in the case of revolution, forming the basis of a new structure of power, or in more limited cases, by integration into the existing social system.

Key Terms

collective behavior (p. 311)
diffuse collectivities (p. 311)
fads (p. 312)
fashions (p. 312)
crazes (p. 312)
public (p. 313)
public opinion (p. 313)
propaganda (p. 314)
crowd (p. 315)
audience (p. 316)
panic (p. 317)
mob (p. 318)
riot (p. 318)
social movement (p. 324)

Review and Discussion Questions

1. What fads have you engaged in? How serious was the behavior? How seriously did you take it at the time? How do you account for your participation? What factors have kept you from participating in fad behavior?

2. When have you spotted propaganda—in terms of an attempt to manipulate public opinion—aimed at you? Think of party slogans, advertising campaigns, and attempts by political candidates to manipulate public opinion. What devices have they relied on? Have they worked? Why or why not?

3. Think of any crowd—whether an audience or an active crowd—of which you were a part. What were some of the norms that emerged and how did they differ from those prevalent outside of the crowd?

4. Several "special interest" movements have emerged in the United States in recent years: antiabortionists, the "gun lobby," environmentalists, the pro-Israel lobby, and others. How have they mobilized their reources to bring about their aims?

5. What are the most important social movements in America today? Which ones are reactionary, which reform, and which revolutionary? Do any of these movements have a greater chance than others to succeed? Why?

6. Several nations, including the United States, were founded after successful revolutionary movements. How were they (or are they being) institutionalized? Can you see any remnants of the original revolutionary impetus?

For Further Study

COLLECTIVE BEHAVIOR Sociologists have tried to improve on the view of collective behavior espoused by Le Bon and others; namely, that such behavior is simply irrational. Two of the most influential attempts are: Ralph Turner and Lewis Killian, *Collective Behavior* (Englewood Cliffs, NJ: Prentice-Hall, 1972); and Neil J. Smelser, *Theory of Collective Behavior* (New York: Free Press, 1963). There have been numerous studies of particular instances of crowd behavior; see, for example: Robert Curvin and Bruce Porter, *Blackout Looting!* (New York: Gardner, 1979). One form of collective behavior that has increasingly occupied sociologists—and others—in recent years is public opinion. Robert S. Erickson and Norman R. Luttberg have analyzed its source and significance in *American Public Opinion: Its Origins, Content, and Impact* (New York: Wiley, 1973). On the role of public opinion polls in politics, see: Charles W. Roll, Jr., and Albert H. Cantril, *Polls: Their Use and Misuse in Politics* (New York: Basic Books, 1973). Finally, for a look at public opinion in socialist nations, see: W. D. O'Connor et al., *Public Opinion in European Socialist Systems* (New York: Praeger, 1977).

SOCIAL MOVEMENTS Two excellent texts on social movements are: Roberta Ash, *Social Movements in America* (Chicago: Markham, 1972) and Anthony Oberschall, *Social Conflict and Social Movements* (Englewood Cliffs, NJ:

Prentice-Hall, 1973). William Gamson's *The Strategy of Social Protest* (Homewood, IL: Dorsey, 1975) presents findings on fifty-three American protest groups. You can get a comprehensive review of the sociological study of social movements in: Robert R. Evans, ed., *Social Movements: A Reader and Source Book* (Chicago: Rand McNally, 1973). Finally, Henry J. Pratt's *The Grey Lobby* (Chicago: University of Chicago Press, 1980) analyzes the "senior citizens movement" and provides a theory of social movements in general.

REVOLUTION Karl Marx and Frederick Engels' *The Communist Manifesto* (New York: International Publishers, 1948) simply and succinctly analyzes what many people feel are the basic antagonisms that lead to revolutions. A very different type of book on revolution is Hannah Arendt's *The Origins of Totalitarianism* (New York: Harcourt Brace Jovanovich, 1973). It is a detailed analysis of the growth of totalitarianism in Nazi Germany and the Soviet Union. You can also find books on specific revolutions, for example: James W. Wilke, *The Mexican Revolution* (Berkeley: University of California Press, 1970); Robert A. Scalapino, ed., *The Communist Revolution in Asia* (Englewood Cliffs, NJ: Prentice-Hall, 1969); and John L. H. Keep, *The Russian Revolution* (New York: Norton, 1976).

UTOPIAS The search for a "perfect" society seems to have occupied people in every generation. The utopian experiments have varied in size from small communes to giant states and in success from unsuccessful anarchist communes to the ongoing Israeli kibbutzim. Marie Louise Berneri conducted a study of utopias from ancient times until the mid-twentieth century in *Journey through Utopia* (New York: Schocken, 1971). For a sociological analysis of American communes, see: Rosabeth Moss Kanter, *Commitment and Community: Communes and Utopias in Sociological Perspective* (Cambridge, MA: Harvard University Press, 1972). For a look at a commune now in its third generation, see: Benjamin Zalocki, *The Joyful Community* (Chicago: University of Chicago Press, 1980).

CHAPTER ELEVEN
Social Change

As we saw in the last chapter, social movements often change society. But social movements, as we'll now see, are only one source of **social change**—a change in social organization, norms, roles, bases for status, or social institutions, which alters the pattern of our relationships with one another. For our study of social change, we'll first look at the nature of social change and then at some of the theories that sociologists have offered to explain the patterns of changes they observe. Finally, we will examine some of the major sources of social change in the spheres of technology, population growth, and urbanization.

THE NATURE OF SOCIAL CHANGE

Some sociologists distinguish between *social* change, which involves social organization, and *cultural* change, which involves changes in the rules of social conduct, ideology, and material elements of a society. While we can make such a distinction in theory, it is not always possible or useful to do so in practice because of the interconnection of social organization and culture (see Chapter 2). For instance, new technological developments, such as computers (an element of culture), have spurred changes in work relationships (an element of social organization), and these new relationships have generated interest in developing new technology, and so forth. In this instance, and many others, it makes little sense to talk about social change without talking about cultural change as well. Thus, although I will use both terms, *social* and *cultural change,* to emphasize certain aspects of change, when I want to emphasize both, I'll just use the term *change.*

Characteristics of Social Change

Social change involves changed relationships among people. In recent decades, for example, to cite one area, there have been many changes in America's acceptance of pornography, including more "adult" bookstores, more open display of pornographic material in magazine stands and theaters, and so on, but these changes in themselves are *not* social changes. Several city governments have managed to partially reverse these changes, for example, without the reversals having much impact on any other aspect of social life. But the rise in pornography *is* a symptom of general social change—a questioning of traditional sexual mores and sexual behavior (see

Chapter 6), changes in family structure, the women's movement, and reforms in morals legislation—which has altered the way in which men and women relate to one another.

Social change usually implies not only changes in the relations between people but also changes within individuals, in their internalized norms and how they define situations. This means that, for example, prohibition was *not* social change. The Eighteenth Amendment to the Constitution outlawed "the manufacture, sale, or transportation of intoxicating liquors" from 1920–1933. But enforcement was impossible because few people accepted the norm that drinking was evil, and most of the nation rejoiced when the amendment was repealed. The Russian Czar Peter the Great (1672–1725) also failed to impose social change and "westernize" his nation by edict. Despite his enthusiasm, the czar failed to "infuse the Russian masses with some soul-stirring enthusiasm" (Hoffer 1951, p. 14).

As we can see, the most dramatic events are not necessarily sources of social change. Gradual trends, however, have often had the far-reaching impact on social organization that distinguishes social change. For example, the fact that the number of women working for wages increased during World War II by over 50 percent was certainly a dramatic change, but not as far-reaching as the more gradual changes of the 1960s and 1970s. During the war, there was little change in attitudes about proper sex-role behaviors; generally, women were simply seen as temporarily filling in for men who were doing "more important" work as soldiers. The status of women remained the same, and they were expected to return to the home when the men came back. As William H. Chafe notes:

"A permanent change in women's economic status . . . required a continued redistribution of sex roles, a more profound shift in public attitudes, and a substantial improvement in the treatment and opportunities afforded the female worker" (1972, p. 150). These developments did not occur in the 1940s—nor in the 1950s or early 1960s.

On the other hand, we saw a reevaluation of women's status as the 1960s and 1970s progressed. And at the same time, the percentage of women in the labor force *gradually* rose from about three-tenths in 1947 to over one-half in 1978 (see Figure 11.1). Although these latter changes were not as abrupt as during the war, they appear to be having a much greater impact on social organizations.

The changing role of women in the work force illustrates another important aspect of social change: a change in one sphere of social life usually entails changes in other spheres. The increased employment of women outside the home, for instance, transforms relations within the family between husbands and wives and between mothers and their children. As it becomes more acceptable for women to work outside the home, it becomes easier for them to marry later in order to pursue a career, to contemplate separation or divorce when married, and to expect fulfillment outside of the home.

As significant social changes occur, new relations of power and new bases of self-interest develop. For instance, America's Progressive movement emerged with the nation's urbanization. As cities grew, businesses concentrated there and tried to gain control of local governments because these governments were controlling access to money, jobs, public works contracts, and other valuable resources. A coalition

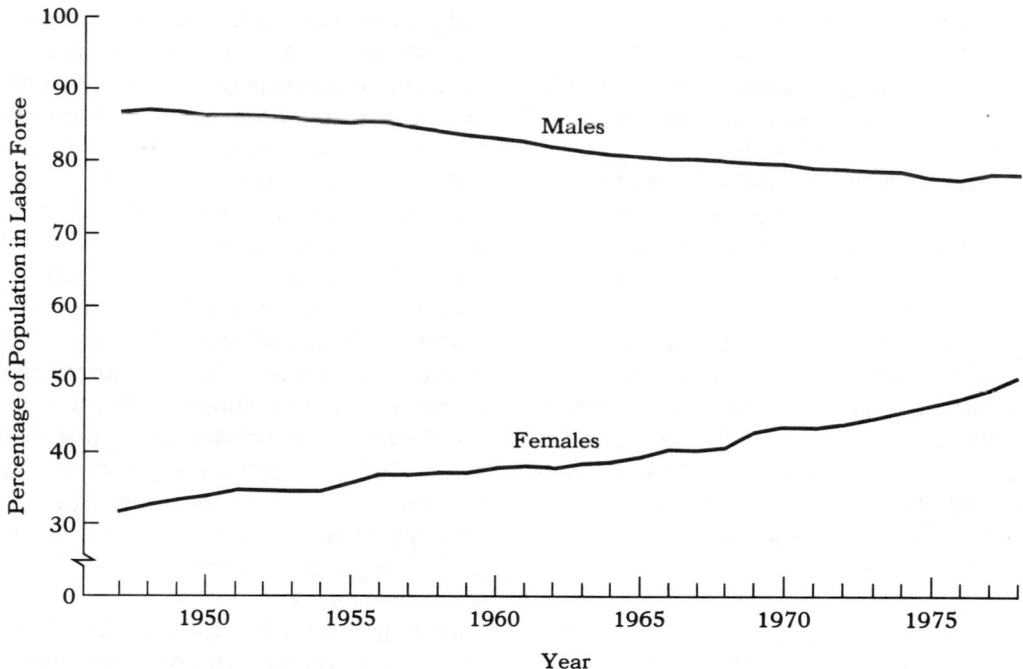

Figure 11.1 Men and Women in the Labor Force in the United States, 1947–1978

SOURCE: *U.S. Department of Labor*, Employment and Unemployment during 1978: An Analysis, *Special Labor Force Report 218, 1979.*

of journalists, liberals, and upper-class reformers formed in response to the business interests, with their own ideas for those resources.

With significant social change, people respond to different motivations and formulate new goals. World War II soldiers in combat fought to defend their fellow GIs, for instance, while many Vietnam GIs had their own immediate safety in mind (Moskos 1977). We can gain a better appreciation of the impact of social change by looking at some goals Americans were expected to have in 1960. A report by a presidential commission included the following goals: increasing the size of the government's bu-

reaucracy (and bureaucrats' pay), developing new education techniques, providing more money for education, and increasing the number of doctors and hospitals (*Goals for Americans* 1960, pp. 3–15). Today, government bureaucracy has become a public villain, and you probably want less, not more, of it. Americans today think teachers should "go back to the basics" and have allowed schools to close rather than vote them more money. Finally, there are so many hospitals in some locations that many beds go unused, and there seems to be an oversupply rather than a shortage of doctors in some areas.

The fact that social change is so complex and involves so many spheres of social life means that we cannot predict all the ramifications of any given change. It also means that social change is essentially irreversible. Of course, revolutionary governments can be overthrown, reform laws repealed, and new forms of technology discarded. But the result of these attempts would not be simply a return to the past because the revolution, reform, or technology would have had many far-flung effects on society. To take an extreme example, if the Soviet regime were overthrown, we would not witness the rebirth of czarist Russia. Rather, installing the new government would involve further social changes and not a return to past conditions.

The Rate and Acceptance of Change

If change is irreversible, it is also inevitable. Change characterizes all societies today; even preliterate societies are changing as their contact with the rest of the world continues to increase. However, not all societies change at the same rate. William F. Ogburn (1936) has identified the major factors that encourage or discourage change (see Table 11.1). In looking at the table, note that the stationary societies and changing ones generally resemble gemeinschaft- and gesellschaft-type societies, respectively. Also, one theme running through the different types of societies is the attitude toward change itself. Modern states are committed to continuing social change, but in the societies Ogburn calls stationary, reverence for tradition predominates.

Ogburn's identification of two types of societies is just a sketch, and we shouldn't let it mislead us into thinking that in so-

cieties like our own change is openly embraced by everyone or that in more traditional societies it is uniformly blocked. The promise of social changes, or their reality, is not accepted uniformly within a society because some people believe that the changes will affect them adversely. Workers, for instance, have sometimes resisted the introduction of new technology because they have been afraid the new machines will cause their layoffs. Citizens' groups have fought the nuclear energy program because of concern about safe disposal of nuclear wastes and possible accidents. The automobile industry has opposed the consumer and ecology movements, which propose bills that threaten industry profits (e.g., mandatory safety features and antipollution devices). Many lawyers have opposed no-fault divorce laws, which threaten to remove the need for many lawsuits. And the American Medical Association has fought any move toward socialized medicine.

Two Kinds of Change—Purposive and Unplanned

The social changes mentioned above are all instances of one kind of change—purposive change. *Purposive change* is change that comes from human action directed to some end. This kind of change includes everything from Soviet five-year plans to revolutions to urban renewal programs to government attempts to promote integrated schools.

Not all social change is purposive, however. Social change can also be *unplanned*. In Chapter 9, we saw the importance of anomie and alienation in the modern world, neither of which were, or are, planned so-

Table 11.1 Characteristics of Stationary and Changing Societies

Stationary Society	Changing Society
No experimentation	New elements tried out in many ways
Belief in fate and the inevitable nature of things	Belief in the idea of progress
Past held in great prestige	Past considered a burden
Elders control information	The young control information, with books
The past guides behavior	Convenience guides behavior
Unchanging laws revered	Laws changed; judged more on content
Specific rules of conduct have the force of morality	Morality has less force than intelligence
No fashions in dress	Prominent fashions in dress
Well mannered	Poor mannered
Human nature suppressed	Human nature encouraged
No individuality: slave of custom	Individuality: customs change
Caste	Class
Sentimental about things	Unsentimental about ever-new things
Art favored	Art turned into fashion
Religion is the outlet of hope; therefore prevents revolt against institutions causing frustration	Religion less moralistic, more generalized, perhaps tied to agents of change
No division between radicals and conservatives	Competing ideologies of radicals and conservatives

SOURCE: *William F. Ogburn, "Stationary and Changing Societies,"* American Journal of Sociology 42 (1936): 16–31.

cial changes. Later in the chapter we will see that some unplanned change comes as an unexpected result of planned change, while other change frequently comes as a result of trends in population movements, urbanization, and technological developments.

The fact of continual changes in our society, the feeling that many of these changes are unplanned and beyond our control, and the interests of various social groups in generating only certain changes has led an increasing number of sociologists, political figures, and the general population to examine what causes change and how it can be controlled. Government leaders and planners want to know how to manage social change, while the leaders of social movements are interested in the best strategies for effecting the changes they are promoting.

Sociologists have studied social change from the discipline's origins in the last half of the nineteenth century. Sociology de-

Real social change requires a fundamental change in values and outlook. Otherwise, particular changes will merely be incorporated into existing patterns of social organization. How much has technological advance changed the status of this third-world woman?

veloped as an attempt to make sense of the many social changes that the Industrial Revolution had brought to traditional society, and early sociologists developed some theories to explain how social change occurs and its historical pattern. In the next section, we will look at these theories.

THEORIES OF SOCIAL CHANGE

Sociologists have developed four main theoretical perspectives on social change: evolutionary, cyclical, functional, and conflict. Each provides an overall context for viewing particular changes.

Evolutionary Theories

Traditional *evolutionary theories* rest on the contention that we can explain all events by a single, overarching principle, namely, that of cumulative progress. Early theorists in this tradition took much of their inspiration from Darwin's theory of biological evolution. In *The Principles of Sociology*, for example, Herbert Spencer (1898) explained its application to social change. Just as organisms have been evolving into more complex forms, Spencer argues, societies have been constantly evolving from primitive to more advanced stages. All social changes—no matter how they appear—are essential for human progress. Spencer was not alone in his view, for the theory of evolution was quite fashionable in intellectual circles in the late nineteenth century.

Because the theory holds that change follows immutable, "natural" laws, social evolutionists believe that governments have no business interfering with the workings of these laws. This fits well with Americans' belief in individual initiative and free market capitalism. It is not surprising, then, that Spencer won many converts among early American sociologists, including William Graham Sumner. We can still hear these echoes among some Americans who oppose government programs to aid the poor, enforce affirmative action, or regulate business practices, as undue interference with our lives.

Spencer's brand of evolutionism, however, has fallen into disfavor. The folkways of primitive and complex societies are now recognized as sometimes being rather similar, as Horace Miner's article on the Nacirema indicates (see Chapter 2). Also, sociologists now view social change as more complex than evolutionary theory allows. More recent evolutionists have attempted to meet these objections. They break sharply from their predecessors by not viewing change as necessarily good or progressive. Nor do they believe that their theory can be applied to all societies at all times. Moreover, they explain change by such factors as technological change, military and economic warfare, and genetics (Lenski 1976; 1975).

Cyclical Theories

Cyclical theories of social change are similar to evolutionary ones in their conception of historical stages through which societies pass. But cyclical theories postulate recurring cycles of the rise and fall of civilizations rather than unending progress.

Certain historians, particularly Oswald Spengler and Arnold Toynbee, have taken a cyclical perspective on history.

Spengler speaks of thousand-year cycles through which all societies go, involving youthful, mature, and disintegrating stages. Toynbee sees societies as being determined by the nature of the challenges they continually face and their responses to those challenges. Whereas Spengler sees a declining trend in Western civilization's present period, however, Toynbee sees an upward progression. However, Pitirim A. Sorokin (1937) has developed the most extensive cyclical theory of social change. He holds that societies alternate between *sensate* stages—in which stress is on personal pleasure and individual freedom—and *ideational* stages—involving the subordination of the collective to some ideal. Sorokin also believes that sensate- and ideational-type societies follow one another as reactions to the deficiencies inherent in each.

Functional Theories

Almost all functional theorists—whether their conclusions tend to be conservative (like those of Talcott Parsons, for example) or radical (like those of Frances Piven and Richard Cloward on welfare [see the Prologue])—share a few basic tenets. One of the most important of these tenets is that social systems tend toward balance, or equilibrium. As Kingsley Davis puts it: "It is only in terms of equilibrium that most sociological concepts make sense" (1949, p. 634). Functionalists believe that any time a disruptive element, such as a war, an economic depression, or an excessively high crime rate, enters the system, social institutions will adjust to assimilate the change. For instance, when international oil prices rose sharply throughout the 1970s, American automakers began man-

ufacturing and advertising more economy cars than at any time in the past, and Americans began to alter their driving patterns slightly to absorb the change. In other words, according to functionalists, social changes occur as institutions adjust to various influences in order to minimize social disruption.

Some functionalists have applied this perspective to develop theories of social change. Talcott Parsons (1966), for example, has conceptualized change and consequent progress in a social system in terms of its increased capacity to adapt to all possible influences on it. But we can find the most comprehensive functionalist theory of change in Emile Durkheim's *The Division of Labor in Society*. As we saw in Chapter 9, Durkheim believes that societies evolve from a state of *mechanical solidarity*—where social bonds are based on likenesses among people—to one characterized by *organic solidarity*—where social bonds rest on the functional interdependence of people.

Functional theories of change are hampered by some of the problems we outlined for functionalism as a theoretical perspective in the Prologue. For one thing, institutions do not always react to restore balance when the system is upset. Despite the automakers' adaptations, as well as government action, we have been unable to solve our energy problem thus far. Nor have institutions mobilized to stop inflation or recurring recession. Change may also be more erratic and less predictable than functionalist theories indicate.

Conflict Theories

In the view of conflict theorists, change occurs through the conflict of group inter-

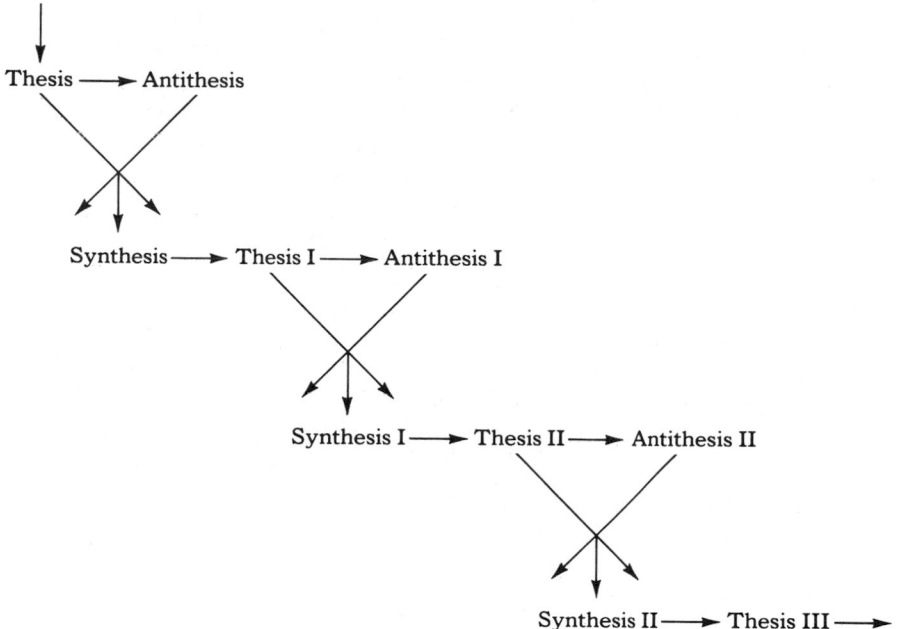

Figure 11.2 Thesis, Antithesis, Synthesis

ests. The central figure among these theorists is Karl Marx. Marx argued that social change occurs through a "dialectical" process. The word *dialectical* comes from a Greek root whose meaning is "to contend," and, as we saw in Chapter 7, Marx views history as the contention for power between different economic groups. There are three important parts to the dialectical process: thesis, antithesis, and synthesis. As Marx analyzed history, the ruling economic group (thesis) of an epoch creates conditions under which another economic group develops in opposition to it (antithesis). The clash of these groups will eventually lead to the overthrow of the old order and the generation of a new social structure (synthesis), whose dominant group would become the thesis of the next epoch, and so on (see Figure 11.2). For instance, the bourgeoisie created the conditions un-

der which the proletariat developed as a class and thus sowed the seeds of its own destruction. That is, in order to organize the capitalist industrial mode of production, the bourgeoisie needed workers, not peasants tied to the land, and through industrialization, it brought large numbers of workers together. For Marx, that reduction of workers to a common condition and bringing them together would lead to the development of class consciousness and contribute to the downfall of the capitalist order and the beginning of a socialist era.

Marx believed that under the capitalist mode of production, technological change would accelerate. The reason for this is that capitalist competition requires that each capitalist constantly develop cheaper means of manufacture in order to maintain competitive prices and generate more profits. "Constant revolutionizing of production, uninterrupted disturbance of all social conditions, everlasting uncertainty and agitation," Marx and Engels wrote in *The Communist Manifesto* (1948 [1848], p. 12), "distinguish the bourgeois epoch from all earlier ones."

The conception of historical process as a dialectical one did not originate with Marx. But while earlier theorists saw the process in terms of conflicting ideas, Marx developed a *materialist* conception, that is, one of contention between people who had different material interests because of their differing relationship to the means of production.

We discussed some of the shortcomings of Marxist theory concerning class struggle in Chapter 7. Here, we need only note that even if all of Marx's predictions have not come to pass, as a theory of the process of social change it can still yield useful results. Many modern conflict theorists, although not necessarily Marxists or believers in the primacy of economic factors, have made fruitful use of the hypothesis that change occurs dialectically through the conflict of group interests.

All of these theories help us to explain certain instances of social change, but none of them is completely convincing. For this reason, most sociologists have turned away from strict adherence to one or another of these theories and instead concentrate on narrower aspects of change. In the remainder of this chapter we are going to look at some principal sources of social change in order to get a better idea of how it occurs.

SOURCES OF SOCIAL CHANGE

In this section, we'll first look at the role of social movements and political institu-

tions in initiating social change, then we'll turn to three important sources of social change that are for the most part unplanned: new developments in technology, demographic changes, and urbanization. These four sources are particularly important because to a large extent they account for the nature of our society today and they are all crucial ingredients in the current struggles of third world countries to industrialize.

Social Movements and Political Institutions

In the last chapter, we looked at social movements, particularly those of reform and revolution, as sources of social change. When victorious, these movements' effects are clear enough—think of the changes brought about by the American Revolution, the Chinese and Russian revolutions, the American labor movement, and so forth. What may not be so obvious is the role that vested interests and the state play as sources of social change. This role is primarily one of attempting to manage social change to maintain as much social stability as possible, so that the changes that occur do so within permissible limits. In this section, we are going to look at two styles of directing social change. One style is that in which vested interests, faced with powerful social movements, attempt to control the direction of social changes they believe are inevitable. In the second style, processes of social change are institutionalized.

ACCOMMODATION TO CHANGE: THE CASE OF NICARAGUA Recent political events in Nicaragua show how even conservative forces, trying to protect their interests, will back some significant changes in order to forestall more drastic ones. A succession of dictators, all of the Somoza family, ruled the Republic of Nicaragua for half a century. It was not surprising, then, that in the late 1970s there was large-scale unrest among the people, who called for Somoza's ouster. It was surprising, however, when Catholic Church and business leaders joined with them, all the more so because the opposition was identified with the nation's Communist movement. In an interview with American reporters, a Nicaraguan business leader cleared up the mystery. Business realized, he explained, that a change was inevitable; it was only a matter of when it would come. The longer it was delayed, he added, the stronger would be the people's support for the Communists. If Somoza did not leave soon, the Communists would triumph and business would lose everything. Thus, to protect their interests, they were backing social change before it was too late. They recognized their nation's instability and felt that only social change could possibly produce social stability; however, they wanted limited change over which they would have some control. Thus, when the leftist Sandanistas triumphed, business was given some role in reconstructing the nation.

INSTITUTIONALIZED CHANGE: THE AMERICAN CASE One of the best examples of institutionalized change is the American governmental system. Consider, for example, the electoral process. By law, Americans have the opportunity to change their president and other officials every four years. And not only is change institutionalized, it is even preferred. Just to make sure of it, Americans ratified the Constitution's Twenty-second Amendment in 1951, prohibiting a president from serving more than two full terms.

In *Democracy in America,* Alexis de Tocqueville observed that the American electoral system manages discontent well by holding elections every two or four years: "When elections come only at long intervals, the state risks overthrow each time." For then defeated candidates and the parties they represent have no *institutionalized* way of fighting back. "But if an equal struggle is soon to be renewed, then the defeated are patient" (1969 [1835], p. 202).

American governments have often attempted to guide social change. Perhaps the most outstanding example of this remains the administration of Franklin D. Roosevelt. Roosevelt's election in 1932 came when it looked like the United States had no answer to the Great Depression. The Roosevelt administration, however, immediately embarked on a radically new program. The National Industrial Recovery Act, for instance, allowed businesses to limit production and fix prices, while also setting important labor codes governing wages and hours and guaranteeing the right of collective bargaining (Piven and Cloward 1971, p. 72). Roosevelt also took American currency off the gold standard; established federal relief agencies, public works, and public employment programs; began regulating stock and bond transactions; created the Federal Deposit Insurance Corporation (FDIC) and the Social Security Administration; and much more. More recent examples of governmental attempts to direct social change include civil rights legislation regarding race and sex, the poverty programs of the 1960s, and attempts to change American norms regarding energy consumption.

Later in the chapter, we will see some other examples of governmental attempts to direct social change, but now we're going to look at some sources of unplanned change, starting with technology.

Technology and Social Change

People have long recognized that technological changes are an important source of social change; some sociologists even argue that they are the single most important source. Historians and archaeologists acknowledge the importance of technology by dating prehistoric and early historic periods according to levels of technology: there is the Old Stone Age (Paleolithic period); the New Stone Age (Neolithic period), which differed from the Old Stone Age by the introduction of agriculture and domesticated animals; the Bronze Age; and the Iron Age. We can see how great an impact the introduction of even a single technological device can have on the character of social relationships in the experience of the Yir Yoront aborigines of Australia, described in Social Change and the Steel Axe, pages 356–57.

The simple introduction of steel axes among the Yir Yoront seems to have played a significant role in destroying their society. To be sure, the change benefited certain *individuals:* it liberated women and young people from the autocratic rule of older men, and it increased technological efficiency. At the same time, it destroyed native relationships, based on native traditions, offering Western values in exchange (Christianity, efficiency, and so on), which did not take hold as a *group* ethos. In any case, the Yir Yoront's experience points to the dual impact of cultural "advances" for social organization:

- Technology can be a *liberating* force, allowing increased production, increased leisure time, and often increased freedoms.
- Technology can also be a *controlling* force, by being limited to certain groups (e.g., those who can afford it), giving them distinct advantages over those who do not have access to the technology.

The experience of the Yir Yoront also illustrates that any new technology can have far-reaching consequences unanticipated by those who introduce it. The introduction of oral contraceptives ("the pill"), for instance, which represents an advance in medical technology, has not only facilitated better family planning (the intended result), but has also led to increased rates of marital sex, freed women and men from the risk of pregnancy to a new degree, and enabled women to have active sex lives and still participate in the labor force—none of which were involved in the original impetus for developing oral contraceptives. Or take another example: better communication and transportation technologies have allowed family members to live hundreds of miles apart from each other and still maintain communication, even seeing one another on occasion. This has meant a change in family relationships, residential patterns, and flexibility in accepting employment. Atomic energy is another case in point. The threat of nuclear war and its attendant global annihilation altered the living patterns of many Americans in the 1950s. People participated in regular air raid drills and built "fallout shelters" in their basements or backyards, stocked with food and water, in hopes of surviving a nuclear war. Even the peaceful uses of

Will the next presidential portrait be done by a computer? Computers are a relatively recent technological advance, with impact on all levels of industry, banking, research, and even the production of cultural artifacts.

atomic energy have had unanticipated results: its potential for catastrophe has spawned new government agencies and an international social movement to protest its use.

We can also speak of technological revolutions in the modern age, when technological changes come so rapidly that their impact on social patterns is revolutionary. The most well known of these, of course, is the Industrial Revolution—the transformation of largely agricultural societies into industrial societies based on a shift from reliance on human and animal strength to machine power. In preceding chapters we discussed some of the many social changes wrought by this change in

the mode of production. Some people believe that the next great technological revolution will be in the field of *informatics* (the technology of processing information). Not only are we creating more complex computers, which can perform more tasks and store more information, but certain kinds of computers are becoming more accessible to the public. However, the largest and most advanced computers tend to be the property of the most powerful and wealthiest organizations in the society because of the high cost of acquiring and maintaining them. This gives these groups a great deal of additional power, as well as an advantage over potential competitors. This fact—and, indeed, the Industrial Rev-

SOCIAL CHANGE AND THE STEEL AXE

Living at the mouth of the Coleman River in northeastern
Australia, the Yir Yoront, like other Australian aborigines, had
no knowledge of metals before their extensive contact with
whites early in this century. Technologically, they lived in
Paleolithic times. Early observers of the tribe noted a group
with a well-developed social structure and belief system. But
when anthropologist Lauriston Sharp (1952) visited the Yir
Yoront in the 1930s, he found a profoundly anomic group,
whose relationships and beliefs had become confused.
Moreover, the elderly, formerly accorded the highest prestige,
were neglected and even mocked, and women were no longer
subject to their male relatives' every whim. The culprit,
according to Sharp: the steel axe, introduced by Europeans to
replace the natives' own stone axes. How could such a simple
change have such a profound effect on Yir Yoront society?

The Yir Yoront used their stone axes to accomplish a
number of vital tasks: hunting, fishing, and gathering; warding
off enemies; building campfires that protected them against
cold and mosquitoes, and special huts that would keep them
dry in the rainy season; and for many other purposes. Now,
anyone—man, woman, or child—could *use* an axe, but only
adult males could *own* one. The skills needed to make an axe—
knowing where the resources were, storing and shaping the
wood and stone—were not considered appropriate for women.
Beyond that, the necessary stone could only be obtained
through "trading partners" in distant tribes, whose Yir Yoront
contacts were primarily older men. In sum, only men could
speak of "my axe," and women and young people needed an
older man's permission if they wanted to use one.

Social relationships revolved around control of the stone
axe, which was an important symbol of masculinity in the
tribe, legitimating the adult male's dominance (Sharp 1952, p.
19). The axe was also associated with the tribe's most
important rituals and beliefs.

The white settlers, however, particularly, the whites who ran the mission, believed that replacing stone axes with steel ones would simply be a boon to "progress" among the Yir Yoront. Unaware of the complexities of Yir Yoront society, they could hardly anticipate the consequences of the technological change they introduced.

The whites gave away steel axes indiscriminately. A person might receive one by chance or at a festival, as payment for an odd job done at the mission, or by impressing the missionaries with outstanding qualities. In other words, the process for obtaining a steel axe was ill-defined, as compared with the rigidly defined behaviors involved in obtaining a stone one. This meant that a person no longer had to defer to older men, who could withhold their stone axes if they were displeased. The Yir Yoront received steel axes in tremendous quantity— often distributed directly to women and children who could now speak of "my axe." "All this," writes Sharp (1952, p. 20), "led to a revolutionary confusion of sex, age, and kinship roles, with a major gain in independence and loss of subordination on the part of those who now owned steel axes." Actually, social control passed from the adult male Yir Yoront to the white society.

Traditional Yir Yoront beliefs crumbled at a rapid rate, along with the group's social organization, built as it was around the ownership of the now superfluous stone axes. Yir Yoront festivals, previously revolving around the stone axe, were no longer any fun, and they attracted fewer and fewer people. The social ideology collapsed; stealing and trespassing, formerly unknown among the Yir Yoront, began to occur, and the group scattered. On one visit, Sharp was struck by the discovery that the older men were stealing his toothpaste. Ignored and ridiculed, they were attempting in vain to restore their lost prestige through a new "toothpaste cult" revolving around this European product.

olution as a whole—points out the tendency toward centralization of power that has also resulted from modern technological advances (Bonnot 1980).

Technological changes are often presented as if they are blind forces over which we have no control and as if they provide us with the solutions to all our problems. But in recent years, many people have begun to recognize the limits of technology. Iran, for instance, has rejected aspects of Western technology introduced by the Shah as being incompatible with Islamic society. More dramatically, the Khmer Rouge in Kampuchea (Cambodia) attempted to obliterate all influences of Western industrialization from their country.

Furthermore, many analysts have begun to recognize that technological developments, if used indiscriminately, can have disastrous social and ecological results. For over a generation, third world nations have been receiving technology from the industrialized nations, much of which has not fit their environmental and social conditions. The nation of Mozambique, for example, ordered several tractors to increase its agricultural production; but its African jungle soil was far too thin for the heavy machines. The tractors proved to be more damaging than useful. The Indian government's attempt at rapid development of the Himalayan foothill region has also had some disastrous consequences. The rapid development and deforestation has left the area liable to flash floods, which can destroy entire villages and cause extensive soil erosion. So the area now has poor soil for farming and an acute shortage of water, which has led to greater poverty among many of the region's residents (Kalapesi 1978).

And even in the United States, we have found that new technology cannot solve all our problems. In response to the current energy crisis, many people now propose solutions requiring less rather than more complex technology: energy from plants, from animal waste, from wind and solar power, and so on. That is, they are proposing a technological change, but one requiring that we reinstitute old technologies instead of developing newer and more complex ones, which may have adverse consequences we cannot control. Gerard Bonnot (1980), a French journalist, has written of a growing disillusionment in the United States and Europe with technological solutions to social problems. But he believes that technological change is progressing nevertheless. The crucial question facing us, he writes, is who will ultimately control that technology—and thereby guide our future social change.

Population and Social Change

Another major source of social change is population change. We'll begin by reviewing the major population processes and population theories and then use them to examine the contemporary social issues of food shortage and birth control. Table 11.2 notes the relationship between population and some other social issues. We will also look for technology's role in order to see how the sources of social change are themselves intertwined with one another. For example, advances in medical technology have greatly increased our life spans, contributing in recent years to concern over the problems of the elderly in developed nations and overpopulation in the developing world.

The scientific study of population is called **demography** and its practitioners,

Table 11.2 Population and Social Problems

Problem	Population's Impact
Housing shortages Energy shortages Hunger Overcrowding Unemployment	Demand is outstripping supply
Illiteracy	Population is rising faster than educational institutions can be built or staffed
Pollution	Concentration of people and industry in smaller areas
Inflation	Greater numbers of people and greater demand drive prices up
Political conflict	Intensifies as more people struggle for limited resources
Endangered wildlife	More and more species are pushed out of their habitats to make way for expanding human population

SOURCE: L. Brown, K. Newland, and B. Stokes, "Twenty-two Aspects of the Population Problem," The Futurist 10 (1976).

demographers. Demographers seek the social reasons for population patterns as well as the impact of these patterns on society. The particular impact of population on social change comes through the three "population processes" of fertility, mortality, and migration.

THE MEANING OF FERTILITY, MORTALITY, AND MIGRATION **Fertility** refers to the number of children being born to a specific population of women. It is often expressed in terms of the **birth rate**, or the annual number of births per 1,000 population (male and female). Several factors may influence fertility. Whether or not we are biologically capable is one, but there are nonbiological factors as well. Fertility has declined in the West, as more women have begun marrying later and working outside the home, for example. Also, increasing divorce lowers the birth rate, as do times of depression, either because people feel they cannot afford the expense of children or because of worry over the uncertain future. Finally, the use of contraceptives and legalization of abortion lower fertility.

Both biological and social factors likewise play a role in the **mortality rate**, or the annual number of deaths in a given population, usually expressed per 1,000 population. Biologically, the human body can only last so long (the oldest *authenticated* span of a human's life is 114 years, although claims have been higher [Weeks 1978, p. 106]). But we know that social factors also influence life spans. For instance, on the average, people live twice as long in the United States as they do in Bangladesh, and, in general, the mortality rate is much lower in industrialized nations than in the developing world. Even within societies, there are variations. People aged sixty-five and over or who are less than one year old have the highest mortality rates, and in the United States, whites live longer than blacks (Weeks 1978, pp. 109–17). Finally, women live longer than men. Some of the factors that explain these differences are less access to physicians and less nutritious diet among the poor, more primitive medical technology in third world countries, and greater stress and greater danger from accidents and homicide for men.

The third population process, **migration,** involves a permanent change of residence. We briefly discussed *international migration* in Chapter 8, when we looked at immigration to the United States. But many people also migrate within societies (*internal migration*)—in search of a better job, for example. But more than a physical change, migration generally means the detachment of individuals from one social system and their engagement in another. International migration involves learning a new language, new customs and norms, different political institutions, and so on. Even migrants who do not cross national boundaries, however, must learn new ways of life. Finally, we must remember that migration is a two-way process; it involves leaving a society or segment of one (emigration) as well as entering another (immigration).

Although historically most population change has not been the result of attempts at purposive social change, societies have tried to exert some control over all three population processes. For example, fertility has been affected by official policies toward birth control; the mortality rate has been lowered by medical technology, often developed through government-funded research or distributed through governments; and governments have often set legal obstacles in the paths of those who wish to migrate. The Soviet Union, for example, limits emigration by refusing exit visas and harassing political emigrants, and the United States limits immigration through quotas. Neither the United States nor the Soviet Union, however, is alone in these restrictive practices. But even if the processes of population change can sometimes be controlled, their impact remains largely uncontrollable.

PERSPECTIVES ON POPULATION For more than two centuries, population theorists have attempted to explain why population grows as it does, as well as its effects on social life. Specifically, theorists, governments, and citizens in general have been concerned with population growth, what it means, and what should be done about it. Debate on these issues has been dominated by the views of Thomas Malthus and Karl Marx, whose opposing ideas are still influential today.

THE MALTHUSIAN VIEW Malthus's *Essay on the Principle of Population* (1798) is the first systematic work on population and, more specifically, on the dangers of overpopulation. His conclusion is that, if no special factors intervene, the human population would increase geometrically (2, 4, 8, 16, 32, 64, 128) every twenty-five years, while the food supply would only grow arithmetically (1, 2, 3, 4, 5, 6, 7).

In 1980 the Cuban government allowed all its citizens who wished to emigrate to the United States. Both nations tried to use the situation to enhance their own prestige: the U.S. by pointing up its "humanitarian" policy and the discontent of many Cubans; Cuba by pointing out the "hypocrisy" of the U.S. policy and meanwhile ridding itself of malcontents. Over 100,000 Cubans came to the United States.

Eventually, this progression would reach a limit, people would starve, the death rate would rise to bring food and population into balance, and the progression would begin anew.

But Malthus was quite aware that "special factors"—war, for example—do intervene. Furthermore: "Sickly seasons, epidemics, pestilence, and plague advance in terrific arrays, and sweep off their thousands and ten thousands . . . gigantic inevitable famine stalks in the rear, and with one mighty blow, levels the population with the food of the world" (1976 [1798], p. 56).

He calls these disasters *positive checks*—positive because they are "divinely ordained" to avert the greater disaster of overpopulation. Malthus was reacting to a vast increase in the number of English poor and to the institutionalization of poor relief, which, he suggests, would undermine one of the positive checks on overpopulation. But, in fact, that increase was largely the result of early industrialization and a massive uprooting of agricultural workers, and not the result of an increase in births (Piven and Cloward 1971, pp. 17–21).

For Malthus, the only feasible way to avoid overpopulation was through the *preventive check* of limiting births. And, at the time, and especially for a clergyman, which Malthus was, the only moral way to limit births was not to have intercourse. His solution was simple, although he doubted that it would be carried out: avoid conception by abstaining from intercourse until the child that might come could be supported. Effectively, this would make sex and reproduction privileges of the wealthy. This argument won over a number of individuals and nineteenth-century governments. Austria and Germany, for instance, refused to grant the necessary permit for marriage unless the applicant had some regular means of support. The unintended result of this restriction on marriage, however, was more illegitimate children (Knodel 1970).

Today, writers about population who share Malthus's gloomy prediction about population growth are known as *neo-Malthusians*. Probably the most famous neo-Malthusian is Paul Ehrlich who, in his book *The Population Bomb* (1968), envisions a future of world war and massive famine as a result of overpopulation. If anything, the picture he paints is more pessimistic than Malthus's. But he parts company with Malthus over the method for controlling population growth. Neo-Malthusians vigorously advocate all methods of birth control, as opposed to Malthus's exclusive reliance on "moral restraint."

THE MARXIAN VIEW   Marx called the *Essay on Population* "schoolboyish" and attributes its success "solely to party interest" (Marx 1906 [1867], p. 675). Confronted with social unrest among the poor and the spread of revolutionary ideas from France,

capitalists and the nobility used Malthus to justify their control of the poor, according to Marx. Marx never did formulate a counter theory of population growth to Malthus's, but he argues that the real issue is not overpopulation as such, but the inability of capitalism to distribute commodities to those who need them. He believes that because labor is the source of value, more people should mean more wealth, not a critical shortage. The problem of "overpopulation" lies with capitalism, not the breeding habits of the poor. It is, in fact, in the interests of the capitalist class, Marx argues, to keep a segment of the working class poor and unemployed in order to keep wages down. At that time in England, for example, there was enough wealth to support all the people adequately, but the nation's capitalist economy funneled most of it to a small group of people: "It is capitalistic accumulation itself that constantly produces . . . a surplus-population" (Marx 1906 [1867], p. 691).

Marx's attack on capitalism as the creator of a population problem implies that socialist societies would not have these problems. Contemporary Marxists, however, while they accept the link between population growth and economic conditions, do not always agree that a socialist society brings an end to all population problems. The Chinese, for example, in facing the realities of making their socialist society work, have instituted programs to limit family size. Besides encouraging female employment and late marriages, they have made many forms of birth control, including sterilization and abortion, easily available (Tien 1973). Even under socialism, then, too many people can be a problem.

Malthus and Marx provided a background for all population studies that fol-

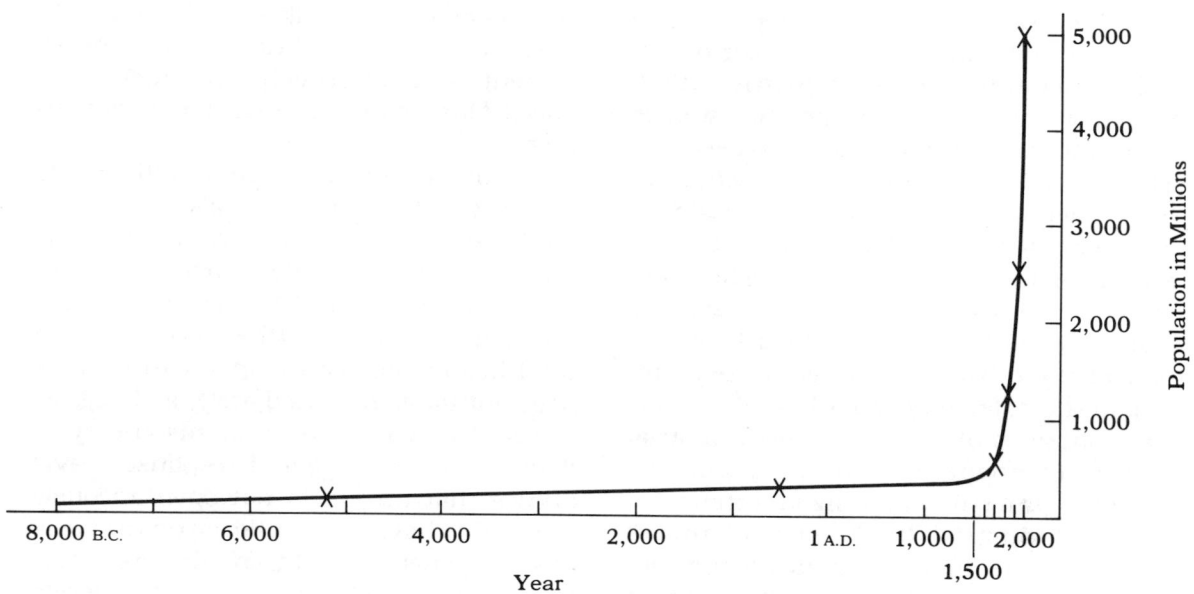

Figure 11.3 The World's Booming Population Growth ("X"s indicate *doubling time.*)

lowed them, and their views reflect opposing views of population problems and policy. Even so, their work on population was not very scientific, and we now must turn to the view offered by modern demographers.

THE THEORY OF THE DEMOGRAPHIC TRANSITION Since it was first formulated in 1929, the *demographic transition theory* has dominated the scientific study of population. This theory attempts to explain the relationship between actual population trends and the changing social and economic conditions associated with industrialization. It begins with the observation that *natural increase* alone—that is, the difference between total births and total deaths—does not explain population growth. We also have to consider fertility and mortality rates; actually, then, the crit-

ical demographic transition is one from high birth and death rates to low ones.

With all the talk in recent years about a world population explosion, it may be hard to imagine that most of human history has been characterized by high rates of mortality and slow (or nonexistent) population growth. From 8000 B.C. to A.D. 1, the population grew at a rate that doubled its size (*doubling time*) every 1,530 years. From then until the beginning of the industrial revolution (about 1750), the doubling time was 1,240 years. Then, population growth began to accelerate, and it reached a doubling time by 1950 of only 122 years. Now, the doubling time is a mere 37 years (see Figure 11.3).

Population growth was slow in preindustrial times because death rates were high. Not only did youth and adults often die in plagues and other calamities, but the

infant mortality rate, the proportion of newborns who die in the first year of life, was consistently high. Philippe Ariès (1962) tells us that the general practice was to have "several children in order to keep just a few . . . . In *Le Caquet de l'accouchee,* we have a neighbor standing at the bedside of a woman who has just given birth, the mother of 'five brats,' and calming her fears with these words: 'Before they are old enough to bother you, you will have lost half of them, or perhaps all of them" (p. 38). In short, fertility had to be high to overcome high mortality. The preindustrial pattern of population growth, then, was one of high fertility and high mortality.

The Industrial Revolution inaugurated a new pattern, as more sanitary living conditions (e.g., better housing, cleaner food and water) and, later, vaccinations and other products of improved medical technology, substantially reduced mortality. Initially, birth rates remained high despite lower mortality. The population pattern of this stage, then, was one of high fertility and low mortality, producing a population explosion. Eventually, however, birth rates also declined, giving us the third pattern of population growth: low fertility and mortality.

The explanation of these changing population patterns is thus a functional one: lower death rates are a function of advanced technology, economic prosperity, and social development; birth rates then go down as a function of the drop in mortality. This theory contains some truth, but there is much that it doesn't explain. For example, population did not begin declining in the most industrialized nation in Europe (Britain) first, but in France. Again, the Moslem population of the Soviet Union, compared with other Moslem populations, has a very high level of education and social development, yet fertility is also high. In other words, factors besides social development, such as the cultural values of the Soviet Moslems in our example, affect fertility.

Another problem with the theory is that it ignores the individual's role in population changes. Yet only that role explains the middle pattern (high birth rates, low death rates). For individuals must notice the altered situation (the lowered death rate) before they can respond to it. This does not happen immediately, as Kingsley Davis (1963) recognizes in his theory of demographic change and response. Davis argues that people do not spontaneously "decide" to have fewer children on the basis of some general social trend (lowered mortality). Such decisions are more concrete and affected by personal interests. For instance, we might begin to notice the economic burden of too many children in someone else's house. Seeing for ourselves the possibility of economic prosperity (the most powerful incentive for keeping births down, according to Davis), we vow not to make the same "mistake." Hence, declining birth rates accompany economic development.

To sum up the perspectives on population, we have two general philosophical or ideological views. The Malthusian view predicts disaster because of continued population growth. The other view, associated with Marx, links the impact of population growth to social organization and the distribution of resources. We also have two scientific theories of population growth. The demographic transition theory explains population change in terms of social changes associated with the Industrial Revolution. To that, Davis adds a symbolic interactionist perspective, seeking out the everyday interpretations made by individuals that determine their actual response to changed conditions. Now, we should be ready to *use* what we have been reading to see some of the ways in which demographic change is related to social change.

POPULATION AND FOOD SUPPLY: WAS MALTHUS RIGHT?

As we look around, we find that the most severe food shortages are in those areas with very high birth rates—Africa, Asia (excluding the Soviet Union, Japan, and Israel), and Latin America. Does that mean that Malthus was right? The answer is yes if we are dealing with a limited amount of food and significant increases in the number of people. But in the foreseeable future the answer is no. There are many other factors besides fertility that contribute to world hunger. For instance, a massive famine that swept rural Russia in the early 1890s was fueled in part by a complex set of laws that kept peasants from leaving their unproductive farms and migrating to other areas (Robbins 1975, p. 6). Today, we actually have the productive capacity to feed everyone, yet 400 million people are currently starving, and millions more are inadequately fed. The problem is one of lopsided distribution. Evenly distributing the food now available to those who need it is hampered by social institutions, customs, and other social elements. For instance, the division of the world's peoples into nations allows us to ignore the well-being of many others in figuring our own interests. So there are actually two separate issues here: food shortages (see Can the Earth Grow More Food?) and food distribution.

It may be somewhat misleading to say that there is a *world* food shortage, because many people have plenty to eat. It is accurate, however, to say that there are drastic shortages in many parts of the world. Africa, for instance, is considered by some to be the most food-deficient continent. Much of it is desert or near-desert, and the rest contains soil without nutrients essential to sustain production. Only Australia has less arable land, but its population is so small that it actually exports grain. Starvation is also common in much of Asia, where a bad harvest or serious crop failure can take millions of lives.

The problem is serious and getting worse. Various solutions have been proposed, some of which see the answer in altering the relationship between a given population and its food supply (reduce the number of people and births; increase agricultural productivity), while others see the solution in more equitable worldwide distribution. In order to evaluate them, however, we must understand the causes of the problem.

Most simply, the problem is one of too many people for the amount of food readily or practically available. One reason for this gap is that warfare and environmental conditions in some third world countries have hampered agricultural production. But the most important source of the present crisis involves the relationship between fertility and mortality. Quite simply, mortality has been dramatically curbed while fertility has remained high in many areas. The Institute of Ecology has identified the logic of the situation:

Technological advances have made possible a tremendous increase in our ability to combat disease, to control our immediate environment and to produce food and other natural materials. Such gains may be used either to increase the

CAN THE EARTH GROW MORE FOOD?

To increase our food supply, we either have to find more acres to farm or increase our crop yield per acre. This is, in part, a technological problem. With the proper technology, we could clear African and South American jungles, drain swamps, irrigate deserts, and obtain up to 75 million acres more farmland in the United States alone—all at a reasonable cost. *Aquaculture*—"farming" the sea for seaweed and algae and managing fish ponds—could also bear rich harvests. And modern technology could increase crop yields in sub-Sahara Africa and elsewhere where people still farm with primitive technology. Why don't we simply apply the technology, then?

There are other problems. Even if the cost of reclaiming those 75 million American acres for farming is reasonable, the rising energy costs of farming them would exceed their possible crop yield because of the soil's poor qualtiy (Pimentel et al. 1976). Furthermore, we have recently seen how the agricultural technology that has been so successful in Europe and North America can be disastrous elsewhere, in Africa and India, for example. And while aquaculture had seemed a solution to world food shortages in the 1960s, subsequent study has cast considerable doubt on that hope.

There are political problems, too. Cities cover many potential acres of farmland in the United States and

welfare of existing individuals or to provide for . . . an added number of people. Insofar as population growth has lagged behind technological growth, at least in some areas of the world, the well-being of individuals has improved. However, in the world as a whole, population growth has consumed the majority of gains. (1971, p. 14)

Since World War II, medical technology has lowered mortality rates significantly, with dramatic strides in the developing nations. In some of these countries, life expectancy is now comparable to that of the industrialized West. A newborn female in Thailand or Malaysia, for example, can expect to live over sixty years (Weeks 1978, p. 128). The major reason for the mortality rate decline has been the control of communicable diseases—which was the reason for Europe's drop in the nineteenth and early twentieth centuries. However, today's decline has been much faster. To take one example, life expectancy in Mexico dur-

metropolitan areas are expanding. There are now 32 million farmable acres just under highways. It would take a massive social movement to tear up those highways, disrupting services and life styles. Environmentalists have objected to the wholesale disappearance of jungles and their unique resources. And, finally, there is the division of the world into independent nations. Australians and North Americans, for instance, are not likely to make heroic, self-sacrificing efforts for people starving in remote corners of the world when they themselves are satisfied.

There has been some success in increasing yields with the introduction of so-called "high yield varieties" of wheat and rice, developed through plant breeding. In India, for example, wheat production rose from 11 million to 27 million tons between 1965 and 1968 (Brown 1973). The high yield varieties alone, however, have not been able to satisfy the growing demand for food in most third world countries.

In short, we might have the technological capacity to significantly increase the worldwide supply of food; however, a number of obstacles block its implementation (specifically, doing so would serve the interests of some people while harming those of others). This means that hopes for solving the global food shortage lie in curtailing population growth—which, we shall see, entails a number of other problems—rather than increasing the amount of food.

ing the 1920s was lower than it was in Europe during the Middle Ages. Today, however, life expectancy in Mexico and Europe is nearly the same. Mexico covered the same territory in mortality control as Europe did, but in one-tenth the time.

While Europeans had to wait for economic development and the discoveries that made gigantic medical advances possible, today's developing nations can relatively cheaply import the technology and knowledge of preventative medicine, often in the form of aid. Sri Lanka's death rate

dropped 40 percent in only one year, when insecticides were used to combat malaria. Unfortunately, though, programs for controlling fertility cannot be instituted as cheaply and as simply as mortality control. Another culture's values and norms cannot be imported like so many commodities. And norms for limiting family size have not emerged in most countries. At one point, India's government got so frustrated that it enforced the sterilization of civil servants who had many children. Even in those countries where mortality remains high, fertility levels ensure fast population growth.

Because of these changes in mortality rates, an estimated 90 percent of the population increase to the year 2000 will come from less-developed nations (Coale 1974, p. 51). To compound the problem, many of these countries are already overcrowded: Indonesia, with the world's fifth largest population, has less than one-sixth the area that the United States has; and although Bangladesh is the eighth largest nation in population, it is smaller in size than New York State (also see Figure 11.4).

In the face of this phenomenal growth, however, there are signs of fertility decline in some small island nations as well as in some larger countries in the developing world. This might signify the first response to a demographic change (lower mortality). But significant changes resulting in population stability or decline are not going to come for many years, and by that time the effects of overpopulation on social life will have long since become disastrous. For this reason, many governments and individuals have decided to intervene and attempt to curb the birth rate through private programs and government policy.

POPULATION POLICY When a government takes steps specifically designed to affect population growth, and does so on a continuing basis, we say it has a **population policy.** When effective, population policies give governments considerable impact on individual and family decisions. For example, whether or not the government makes contraceptive devices freely available will probably alter a population's sex life materially. In fact, the most obvious element of a population policy involves legislation and other actions on contraception and abortion, that is, on birth control.

Not everyone agrees that governments should have population policies. Some feel that governments have no right to interfere in family decisions. Whether right or not, however, the fact is that an increasing number of governments have developed population policies aimed at curbing the birth rate. In 1978, the United Nations Fund for Population Activities reported: "It is noteworthy that only 8 of the 114 developing countries surveyed by the UN restrict access to modern methods of fertility regulation. Eighty-two developing countries provide either direct or indirect support to regulation efforts" (Salas 1978, p. 18). However, there are still countries, such as Burma and Saudi Arabia, where you would have a difficult time obtaining contraceptives. Some other countries pay lip service to the principle of population control but do not actively pursue it. And, on the other hand, the Brazilian government, for one, feels it needs population growth "to occupy the sparsely inhabited north and west regions; to create a strong international market for trade and industry; and to meet the minimum population requirement to become a major world power" (Nortman 1975, p. 28). But the number of developing nations actively opposing birth control is small.

Attempts at direct and harsh methods of birth control have met with considerable popular resistance where they have been tried. For example, the Austrians and Germans, who tried to implement a Malthusian policy, only changed the legal status of the children born, not their numbers; and the Indian government's sterilization program helped to defeat that government. Thus most countries have used indirect

Putting Population on the Map Sizes represent 1977 populations (figures in millions), World population: 4.1 bn

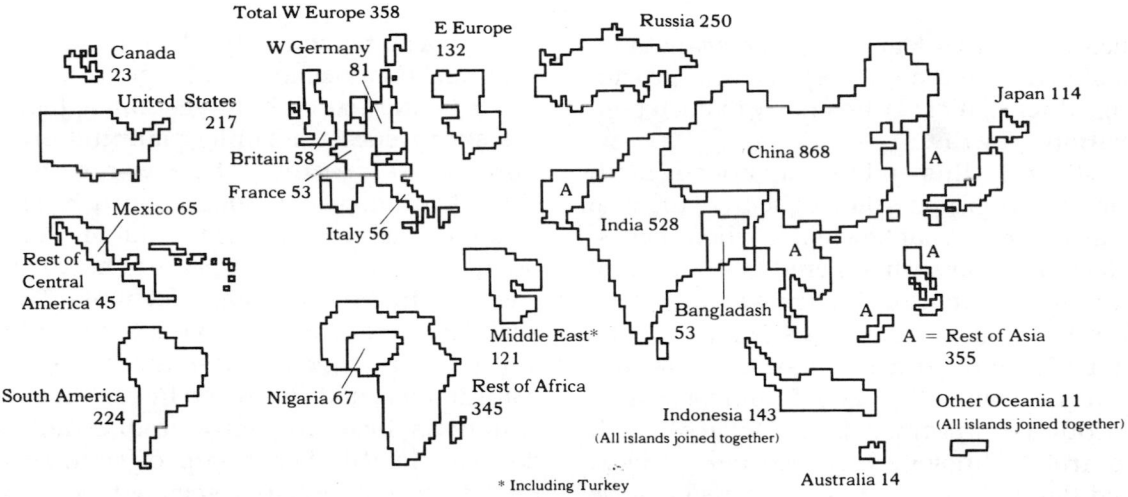

SOURCE: The Economist, 10–16 February 1979, p. 39. Reprinted by permission.

The World's Nations in Order of Their Population Size

1. China	34. Afghanistan	66. Sweden	99. Israel
2. India	35. Morocco	67. Syria	100. Jordan
3. USSR	36. Algeria	68. Ecuador	101. Laos
4. USA	37. East Germany	69. Zimbabwe	102. Lebanon
5. Indonesia	38. Nationalist China	70. Switzerland	103. New Zealand
6. Japan	(Taiwan)	71. Cameroon	104. Papua New Guinea
7. Brazil	39. North Korea	72. Yemen	105. Paraguay
8. Bangladesh	40. Sudan	73. Angola	106. Puerto Rico
9. Pakistan	41. Peru	74. Polovia	107. Sierra Leone
10. Nigeria	42. Tanzania	75. Guatemala	108. Somalia
11. Mexico	43. Czechoslovakia	76. Mali	109. Uruguay
12. West Germany	44. Sri Lanka	77. Tunisia	110. Central African Empire
13. Italy	45. Kenya	78. Upper Volta	111. Costa Rica
14. United Kingdom	46. Netherlands	79. Denmark	112. Liberia
15. France	47. Australia	80. Dominican Republic	113. Libya
16. Vietnam	48. Nepal	81. Finland	114. Nicaragua
17. Philippines	49. Venezuela	82. Guinea	115. Panama
18. Thailand	50. Malaysia	83. Haiti	116. Togo
19. Turkey	51. Uganda	84. Ivory Coast	117. Botswana
20. Egypt	52. Iraq	85. Malawi	118. Congo
21. Spain	53. Hungary	86. Niger	119. Gabon
22. South Korea	54. Chile	87. Senegal	120. Gambia
23. Poland	55. Ghana	88. Zambia	121. Guyana
24. Iran	56. Belgium	89. Burundi	122. Kuwait
25. Burma	57. Cuba	90. Chad	123. Mauritania
26. Ethiopia	58. Portugal	91. El Salvador	124. Bhutan
27. South Africa	59. Bulgaria	92. Hong Kong	125. Mauritius
28. Argentina	60. Greece	93. Norway	126. Timor
29. Zaire	61. Mozambique	94. Rwanda	127. Iceland
30. Columbia	62. Saudi Arabia	95. Albania	128. Greenland
31. Canada	63. Austria	96. Benin	129. Spanish Sahara
32. Yugoslavia	64. Kampuchea (Cambodia)	97. Honduras	130. Namibia
33. Romania	65. Madagascar	98. Ireland	131. Mongolia

Figure 11.4 National Areas in Proportion to Population Size

SOURCE: John R. Weeks, Population: An Introduction to Concepts and Issues (Belmont, CA: Wadsworth Publishing Company, 1978). Reprinted by permission.

means such as legislating the availability of abortion and contraception and providing education programs to try to curb population growth.

Despite this indirect approach, birth control programs still frequently run into a number of roadblocks. In some cases, efforts have been hampered by traditional beliefs and emotions. They may fly in the face of religious traditions (e.g., Catholic and Moslem); and some people may feel that the availability of birth control devices encourages promiscuity. Modern birth control technology can also be complex, and family planning programs also involve distributing information about that technology—specifically where to obtain it and how to use it, as well as general information about contraceptives, abortion, and sterilization. These activities require trained personnel, who are not always available in large numbers. Finally, and perhaps most importantly, family planning workers in almost every society have to contend with strong *pronatalist* pressures, that make having children—sometimes many children—normative and discourage childlessness. Even in the United States, childless couples are often asked by relatives if "something is wrong" with the marriage, since there are no children. More critical for our discussion, however, are the pronatalist pressures in third world nations, which have frustrated family planning there. The Yoruba of Nigeria, for instance, still find families with less than four children "horrifying" (Ware 1975). In Arabic North Africa, having many children still signifies being a "manly" father. And in rural India, women can only gain any status in their communities by bearing many children: "For all but a relatively few, a woman's destiny lies in her procreation; the mark of her

success as a person is her living, thriving children" (Mandelbaum 1974, p. 16).

It is still too early to accurately judge the effectiveness of family planning on a world scale. It seems to have worked best (e.g., Taiwan, Hong Kong, South Korea) where it has accompanied social and economic development. It appears to have lowered fertility in Guatemala, Colombia, Turkey, and some other countries, but fertility still remains high in these areas. Family planning has had almost no impact in other nations, including Kenya, India, and Indonesia. In this last group of countries, neither government nor society has really actively supported these efforts (Caldwell 1975). One of the success stories of birth control appears to be that of the People's Republic of China. The socialist restructuring of Chinese society has drastically reshaped sex roles, putting men and women on a more equal footing, thus allowing women other sources of social respect than only that of bearing and caring for children. People are expected to delay marriage and parenthood to further their education and work in service to the people; and official and unofficial sources apply a great deal of social pressure to limit births (Sidel 1972). Together with the spread of contraceptives and the intensive economic development that has taken place in China in the past three decades, these policies have significantly reduced China's population growth.

As world population continues to increase, population policy and the politics of food distribution are likely to become almost every government's central concern. In the end, no people that does not limit population growth will be able to escape eventual catastrophe.

The relationship between population

and food, as we have seen, revolves mainly around the population processes of fertility and mortality. Urbanization, the last major source of social change we will consider in this chapter, on the other hand, focuses on migration.

Urbanization

Urbanization—the general movement of people from rural to urban areas—has become a worldwide phenomenon. Whereas less than 3 percent of the world's population lived in cities in 1800, more than 40 percent do so today. It is projected that by 1990, the majority of the world's population will live in cities of 100,000 people or more. This shift in the concentration of population is due almost exclusively to migration and not natural increase. In this section, we are going to look at the process of urbanization and related population movements, concentrating primarily on the United States. Then, we'll look at the impact of urbanization on social change.

THE GROWTH OF AMERICAN CITIES
With about three-fourths of the American population living in urban areas today, it is difficult to imagine that before 1914 most Americans were rural dwellers. It is even more difficult to imagine a United States with only five percent of its population urban residents, but that was what the first census found in 1790. America's urbanization proceeded apace with industrialization, starting out slowly and then accelerating rapidly after the Civil War (see Figure 11.5).

Although American industry began developing from the start of the new nation, the frontier—whether the Ohio River Valley, the Mississippi, or California—offered more opportunity for earning a living than did the fledgling industries located in the cities of the East. By the Civil War's outbreak, only one of every five Americans lived in a city.

But in the decades following the war a combination of factors led to a tremendous growth of the cities. In the South, slavery ended and the rural economy was in shambles. Furthermore, new developments in agricultural technology made it possible for fewer laborers to produce the same amount. Agricultural workers in Europe and the United States were thus forced off the land, and many migrated to the cities of America. They were attracted by the promise of jobs in now rapidly expanding industries, mostly in the northeastern and north central states. Some of those uprooted, it is true, didn't migrate to the cities but moved further west to try their hand at farming, but by the end of the century, this opportunity had narrowed considerably, for much of the free land available under the Homestead Act had been already claimed. And ranchers, railroad and oil magnates, and others had bought many other acres of land.

Rural to urban migration continued in the twentieth century. Particularly significant was the migration of extensive numbers of blacks from the rural South to the cities of the North, beginning about 1910 and lasting until quite recently. Between 1940 and 1960 alone, over 3 million more blacks migrated from South to North, than from North to South (Kerner Commission 1968, p. 240).

Even though the city offers its citizens such unique benefits as varied job oppor-

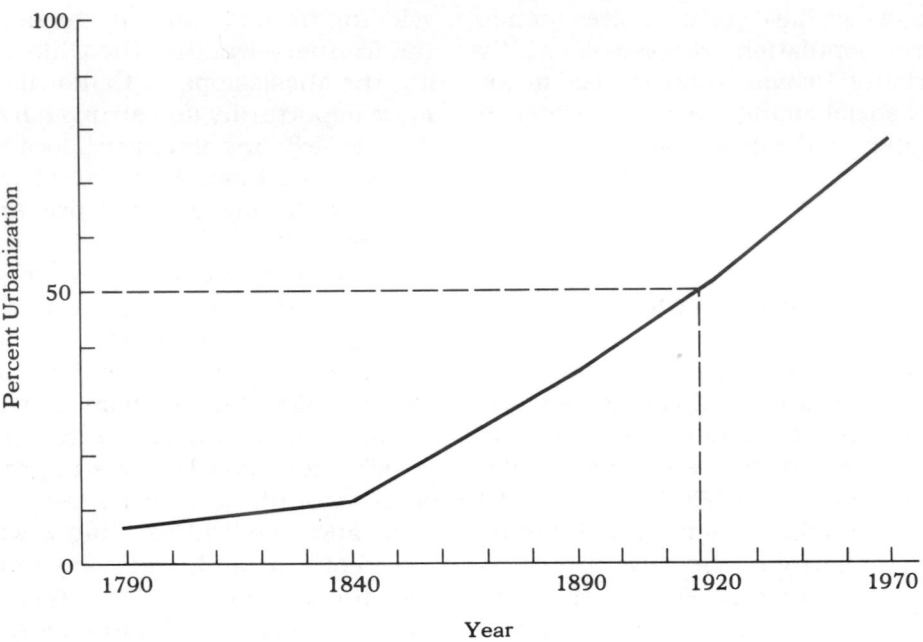

Figure 11.5   Urbanization of the United States, 1790–1970

SOURCE: U.S. Department of Commerce, Statistical Abstract of the United States,
1979 (Washington, DC: Government Printing Office, 1979, p. 28).

tunities, cultural facilities, multiple educational opportunities, social welfare, interaction with a broad spectrum of people, and so on, in recent years we have witnessed an extensive migration away from city centers to suburbia. Before examining the influence of urbanization on social change, we should briefly review this trend.

SUBURBANIZATION   *Suburbs*—communities located near central cities—are not new, but their current popularity is. So many people have moved from city to suburb in recent decades that by 1970 more Americans were living in big city suburbs than in the cities themselves. Migration

has been extensive enough to cause analysts to develop a new demographic category: the *metropolitan area* or, more technically, the **Standard Metropolitan Statistical Area (SMSA)**. The SMSA includes both the city proper and the surrounding area which, because of economic and other ties (e.g., jobs, commercial centers), can be considered part of the same unit as the city. SMSAs even cross state lines: both the New York and Philadelphia SMSAs include parts of New Jersey, and the Chicago SMSA extends into Indiana. The need for this new category signifies the suburb's prominence. Paradoxically, the SMSA also signifies that the influence of cities is extended as people move into areas

Whether American cities are dying or experiencing a rebirth depends on whether we see in them unique cultural, economic, and interactional possibilities—or crime, pollution, poverty, and poor schools.

around them. The high tide of suburbanization in the United States occurred between 1950 and 1970, but the migration
now appears to have peaked.

URBANIZATION AND SOCIAL CHANGE

The influences of urbanization on social
life and social organization have been many
and far-reaching. Let's look first at the impact of the suburbanization movement on
social life in the central city and then at
the more general impact of urbanization.

Many city-to-suburb migrants have
been from the middle and upper-middle
classes. Their migration has meant a
crumbling "tax base" for the central cities.
The suburbanites continue to use the city
by day, commuting to their jobs, but leave
its financial support to the relatively poorer
people who remain in the city. The continued need for city maintenance and public
services (e.g., police, firefighters, road re-
pair) coupled with the decline in revenues
because of the flight of higher income
groups has severely strained many city
budgets. Eventually, more cities might follow Cleveland, Ohio, which in 1979 became
the first American city to default on its
loans since the Great Depression.

At the same time, suburbanization has
helped blacks gain control of the political
machinery in a number of large cities. The
fact that the migrants to the suburbs have
been disproportionately white has left a
concentration of blacks in the central cities.
(In 1970, according to the U.S. Census, 40
percent of the country's whites lived in suburbs, while only 16 percent of its blacks
did.) Blacks as a result have been able to
gain more political power. There are black
mayors in major cities, black-led city councils, blacks on school boards, even black
patronage appointees.

More generally, urbanization has been
a major element in the shift from gemein-
schaft- to gesellschaft-type of social relations. In contrast to the informal relations
of the village, which are characterized by
personal acquaintance with one another,
the extensiveness of city populations means
that relationships are likely to be more impersonal and social controls more formal.
The pioneering American sociologist of urban life, Louis Wirth (1938), has also pointed out that the size and diversity of city life
allows for a greater division of labor than
in rural areas and, through constant contact, encourages inhabitants to become
more tolerant of different life-styles and
beliefs. The city also provides inhabitants
with various and conflicting sources of information—speeches, dramatic presentations, political activities, newspapers,
books, and the like.

In order to provide for the needs of city
populations, bureaucracies must be developed to coordinate activities and provide
services. The density of population that
characterizes cities, for example, has meant
that generally sewage, air and water pollution, carbon monoxide from vehicular
traffic, and garbage are more concentrated
and require formal regulation.

These are only a few of the changes
brought on by urbanization. Another is
that it provides the opportunity for social
movements to grow, since many people
concentrate together. But the greatest impact it is now having is in the third world.

URBANIZATION IN THE THIRD WORLD

The growth of large cities and giant metropolitan areas in the industrialized West
has been accomplished by the relative de-
pletion of the rural populations of those
nations. This pattern does not hold for the

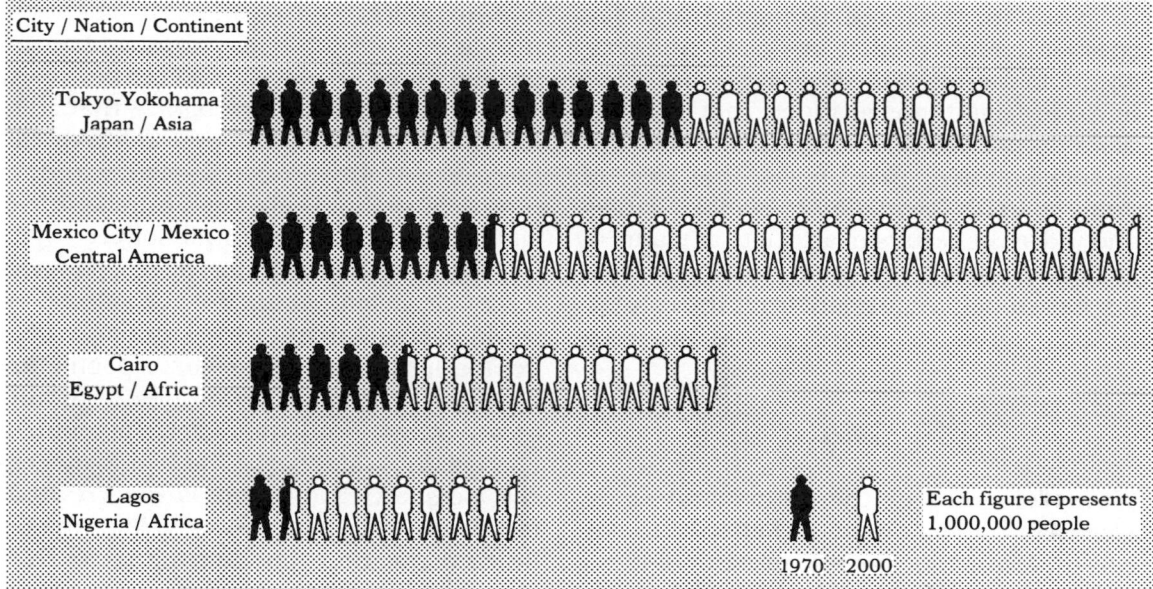

Figure 11.6 Population of Selected Cities, 1970 and 2000

SOURCE: *Rafael M. Salas, "What Population Changes Portend."* Atlas World Press Review *(Dec. 1978): 15–18.*

third world, however. The number of large cities in the third world has skyrocketed, and according to United Nations' projections, (see Figure 11.6) many of them should "expand to sizes hitherto unknown to planners" (Salas 1978). Cairo's population, for example, will have tripled between 1970 and 2000; Mexico City's population will be nearly four times its present size; and Lagos, Nigeria, will grow to just under seven times its current size. But in many cases, the proportion of urban to rural inhabitants has remained substantially unchanged. While it is true that the major force for urban growth is migration from country to city, the rural birth rate is so high that the rural population keeps replenishing its numbers. The third world is

thus witnessing the growth of many large cities, but not much *urbanization.*

In contrast to cities in the industrialized world, those in developing nations are not attracting population on the basis of increased industry or other job opportunities. The sheer numbers of people in the countryside seems to be the major pressure behind movement to the cities. As a result, the cities do not prosper from the migration; instead, they sprout the most impoverished slums in urban history. Yet, the migrants keep coming, apparently seeing more hope in even these desperate conditions than in the countryside. What the results of this population shift will be is not clear, but it is certain that it will remain a force for social change.

Our study of social change and its sources hasn't yielded any clear answers about many aspects of society, and it is obvious that there is much that sociologists do not yet understand about society or social change. But the fact that we can analyze many elements of social change and judge the results of attempts at planned change is a positive sign of sociology's usefulness in helping us construct the future.

SUMMARY

We have looked at the nature and some sources of social change—a change in social organization, norms, roles, activities, or social institutions that alters the pattern of relationships among people. Social change often has far-reaching ramifications and its effects usually are irreversible. Some social change is inevitable in every society, although societies differ in the rate at which they change.

Various theories have been proposed to account for what some sociologists believe are long-range patterns of change. Evolutionary theorists view history in terms of linear human progress; cyclical theorists, by contrast, see civilizations as proceeding through cycles of rise and decline. Functional theorists believe that social systems tend toward equilibrium, stressing the capacity of societies to adapt to social change. Finally, conflict theorists argue that change occurs through the conflict of group interests.

In this chapter, we saw how groups react to change and how in modern societies like our own, change is institutionalized through the governmental process. Some writers consider technology, another source of social change, to be the crucial

one in understanding modern life. Technology can be both a liberating and a controlling force in society. Recently, many writers have begun to recognize that technology, if applied indiscriminately, can have disastrous effects on society and on nature, and that there are a number of social problems that it cannot solve.

Population growth has been a powerful force for social change in the modern world. Demography, the scientific study of population, looks at the three population processes of fertility (birth rates), mortality (death rates), and migration (permanent changes in residence). The two early general perspectives on population grew out of concern over mass poverty. Malthus believed population was growing faster than food supply, and that only positive checks (war, famine, plague) and preventive checks (sexual abstinence) would stop future disaster from overpopulation. Marx, on the other hand, argued that the central issue was not overpopulation but the interests of the capitalist class in maintaining a mass of unemployed workers and control over the distribution of resources. The dominant scientific perspective (demographic transition theory) sees population change in terms of social structure: prosperity lowers mortality which lowers fertility. Davis cautions against too simple an explanation, however, and notes that individuals must first recognize lowered mortality before responding to it by reducing the number of children they bear.

Technological advances, particularly since World War II, have decreased mortality in the developing world. One result is a rapidly expanding population and a shortage of food. The advances were imported from the industrialized nations, but the changes in norms, institutions, and so on required to lower fertility could not be so simply imported. Thus governments have tried to limit births by adopting population policies (family planning, legalizing abortion) designed to lower fertility, which might not be adequate long-term solutions unless accompanied by industrialization.

Urbanization—the movement of people from the country to the city—has become a worldwide phenomenon. The United States is 74 percent urban; until 1914, it was mostly rural. Industrialization in the late nineteenth and early twentieth centuries made cities a seemingly endless source of jobs, and millions of Americans migrated to them from the farm. Recent years have seen a trend by mainly white middle- and upper-middle-class urbanites to move into suburbs, creating metropolitan areas. Although they continue to use the cities by day, the suburbanites leave their upkeep to a large number of poor people. These two demographic trends have had an impact on many aspects of social life.

Key Terms

social change (p. 343)
demography (p. 358)
fertility (p. 359)
birth rate (p. 359)
mortality rate (p. 359)
migration (p. 360)
infant mortality rate (p. 364)
population policy (p. 368)
urbanization (p. 371)
Standard Metropolitan Statistical Area (SMSA) (p. 372)

Review and Discussion Questions

1. What factors make regular social change inevitable in modern societies? Take the

United States as an example. What significant changes do you foresee for the near future? What problems will persist? How will we deal with others?

2. We in the United States are used to hearing about ever-new advances in technology—from food processors to microcomputers. What role will technology play in America's future? How will it figure in stimulating the social change to solve the "energy crisis" and other social problems? How will it fail?

3. Can you find examples of all three population patterns identified by the demographic transition theory (high fertility and mortality rates; high fertility, low mortality; low fertility and mortality) in the world today? How do you account for the different patterns various societies display?

4. Since 1973, the oil exporting nations have been using their oil to further their own national interests. Should the United States do the same with its surplus grain? Why or why not? What are the major issues involved? Conduct a debate between partisans of each side.

5. Some observers say they detect a movement of population from suburb to city in recent years. Others disagree. What do you think? What factors might lead to such a movement? What do you see as the long-term outlook? What will happen to the people now living in the city?

For Further Study

CHANGE Whereas early sociologists used to speak of the transition from rural to industrial society as the major pattern of contemporary social change, many sociologists now talk about the transition to a "postindustrial" society. Two good presentations of this concept are: Daniel Bell, *The Coming of Post-Industrial Society* (New York: Basic Books, 1976); and Amitai Etzioni, *The Active Society: A Theory of Societal and Political Processes* (New York: Free Press, 1968). You can read two good case studies of cultural change in: R. W. Wilson et al., *Value Change in Chinese Society* (New York: Praeger, 1979); and George M. Foster, *Tzintzuntzan: Mexican Peasants in a Changing World* (New York: Elsevier, 1979). Finally, a good textbook on social change is Steven Vago's *Social Change* (New York: Holt, 1980).

TECHNOLOGY There are a few books that principally deal with how we can live in our highly technical society, with particular emphasis on population. See: Paul Ehrlich and Anne H. Ehrlich, *Population, Resources, Environment* (San Francisco: Freeman, 1972); and G. Tyler Miller, Jr., *Living in the Environment* (Belmont, CA: Wadsworth, 1975). For perhaps the best study of how modern society has become technological in character, see: Jacques Ellul, *The Technological Society* (New York: Vintage, 1964).

POPULATION IN THE UNITED STATES With our focus on the world food shortage, we largely concentrated on population in the third world. But population is an active issue within the United States as well. You can find current data from such government publications as *Population Bulletin, Current Population,* and *Statistical Abstract of the United States.* An excellent reader on population issues in the United States is: Charles Westoff and R. Parke, eds., *Social and Demographic Aspects of Population Control and the American Future* (Washington, DC: Government Printing Office, 1972). Although a bit old, Lee Rainwater's *And the Poor Get Children* (Chicago: Quadrangle, 1960) is a readable and insightful probe into the obstacles facing family planning attempts among America's poor. A more general work is Bernard Berelson's *Population Policy in Developed Countries* (New York: McGraw-Hill, 1974). Finally, an excellent text that relates issues of population to social problems is John R. Weeks' *Population: An Introduction to Concepts and Issues* (Belmont, CA: Wadsworth, 1978).

URBANIZATION Early in this century, Georg Simmel made what remains a basic statement about the city in "The Metropolis and Mental Life," in *The Sociology of Georg Simmel,* ed. Kurt Wolff (New York: Free Press, 1950). Simmel contrasted the city dweller's progressive alienation with the developing city culture. For a unique perspective on city social problems and a critique of urban renewal decisions, see: Jane Jacobs, *The Death and Life of Great American Cities* (New York: Random House, 1961). There are also many good texts on urban sociology, such as: Claude S. Fischer, *The Urban Experience* (New York: Harcourt Brace Jovanovich, 1976). Finally, for a review of the urbanization process—in both the United States and abroad—see the collection: *Urbanization and Counter-Urbanization,* edited by Brian J. L. Berry (Beverly Hills, CA: Sage, 1976).

Afterword

Each section of this book became the foundation for our study of the one that followed. We began with a Prologue that focused on the relationship between sociology and one particular individual—you. Only after establishing that relationship could we proceed to Part One and apply sociology to the relationship that all individuals have with society. One of our primary goals in that section was to recognize how rooted we all are in social structure, and are in that sense, social beings. From there, we went beyond the individual level to a study of social structure itself in Part Two. In that section we saw the reality of society's structure apart from individuals. And on the basis of the knowledge gained in Parts One and Two, we were able to analyze the broad social processes of change.

Yet, running throughout our study, regardless of the particular topic, was the theme of social control as an active, directing force in our lives. We saw that social control is far more pervasive than the various social controllers, like the police, and that we internalize social control as an aspect of our selves early in our socialization. We thereby become the principal enforcers of our own social control by limiting our behaviors to a set of socially acceptable alternatives. In Erich Fromm's apt phrase, we learn to "want to do" what we "have to do." To be sure, we also saw that social life would not be possible were it not for the regularity and predictability of behavior that social control ensures. But, people, for the most part, support the status quo, including those aspects of it that perpetuate social inequalities (whether between economic classes, women and men, racial and ethnic groups, or age strata). So, in fact, both social structure and our own "complicity" underlie such injustices.

Our understanding of social control also played an important role in our view of change. We viewed change, for the most part, positively—although not entirely so. But, we also viewed it as inevitable, In the contemporary setting, in particular, societies will experience either gradual change (e.g., the United States) or revolution (e.g., Iran). Conservative as well as radical groups have recognized the need for change, as we saw in the case of Nicaragua, and will struggle to manage the change in ways that further their particular interests. We also observed that social mechanisms of conflict, technological progress, and so forth, which characterize modern heterogeneous societies and help maintain their unity, also make change inevitable.

The Promise of Sociology

The role of the sociologist is to analyze this social world and attempt to make some sense of it. You have now become familiar with some of the tools of the sociologist's trade. For instance, you have learned a new language—one that includes terms like socialization, norm, role, and stratification. It also includes familiar words but gives them more precise meanings: compare, for instance, the ordinary usage of culture, performance, or class with the sociological meanings of these terms. These words are important because they are the concepts that sociologists use to organize their view of the world so they can study and analyze it. Think of the insight and understanding of social inequality that the concepts of stratification, social class, and prestige yield together.

Of course, a professional sociologist can best utilize these concepts for understanding social reality. But you do not have to be a professional to use them. (For example, I can take a hammer and saw and put together an adequate bookcase—although a carpenter could make a beautiful one.) To take other, more related examples, certain police academies offer mandatory courses in sociology as part of recruits' police training. A number of businesses have sent employees to college for training that usually includes several sociology courses. And the University of Pennsylvania's Wharton School—one of the nation's top business colleges—requires its students to take sociology and even offers a major in the discipline.

If you do not happen to be considering one of the above categories, however, you might wonder how you can employ your new way of seeing. To begin with, your understanding of social reality will help you become a more aware citizen. You should be able to better cut through the bias and misinformation that often accompany political statements. You should have a better understanding of why candidates would make certain statements (to tap some basic American value, for example). Similarly, you should now have a firmer grasp of the dynamics underlying public debates on such issues as abortion on demand, busing, welfare, and the like. If you are planning a career in business or are already involved in one, you should recognize the value of your newly learned way of seeing for understanding market trends (consumer behavior), to give one example.

Most importantly, this sociological way of seeing will stand you in good stead for achieving a certain degree of control over your behavior. For you will be able to recognize the special interests that are served by even the most altruistic social movements. You will understand the basis in social control for many pious sounding statements. And, too, you should appreciate the substantive contributions that are offered beneath the cant in many public pronouncements. But, like any other faculty, your sociological imagination, this way of seeing, will only be maintained if you use it—long after your final exam in sociology class.

Glossary

Abstraction: The process of identifying the element(s) common to several situations (Prologue).

Achieved status: The social rankings that must be earned in some way (Chapter 2).

Acute anomie: Anomic situation in which there are no authoritative norms to follow (Chapter 9).

Affinal ties: Family relations based on choice or selection (Chapter 6).

Ageism: Prejudice or discrimination on the basis of age (Chapter 8).

Agencies of socialization: Groups or institutions that carry socialization out (Chapter 1).

Aggregate: A number of persons who happen to be in the same place at the same time but who don't share a common consciousness or interact regularly (Chapter 5).

Alienation: The intense feeling of separation from the world, from other people, and/or our own self (Chapter 9).

Altruistic suicide: That type of suicide, according to Durkheim, which occurs because the individual is overly integrated into society and has no sense of individual worth (Chapter 9).

Anomic suicide: That type of suicide, according to Durkheim, which occurs because society is unable to provide any coherent and practical guides for conduct (Chapter 9).

Anomie: A state of society in which major norms are either unclear or missing (Chapter 9).

Anticipatory socialization: Using one role to learn how to play another (Chapter 3).

Ascribed status: The social rankings we hold over which we have no control (Chapter 2).

Assimilation: The process by which an individual or group is integrated with the culture and society of the host country (Chapter 8).

Audience: A crowd that assembles to witness an event (Chapter 10).

Authority: The right—legal, moral, religious, or whatever—to command behavior (Chapter 5).

Bilateral descent: Descent system tracing kinship on both the mother's and father's sides of the family (Chapter 6).

Birth rate: The annual number of births per 1,000 population (male and female) (Chapter 11).

Bourgeoisie: The class of owners of the means of production (Chapter 7).

Bureaucratic organization: A formal organization that operates according to defined rules and whose authority structure is hierarchal and centralized (Chapter 5).

Caste system: Stratification system in which individuals are born into a specific social rank—their parents'—and can never leave it (Chapter 7).

Charismatic authority: Authority based on the special personal qualities of an individual (Chapter 5).

Class (Marx): Those people who are in fundamentally the same relationship to a society's means of production (Chapter 7).

Class (Weber): People with similar life chances as determined by economics (the possession of goods and opportunities for income) (Chapter 7).

Class consciousness: Group consciousness among members of the same class, whereby they recognize their essential common interests and formulate a plan of action in pursuit of them (Chapter 7).

Class system: Stratification system that allows movement between strata (Chapter 7).

Collective behavior: Relatively transient, similar, or related behavior of a number of people (Chapter 10).

Collective conscience: All the beliefs and sentiments common to average citizens of the same society (Chapter 9).

Concepts: Simple names for complex items and ideas (Prologue).

Conflict theory: That sociological perspective which sees groups competing for values and resources as the basis of social action (Prologue).

Conformity: Behavior according to social expectations; in anomie theory, it is acceptance of both the cultural goal of success and the approved means for reaching it (Chapter 4).

Consanguinal ties: Family relationships based on blood ties (Chapter 6).

Crazes: Intense and volatile behavior widely engaged in for a brief time, which then declines abruptly in popularity, often having severe consequences (Chapter 10).

Crowd: An unorganized collection of people who have temporarily assembled at the same time (Chapter 10).

Cultural diffusion: The process by which one culture acquires elements of another (Chapter 2).

Cultural lag: The situation when one part of a culture—usually the material—changes more rapidly than another—usually the ideological (Chapter 2).

Cultural relativism: The belief that we can understand the customs, beliefs, and values of other cultures only on the basis of the culture's own standards and not our own (Chapter 2).

Culture: All human products and activities that are not strictly biological in origin. It is that complex whole which includes knowledge, beliefs, art, morals, law, custom, and any other capabilities and habits acquired by individuals as members of society (Chapter 2).

Demography: The scientific study of population (Chapter 11).

Deviance: The failure to live up to socially held expectations (Chapter 4).

Diffuse collectivities: Persons who have little or no contact with one another but express similar behavior or attitudes (Chapter 10).

Discrimination: The actual behavior of denying access to social rewards to persons simply on the basis of their group membership (Chapter 8).

Egoistic suicide: That type of suicide, according to Durkheim, which occurs because the individual has very weak social ties (Chapter 9).

Endogamy: The requirement that we marry within our own group (Chapter 6).

Equalitarian: Family authority structure in which husband and wife wield equal power over children and decision making (Chapter 6).

Ethnic groups: Groups whose members are held together by race, religion, national origin, or some combination of these (Chapter 2).

Ethnocentrism: The tendency for people to see their own culture as superior to others (Chapter 2).

Exogamy: The requirement that we marry outside our own group (Chapter 6).

Extended family: More than one nuclear family related to each other by blood or marriage (Chapter 6).

Fads: Behavior widely engaged in for a brief time and which then declines abruptly in popularity (Chapter 10).

False consciousness: A belief about our place in the world and our interests that is based on an illusory sense of objective reality (Chapter 7).

Family: A group of two or more individuals who live together for an extended period of time; who are recognized by their society as being bonded by marriage, blood relationship, or *adoption;* and who are responsible for the care of their offspring (Chapter 6).

Family of orientation: The family into which we are born (Chapter 6).

Family of procreation: The family we generate ourselves (Chapter 6).

Fashions: Similar styles of appearance (e.g., dress, hairdos, furniture, or other chosen items) by large numbers of people at a given time (Chapter 10).

Fertility: The number of children being born to a specific population of women, usually expressed in terms of the birth rate (Chapter 11).

Folkways: The customary ways of doing things (Chapter 2).

Formal organization: A collection of interrelated groups formed to accomplish a specific purpose and operating according to an explicit set of rules (Chapter 5).

Front: The part of our performance that we regularly use to define the situation for those who observe us in it (Chapter 3).

Functionalism: That sociological perspective which focuses on the interrelationship of social structures and groups (Prologue).

Gemeinschaft: A type of society characterized by a tightly knit community built around the principle of traditional authority (Chapter 5).

Gender identification: The process by which we learn what our sex is and the cultural characteristics associated with it (Chapter 8).

Generalized other: Our impression of society as a whole, on which we base our expectations of individual behavior (Chapter 1).

Gesellschaft: A type of society where calculation and rationality guide conduct (Chapter 5).

Groups: Collections of people who share a common identity and interact with one another in a patterned way (Chapter 5).

Horizontal social mobility: Movement from onc position to another of the same rank (Chapter 7).

Ideology: A comprehensive view of the world justified by an appeal to basic social values (Chapter 2).

Infant mortality rate: The proportion of newborns who die in the first year of life (Chapter 11).

Innovation: The process by which cultures produce their own cultural elements (Chapter 2).

Innovation (in anomie theory): Acceptance of the cultural goal of success, but not the approved means for attaining it; instead, an unorthodox means of achieving success is substituted (Chapter 4).

Institutional sexism: Sexism that pervades our customary ways of life (Chapter 8).

Interest group: A group whose reason for existence is to promote its interests in competition with other groups, usually in the political arena (Chapter 5).

Internalize: The process in socialization whereby we take on learned behavior as our own (Chapter 1).

Labeling theory: The perspective that attempts to understand deviance in terms of how people come to be labeled by others, and the effect of those labels on their subsequent careers (Chapter 4).

Life chances: Our opportunity to enjoy various goods, living conditions, and experiences (Chapter 7).

Material culture: The physical objects that members of a human society make use of (Chapter 2).

Matriarchy: Family authority structure giving the mother wide-ranging power over most, if not all, aspects of family life (Chapter 6).

Matrilineal: Descent system tracing kinship only on the mother's side of the family (Chapter 6).

Matrilocality: Residence of a married couple with the wife's parents (Chapter 6).

Mechanical solidarity: Social solidarity based on similarity among individuals (characterizes gemeinschaft-type societies) (Chapter 9).

Migration: A permanent change of residence, involving detachment from one social system and engagement in another (Chapter 11).

Minority: A group within a larger society that, because of its physical or cultural characteristics, is denied equal participation in the life of that society (Chapter 8).

Mob: An emotionally aroused crowd whose members are ready to engage in violent action (Chapter 10).

Monogamy: The marriage of two people (Chapter 6).

Mores: Norms that regulate moral behavior and generally carry severe sanctions (Chapter 2).

Mortality rate: The annual number of deaths in a given population, usually expressed per 1,000 population (Chapter 11).

Neolocality: Residence of a married couple apart from their parents (Chapter 6).

Nonmaterial culture: The intangibles—beliefs, values, rules of behavior (norms) that shape our understanding of the world around us and of ourselves (Chapter 2).

Norms: Shared standards of behavior rooted in values and enforceable (Chapter 2).

Nuclear family: One set of parents and their dependent children (Chapter 6).

Organic solidarity: Social solidarity based on differences among individuals and their mutual interdependence (characterizes gesellschaft-type societies) (Chapter 9).

Panic: A collectivity's hasty, fearful, and unorganized reaction to a perceived direct threat (Chapter 10).

Parties: Groups whose only purpose is to acquire social power (Chapter 7).

Patriarchy: Family authority structure giving the father wide-ranging power over most, if not all, aspects of family life (Chapter 6).

Patrilineal: Descent system that traces kinship only on the father's side of the family (Chapter 6).

Patrilocality: Residence of a married couple with the husband's parents (Chapter 6).

Peer group: Three or more people of about the same age and social rank who associate with one another (Chapter 1).

Performance: That part of our behavior that is solely intended to make an impression on our audience (Chapter 3).

Polyandry: The marriage of one woman to more than one man (Chapter 6).

Polygamy: A general term referring to plural marriage (Chapter 6).

Polygyny: The marriage of one man to more than one woman (Chapter 6).

Population policy: Measures taken by a government on a continuing basis specifically designed to affect population growth (Chapter 11).

Power: A general term referring to our ability to secure another's obedience (Chapter 5).

Prejudice: An inflexible, hostile belief about the members of a particular group (Chapter 8).

Primary group: A group whose members interact with each other on a direct, face-to-face, and often long-lasting basis (Chapter 5).

Primary socialization: Socialization that begins at birth and continues throughout childhood and adolescence (Chapter 1).

Professionalization: The process by which the members of a profession or occupation—as a group—acquire the exclusive right to practice a skill and to train and admit new members (Chapter 3).

Proletariat: The class of workers who neither own nor control the means of production (Chapter 7).

Propaganda: The manipulation of ideas through an appeal to people's emotions and prejudices (Chapter 10).

Public: A collection of people who share an interest in and express their attitudes about a given value (Chapter 10).

Public opinion: The sum of views expressed by a public on a given issue (Chapter 10).

Race: In a sociological sense, a category of persons whom others define as sharing similar innate physical characteristics (Chapter 8).

Rational/legal authority: Authority based on rules (Chapter 5).

Rebellion: In anomie theory, replacement of an approved cultural goal of success and the proper means for attaining it, with new ones (Chapter 4).

Reference group: The group you use to measure your own social standing or life course, whether or not you are actually a member of it (Chapter 5).

Religion: A unified system of beliefs and practices relative to sacred things, which unite into a single moral community called a church, all those who adhere to them (Chapter 6).

Resocialization: A frequently rapid and intense process, requiring a radical change in behavior and attitudes (Chapter 1).

Retreatism: In anomie theory, rejection of both socially prescribed goals and means (Chapter 4).

Riot: General public violence generated by a mob (Chapter 10).

Ritualism: In anomie theory, overconformity to socially approved means for success when hope of attaining the goal of success has faded (Chapter 4).

Role: A collection of activities regularly performed by the occupant of a specific social position (Chapter 3).

Role conflict: A situation in which contradictory expectations are made upon us: either conflict between roles (interrole); conflict over how to play a single role (intrarole); or conflict between our role expectations and our sense of self (self-role) (Chapter 3).

Role expectations: The norms that define a role for everyone who might play it, want to play it, or observe it (Chapter 3).

Role set: The pair or cluster of roles in which each role takes its meaning from its relationship to the others and cannot exist without them (Chapter 3).

Role taking: The process by which we internalize role expectations (Chapter 3).

Sacred: Awe-inspiring phenomena that are ultimately beyond our power to understand completely, and set apart by religious beliefs (Chapter 6).

Sanction: That part of a norm—stated or not, specific or general—that indicates a proper re-

action to either the violation of or adherence to the norm (Chapter 2).

Scientific method: Forms of inquiry and rules of evidence that are designed to minimize the investigator's subjective influence as much as possible (Prologue).

Secondary deviance: Deviant behavior generated in the labeled person solely by the fact of being labeled (Chapter 4).

Secondary group: A group whose members interact on a relatively impersonal basis (Chapter 5).

Secondary socialization: Socialization that occurs beyond adolescence (Chapter 1).

Self: The conscious sense of who we are (Chapter 1).

Sexism: Prejudice or discrimination on the basis of sex (Chapter 8).

Significant others: Individuals who, because of our emotional attachment to them or their control over resources we need, exercise the greatest influence on our self-concept (Chapter 1).

Simple anomie: An anomic situation arising from a conflict of norms (Chapter 9).

Sociability: Any situation in which the participating individuals suppress their individual interests and concerns in order to assure relatively conflict-free interaction (Chapter 3).

Social category: A number of people who share a trait (e.g., hair color, age, or sex) that we use to associate them together (Chapter 5).

Social change: A change in social organization, norms, roles, bases for status, or social institutions, which alters the pattern of our relationships with one another (Chapter 11).

Social control: The containment of our behaviors within socially approved boundaries (Chapter 1).

Social disorganization: The disruption of a preexisting social organization in such a way that previously normal social control breaks down (Chapter 9).

Social facts: Every way of acting which is general throughout a given society (Prologue).

Social institutions: Persistent patterns of expected behavior, which are built around enduring social needs (Chapter 6).

Socialization: The social process through which we gain our sense of self and learn the values of our society (Chapter 1).

Social mobility: Movement from one social position to another (Chapter 7).

Social movement: A concerted effort by a large number of people over an extended period of time to effect (or block) social change (Chapter 10).

Social organization: The patterned regularity of our social actions and beliefs (Chapter 5).

Social stratification: The unequal distribution of valued resources among different categories of people in society (Chapter 7).

Social structures: The customary patterns of interaction evident in institutions, groups, occupations, and the like (Prologue).

Sociology: The scientific study of social relationships among human beings (Prologue).

Standard Metropolitan Statistical Area (SMSA): A city plus the surrounding area which, because of economic and other ties, can be considered part of the same unit as the city (Chapter 11).

Status group: A number of people with roughly similar life chances, based on their prestige (Chapter 7).

Status symbols: Things that indicate the possessor is worthy of respect because they are associated with high-status people (Chapter 7).

Stereotypes: Distorted portraits of supposed group characteristics used to interpret the actions of all members of the group (Chapter 8).

Subculture: A distinct way of life practiced by a group living within a larger society (Chapter 2).

Symbol: Something that stands for something else (Prologue).

Symbolic interactionism: That sociological perspective which concentrates on interacting individuals (Prologue).

Taboos: Norms the violations of which are considered a serious threat to society's moral functioning (Chapter 2).

Techniques of neutralization: Subcultural redefinition of deviant behavior to accord it with dominant social norms (Chapter 4).

Technology: The sum total of all the methods that a society's members use to accomplish their tasks (Chapter 2).

Theory: A proposition that organizes and emphasizes certain concepts, showing the relationships among them (Prologue).

Total institutions: Places where individuals are cut off from the rest of society and put under constant supervision (Chapter 1).

Traditional authority: Authority based on conformity to the way things have always been done (Chapter 5).

Urbanization: The general movement of people from rural to urban areas (Chapter 11).

Values: Broad social definitions of what is good, right, or preferred (Chapter 2).

Variable: Any property that can change and be measured (Prologue).

Vertical social mobility: Movement either upward or downward between ranks in a stratification system (Chapter 7).

References

Ahlstrom, Sydney E. 1972. *A Religious History of the American People.* New Haven, CT: Yale University Press.

———. 1978. "National Trauma and Changing Religious Values." *Daedalus* **107** (Winter): 13–29.

Allworth, Edward, ed. 1971. *Soviet Nationality Problems.* New York: Columbia University Press.

American Friends Service Committee. 1971. *Struggle for Justice.* New York: Hill & Wang.

American Jewish Committee. 1979. *The American Jewish Year Book.* Philadelphia: Jewish Publication Society.

Amir, Menachem, and Yitzchak Berman. 1970. "Chromosomal Deviation and Crime." *Federal Probation* **34**: 55–62.

Anderson, Jack. 1978. "The Federal Coverup of White-Collar Crime." *Chicago Sun-Times* 1 May.

Arendt, Hannah. 1963. *Eichmann in Jerusalem: A Report on the Banality of Evil.* New York: Viking Press.

Ariès, Philippe. 1962. *Centuries of Childhood: A Social History of Family Life.* Translated by Robert Baldick. New York: Vintage Books.

Asch, Solomon. 1955. "Opinions and Social Pressure." *Scientific American* **193** (5): 31–35.

Bahr, Howard M. 1973. *Skid Row: An Introduction to Disaffiliation.* New York: Oxford University Press.

Ball, Samuel, and Gerry Bogatz. 1970. *The First Year of Sesame Street: An Evaluation.* Princeton, NJ: Educational Testing Service.

Baltzell, E. Digby. 1964. *The Protestant Establishment: Aristocracy and Caste in America.* New York: Vintage Books.

Baron, Harold M. 1975. "Postscript—1974." In *Majority and Minority: The Dynamics of Racial and Ethnic Relations,* edited by Norman R. Yetman and C. Hoy Steele. Boston: Allyn and Bacon.

Bascom, William. 1969. *The Yoruba of Southwestern Nigeria.* New York: Holt, Rinehart and Winston.

Becker, Howard S. 1952. "Social Class Variations in the Teacher-Pupil Relationship." *Journal of Educational Sociology* **25**: 451–65.

———. 1963. *Outsiders: Studies in the Sociology of Deviance.* New York: Free Press.

Bell, Robert R., and J. B. Chaskes. 1970. "Premarital Sexual Experience Among Coeds, 1958 and 1968." *Journal of Marriage and the Family* **32**: 81–85.

Benkin, Richard L. 1978. "Ethnicity and Organization: Jewish Communities in East Europe and the United States." *Sociological Quarterly* **19**: 614–25.

———, and Grace DeSantis. 1978. "Creating Ethnicity." Paper presented at the annual meeting of the Midwest Sociological Society, Omaha, NB.

Bentham, Jeremy. 1948 [1776]. "A Fragment on Government." In *A Fragment on Government and An Introduction to the Principles of Morals Legislation,* edited by W. Harrison. Oxford: Blackwell Scientific Publications.

Berger, Peter. 1963. *Invitation to Sociology: A Humanistic Perspective.* Garden City, NY: Doubleday & Company.

Bergman, J. 1974. "Are Little Girls Being Harmed

by Sesame Street?" In *And Jill Came Tumbling After: Sexism in American Education,* edited by J. Stacey, S. Bereaud, and J. Daniels. New York: Dell Publishing Company.

Bernard, Jessie. 1973. *The Sociology of Community.* Glenview, IL: Scott, Foresman and Company.

Black, Donald, and Albert J. Reiss, Jr. 1970. "Police Control of Juveniles." *American Sociological Review* 35: 63–77.

Blau, Peter M. 1963. *Dynamics of Bureaucracy: A Study of Interpersonal Relationships in Two Government Agencies.* Chicago: University of Chicago Press.

Blauner, Robert. 1964. *Alienation and Freedom: The Factory Worker and His Industry.* Chicago: University of Chicago Press.

Blumer, Herbert. 1951. "Elementary Collective Groupings." In *New Outline of the Principles of Sociology,* edited by A. M. Lee. New York: Barnes & Noble.

Blumstein, Philip W., and Pepper Schwartz. 1975. "Lesbianism and Bisexuality." In *Sexual Deviance and Sexual Deviants,* edited by Erich Goode and Richard Troiden. New York: William Morrow & Company.

Bonnot, Gérard. 1980. "The Coming Age of Telematics." *Le Nouvel Observateur.* Reprinted in *Atlas World Press Review* (Feb.): 21–23.

Bottomore, T. B. 1966. *Classes in Modern Society.* New York: Vintage Books.

Brodsky, Annette M. 1973. "The Consciousness-Raising Group as a Model of Therapy with Women." *Psychotherapy: Theory, Research, and Practice* 10: 24–29.

Broverman, I. K., et al. 1970. "Sex-role Stereotyping and Clinical Judgments of Mental Health." *Journal of Consulting Psychology* 34: 1–7.

Brown, Lester. 1973. "Population and Affluence: Growing Pressures on World Food Resources." *Population Bulletin* 29 (2).

———, Kathleen Newland, and Bruce Stokes. 1976. "Twenty-two Aspects of the Population Problem." *The Futurist* 10: 238–51.

Brown, Roger. 1965. *Social Psychology.* New York: Free Press.

Brown, Scott Campbell. 1979. "Educational Attainment of Workers—Some Trends from 1973 to 1978." *Monthly Labor Review* (Feb): 54–58.

Brownmiller, Susan. 1975. *Against Our Will: Men, Women and Rape.* New York: Simon & Schuster.

Burks, R. V. 1961. *The Dynamics of Communism in Eastern Europe.* Princeton, NJ: Princeton University Press.

Butler, Robert, and Myrna Lewis. 1976. *Sex after Sixty.* New York: Harper & Row.

Caldwell, J. 1975. "The Containment of World Population Growth." *Studies in Family Planning* 6: 429–36.

Campbell, E. 1969. "Adolescent Socialization." In *Handbook of Socialization Theory and Research,* edited by D. A. Goslin. Chicago: Rand McNally & Company.

Carden, Maren Lockwood. 1978. "The Proliferation of a Social Movement: Ideology and Individual Incentives in the Contemporary Feminist Movement." In *Research in Social Movements, Conflict, and Change,* Vol. 1, edited by Louis Kriesberg. Greenwich, CT: JAI Press.

Carron, Alain-Marie. 1978. "Two Societies: 'Social Dynamite.' " *Le Monde.* Excerpted in *Atlas World Press Review* (Aug): 54–55.

Castro, Fidel. 1969. *Fidel Castro Speaks.* New York: Grove Press.

Chafe, William H. 1972. *The American Woman: Her Changing Social, Economic, and Political Roles, 1920–1970.* New York: Oxford University Press.

Chambliss, William J., and Robert J. Seidman. 1971. *Law, Order, and Power.* Reading, MA: Addison-Wesley Publishing Company.

Clanton, Gordon, and Chris Downing, eds. 1975. *Face to Face to Face.* New York: E. P. Dutton & Company.

Cloward, Richard A., and Lloyd E. Ohlin. 1960. *Delinquency and Opportunity.* New York: Free Press.

Coale, Ansley J. 1974. "The History of the Human Population." *Scientific American* 231 (3): 40–51.

Cohen, Albert. 1955. *Delinquent Boys: The Culture of the Gang.* Glencoe, IL: Free Press.

Cole, Charles Lee. 1977. "Cohabitation in Social Context." In *Marriage and Alternatives: Exploring Intimate Relationships,* edited by Roger Libby and Robert N. Whitehurst. Glenview, IL: Scott, Foresman and Company.

Coleman, James S. 1961. *The Adolescent Society: The Social Life of the Teen Ager and Its Impact on Education.* New York: Free Press.

———. 1961a. "Athletics in High School." *The Annals of the American Academy of Political and Social Science* **338** (Nov): 33–43.

———, et al. 1966. *Equality of Educational Opportunity.* Washington, DC: Government Printing Office.

Coleman, Richard P., and Lee Rainwater. 1978. *Social Standing in America: New Dimensions of Class.* New York: Basic Books.

Collins, Randall. 1971. "Functional and Conflict Theories of Education Theory and Research." *American Sociological Review* **36**: 1002–19.

———. 1975. *Conflict Sociology: Toward an Explanatory Science.* New York: Academic Press.

Cooley, Charles H. 1924. *Social Organization: A Study of the Larger Mind.* New York: Charles Scribner's Sons.

Coser, Lewis A. 1956. *The Functions of Social Conflict.* New York: Free Press.

Coward, B. E., J. R. Feagin, and J. A. Williams, Jr. 1974. "The Culture of Poverty Debate: Some Additional Data." *Social Problems* **21**: 621–34.

Curtis, Richard F., and Elton F. Jackson. 1977. *Inequality in American Communities.* New York: Academic Press.

Dahrendorf, Ralf. 1959. *Class and Class Conflict in Industrial Society.* Stanford, CA: Stanford University Press.

———. 1967. *Society and Democracy in Germany.* Garden City, NY: Doubleday & Company.

David, Deborah S., and Robert Brannon. 1976. "The Male Sex Role: Our Culture's Blueprint for Manhood, and What It's Done for Us Lately." In *The Forty-Nine Percent Majority: The Male Sex Role,* edited by Deborah S. David and Robert Brannon. Reading, MA: Addison-Wesley Publishing Company.

Davies, James C. 1969. "The J-Curve of Rising and Declining Satisfactions as a Cause of Some Great Revolutions and a Contained Rebellion." In *Violence in America: Historical and Comparative Perspectives,* edited by H. D. Graham and T. R. Gurr. Washington, DC: National Commission on the Causes and Prevention of Violence.

Davis, Fred. 1967. "Focus on the Flower Children: Why All of Us May Be Hippies Someday." *Trans-action* **5**: 10–18.

Davis, Kingsley. 1947. "Final Notes on a Case of Extreme Isolation." *American Journal of Sociology* **52**: 432–37.

———. 1949. *Human Society.* New York: The Macmillan Company.

———. 1963. "The Theory of Change and Response in Modern Demographic History." *Population Index* **29** (4): 345–66.

———, and Wilbert Moore. 1945. "Some Principles of Stratification." *American Sociological Review* **10**: 242–49.

Dean, D. G., et al. 1975. "Cultural Contradictions and Sex Roles Revisited: A Replication." *Sociological Quarterly* **16**: 207–15.

de Beauvoir, Simone. 1952. *The Second Sex.* New York: Alfred A. Knopf.

———. 1972. *The Coming of Age.* New York: Warner Books.

de Grazia, Sebastian. 1948. *The Political Community: A Study of Anomie.* Chicago: University of Chicago Press.

DeSantis, Grace, and Richard Benkin. 1980. "Ethnicity without Community." *Ethnicity* **7**: 137–43.

de Zulueta, Tana. 1980. "Abolishing Mental Hospitals." *Guardian* (London). Reprinted in *Atlas World Press Review* (Feb): 57.

Dollard, John. 1937. *Caste and Class in a Southern Town.* New Haven, CT: Yale University Press.

Dugdale, Richard. 1877. *The Jukes: A Study in Crime, Pauperism, Disease, and Heredity.* New York: G.P. Putnam's Sons.

Durkheim, Emile. 1951 [1897]. *Suicide: A Study in Sociology.* Translated by John A. Spaulding and George Simpson. New York: Free Press.

———. 1964 [1893]. *The Division of Labor in Society.* Translated by George Simpson. New York: Macmillan and Co.

———. 1964a [1895]. *The Rules of Sociological Method.* Translated by Sarah A. Solovay and John H. Mueller. New York: Free Press.

———. 1965 [1915]. *The Elementary Forms of Religious Life.* Translated by Joseph Ward Swain. New York: Free Press.

Ehrlich, Paul. 1968. *The Population Bomb.* New York: Ballantine Books.

Einstein, Albert. 1949. *The World as I See It.* Translated by Alan Harris. New York: The Wisdom Library.

Elkin, Frederick. 1960. *The Child and Society: The Process of Socialization.* New York: Random House.

Ellis, Godfrey J., Gary R. Lee, and Larry R. Petersen. 1978. "Supervision and Conformity: A Cross-cultural Analysis of Parental Socialization Values." *American Journal of Sociology* 84: 386–403.

Engels, Frederick. 1972 [1902]. *The Origin of the Family, Private Property and the State.* New York: International Publishers.

Etzioni, Amitai. 1961. *Complex Organizations.* New York: Free Press.

Eysenck, H. J., and D. K. B. Nias. 1978. *Sex, Violence and the Media.* New York: St. Martin's Press.

Featherman, David L., and Robert M. Hauser. 1976. "Changes in the Socioeconomic Stratification of the Races." *American Journal of Sociology* 82: 621–51.

———, and Robert M. Hauser. 1977. *The Process of Stratification: Trends and Analysis.* New York: Academic Press.

Foy, Eddie, and Alvin F. Harlow. 1928. *Clowning through Life.* New York: E. P. Dutton & Company.

Frazier, Nancy, and Myra Sadlek. 1973. *Sexism in School and Society.* New York: Harper & Row.

Freedman, Jonathan L., and Scott C. Fraser. 1966. "Compliance without Pressure: The Foot-in-the-Door Technique." *Journal of Personality and Social Psychology* 4: 117–24.

Freeland, Richard M. 1974. *The Truman Doctrine and the Origins of McCarthyism.* New York: Schocken Books.

Freud, Sigmund. 1953 [1916]. *A General Introduction to Psychoanalysis.* New York: Pocket Books.

Fried, Marc. 1974. *The World of the Urban Working Class.* Cambridge, MA: Harvard University Press.

Friedenberg, Edgar Z. 1963. *Coming of Age in America.* New York: Vintage Books.

Friedl, Ernestine. 1975. *Women and Men: An Anthropologist's View.* New York: Holt, Rinehart and Winston.

Fromm, Erich. 1941. *Escape from Freedom.* New York: Avon Books.

———. 1949. "Psychoanalytic Characterology and Its Application to the Understanding of Culture." In *Culture and Personality,* edited by S. S. Sargent and M. W. Smith. New York: Viking Press.

———. 1955. *The Sane Society.* New York: Holt, Rinehart and Winston.

———. 1956. *The Art of Loving.* New York: Harper & Row.

Gagnon, John H. 1977. *Human Sexualities.* Glenview, IL: Scott, Foresman and Company.

———, and William Simon. 1973. *Sexual Conduct.* Chicago: Aldine Publishing Company.

Gans, Herbert. 1962. *The Urban Villagers.* New York: Free Press.

———. 1974. *Popular Culture and High Culture.* New York: Basic Books.

———. 1977. "The Uses of Poverty: The Poor Pay All." In *Social Problems: The Contemporary Debates,* edited by John B. Williamson, Jerry F. Boren, and Linda Evans. Boston: Little, Brown and Company.

Garfinkel, Harold. 1967. *Studies in Ethnomethodology.* Englewood Cliffs, NJ: Prentice-Hall.

Garland, Parker. 1974. "Enrollment in American Two-Year Colleges, 1973–74." *Intellect* (Apr): 469.

Gerlach, Luther P., and Virginia H. Hine. 1970. *People, Power, Change: Movements of Social Transformation.* Indianapolis: The Bobbs-Merrill Company.

Giddens, Anthony. 1973. *The Class Structure of Advanced Societies.* New York: Harper & Row.

Giele, Janet Zollinger. 1975. "Changing Sex Roles and the Future of Marriage." In *Contemporary Marriage: Structure, Dynamics and Therapy,* edited by Henry Gruenbaum and Jacob Christ. Boston: Little, Brown and Company.

Glazer, Nathan, and Daniel Patrick Moynihan. 1963. *Beyond the Melting Pot.* Cambridge, MA: MIT Press.

Glenn, Norval D., and Ruth Hyland. 1967. "Religious Preference and Worldly Success: Some Evidence from National Surveys." *American Sociological Review* 32: 73–75.

Glick, Paul C., and Arthur J. Norton. 1971. "Frequency, Duration, and Probability of

Marriage and Divorce." *Journal of Marriage and the Family* 33: 307–17.

Glock, Charles Y., and Rodney Stark. 1965. *Religion and Society in Tension*. Chicago: Rand McNally & Company.

Glueck, Sheldon, and Eleanor Glueck. 1956. *Physique and Delinquency*. Harper and Brothers.

Goals for Americans: The Report of the President's Commission on National Goals. 1960. Henry M. Wriston, chairman. Englewood Cliffs, NJ: Prentice-Hall.

Goddard, Henry. 1914. *Feeblemindedness: Its Causes and Consequences*. New York: Macmillan and Company.

Goffman, Erving. 1959. *The Presentation of Self in Everyday Life*. Garden City, NY: Doubleday and Co.

———. 1961. *Asylums*. Garden City, NY: Doubleday & Company.

Goldberg, Herb. 1976. *The Hazards of Being Male*. New York: Signet Books.

Goldman, Paul, and Donald R. Van Houten. 1977. "Managerial Strategies and the Worker: A Marxist Analysis of Bureaucracy." *Sociological Quarterly* 18: 108–25.

Goode, William J. 1960. "A Theory of Role Strain." *American Sociological Review* 25: 483–96.

———. 1960a. "Illegitimacy in the Caribbean Social Structure." *American Sociological Review* 25: 21–30.

Gordon, Milton M. 1964. *Assimilation in American Life*. New York: Oxford University Press.

Goring, Charles. 1913. *The English Convict: A Statistical Study*. London: H. M. Stationery Office.

Gough, E. Kathleen. 1959. "The Nayars and the Definition of Marriage." *Journal of the Royal Anthropological Institute* 89: 23–34.

Greeley, Andrew. 1976. *Ethnicity, Denomination, and Inequality*. Beverly Hills, CA: Sage Publications.

Griffin, Larry J., and Karl L. Alexander. 1978. "Schooling and Socioeconomic Attainments: High School and College Influences." *American Journal of Sociology* 84: 319–47.

Gross, Neal, A. W. McEachern, and W. S. Mason. 1957. *Explorations in Role Analysis: Studies of the School Superintendency Role*. New York: John Wiley & Sons.

Guest, Iain. 1979. "The Year of the Child." *New Internationalist*. Excerpted in *Atlas World Press Review* (Mar): 46.

Guinther, John. 1976. *Moralists and Managers: Public Interest Movements in America*. Garden City, NY: Doubleday & Company.

Hancock, Graham. 1979. "Is There Life after 65?" *New Internationalist*. Excerpted in *Atlas World Press Review* (Dec): 32–33.

Haney, Craig, Curtis Banks, and Philip Zimbardo. 1973. "A Study of Prisoners and Guards in a Simulated Prison." In *Readings about the Social Animal*, edited by Elliot Aronson. San Francisco: W. H. Freeman and Company.

Hardy, James D., Harold G. Wolff, and Helen Goodell. 1952. *Pain Sensations and Reactions*. Baltimore: Williams & Wilkins Company.

Harris, Marvin. 1974. *Cows, Pigs, Wars, and Witches*. New York: Random House.

Harris, Norman C., and John F. Geede. 1977. *Career Education in Colleges*. San Francisco: Jossey-Bass.

Harrison, Barbara G. 1973. *Unlearning the Lie: Sexism in School*. New York: William Morrow & Company.

Heer, David M. 1974. "The Prevalence of Black-White Marriage in the United States, 1960 and 1970." *Journal of Marriage and the Family* 36: 246–58.

Heilbroner, Robert L. 1966. *The Limits of American Capitalism*. New York: Harper & Row.

Helfgot, Joseph. 1974. "Professional Reform Organizations and Their Active Members: A Research Summary." *Journal of Social Issues* 29: 475–91.

Heydebrand, Wolf. 1977. "Organizational Contradictions in Public Bureaucracies: Toward a Marxian Theory of Organizations." *Sociological Quarterly* 18: 83–107.

Hirschi, Travis. 1969. *Causes of Delinquency*. Berkeley: University of California Press.

Hobbes, Thomas. 1968 [1651]. *Leviathan*. Baltimore: Penguin Books.

Hochschild, Arlie R. 1973. *The Unexpected Community*. Berkeley: University of California Press.

Hodge, Robert W., Paul M. Siegel, and Peter H. Rossi. 1964. "Occupational Prestige in the

United States, 1925–63." *American Journal of Sociology* **70**: 286–302.

Hoffer, Eric. 1951. *The True Believer.* New York: Harper & Brothers.

Hoover, Kenneth R. 1976. *The Elements of Social Scientific Thinking.* New York: St. Martin's Press.

Horner, Martina. 1972. "Toward an Understanding of Achievement Related Conflicts in Women." *Journal of Social Issues* **28**: 157–75.

Horowitz, Irving Louis. 1972. *Foundations of Political Sociology.* New York: Harper & Row.

———, and James E. Katz. 1975. *Social Science and Public Policy.* New York: Frederick A. Praeger.

Hunt, Chester L., and Lewis Walker. 1974. *Ethnic Dynamics: Patterns of Intergroup Relations in Various Societies.* Homewood, IL: Dorsey Press.

Hunt, J. McVicker. 1969. *The Challenge of Incompetence and Poverty.* Urbana: University of Illinois Press.

Huntington, Samuel P. 1968. *Political Order in Changing Societies.* New Haven, CT: Yale University Press.

Hurley, Rodger. 1969. *Poverty and Mental Retardation: A Causal Relationship.* New York: Random House.

Institute of Ecology. 1971. *Man in the Living Environment: A Report on Global Ecological Problems.* Madison, WI: University of Wisconsin Press.

Iorizzo, Luciano J. 1970. "The Padrone and Immigrant Distribution." In *The Italian Experience in the United States,* edited by S. M. Tomasi and H. M. Engel. Staten Island, NY: Center for Migration Studies.

Jacobs, Jane. 1961. *The Death and Life of Great American Cities.* New York: Vintage Books.

James, William. 1961 [1901]. *The Varieties of Religious Experience.* New York: The Macmillan Company.

Janis, Irving L., et al. 1964. "The Problem of Panic." In *Panic Behavior: Discussion and Readings,* edited by Duane P. Schultz. New York: Random House.

Janson, H. W. 1970. *History of Art.* Englewood Cliffs, NJ: Prentice-Hall.

Jencks, Christopher, and David Reisman. 1968. *The Academic Revolution.* Garden City, NY: Doubleday & Company.

———, et al. 1972. *Inequality: A Reassessment of the Effect of Family and Schooling in America.* New York: Basic Books.

Jensen, Arthur R. 1969. "How Much Can We Boost I.Q. and Scholastic Achievement?" *Harvard Educational Review* **39**: 1–123.

Johnson, Chalmers. 1969. "Building a Communist Nation in China." In *Communist Revolution in Asia: Tactics, Goals, and Achievements,* edited by Robert A. Scalapino. Englewood Cliffs, NJ: Prentice-Hall.

Judah, J. Stillson. 1978. "The Hare Krishna Movement." In *Religious Movements in Contemporary America,* edited by Irving I. Zaretsky and Mark P. Leone. Princeton, NJ: Princeton University Press.

Kaats, Gilbert, and Keith E. Davis. 1970. "The Dynamics of Sexual Behavior of College Students." *Journal of Marriage and the Family* **32**: 390–400.

Kalapesi, Dhun M. 1978. "Overdevelopment in the Himalayas." *Sunday Standard* [New Delhi]. Excerpted in *Atlas World Press Review* (Aug): 44.

Kalleberg, Arne L., and Larry J. Griffin. 1980. "Class, Occupation, and Inequality in Job Rewards." *American Journal of Sociology* **85**: 731–68.

Kanter, Rosabeth Moss. 1970. "Communes." *Psychology Today* (July): 53–57,78.

———. 1977. "Some Effects of Proportion of Group Life: Skewed Sex Ratios and Responses to Token Women." *American Journal of Sociology* **82**: 965–90.

Kass, Roy. 1977. "Recent Changes in Male Income." *Sociological Quarterly* **18**: 367–77.

Kephart, William M. 1976. *Extraordinary Groups: The Sociology of Unconventional Life-Styles.* New York: St. Martin's Press.

Kerner Commission. 1968. *Report of the National Advisory Commission on Civil Disorders.* Otto Kerner, chairman. Washington, DC: Government Printing Office.

Kierkegaard, Søren. 1962 [1847]. *The Present Age and Of the Difference between a Genius and an Apostle.* Translated by Alexander Dru. New York: Harper & Row.

King, Martin Luther. 1969. "Letter from Birmingham City Jail." In *Civil Disobedience:*

Theory and Practice, edited by Hugo Adam Bedau. New York: Pegasus.

Knight, Arthur. 1957. *The Liveliest Art*. New York: The Macmillan Company.

Knodel, John. 1970. "Two and a Half Centuries of Demographic History in a Bavarian Village." *Population Studies* **24**: 353–69.

Knudson, Ruth B., ed. 1974. *Women and Success: The Anatomy of Achievement*. New York: William Morrow & Company.

Kohn, Melvin. 1976. "Occupational Structure and Alienation." *American Journal of Sociology* **82**: 111–30.

Kolko, Gabriel. 1963. *The Triumph of Conservatism: A Reinterpretation of American History, 1900–1916*. Glencoe, IL: Free Press.

Komarovsky, Mirra. 1976. *Dilemmas of Masculinity*. New York: W. W. Norton and Company.

Krauss, Irving. 1976. *Stratification, Class, and Conflict*. New York: Free Press.

Lake, Alice. 1975. "Are We Born into Our Sex Roles or Programmed into Them?" *Women's Day* (Jan): 24–25.

Lampman, R. J. 1962. *The Share of Top Wealth-Holders in National Wealth*. Princeton, NJ: Princeton University Press.

Latane, Bibb, and Judith Rodin. 1969. "A Lady in Distress: Inhibiting Effects of Friends and Strangers on Bystander Intervention." *The Journal of Experimental Social Psychology* **5**: 189–202.

Latham, Earl. 1952. *The Group Basis of Politics*. Ithaca, NY: Cornell University Press.

Lazarsfeld, Paul F., Bernard Berelson, and Hazel Gaudet. 1948. *The People's Choice: How the Voter Makes Up His Mind in a Presidential Campaign*. New York: Columbia University Press.

Lazerwitz, Bernard. 1964. "Religion and Social Structure in the United States." In *Religion, Culture and Society*, edited by Louis Schneider. New York: John Wiley & Sons.

Le Bon, Gustave. 1960 [1895]. *The Crowd*. New York: Viking Press.

Lee, Gary R., and Robert W. Clyde. 1974. "Religion, Socioeconomic Status, and Anomie." *Journal for the Scientific Study of Religion* **13**: 35–47.

Lefkowitz, Monroe, Robert R. Blake, and Jane Srgley Mouton. 1955. "Status Factors in Pedestrian Violations of Traffic Signals."

Journal of Abnormal and Social Psychology **51**: 704–6.

Lemert, E. M. 1972. *Human Deviance, Social Problems, and Social Control*. Englewood Cliffs, NJ: Prentice-Hall.

Lenski, Gerhard. 1966. *Power and Privilege: A Theory of Social Stratification*. New York: McGraw-Hill.

———. 1975. "Social Structure in Evolutionary Perspective." In *Approaches to the Study of Social Structure*, edited by Peter Blau. New York: Free Press.

———. 1976. "History and Social Change." *American Journal of Sociology* **82**: 648–64.

Levin, Murray B. 1960. *The Alienated Voter: Politics in Boston*. New York: Holt, Rinehart and Winston.

Levine, Irving M., and Judith M. Herman. 1971. "The New Pluralism." In *Overcoming Middle Class Rage*, edited by Murray Friedman. Philadelphia: Westminster Press.

Lewis, Diane. 1978. "The Black Family: Socialization and Sex Roles." In *The Black Family: Essays and Studies*, edited by Robert Staples. Belmont, CA: Wadsworth Publishing Company.

Libby, Roger, and Robert N. Whitehurst, eds. 1977. *Marriage and Alternatives: Exploring Intimate Relationships*. Glenview, IL: Scott, Foresman and Company.

Liebow, Elliot. 1967. *Tally's Corner: A Study of Streetcorner Men*. Boston: Little, Brown and Company.

Linton, Ralph. 1936. *The Study of Man: An Introduction*. New York: Appleton-Century Crofts.

Lipset, Seymour Martin, and Reinhard Bendix. 1959. *Social Mobility in Industrial Society*. Berkeley: University of California Press.

Lyman, Stanford M. and Marvin B. Scott. 1967. "Territoriality: A Neglected Sociological Dimension." *Social Problems* **12**: 236–49.

MacCannell, Dean. 1976. *The Tourist: A New Theory of the Leisure Class*. New York: Schocken Books.

Maccoby, Eleanor, and Carol Nagy Jacklin. 1974. *The Psychology of Sex Differences*. Stanford, CA: Stanford University Press.

Mackay, C. 1962 [1841]. *Extraordinary Popular Delusions and the Madness of Crowds*. New York: Farrar, Straus & Cudahy.

Mainardi, Pat. 1970. "The Politics of Housework." In U.S. Congress, House Special Subcommittee on Education of the Committee on Education and Labor, *Discrimination Against Women.* 91st Congress, Second Session, Part 1. Washington, DC: Government Printing Office.

Malinowski, Bronislaw. 1927. *Sex and Repression in Savage Society.* London: Kegan Paul, Trench, Trubner & Company.

———. 1974 [1930]. "Parenthood, the Basis of Social Structure." In *The Family: Its Structures and Functions,* edited by Rose L. Coser. New York: St. Martin's Press.

Malthus, Thomas. 1976 [1798]. *An Essay on the Principle of Population.* New York: W. W. Norton & Company.

Mandelbaum, David G. 1974. *Human Fertility in India.* Berkeley: University of California Press.

Mannheim, Karl. 1936. *Ideology and Utopia.* New York: Harcourt, Brace and World.

Mansfield, Roger. 1973. "Bureaucracy and Centralization: An Examination of Organizational Structure." *Administrative Sciences Quarterly* 18: 477–88.

Marty, Martin E., Andrew Greeley, and Stuart Rosenberg. 1968. *What Do We Believe?* New York: Meredith Press.

Marx, Karl. 1906 [1867]. *Capital* Vol. I. Translated by Samuel Moore and Edward Aveline. New York: The Modern Library.

———. 1956 [1843–80]. *Karl Marx: Selected Writings in Sociology and Social Philosophy.* Translated by T. B. Bottomore. New York: McGraw-Hill.

———. 1963 [1844]. *Karl Marx: Early Writings.* Translated by T. B. Bottomore. New York: McGraw-Hill.

———, and Frederick Engels. 1948 [1848]. *The Communist Manifesto.* New York: International Publishers.

Mauss, Marcel. 1967 [1925]. *The Gift.* New York: W. W. Norton and Company.

Mayhew, David. 1977. *Congress: The Electoral Connection.* New Haven, CT: Yale University Press.

McCarthy, John D., and Mayer N. Zald. 1977. "Resource Mobilization and Social Movements." *American Journal of Sociology* 82: 1212–41.

Mead, George Herbert. 1934. *Mind, Self and Society.* Chicago: University of Chicago Press.

Mead, Margaret. 1968 [1935]. *Sex and Temperament in Three Primitive Societies.* New York: Dell Publishing Co.

Merton, Robert K. 1968. *Social Theory and Social Structure.* New York: Free Press.

Messenger, John C. 1976. "Sex and Repression in an Irish Folk Community." In *Sex Research: Studies from the Kinsey Institute,* edited by Martin S. Weinberg. New York: Oxford University Press.

Meyer, John F. 1977. "The Effects of Education as an Institution." *American Journal of Sociology* 83: 55–77.

Meyers, Jerome K., and Lee L. Bean. 1969. *A Decade Later: A Follow-up of Social Class and Mental Illness.* New York: John Wiley & Sons.

Michelotti, Kopp. 1978. "Educational Attainment of Workers, March 1977." U.S. Department of Labor. Bureau of Labor Statistics. Special Labor Force Report 209.

Michels, Robert. 1962 [1911]. *Political Parties: A Sociological Study of the Oligarchical Tendencies of Modern Democracy.* Translated by Eden and Cedar Paul. New York: Collier Books.

Milgram, Stanley. 1961. "Nationality and Conformity." *Scientific American* (5): 45–51.

———. 1963. "Behavioral Study of Obedience." *Journal of Abnormal and Social Psychology* 67: 371–78.

Miller, Perry. 1956. *Errand into the Wilderness.* Cambridge, MA: Harvard University Press.

Miller, S. M., and Pamela Roby. 1970. *The Future of Inequality.* New York: Basic Books.

Mills, C. Wright. 1956. *The Power Elite.* New York: Oxford University Press.

———. 1959. *The Sociological Imagination.* New York: Oxford University Press.

Miner, Horace. 1956. "Body Ritual among the Nacirema." *American Anthropologist* 58: 503–7.

Moscovici, S., E. Lage, and M. Naffrechoux. 1969. "Influence of a Consistent Minority on the Responses of a Majority in a Color Perception Task." *Sociometry* 32: 365–80.

Moskos, Charles A., Jr. 1977. "Why Men Fight: American Combat Soldiers in Vietnam." In *The Study of Society: An Integrated Anthology,* edited by Peter I. Rose. New York: Random House.

Murdock, George P. 1949. *Social Structure.* New York: The Macmillan Company.

Nash, Jeffrey. 1975. "Bus Riding: Community on Wheels." *Urban Life and Culture* 4: 99–124.

National Center for Productivity and Quality of Working Life. 1977. *Productivity and Job Security: Retraining to Adapt to Technological Change*. Winter.

National Jewish Population Study. 1974. Fred Massarik, scientific director. New York: Council of Jewish Federations and Welfare Funds.

Nelli, Humbert. 1970. *The Italians in Chicago: 1880–1930*. New York: Oxford University Press.

Nelson, Richard R., and David A. Levy. 1977. "State Labor Legislation Enacted in 1977." *Monthly Labor Review* (Dec): 3–24.

Newfield, Jack, and Jeff Greenfield. 1972. *A Populist Manifesto*. New York: Warner Paperback Library.

Nisbet, Robert A. 1974. *The Sociology of Emile Durkheim*. New York: Oxford University Press.

———, with Robert G. Perrin. 1977. *The Social Bond*. New York: Alfred A. Knopf.

Noel, Donald L. 1968. "A Theory of the Origin of Ethnic Stratification." *Social Problems* 16: 157–72.

Nortman, Dorothy. 1975. "Population and Family Planning Programs: A Factbook." *Reports on Population/Family Planning, No. 2*. New York: Population Council.

Novak, Michael. 1972. *The Rise of the Unmeltable Ethnics*. New York: The Macmillan Company.

Oberschall, Anthony. 1973. *Social Conflict and Social Movements*. Englewood Cliffs, NJ: Prentice-Hall.

Ogburn, William F. 1936. "Stationary and Changing Societies." *American Journal of Sociology* 42: 16–31.

———. 1964. "Cultural Lag as Theory." In *William F. Ogburn on Culture and Social Change*. Chicago: University of Chicago Press.

O'Neill, Nena, and George O'Neill. 1972. *Open Marriage: A New Life Style for Couples*. New York: Avon Books.

Orenstein, Alan, and William R. F. Phillips. 1978. *Understanding Social Research: An Introduction*. Boston: Allyn and Bacon.

Padgaonkar, Dileep. 1978. "Islam's Fundamentalist Wave." *Times of India*. Excerpted in *Atlas World Press Review* (Feb): 49.

Parsons, Talcott. 1966. *Societies: Evolutionary and Comparative Perspectives*. Englewood Cliffs, NJ: Prentice-Hall.

Pavalko, Ronald M. 1977. "Racism and the New Immigration: Toward a Reinterpretation of the Experience of White Ethnics in American Society." Paper presented at the annual meeting of the American Sociological Association, Chicago.

Peck, Cornelius. 1967. "Nationalism, 'Race' and Developments in the Philippine Law of Citizenship." *Journal of African and Asian Studies* 2: 128–43.

Perlman, Daniel. 1974. "Self Esteem and Sexual Permissiveness." *Journal of Marriage and the Family* 36: 470–73.

Perrow, Charles. 1979. *Complex Organizations: A Critical Essay*. Glenview, IL: Scott, Foresman and Company.

Pimentel, D., et al. 1976. "Land Degradation: Effects on Food and Energy Resources." *Science* 194: 149–55.

Piven, Frances Fox, and Richard A. Cloward. 1971. *Regulating the Poor: The Functions of Public Welfare*. New York: Vintage Books.

———, and Richard A. Cloward. 1977. *Poor People's Movements: Why They Succeed, How They Fail*. New York: Pantheon.

Pleck, Joseph. 1976. "My Male Sex Role—and Ours." In *The Forty-Nine Percent Majority: The Male Sex Role*, edited by Deborah S. David and Robert Brannon. Reading, MA: Addison-Wesley Publishing Company.

Pospisil, Leopold. 1963. *The Kapauku Papuans of West New Guinea*. New York: Holt, Rinehart and Winston.

Quinney, Richard. 1970. *The Problem of Crime*. New York: Dodd, Mead & Company.

Rabkin, Leslie, and Karen Rabkin. 1969. "Children of the Kibbutz." *Psychology Today* 3 (Sept): 40–46.

Radcliffe-Brown, A. R. 1922. *The Andaman Islanders*. New York: Free Press.

Reasons, Charles. 1974. "The Politics of Drugs: An Inquiry into the Sociology of Social Problems." *Sociological Quarterly* 15: 381–404.

Reckless, Walter C. 1969. "The Use of the Death

Penalty—A Factual Statement." *Crime and Delinquency* **15**: 43–56.

Reissman, Frank. 1977. "Men's Groups: The Lost Art of Talking to Each Other." In *Our Sociological Eye: Personal Essays on Society and Culture,* edited by Arthur B. Shostak. Port Washington, NY: Alfred Publishing Company.

Riesman, David. 1950. *The Lonely Crowd.* New Haven, CT: Yale University Press.

Righter, Rosemary. 1980. "The Dangerous Imbalance." *Sunday Times* (London). Excerpted in *World Press Review* (Mar): 39–40.

Robbins, Richard. 1975. *Famine in Russia 1891–92: The Imperial Government Responds to a Crisis.* New York: Columbia University Press.

Roberts, Alan, and Milton Rokeach. 1956. "Anomie, Authoritarianism, and Prejudice: A Replication." *American Journal of Sociology* **61**: 355–58.

Roethlisberger, Fritz J., and William J. Dickson. 1939. *Management and the Worker.* Cambridge, MA: Harvard University Press.

Rosenberg, Bernard, and Irving Howe. 1974. "American Jews: Are They Turning Right?" *Dissent* **21**: 30–45.

Rosenberg, George S. 1970. *The Worker Grows Old.* San Francisco: Jossey-Bass.

Rosenhan, David R. 1973. "On Being Sane in Insane Places." *Science* **179**: 250–58.

Rosenkrantz, P., et al. 1968. "Sex-Role Stereotypes and Self-Concepts in College Students." *Journal of Consulting and Clinical Psychology* **32**: 287–95.

Rosow, Irving. 1967. *Social Integration of the Aged.* New York: Free Press.

Rousseau, Jean Jacques. 1913 [1754]. *The Social Contract/Discourses.* Translated by G. D. H. Cole. London: J. M. Dent & Sons.

Royko, Mike. 1971. *Boss: Richard J. Daley of Chicago.* New York: E. P. Dutton & Company.

Rubin, J. Z., F. J. Provenzano, and Z. Luria. 1974. "The Eye of the Beholder: Parents' Views on Sex of Newborns." *American Journal of Orthopsychiatry* **44**: 512–19.

Salas, Rafael M. 1978. "What Population Changes Portend." *United Nations Fund for Population Activities, Annual Report.* Excerpted in *Atlas World Press Review* (Dec): 15–18.

Saldahna, S., et al. 1975. "American Catholics—Ten Years Later." *The Critic* (Jan-Feb): 14–21.

Samuda, Ronald J. 1975. *Psychological Testing of American Minorities: Issues and Consequences.* New York: Dodd, Mead & Company.

Schachtel, Ernest. 1961. "On Alienated Concepts of Identity." *Journal of Humanistic Psychology* **1**: 110–21.

Schwartz, David. 1973. *Political Alienation and Political Behavior.* Chicago: Aldine Publishing Company.

Seagull, Louis M. 1977. *Youth and Change in American Politics.* New York: New Viewpoints.

Seeman, Melvin. 1959. "On the Meaning of Alienation." *American Sociological Review* **24**: 783–91.

———. 1966. "Antidote to Alienation: Learning to Belong." *Trans-action* **3**: 34–39.

Sexton, Patricia. 1964. *Education and Income.* New York: Compass Books.

Sharp, Lauriston. 1952. "Steel Axes for Stone Age Australians." *Human Organization* **11**: 17–22.

Sheldon, William H. 1949. *Varieties of Delinquent Youth.* New York: Harper & Brothers.

Sherif, M., and C. W. Sherif. 1953. *Groups in Harmony and Tension: An Integration of Studies on Intergroup Relations.* New York: Harper & Brothers.

Sidel, Ruth. 1972. *Women and Child Care in China.* New York: Hill and Wang.

Simmel, Georg. 1950. *The Sociology of Georg Simmel.* Translated, edited, and introduced by Kurt H. Wolff. New York: Free Press.

Simon, William and John H. Gagnon. 1976. "The Anomie of Affluence: A Post-Mertonian Conception." *American Journal of Sociology* **82**: 356–78.

Smelser, Neil J. 1963. *Theory of Collective Behavior.* New York: Free Press.

Smith, Adam. 1961 [1776]. *An Inquiry into the Nature and Causes of the Wealth of Nations.* London: Methuen & Co.

Smith, James D., and Stephen D. Franklin. 1974. "The Concentration of Personal Wealth." *American Economic Review* **64**: 162–67.

Sommer, Robert. 1976. *The End of Imprisonment.* New York: Oxford University Press.

Sommers, Dixie, and Alan Eck. 1977. "Occupational Mobility in the American Labor Force." *Monthly Labor Review* (Jan): 3–19.

Sorokin, Pitirim A. 1937. *Social and Cultural Dynamics.* 4 vols. New York: American Book Company.

Sowell, Thomas. 1978. "Ethnicity in a Changing America." *Daedalus* 107 (Winter): 213–37.

Spangler, E., M. A. Gordon, and R. M. Pipkin. 1978. "Token Women: An Empirical Test of Kanter's Hypothesis." *American Journal of Sociology* 84: 160–70.

Spencer, Herbert. 1898. *The Principles of Sociology.* New York: D. Appleton & Company.

———. 1961 [1874]. *The Study of Sociology.* Ann Arbor: University of Michigan Press.

Stark, Rodney, and Charles Y. Glock. 1970. *American Piety: The Nature of Religious Commitment.* Berkeley: University of California Press.

Stebbins, Robert D. 1969. "Studying the Definition of the Situation: Theory and Field Research Strategies." *Canadian Review of Sociology* 6: 193–211.

Stephens, Joyce. 1976. *Loners, Losers, and Lovers.* Seattle: University of Washington Press.

Sumner, William Graham. 1906. *Folkways.* Boston: Ginn and Company.

Surgeon General's Scientific Advisory Committee on Television and Social Behavior. 1972. *Television and Growing Up: The Impact of Televised Violence.* Washington, DC: Government Printing Office.

Sutherland, Edwin H. 1947. *Principles of Criminology.* Philadelphia: J. B. Lippincott Company.

Syfers, Judy. 1973. "Why I Want a Wife." In *The First Ms. Reader.* New York: Warner Paperback Library.

Sykes, Gresham, and David Matza. 1957. "Techniques of Neutralization: A Theory of Delinquency." *American Sociological Review* 22: 667–69.

Szymanski, Albert. 1976. "Racial Discrimination and White Gain." *American Sociological Review* 41: 403–14.

Teitelbaum, Michael S. 1975. "Population Theory and the LDCs." *Science* 188: 420–25.

Thernstrom, Stephan. 1973. *The Other Bostonians: Poverty and Progress in the American Metropolis, 1880–1970.* Cambridge, MA: Harvard University Press.

Thomas, Charles W., and Robin J. Cage. 1977. "The Effect of Social Characteristics on Juvenile Court Dispositions." *Sociological Quarterly* 18: 237–52.

Thomas, W. I., with Florian Znaniecki. 1920. *The Polish Peasant in Europe and America.* 5 vols. Chicago: University of Chicago Press.

Tien, H. Yuan. 1973. *China's Population Struggle.* Columbus: Ohio State University Press.

Tiryakian, Edward A. 1974. "Neither Marx nor Durkheim . . . Perhaps Weber." Paper presented at the annual meeting of the American Sociological Association, Montreal.

Toqueville, Alexis de. 1955 [1856]. *The Old Regime and the French Revolution.* Translated by Gilbert Stuart. Garden City, NY: Doubleday & Company.

———. 1969 [1835]. *Democracy in America.* Translated by George Lawrence. Garden City, NY: Doubleday & Company.

Toennies, Ferdinand. 1957 [1887]. *Community and Society.* Translated by Charles P. Loomis. New York: Harper & Brothers.

Tumin, Melvin. 1967. *Social Stratification.* Englewood Cliffs, NJ: Prentice-Hall.

Turner, Ralph, and Lewis Killian. 1972. *Collective Behavior.* Englewood Cliffs, NJ: Prentice-Hall.

Udry, J. Richard. 1974. *The Social Context of Marriage.* Philadelphia: J. B. Lippincott Company.

United States Department of Commerce. 1973. *Statistical Abstract of the United States, 1973.* Washington, DC: Government Printing Office.

———. 1977. *Social Indicators: 1976.* Washington, DC: Government Printing Office.

———. 1979. *Money Income in 1977 of Families and Persons in the United States.* Washington, DC: Government Printing Office.

———. 1979a. *Statistical Abstract of the United States, 1979.* Washington, DC: Government Printing Office.

———. 1979b. *Current Population Survey: Consumer Income.* Series P-60. Number 118. March. Washington, DC: Government Printing Office.

United States Department of Justice. Federal Bureau of Investigation. 1979. *Crime in the United States—1978.* Washington, DC: Government Printing Office.

United States Department of Labor. Bureau of Labor Statistics. 1977. *Work Experience of the Population, 1976.* Special Labor Force Report 201.

———. 1978. "Survey Shows Weekly and Hourly Earnings for Major Groups of Workers." USDL 78–842.

———. 1978a. *Marital and Family Characteristics of Workers, 1970 to 1978.* Special Labor Force Report 209.

———. 1978b. *Occupational Earnings and Wage Trends in Metropolitan Areas, 1977.* Summary 78–2.

———. 1979. *Women in the Labor Force: Some New Data Series.* Report 575.

———. 1980. *Employment and Unemployment during 1979: An Analysis.* Special Labor Force Report 234.

———. 1980a. "The Employment Situation: January 1980. USDL 80–65.

United States Public Health Service. 1975. *Selected Vital and Health Statistics in Poverty and Non-poverty Areas of Nineteen Large Cities: United States: 1969–71.* Washington, DC: Government Printing Office.

———. 1976. "Advance Report on Final Natality Statistics, 1974." *Monthly Vital Statistics Report* (Feb): 1–5.

Van Dusen, Roxann A., and Eleanor Bernert Sheldon. 1976. "The Changing Status of American Women: A Life Cycle Perspective." *The American Psychologist* 31: 106–16.

Verba, Sidney, and Norman H. Nie. 1972. *Participation in America.* New York: Harper & Row.

Walum, Laurel Richardson. 1977. *The Dynamics of Sex and Gender: A Sociological Perspective.* Chicago: Rand McNally & Company.

Ware, Helen. 1975. "The Limits of Acceptable Family Size in Western Nigeria." *Journal of Biosocial Science* 7: 273–96.

Warren, Roland I. 1963. *The Community in America.* Chicago: Rand McNally & Company.

Weber, Max. 1946 [1906–24]. *From Max Weber: Essays in Sociology,* edited by H. H. Gerth and C. W. Mills. New York: Oxford University Press.

———. 1947 [1925]. *The Theory of Social and Economic Organization.* Translated by Talcott Parsons and A. M. Henderson. Glencoe, IL: Free Press.

———. 1958 [1904]. *The Protestant Ethic and the Spirit of Capitalism.* Translated by Talcott Parsons. New York: Charles Scribner's Sons.

Weeks, John R. 1978. *Population: An Introduction to Concepts and Issues.* Belmont, CA: Wadsworth Publishing Company.

Weitz, Shirley. 1977. *Sex Roles: Biological, Psychological, and Sociological Foundations.* New York: Oxford University Press.

Weitzman, Lenore J. 1975. "To Love Honor and Obey." *The Family Coordinator* 24: 543–47.

———, et al. 1972. "Sex-Role Socialization in Picture Books for Preschool Children." *American Journal of Sociology* 77: 1125–50.

Welch, Claude, Jr., and Mavis Bunker Taintor. 1972. *Revolution and Political Change.* Belmont, CA: Duxbury Press.

Westoff, Charles F., and Larry Bumpass. 1973. "The Revolution in Birth Control Practices of U.S. Roman Catholics." *Science* 179: 41–44.

———, and Normal B. Ryder. 1969. "Recent Trends in Attitude toward Fertility Control and in the Practice of Contraception in the United States." In *Fertility and Family Planning: A World View,* edited by S. J. Behrman, Leslie Corsa, Jr., and Ronald Freedman. Ann Arbor: University of Michigan Press.

White, Walter. 1969 [1928]. *Rope and Faggot.* New York: Arno Press.

Wilson, John. 1978. *Religion in American Society: The Effective Presence.* Englewood Cliffs, NJ: Prentice-Hall.

Wirth, Louis. 1938. "Urbanism as a Way of Life." *American Journal of Sociology* 44: 1–24.

Wollstonecraft, Mary. 1975 [1792]. *A Vindication of the Rights of Women.* New York: Penguin.

Wolman, C., and H. Frank. 1972. "The Solo Woman in a Professional Peer Group." Working Paper No. 136. Philadelphia: The Wharton School, University of Pennsylvania.

Women on Words and Images. 1975. *Dick and Jane as Victims: Sex Stereotyping in Children's Readers.* Princeton, NJ: Women on Words and Images.

Wright, James D. 1978. "In Search of the New Working Class." *Qualitative Sociology* 1: 33–57.

———, and R. Hamilton. 1978. "Work Satisfaction and Age: Some Evidence for the 'Job Change' Hypothesis." *Social Forces* 56: 1140–58.

Yalom, Irvin D., and Morton A. Lieberman. 1971. "A Study of Encounter Group Casualties." *Archives of General Psychiatry* 25: 16–30.

Yancey, William L., Eugene P. Ericksen, and Richard N. Juliani. 1976. "Emergent Ethnicity: A Review and Reformulation." *American Sociological Review* 41: 391–403.

Young, Virginia Heyer. 1970. "Family and Childhood in a Southern Negro Community." *American Anthropologist* 72: 269–88.

Zangwill, Israel. 1909. *The Melting Pot.* New York: The Macmillan Company.

Zashin, Elliot. 1978. "The Progress of Black Americans in Civil Rights: The Past Two Decades." *Daedalus* 107 (Winter): 239–62.

Zborowski, Mark. 1953. "Cultural Components in Responses to Pain." *Journal of Social Issues* 8: 16–31.

Name Index

Subject Index

To the owner of this book:

I hope that you enjoyed SOCIOLOGY: A WAY OF SEEING as much as I enjoyed writing it. I would like to know as much about your experience as you care to offer. Only through your comments and those of others can I learn how to make this a better text for future readers.

School   Your Instructor's Name

1. What did you like most about SOCIOLOGY: A WAY OF SEEING?

2. What did you like least about the book?

3. Were all the chapters of the book assigned for you to read? If not, which ones weren't?

4. Were any chapters or concepts particularly difficult for you? If so, which ones?

5. How useful were the graphics (figures, tables, cartoons, photographs), and how would you compare them to those in other college texts you have used?

6. In the space below or in a separate letter, please let me know any other comments about the book you'd like to make. For example, are there any topics I did not cover that you would have liked to learn about? I'd be delighted to hear from you!

Optional: Your Name   Date

May Wadsworth quote you, either in promotion for SOCIOLOGY: A WAY OF SEEING or in future publishing ventures?   Yes   No

Yours sincerely,

FOLD HERE